CW00408588

DAILY LIFE
IN REMBRANDT'S HOLLAND

Other books in the *Daily Life* series published by
Stanford University Press

Daily Life

in

REMBRANDT'S HOLLAND

Paul Zumthor

Translated from the French by Simon Watson Taylor

STANFORD UNIVERSITY PRESS
STANFORD, CALIFORNIA
1994

Stanford University Press publications are distributed
exclusively by Stanford University Press within
the United States, Canada, and Mexico; they are
distributed exclusively by Cambridge University
Press throughout the rest of the world.

Cover illustration: Reinier Nooms (Zeeman)
(Netherlands, c. 1623–1667), a detail of *The Block
House, Views of Ships* c. 1660. Etching, plate 8 from
the *36 Views of Amsterdam*. Courtesy of the Stanford
University Musuem of Art, The Robert M. Loeser
Collection. 1944.2.27

CONTENTS

To

A. H. Van der Weel

As for this country's way of life, I assure you that I find very little difference from our own. In some matters you will find more polish here; in others, more plainness. But the delights of freedom are as deeply felt here as in any other country.

Letter from BUZENVAL, 2nd January 1593

N O R T H   S E A

Kenne

Cat
Rijns
Scheveninge
The Hague

S

Brielle

Brouvershaven
Schouwen
Zierikzee

Walcheren
Middelburg
Flushing

Z E E L A N D

L A N D S   O F

Ghent

Scheldt

HOLLAND IN THE
SEVENTEENTH CENTURY

· MILES ·
10   0   10   20   30

CHARLES GREEN

INTRODUCTION

The title of this book, *Daily Life in Rembrandt's Holland*, should be taken strictly to mean the years 1606 to 1669, the artist's lifetime. The choice of these years as limits is not entirely arbitrary. What the Dutch refer to as their 'golden age', the classic era of their civilisation, extended no further than a human lifetime: its beginning, between 1600 and 1610, corresponded with the period in French history which saw the end of Henri IV's reign, and it drew to a close between 1675–80 while Louis XIV was at the very height of his power.

Historically – as much on the political level as on that of ideas and forms of expression – this period can be divided into three stages. Until 1621 the gradual slackening in the war against Spain, the financial difficulties resulting from this war, and the eventual truce, combined to bring about a profound reaction in which some balance was sought between a still exuberant vitality and the wisdom inspired by a dearly won success. From 1621 to 1650 the Netherlands participated, with mixed fortunes, in the Thirty Years War in Europe, while, at the same time, they founded and consolidated their overseas empire and accumulated vast riches within their own frontiers. After 1650, the abolition of stadtholderates (provincial governorships) turned the Republic into a confederation of an economic rather than political nature, entirely dominated by the province of Holland and by the merchants of Amsterdam; a republic whose visible glory concealed the corruption resulting from its very prosperity.

In order to make it easier for the reader to establish the necessary references, I give at this juncture a brief chronology of events:

6th January 1579   'Union of Arras', between the ten Catholic provinces of the southern Netherlands, under Spanish control.

23rd January 1579	'Union of Utrecht', between the seven northern provinces: Holland, Zeeland, Utrecht, Gelderland, Overijssel, Groningen and Friesland – The regions subsequently captured from Spain formed the 'Land of the States-General'.
10th July 1584	Assassination of William the Silent.
1584–7	The title of Governor-General of the Provinces is offered to the Duke of Leicester, who will thus ensure an English protectorate.
1584–97	First navigations in arctic waters, and in the directions of the Far East and America.
1585	The fall of Antwerp – Maurice of Nassau becomes Stadtholder.
1588	After Leicester's resignation Maurice takes over the government of the country – Defeat of Spain's 'Invincible Armada'.
c. 1590	First Dutch navigations in the Mediterranean.
1602	Foundation of the Dutch East India Company.
1609	Negotiation of a truce with Spain lasting twelve years.
1618–19	Political, social and religious conflicts, especially between the followers of Gomarus and those of Arminius (known as counter-remonstrants and remonstrants), and between Maurice and Oldenbarnevelt – Synod of Dordrecht; Oldenbarnevelt condemned to death: triumph of the popular party, of the Gomarists (counter-remonstrants), and of Maurice.
1619	Foundation of Batavia.
1621	Resumption of war.

1625	Death of Maurice – His brother, Frederick Henry, succeeds him.
1629	Capture of 's Hertogenbosch.
1637	Capture of Breda.
October 1639	Naval victory of Tromp over Oquendo: defeat of Spain's final campaign against the United Provinces.
1647	Death of Frederick Henry – His son, William II, succeeds him.
30th January 1648	Signing of the Treaty of Westphalia at Münster, confirming the independence of the United Provinces.
1650	Conflict between William II and the States-General about dismissal of troops – Death of William II – Birth of the future William III.
1651	Abolition of the post of Stadtholder (except in Friesland and in the province of Groningen) – The 'Navigation Act' leads to a period of hostilities between the Republic and England.
1652	Foundation of a colony at the Cape of Good Hope.
1652–4	First war against England.
1653–72	Johan De Witt, 'Grand Pensionary' of the province of Holland, assumes effective control of the Republic.
1665–7	Second war against England.
April 1672	Louis XIV invades the Republic: occupies Utrecht, Guelders, Overijssel – A popular uprising forces the States to re-establish the stadtholdership in favour of William III.
20th August 1672	Assassination of Johan De Witt.
End of 1673	William III repels the French troops.
February 1674	Peace with England.
1677	William III marries the daughter of the future James II.

August 1678   Treaty of Nijmegen.

1685   Revocation by Louis XIV of the edict of Nantes – Influx into Holland of French refugees.

1689   William III becomes King of England, ruling jointly with his wife.

The Republic presented considerable diversity between its different parts, and in this sense the use of the name 'Holland' to designate the entire country (a habit already widespread in seventeenth-century Europe) was quite improper. It is true that, despite its modest dimensions, the province of Holland was rich and powerful enough to attract more attention from abroad than all the other provinces put together. Nevertheless, local custom had long sanctioned the use of the name *Nederland* (Netherlands) for those territories brought together by the Union of Utrecht, and in this book I have used these words in their proper sense: *Holland* for the province, and *Netherlands* for the United Provinces, though for reasons of brevity the word 'Holland' is used in its general acceptance in chapter headings. A distinction is also made between the United Provinces and the southern Netherlands under Spanish jurisdiction; for simplicity's sake I refer to the latter as *Belgium*, although they were usually called *Brabant* in the seventeenth century.

The 'Land of the States-General', being Catholic and administered collectively by the Provinces, remained on the fringe of the political scene, but a semblance of national unity was induced by the proximity of their southern and eastern 'foreign neighbours'. This unity was cemented by the actions of men as remarkable as Maurice of Nassau and Oldenbarnevelt, and was able to embrace the various mutually exclusive political and theological factions.

The war against Spain served to create many common interests but, at the same time, it was fought with the aim of asserting the principle of self-government at the local level. In the Republic, sovereignty derived from the elected municipal corporations but since the sixteenth century these had perpetuated themselves by co-option, thus assuring power to local notabilities. A municipal corporation consisted of a legislative Council (thirty-six members in Amsterdam), municipal magistrates (nine in Amsterdam) constituting a tribunal, and burgomasters (four in Amsterdam) who were executive officials, together with treasurers and a pensionary (legal adviser). It thus formed a miniature republic, federated to its fellow-corporations within the province's boundaries. The province itself exercised plenary powers, possessing its own government of similar structure to the corporations. The provincial council, formed of town delegates and those of the nobility, bore the title 'States'; the deliberative functions were entrusted to corporative bodies rather than individual deputies. In the States of Holland, for instance, each town had one person entitled to speak and vote, and the nobility also had one such representative. Gelderland and Overijssel allowed far greater representation to the nobility. Only Friesland and Groningen gave the peasants a voice in council deliberations; in these provinces the villages grouped themselves in bailiwicks or *Ommelanden* constituting communities with public rights. The central government, sitting in The Hague, was really nothing more than a conference of ambassadors from the provinces, with the States-General as its essential organ. As a consequence, discussion was less frequent than diplomacy, trickery and haggling. Rather than being a sovereign council, the States-General played the role of representatives of provincial sovereignty. The Union existed solely in virtue of the provinces' agreement, and even the least conflict of interests was quite capable of endangering such agreement. In 1648 Zeeland found itself on the verge of secession. Unity was always re-established finally, but these vicissitudes ruled out the possibility of any long-term political policy.

The Stadtholder occupied an ambiguous position in the enacting terms of the constitution. He was head of the military establishment and possessed privileges such as the granting of free pardons and the nomination of certain magistrates, yet he was not empowered to exercise either judicial or fiscal control and his office was not even unique in the Republic, since Friesland and Groningen had their own Stadtholder from the beginning of the seventeenth century. The individual 'reigning' at The Hague was more an arbiter than an initiator in political matters; on the emotional plane he was viewed as a national symbol by the majority of Dutchmen.

At this stage it may be appropriate to present a genealogical table of the family of Orange-Nassau from the sixteenth to the seventeenth centuries:

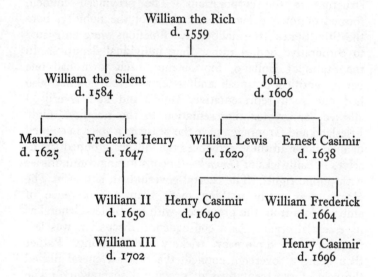

The members of the junior branch, from William Lewis onwards, were Stadtholders of Friesland and Groningen.

During the course of the sixteenth century a double revolution had shaken this nation of peasants and fishermen, which had hitherto remained aloof from the great march of civilisation. Anti-papist faith combined with resistance to Spain provided the Dutch with the energy they needed to tear themselves from the mediocrity of their past and open up a hitherto unknown highway leading to financial wealth and high cultural gains. The war had been conducted in conditions which often necessitated extreme heroism, so that a relatively unsophisticated society suddenly found itself called upon to answer extraordinary demands; this very pressure provoked the sudden upsurge of something approaching creative genius among the flower of the nation. This élite continued on its course with unabated energy once the war was over, opening up new and sometimes sterile perspectives, and permitting itself the luxury of creating works of art. The last and most brilliant flames of this genius flared up during the few years comprising the 'golden age'. But after the Westphalia peace treaty fewer and fewer individuals retained their creative inspiration. And with the crisis of 1672 the flame was extinguished.

P. Z.

Amsterdam, March 1959.

NB—As far as possible, I have given uniformity to the numerical data provided by different historical documents. The various monetary denominations have been converted to florins, and the old measures of length and capacity changed to modern units.

CHAPTER ONE

THE BACKGROUND OF DAILY LIFE

*The Town: Appearance, Maintaining Order—The Country-
side—Highways and Canals.*

THE TOWN: *Appearance*
William Temple, who was English ambassador to The
Hague and published a long report on the Netherlands in
1673, admired 'the beauty and strength'[1] of Dutch towns.
The 'golden age' was indeed an era of huge investments in
the field of construction and town-building. The wealthy
bourgeois gloried in the splendour of his town as, in other
countries, he valued his family heritage.

A reddish-brown, black or pink line across the uniform
green of the meadows, with possibly the outline of dunes
against the far horizon, provided a typical view of those
towns built on flat ground. Except in the east and north
of the country, as at Nijmegen, the terrain did not provide
the rising ground which in France and Germany, for example,
served as a focal point for the town. A few towers, a belfry,
some roof-tops would be outlined low down under the vast
Dutch sky, misty either with drizzle or with a soft light;
and there would be a long brick wall and an earth-bank. At
the beginning of the seventeenth century most towns were
still surrounded by ramparts – brick walls or fortifications,
battlements with loopholes, turrets, moats. Here and there
the heavy gateway with its drawbridge would sometimes
open, as at Zutphen, not onto a road but onto a canal spanned
by its arch.

These fortifications were no longer really used for defence.
Grass and trees were planted, or they were turned into

promenades. By about 1670 Leyden still had large deep moats, but its ramparts had become nothing more than a long grassy bank bordered by a quickset hedge, and adorned on the outside by a brick façade with occasional bastions. The ancient strongholds which previously flanked the gateways had nearly all been demolished. Those which survived were mostly preserved for purely aesthetic reasons, unless the place in question was of exceptional military importance. A massive tower housed the clock, and the two or three floors beneath the clock were used for municipal purposes, providing premises for the watch, the guilds, and literary clubs known as 'chambers of rhetoric'. The gateway of Hoorn, built of brick and grey stone, was decorated with the city's arms and flanked by two heavy round towers, so that the street beneath had to curve sharply around it. The gateway of Zierikzee was of whitewashed brick surmounted by battlements.

Most Dutch cities were built according to one or other of three standard plans; round-shaped, with more or less circular streets, as was the case with Leyden, Haarlem and Gouda; or almost square-shaped with straight streets, as in Delft and Alkmaar; or else verging into a narrow or broad point between two straits, as in Dordrecht or Medemblik. Alongside the principal canal forming its axis stood frontages of different heights and covered butchers' stalls. Another canal, straddled by a hog-back bridge, might lead to the long market-place dominated by the building which housed the inspector of weights and measures; there, also, would be the meat-market, and that symbol of municipal enfranchisement, the Town Hall; and, soaring above a row of pointed roofs, the nave of a long Gothic church, as at Gouda. This main square provided the centre around which local life revolved.

Although at the beginning of the seventeenth century the ground in most of the towns was still sand or clay, the municipalities soon began to provide hard surfaces for the main square and the chief streets leading up to it, thus hoping to promote commercial traffic. By about 1650 most of the main streets in the towns were paved, and the

Calvinist preachers complained about the spread of such blameworthy luxury. The road surface was usually of two kinds: the material in the middle of the road, used by carriages and carts, was of rough stone or brick; but alongside the houses, and on the canal side, a pavement of small, hard, tightly packed bricks was provided for pedestrians. In other words, the typical Dutch street usually had a canal flowing between its double row of houses and its double roadway. Even in the country the peasants' houses were surrounded by ditches. The Dutch always seem to have associated their habitat with the presence of water. In wealthy districts the canal was very often flanked by large trees – elms or lindens; these spread out over the black water, whose sandy bottom acted as a mirror in the sunshine, so that the surface reflected their branches, mingled with the reflections of the tall baroque façades and their latticed windows with green shutters thrown back.

The whole town was not yet included in these works of improvement, street paving. Really sewer-like unpaved streets still existed, and were found particularly in the old, poor districts, whose ancient wooden houses jutted out over the pathway, with upper storeys facing each other so closely – when there was no canal between – that one could shake hands across the street. Here, a heterogeneous population swarmed, living on the brink of misery, at least in the large towns. The difficulty of accommodation continued throughout the 'golden age', and the increase in population, together with profiteering by landlords, turned these hovels into barracks. Speculators bought these houses, partitioned the rooms to increase the number of apartments available, and let them at exorbitant prices. Leyden, Amsterdam and Weesp never succeeded in getting rid of their slums nor of those who exploited them.

Even in the principal streets some wooden houses still remained. However, new building was now all done in brick; light sandstone was usually used to decorate the façades, and foliated cusps embellished their bases. Freestone was still a luxury. The first houses for which these materials were used copied the style of older buildings and the

3

storeys facing the street were staggered. Later there was more regularity, and the buildings also tended to become less cramped in width; in fact, when sufficient ground was available, builders began to construct houses which were wider than they were high. The opposite, however, still remained much more usual, although it was true that the height of the windows gave a passer-by the impression that the frontages were narrower than they really were.

The Dutch town contained very few large houses. Relatively small structures were preferred, separated from each other, even right in the centre of town, although the gap between the houses was sometimes only an inch or two. A house was usually designed for only a single family. Since the steadily increasing population made new housing mandatory, additional accommodation was provided by extending the town boundaries rather than by adding storeys to the existing houses, and these boundary extensions were sometimes considerable. The new buildings had two – or more rarely three – storeys above street-level. In Amsterdam a few houses had four or even as many as seven storeys, and as the century advanced the height of his house became increasingly a symbol of his wealth for the prosperous citizen.

A Dutch house seldom had more than five or six front casement-windows, but tended to stretch fairly far back. The climate had such a rapid corrosive action on all building materials that it was usual to tar the outside walls, and the town took on a predominantly dark hue relieved by the paleness of the sandstone ornamentation. Many of the houses were bow-fronted, a peculiarity which can be ascribed to the architects' idea that the curve would prevent the rain coming in. The lowest storey was a kind of vault whose floor was level with the surface of the canal and thus below street-level; it was separated from the street by a ditch more than a foot wide, covered by gratings. An outside staircase of four or five steps gave access to it. The ground floor was sometimes slightly above street-level and opened onto the roadway by a central door, either with or without a flight of steps, and had small leaded windows. Level with the tops of these windows, a sort of horizontal

4

canopy (called a *luifel*), usually of painted wood, ran the length of the frontage and protected from rain and sun that part of the pavement where the craftsman worked, and where the merchant took the air on summer evenings on a bench placed at either end of the house-front. These projections gradually disappeared during the course of the century. Just above the protective canopy appeared the first and second storey windows. The second storey, under the eaves, had usually only a single casement-window; but if it served as a merchant's loft a great door would open into space, above which would be a large hook used to hoist up merchandise. A tiled roof, with very steep side-panels, formed a pediment on the top of the façade which sometimes contained a dormer-window. The architects of this century made this type of window one of the main exterior embellishments of houses, enlarging them with occasional square shields extending further than the outer line of the roof on both sides.

Such was the typical Dutch citizen's house. The details varied tremendously, according to the wealth and rank of the owner. The grander houses had no canopy, but had shuttered windows at street-level whose sills and casements were decorated with caryatids, lions or mythological figures. Pilasters lined the house-frontage, and later the wall-bases were made of marble, sometimes lined with faience. The houses of plain folk were lower, being rarely more than one storey high, and the single refinement that they offered to the eye of the beholder was the varnish covering the wooden parts: window-frames, doors, and shutters. This varnish – green, red, brown, or white – protected the fragile material from the damp air. It was this glaze, even more than the brickwork, which gave a Dutch street its smart appearance.

But the street was more than just a row of façades and a passageway. It exercised a sociological if not a political function: particular streets were devoted to individual trades – for example, coopers, bootmakers or bakers. The concentration of identical activities in a single place made it much easier for the various guilds to exercise effectively the rights of control which they possessed. In Utrecht, tailors were empowered to make arrests in their own streets and to imprison clandestine workers or those who refused to become members of their guild. A town thus became a conglomeration of little worlds, each with its own atmosphere, local gossip and special smells. From house to house people kept watch on each other and upheld established order. The trades gave their names to the streets and districts: Glassblowers' Canal, Wine Harbour, Cheese Street, the Street of Flowers, Spice Street, Blacksmiths' River, and so on. Amsterdam, disdaining such realism, named its three great semi-circular canals in terms of an imaginary hierarchy: the Emperor's Canal, the Princes' Canal and the Lords' Canal.

Often, even the house itself took its name from the profession of its occupant. The wealthy inscribed their family name and coat of arms on the pediment above the main door. The frontages of less exalted houses carried a cast-iron sign upon which was painted a realistic or allegorical design indicating the owner's trade, or at least the virtues particularly admired in that establishment: a pot for the potter; scissors, or Saint Martin tearing his cloak, for the tailor. People would talk, for instance, of 'going to the Scissors'. In one particular sales contract a house was described as 'the House of the Bell, in the main street, opposite the Brush, near Ironmongers' Street, in Dordrecht'. A pious bourgeois who had built three houses side by side might call them Faith, Hope and Charity and decorate the fronts with appropriate biblical figures. Others took their theme from literature, and Amsterdam, for instance, had its house of the 'Four Sonnes of Aymon'. In villages, people sometimes simply nailed a board to a tree near the front door. With the rapid expansion of handicrafts and commerce during the seventeenth century, these signs multiplied. Dordrecht was famous for the number and variety of its signs. Some people commissioned well-known artists to design them. Sometimes, too, a single house sported several signs, because the new owner had decided to keep his predecessors' signs as decorations. Pastry-cooks displayed pictures of Saint Nicholas or Saint Osbert, or simply an oven, while doctors displayed a urinal vessel. The surgeon stuck up outside his door or window a pole with a yellow tip and white, red and blue stripes; of these emblematic colours the white signified that here one could get teeth pulled and fractures treated, the red that one could undergo bleeding, and the blue that one could get a shave. The walls of smoke-rooms featured paintings which often represented a peasant or a sailor, sometimes a famous navigator, pipe in hand, with some motto forming a halo around his head.[2]

The boats on the canals, the carts, buckets and barrels used for transporting food produce, were painted blue, red, green and black in areas of contrasting colour. But Dutch towns were full of sound as well as colour. The din of workshops, the cries of merchants, the rolling of carriages combined to produce a noise which was, however, still feeble compared to the deafening cacophony of the streets of France.[3] From hour to hour the air vibrated with the strokes of innumerable bells. Change-ringing was becoming a national art in Holland. Many of the chimes were famous, especially those of Amsterdam's Old Church, the Church of Saint John at 's Hertogenbosch, Utrecht Cathedral, Saint Servatius at Maastricht and the office of weights and measures in Alkmaar. Some of these chimes had more than a hundred bells.[4]

Waste land, and even meadows and fields, still studded most of the towns as in medieval times. In expanding cities these empty spaces were used for building, or else converted into 'malls' – long avenues designed for strolling and for various public games, bordered by trees, and with taverns nearby. The Utrecht mall, designed in 1637, was nearly half a mile long and was considered to be the most beautiful in Europe, especially because of the beauty of the lindens which shaded it. The linden was, in fact, the favourite ornamental tree in Dutch towns. In the new district in the north-east of the town, the Amsterdam corporation created a public park, an entirely new idea at the time. At The Hague, alongside a natural park called

7

The Wood, a mall was constructed, as well as a grass plot where a few wild animals were kept in cages. Vast oak-trees grew here at random on slightly undulating ground and the spot became a favourite promenade for fashionable people. The Hague was a residential town, and so was more concerned than were commercial cities in developing forms of beauty to stimulate leisure and flatter people's vanity. The few canals which wended their way through the town contained water that was fresher and clearer than elsewhere, and no barges were to be seen making their way along them from one district to another; so the town lacked the stir and bustle of the trading ports. The Wood was a smart district which contained ambassadors' mansions and the palaces of the Princes of Orange, constituting a solid quadrilateral dominated by the spire of its church, and preceded by a broad lake stocked with fish. The Hague was impressive because of its gay and noble atmosphere; it was a capital with an almost French atmosphere and an urbanity that had no equal in the Netherlands.

Nine miles to the north, the traveller bound for Amsterdam would come to Leyden, entering the city by one of the eight gates in the ramparts. Leyden, a great industrial town with a world-famous university, was fifteen miles from Haarlem, twenty-one miles from Amsterdam, thirty miles from Utrecht, fifteen from Gouda, nine from Delft, and was the nucleus of this collection of cities which constituted essentially the province of Holland.

Towards the south, in the heart of the province, lay Rotterdam, eighteen miles from the sea, rising on either bank of the Maas's wide mouth. At high tide even the largest vessels were able to sail into the very heart of the city. There the merchants' houses were noteworthy in that their opposite frontages each overlooked a quay. During the seventeenth century the municipal council was faced with the urgent necessity of constructing new dwellings, and gave up to private citizens the space hitherto occupied by the navy yards, which were transferred to huge docks approached by waterways, all specially constructed in the fields to the west of the town.

There were other towns which were the equal of Amsterdam in terms of activity and energy: Rotterdam; Dordrecht, up-stream; Middelburg, the capital of Zeeland, on the island of Walcheren. But Amsterdam had nothing to fear from them. After the destruction of Antwerp she had forged too far ahead. The ports of Enkhuizen and Hoorn on the Zuider Zee, the country's most important towns during the sixteenth century, gradually became dead cities and soon joined the two other small towns of this inland sea, Medemblik and Monnikendam, in their somnolence.

Amsterdam was one of the great cities of the West during this era, the wonder of the civilised world, less perhaps for its beauty than for its intense vitality. It was an enormous town for this period: at the beginning of the eighteenth century it took almost two hours to walk from one end to the other of the semi-circular canals along the banks of which the city was built. It spread out like a fan around its centre – the harbour, the Stock Exchange, the Town Hall and the Damplein – and retained its organic centralisation while still growing steadily. The harmony of its town planning was its chief attraction. Amsterdam was the spiritual centre of the Union, and offered to the mind and the imagination complete freedom and the most favourable economic conditions. It was the centre of all commerce, and its activities were world-wide; these factors endowed its inhabitants with a spirit of independence and a permanent distrust of anything emanating from The Hague. The town's economic vocation was manifest in the number of warehouses packed tightly alongside its canals, among footbridges that could be raised and lowered, and elegant arcaded bridges leading to the heart of the fashionable districts. These tall buildings mingled with the houses of skilled tradesmen giving directly onto both street and water, at the foot of which were stacked the boxes, sacks, barrels and tuns which the port's lighters had unloaded from ships in the harbour. Throughout the town a need for down-to-earth efficiency was apparent in a context of often abortive aesthetic ventures. This metropolis was built on land seemingly least propitious for its development – the marshes

9

formed at the mouth of the Amstel in the Ij's inlet. The
original cluster of structures was raised on a few strips of
land projecting at right angles into the river's mouth.
Later, this nucleus of a town was enveloped by a semi-
circular canal, the *Singel* or 'Belt'. The builders were
constructing upon sodden land which invariably revealed
water at a depth of a few feet everywhere they dug. For
this reason, all the houses of Amsterdam were built on
pilings made of long, stout beams in trestle form driven into
the spongy soil and taking the place of ordinary foundations.
Hence the ironical popular verse of the time:

> *The great town of Amsterdam*
> *is built on piles, until*
> *The day the whole place tumbles down:*
> *then who will pay the bill?*[5]

A brick wall surrounded the town, reinforced by innumerable stone arches, under which many destitute
families lived in appalling squalor. Twenty-six gateways on
the inner side of the moat opened onto the same number of
roads converging upon the old town, where the Amstel
dispersed its waters in the old port's numerous waterways.
To the north the old town emerged into the old port, was
penetrated by it, and prolonged itself by the district of
'Islands' – narrow lanes lined with warehouses and cut by
bridges with rats roaming at night. Towards the east it
spread out in a network of squalid alleys where hovels
adjoined elegant mansions. The influx of Jewish refugees
from Portugal and Spain, followed by Walloon and Flemish
Protestants, had made it necessary, even before 1600, to
enlarge the original city. In 1601 the town's diameter was
extended, but by a mere four hundred feet. The paltry
amount of additional space thus won was built over in a few
years. With a view to further expansion of the city, the
marshes to the east of the town were drained. Nothing
was left to chance: in 1610 a complete plan was submitted
for the approval of the municipal council. Two years later
work started. The old ramparts were demolished but the
high towers which had dominated them were preserved and,

thenceforward, found themselves scattered throughout the centre of town. Three great canals were dug, following the circular line of the 'Belt', and fairly widely spaced so that deep gardens could be built behind the houses. The plan was most ambitious, tripling the size of the old town and giving it the considerable surface of about 1,800 acres which already proved insufficient. New projects were put into effect in 1615, in 1658 and in 1660. From 1648 onwards the inner suburbs became a huge construction site. The islands of the Ij were connected to the town, and a fresh semi-circle of residential districts was also built, broader than the preceding ones and intersected by passageways along which shops were built. By 1672 the loop of the Amstel had been reached and the semi-circular scheme had to be abandoned in favour of the almost rectangular district built on the far side of the river and known as the 'Plantation'. At this stage Amsterdam had become an entirely renovated town from which the last vestiges of medieval construction had disappeared. But an economic recession threatened as a result of the freezing of a huge capital sum in investments, necessitated by these extensions to the town. The construction of the new bastions alone had cost eleven million florins, and the new town hall eight million.[6] In government circles a number of people expressed their anxiety on this subject to William Temple.[7]

At least this half-century of feverish construction produced several works of genuine artistic merit, especially the monumental town hall in the Damplein, now the Royal palace. The size and bulk of this edifice constituted a challenge to the nature of the sub-soil, a challenge enhanced by the choice of material, freestone, and thousands of pilings were necessary. The corporation was so anxious to spare unnecessary disappointment to the townsfolk that, in adopting the project, it refused to announce any date for completion of the work. This prudence may possibly have been influenced, too, by a superstitious fear, since Antwerp had been destroyed the very same year that its town hall had been completed. Work started on the 'palace' in 1648 and it was inaugurated in 1656. The final result was a vast rectangular mass with a dome and bell-turret, in Louis XIV style, which astonished French travellers because it had neither a flight of steps leading up to it nor even a main entrance; [8] in fact the entire length of the façade was occupied by seven small doors of identical size at street-level. The reason remains mysterious. Perhaps they symbolised the seven provinces of the Union, or were a sign of civic equality, or were intended to deprive potential rioters of a focal point. In any case, it is true that the building housed not only the communal services but also the law-court, the arsenal, the bank of Amsterdam's treasury and, in its basements, the prisons. Most visitors during the seventeenth century never tired of praising this architectural achievement, and Vondel wrote enthusiastically about it. The palace of Amsterdam did, indeed, testify magnificently to a desire for power. An allegorical sculpture in stone was commissioned: the four quarters of the world offering their tribute to the divine City.

Other towns of the Netherlands possessed more genuinely beautiful town halls than that of Amsterdam, but none could match it in sheer splendour. Travellers admired Dordrecht's town hall, and particularly that of Gouda with its plain grey stone, set askew in the very middle of the main square and dating from the middle of the fifteenth century.

Although the country was lacking in architectural monuments, it was still able to display during its 'golden age' some beautiful remnants of its past – imposing ruins, such as the medieval castle of Leyden, and curious unfinished buildings, such as the massive square belfry of Zierikzee whose builders had intended to make it the world's highest tower. Utrecht cathedral, built in late Gothic style, its 328-foot tower dominating the entire province, was constructed on a vast scale. Its nave was weakened by a hurricane and suddenly collapsed on the evening of 1st August 1674 just after the end of vespers; it was never rebuilt, but the transept was converted into a new nave, and was big enough to form a large church on its own.

Nearly all the country's churches were old Catholic edifices taken over by the Protestants, and they had all suffered from the wave of iconoclasm which had accompanied the initial stages of the religious conflict. These churches usually had a stark exterior, since the climate was apt to gnaw away the brick and sandstone and blunt the edges of the mouldings; inside they were almost bare – a pulpit, a lectern, pews, limewashed walls, no pictures. The chancel often contained the tombs of a few wealthy individuals. The Protestant Church was not a sacred place in the sense in which the Catholics understood the phrase: the people strolled around in it when the weather was bad, held meetings in it and gave concerts there.

Small towns did not always possess real churches, and so sometimes improvised huts known as 'houses of prayer'. This was the case, for instance, at Zaandijk in 1638, when Borstius was sent there as minister. But his oratorical talent soon attracted such crowds to his sermons that, in his wretched little church, 'the congregation became ill because of the lack of space, or complained of headaches so severe that they were afraid to return . . . and young children even fainted away in the arms of their mothers and were taken for dead.'⁹ A larger building had to be constructed, and when this was completed in 1642 the materials of the old building were sold for nine hundred florins; the purchaser transported the rubble to Kaag and used them to build a farmhouse.

The century's progress witnessed a marked evolution in the art of building. At its close, the sixteenth century had broken away finally from the Gothic style, and had begun to multiply articulations and emphasise contrasts that blended into the plasticity of the whole structure; the Haarlem meat-market provides an example of this new tendency.

Churches built after 1600 abandoned the traditional formula of chancel, transept with chapels and nave. The Lutheran Church of Amsterdam was built with a circular outline, as were the *marekerk* of Leyden and some others. It was no longer a question of directing the eyes of the faithful towards the east but of directing their ears towards a centre, namely the pulpit.

The Dutch Renaissance became exposed to Italian influences, and in architecture ornamentation began to lose its solid character and assume the form of decorative traceries superimposed upon a plain background. Architectural manuals of the time were full of the Italian spirit until the middle of the century, when French classicism asserted an ever-increasing influence which by the close of the century was triumphant.

With the advance of the century house-building showed an increasing tendency towards massiveness and luxurious ornamentation, especially as far as the aristocracy was concerned. Exterior design became closed in once again and the various segments blended into each other without breaks. At the same time dimensions increased. The Mauritshuis at The Hague and the Trip house at Amsterdam provided examples of this trend. Ornamentation became more homogeneous than previously, and more scientifically disposed. Houses were decorated with columns, pilasters, cornices, gargoyles, scrolled window and door frames, tritons, satyrs, birds, acanthus leaves, and sometimes – in typically Dutch fashion – with a stylised scene from daily life. But the prestige of the Parisian decorative fashions finally exhausted native inspiration, and from then on specialisation entered the relationship between architect and decorator, with the former reduced to the status of a mere builder of walls.[10]

Maintaining Order
The Netherlands, and the province of Holland in particular, presented a phenomenon of urban concentration which was unique in seventeenth-century Europe. The data we possess about the population of the various towns during that era require interpretation but remain most eloquent. Censuses in those days were undertaken solely for fiscal reasons, and the numbers they record may be considered smaller than the actual figures. The 1622 census, for instance, designed to establish the scale of a special personal tax, excluded sailors, soldiers serving in the Indies, vagabonds, non-domiciled foreigners and prisoners held in the public gaols;

on the other hand, it included the inmates of reformatories and charitable institutions. On this basis the following results were obtained:

The entire province	.	672,000 inhabitants
Amsterdam	.	105,000	,,
Leyden.	.	45,000	,,
Haarlem	.	39,000	,,
Delft	.	23,000	,,
Enkhuizen	.	21,000	,,
Rotterdam	.	19,500	,,
Dordrecht	.	18,300	,,
The Hague	.	16,000	,,

The census taken in Amsterdam in 1630, to prepare the way for the distribution of provisions on the occasion of a famine, gave the city's population as 115,000. The study of registry office figures of the period reveal a total of some 140,000 inhabitants of Amsterdam in 1640.[11] The population must, then, have grown by some twenty-five or thirty thousand people during the eighteen years preceding the city's second extension scheme. This increase in urban population was not confined to Amsterdam: by about 1700 The Hague had absorbed fifty thousand inhabitants, and Rotterdam eighty thousand.[12]

Such figures give some idea of the acute problems confronting the ill-equipped craftsmen of the period, not only in the field of house construction but also in that of public services. The main problem concerned public highways and traffic. The introduction of paved streets had followed shortly upon the advent of private carriages. William the Silent's wife, Louise de Coligny, is credited with having imported from France the first 'coach' (that is to say, a carriage with springs) to be seen in Holland. At first this novelty made little stir, and at the beginning of the seventeenth century it was still almost unknown outside The Hague; the most distinguished citizens still travelled on horseback or in hired carts. A few coaches began to make an appearance in Amsterdam and Dordrecht about 1610. Then suddenly the fashion spread. Even so, the number of these vehicles remained more than modest in comparison with those in France at that time, and in 1671 Utrecht still had less than a hundred.

However, these heavy, luxurious coaches were soon faced with competition from lighter vehicles, such as gigs lined with leather, barouches and cabs, all of French origin. From mid-century onwards fewer and fewer horsemen were to be seen.[13]

This evolution added considerably to the volume of traffic. In Amsterdam most of the streets were so narrow that a coach took up the entire carriage-way. In 1615 a scheme was devised for making all the roads leading to the bread market 'one-way streets' for commercial traffic, but by 1634 the situation appeared so hopeless that the municipal corporation simply forbade private carriages to circulate within the urban limits. But the moment this measure was adopted it was seen that the hardship fell mainly upon the most prosperous citizens, and members of the town council at that. So the law was modified, and people returning from an excursion or a voyage were allowed to travel by carriage as far as their own door, provided that they took the shortest route.

Apart from the narrowness of the streets, traffic in Amsterdam faced another major obstacle – the many steeply inclined hog-backed bridges. These posed insoluble problems of traction up to the bridge's summit and of braking when going down the other side. In 1664 a wagoner of French extraction had the idea of constructing a new type of vehicle by adapting a coach's superstructure to the chassis of a sledge, and this 'slide carriage' met immediately with tremendous success; in a few years its use had spread throughout the towns of the Union and it became a familiar and picturesque sight everywhere in the Netherlands. The upper part of the vehicle reproduced every type of open or closed carriage then in fashion, and sledges were also designed for transporting goods and merchandise within the towns. Various accessories were wedged under the iron slides at appropriate moments: greased rags to help them on, and wads of straw to slow them up. Driving such a vehicle was a difficult art. The driver trotted briskly along at the right of the sledge, reins and whip in his right hand, while his left hand kept the load steady. Without ever stopping, he guided the horses, ran forward when necessary with his greased rags or bundle of hay and pitched into the canal at the end of a cord a keg perforated with holes which he used for sprinkling the road in front of him. Nothing was allowed to slow the pace down, and pedestrians had to keep a sharp look-out. Indeed the pedestrian ran very real risks, especially after nightfall, since the sledges circulated in the streets without lanterns.

Carriages and sledges had become commonplace by 1670. The wealthier bourgeois decorated them with gilding and precious stuffs, and painted them bright colours. Anyone who did not possess his own vehicle was able to hire one, and taxi ranks for travellers and for merchandise were set up in the Dam, with stables and drinking-troughs. A traveller wanting to hire a carriage rang a bell and several coachmen would then dash forward. They each threw a dice in turn, the highest number winning the fare.

The municipal corporations had a police force at their disposal, charged with maintaining public order, seeing that statutes were carried out and executing the sentences handed down by the magistrate's court. It must be said that their efficacy was more than dubious. The choice of a 'super-bailiff', the head of the police establishment, rested more on social considerations than on those of competence. Some towns sold the post of police chief to the highest bidder, and there was no lack of candidates. An occupant of the office who was sufficiently unscrupulous or had a chequered past derived a dual advantage from it: first, it provided him with legal protection, and secondly it allowed him to make huge profits by multiplying fines arbitrarily. But more often the super-bailiff would be a member of some rich local family who would never deign to sink to such levels of corruption, and delegated his powers to an assistant bailiff, a shady character who was the direct chief of the police agents. These agents had such an evil reputation that respectable citizens kept their distance; the literature of the period expresses complete contempt for them and expatiates upon their corruption.

A sworn official, the gate-keeper, and a special guard kept watch over the town at night. In those districts which had preserved their fortified gateway, the gate-keeper lived on the lower floor. His functions consisted in opening the gates in the morning and closing them again at night, according to a time-table laid down by the corporation. Every evening, after locking up, he deposited the keys with the burgermaster or at the town hall and went to fetch them again in the morning.

The night-guard assembled in a room adjacent to his lodgings. Originally its members were drawn from bourgeois citizens engaged by the corporation on short-term contracts. But in 1620 Amsterdam replaced these by a corps of 158 professional soldiers, forming a company under the command of a captain, lieutenants and sergeants. In 1672 their number was increased to 280 by the creation of a second company, and to facilitate control the city was divided up into seventy districts. By 1685 the guard's strength was about 560 men, and the number of districts had increased to 138. A similar organisation existed in every town in the country and even in some villages.

Every evening, about ten o'clock, the rolling of a drum called the guard on parade. The officers formed the patrols and distributed equipment: a lantern, a hand-rattle and a pike or halberd. The patrol was sometimes accompanied by a dog. The round followed a fixed itinerary, and the men advanced slowly and purposefully through the deserted streets and alongside the unlit canals. Their task consisted mainly of escorting home those who had lost their way, arresting anyone breaking the law by walking abroad without a lantern in his hand, helping drunkards to their feet, notifying citizens who had failed to close their door or window securely, chasing burglars and keeping a look-out for possible fires. The rattle served as an alarm-signal and enabled the guard to summon the civil militia to the rescue in case of need. The schedules of the patrols varied according to the season and the particular place, but during the winter the guard was usually back in its quarters by four in the morning.

Sometimes belated citizens or bands of students would come up against a patrol, refuse to comply with its orders, and resort to blows. In such cases the miscreants could expect to meet with the full rigours of justice. Parival relates, for instance, that a gentleman of quality, emerging from some debauchery one night in The Hague, killed a guard. No intercession availed and offers of large sums of money were fruitless. Nothing could save him, and he was duly beheaded to serve as a public example.[14] However, the night guards' reputations were as unsavoury as those of the police; they were brutal, corruptible and more often to be found sitting in taverns than patrolling the streets, especially during the long winter nights. Some of them, indeed, were popularly supposed to be hand in glove with highwaymen and even arsonists.

Most towns also possessed night watchmen provided with trumpets who kept watch from the tops of the rampart towers. These excessive precautions may seem astonishing, but one must bear in mind that through the centuries total darkness presented terrible natural dangers to the honest man asleep in his bed. Everything which menaced his house, his belongings, his very existence became vastly more powerful during the night, and he was constantly assailed by the spectre of fire, theft, assassination; in Holland, too, there was the added danger of falling into a canal, none of which had parapets.

All these considerations justified the curfew and the multiplication of regulations (which never proved adequate) relating to public illumination. Guards, and individuals authorised to walk abroad at night, were obliged to carry a lantern or torch. But despite these measures, until about 1670 sunset plunged Dutch towns into darkness every evening, and moonlight scarcely penetrated the narrow streets or the avenues overhung with trees. From the sixteenth century onwards sporadic attempts had been made to contend more effectively with the night; in Dordrecht, for example, the town hall, the guard-house and a few other public buildings were lit by candles set in recesses and, in 1600, 4,266 candles are recorded as having been burnt during the year. In other places, small oil-lamps were attached to the corners of municipal buildings and at the entrances of dangerous bridges. In 1579 the tavern-keepers of Amsterdam received an order to hang an oil-lamp above their doors after ten in the evening, but they obeyed so unwillingly that the statute had to be renewed in 1587. In any case, the amount of light produced in this way was practically useless. In 1595 the municipal corporation decreed that in every street one house out of twelve, at equal intervals, must have an iron bracket attached to its frontage, on which a lantern was to be hooked. The order was obeyed. But the candle in the lantern was expensive and people often 'forgot' to light it. In 1597 the city had to create a corps of lantern-lighters, and another corps of collectors charged with levying a special tax for the upkeep of these functionaries. Just one technical difficulty rendered these efforts nugatory: the candles simply did not give out an adequate light.

It was only in 1669 that an effective system of public lighting finally appeared. In that year the artist Jan van der Heyden presented to the Amsterdam corporation a project for oil-lamps, specially adapted for outdoor use, to be distributed throughout the town in large numbers. This invention aroused great enthusiasm, and van der Heyden was awarded the title of 'Inspector of public lamps' and given the direction of the corps of lantern-lighters. From that time on, at nightfall, one could see the lighters perambulating the town, carrying their ladder and the rag with which they wiped away the oil obscuring the lamp's horn window-panes. In 1679, 133 lamps illuminated the city in this manner[15]; ten years later there were no less than 2,400 lit simultaneously each evening, and whose oil-level was regulated according to the length of the night. Other cities imitated Amsterdam. Jan van der Heyden's lamps were adopted by The Hague in 1678, and by Hoorn in 1682. But less important localities possessed no form of public lighting whatsoever until the end of the century.

Among the perils which the night harboured was one that street-lighting not only did not eliminate but, to some extent, increased: fire. The number of wooden buildings, the narrowness of the public thoroughfares and, above all, the primitive nature of fire-fighting equipment made fires by far the worst menace that a town had to fear. The special illuminations set up at certain festivals, with pitch or tar as fuel, were additional fire hazards. In 1665 a procession at Roermond caused a fire which razed the town; in 1667 fire entirely destroyed the village of Marken and in 1655 that of Rijp. In 1651, while the new town hall of Amsterdam was in course of construction, the old building, already partly pulled down, burst into flames under mysterious circumstances and burnt down; large quantities of silver coins deposited in its vaults melted, and some of the archives were destroyed. Flames, driven by the wind, licked across the Damplein and very nearly spread to the palace under construction.

Public opinion treated these conflagrations as natural catastrophes provoked by divine anger, but the authorities, fortunately, were rather more rational and did their best to prevent fires and to fight them when they broke out. At Wormer, the centre of the important biscuit-making industry, a special bell was installed in 1604 which announced the moment when the ovens were fired and again when they were slaked; baking was forbidden outside these hours. The materials used for building chimneys, and their shape and size, were laid down by law everywhere.

All the towns and many villages operated a signalling system, which was in the hands of the watchmen and the night-guard. In case of alarm, the guard turned his rattle in the opposite direction, thus producing a readily identifiable and dismal sound; the watchman blew a blast on his trumpet and then hung a lantern on the tower parapet facing the direction in which he had seen flames. At this signal the citizens hastily equipped themselves and came running. The relative efficiency of the Dutch system was a result of the abundance of fire-fighting equipment and the excellence of its upkeep. At Leyden the municipal fire service disposed of a dozen ladders, four hundred torches, four hundred and thirty-eight leather buckets and two ships' sails each sixty-five feet long which were soaked in water and thrown over buildings in flames. In addition, each district possessed four thirty-runged ladders, two of twenty-three rungs and eight of ten rungs, four hundred torches and two sails. Finally, each person inhabiting a lodging with a rateable value of one to thirty florins had to own a bucket in good condition, each house rated from thirty to two hundred florins had to have a small ladder, houses rated from two hundred to six hundred florins two ladders and houses rated at over six hundred florins two ladders and a bucket. Business premises were subject to similar regulations: a beer-house was assessed six buckets, a weaving-works four buckets, a bakery two. Each year, during April, the municipal authorities made an inspection tour of all this equipment; every citizen stood in front of his door by the side of his display of buckets and ladders while the officials proceeded slowly down the street examining it all. This method of organisation was more or less identical in all the towns. Jan van der Heyden also played a role in this field. As a result of the violent fire which destroyed the Navy's rope storeroom in Amsterdam on 12th January 1673, he persuaded the corporation to adopt a pump he had invented; this was worked by a syringe and a system of pipes and was capable of throwing a jet of water as thick as an arm and powerful enough to reach the roof-tops of the highest houses.

The services of public hygiene may seem rudimentary to us today, but, at the time, they largely justified the Netherlands' reputation for cleanliness.

In every town officials exercised control, in the name of the interested guilds, over the marketing of perishable foodstuffs such as meat, fish, wine and even wheat. In the absence of any means of refrigeration, and in view of the relative slowness of transportation, the corporations of the large towns were particularly concerned with the control of fish, and complicated statutes were enacted. At The Hague, for instance, the fish brought in from the port of Scheveningen was not allowed to enter the town by the quickest route but, rather, alternatively from the north and from the south, so that each district in turn might have its share of freshly caught fish. All waste products had to be removed to outside the city limits within half an hour of market closing time. At Utrecht, stale wine was thrown into the canal, and it was forbidden to use spoiled wheat, although its sale in the villages of the province was authorised.

Foreign travellers of the period invariably commented on the cleanliness of Dutch streets. Every bourgeois washed, or had washed, the pavement and roadway outside his house, and sometimes sprinkled them with fine sand. At Broek the street-paving was scrubbed with brushes, and the corporation pushed its zeal to the point of forbidding the inhabitants to satisfy the needs of nature in the street. Broek Alkmaar and Leyden rivalled each other in cleanliness, and foreign visitors were hard put to decide which town deserved first prize in this field.[16] However, Leyden suffered gravely from the nature of its canals, which contained currentless water that was often stagnant and evil-smelling. An attempt was made to remedy this state of affairs by digging a waterway as far as the sea, but the project had to be abandoned since it would have involved cutting through the line of dunes at Catwijk and so endangering a part of the province lying below sea-level. The canals remained an insalubrious feature of these well-groomed towns. Town drainage was unknown in the Netherlands of the seventeenth century, and dirty water and rubbish was simply dumped into the canal. Occasionally dredgers would pass along the canals removing the accumulated sludge from their bottoms. Even so, the atmosphere in the towns became most unwholesome during the hot season.

At least the rubbish that accumulated on the roadway could be disposed of. Whereas in France, at that time, streets had a slightly concave surface with a gutter running along the middle, in Holland the streets were convex and gutters ran along each side of the road. Movable planks covered them. The citizens living along these streets were responsible for keeping the gutter clean and keeping the planks in good condition the length of their house-frontages. At The Hague a municipal roadman was specially charged with sprinkling the courtyard of the

Voorhout with water several times a day in summer. He accomplished this with the aid of a watering-cart drawn by horses, a unique procedure in that age.

THE COUNTRYSIDE

Geography in the seventeenth century had isolated the Netherlands from the rest of Europe. On one side was the sea, on the other sandy moors and marshland; the country seemed to be surrounded by 'deserts'.[1] The Rhine and the Maas, known as the 'great rivers', separated Dutch territory from Flanders and Spanish Brabant with a confusion of deltas sending out innumerable branches and inlets with ill-defined banks. Willows grew in this region, rooted in exhausted soil whose erosion was only partly prevented by lines of tarred stakes. In some places thin strips of marsh-land, where reeds flourished and ducks nested, separated these barriers from the firm river-bank. A dike skirted the broad Biesbosch swamp, and along it ran the highway shaded by linden trees. Beyond lay the absolute flatness of the Dutch countryside, cut by canals and ditches.

A traveller coming from France had the choice of two routes into the interior of the country. One, which today we would call a tourist route, skirted the sea and was less a road than a promenade of fine sand flanked by tall dunes dotted with spikes of gorse; this long beach stretched in an almost straight line for more than sixty miles, from the mouth of the Rhine to the vicinity of Helder. At its northern extremity a relatively recent catastrophe had cut off the island of Texel from the mainland. During the seventeenth century one could still see great tree-trunks rising from the bed of the newly formed branch of the sea. Boats' anchors sometimes became inextricably entangled with them, and fishermen avoided throwing their nets in these waters. Beyond stretched the whole Zuider Zee, a dangerous sea whose surface occasionally revealed the humps of sandbanks. The winds produced heavy swells and the shallowness of the water necessitated the constant use of narrow straits between the shallows and the islands of Marken, Schokland, Urk and Wieringen.

The other route was the one normally taken. It gave access to the great towns of Holland as well as to the country's central and northern provinces and crossed through a region which was then still two-thirds under water and abounded in rivers, lakes, ponds and swamps. The earth seemed to melt away in these parts, and boats provided the only convenient means of getting from one place to another; villages were rarer here than in any other part of the Netherlands. To the north stretched the districts of 'northern Holland' with their highways bordered by great trees. To the east lay the province of Utrecht, traversed by the beautiful River Vecht winding its serpentine way under the shade of tall trees. To the north-east, on the coast of Zuider Zee, the region of wooded dunes called the Gooi formed an extension of Gelderland with its heaths and vast forests peopled with great flocks of sheep, wild boars, castles and legends. From there, spanning the River Ijssel, the roads led northwards again, crossing the desert-like province of Drenthe whose infertile lands were interspersed with clumps of oak trees and with pathetic 'castles'. The roads then passed through the sparsely populated territory of Groningen which was, nevertheless, one of the best cultivated and most prosperous provinces of the Union. From its small coastal ports one could reach the Frisian islands, teeming with pheasants and sea-birds, and the most southerly point on the migration routes of seals. Towards the west, Friesland, studded with lakes but with comparatively few canals, displayed its fields bordered by hedges and its copses. From there, embarking at Harlingen, the traveller could go downstream again by sailing-boat in the direction of Zeeland, with its fertile islands spreading through the immense stretch of water where the Rhine, the Maas and the Scheldt gradually became a sea.

Mildness and changeableness characterised the climate of this country. Winters and summers were generally temperate, all the seasons were windy, it rained a lot but snowed rarely. Ice forming on lakes or canals seldom lasted more than a few days, or a few weeks at the most. In some years the waters did not freeze at all, and in 1630, for example, the winter is recorded as having been abnormally warm. The scourge of this country was the humidity of its atmosphere, resulting in continuous mists. Amsterdam was particularly unfortunate in this respect, since the marshes surrounding the city gave rise to more fogs there than anywhere else. In fact, natural climatic conditions may be considered to have been rather rough, and foreigners who lived long enough in the Netherlands to feel its long-term effects tended to complain of headaches, rheumatism and somnolence. Saumaise and Descartes both complained that the softness of the air was prejudicial to intellectual activity.[2]

The Dutch countryside was monotonous and yet immensely charming. The large number of waterways created a marvellous impression of variety in uniformity, and the windmills became picturesque symbols of the Dutch landscape. Many distinguished foreigners made visits to Holland during this era; they were attracted simply by its beauty and may be considered tourists before the invention of tourism. The impressions they brought back from their travels were composed of mixed memories in which the countryside provided the basic harmony, the pleasant and confused background against which the 'magnificence' of the towns stood out.

In fact, the Netherlands remained essentially urban in character, especially the province of Holland. The many towns were usually rich and always heavily populated and collectively they dominated the life of the nation, determining its customs, its politics and its spiritual orientations. The country districts played only a passive role; they followed where the towns led. However, in the densely populated western and southern provinces, which lacked those vast empty spaces typical of the surrounding countries, the distinction between towns and villages (as we understand the terms) was ill-defined, being based entirely on the community's legal status. The status of township was bestowed only on built-up areas surrounded by ramparts, possessing a municipal toll-house and sending deputies to the provincial States. In the province of Holland only eighteen localities carried this title: they were Amsterdam, Leyden, Haarlem,

Delft, Gouda, Dordrecht, Rotterdam, Gorkum, Schiedam, Schoonhoven, Brielle, Alkmaar, Hoorn, Enkhuizen, Medemblik, Edam, Monnikendam and Purmerend. Several of these remained, in fact, straggling villages throughout the seventeenth century, while on the other hand some important localities, including The Hague, were still considered officially to be villages. The 'village' of Zaandam was an important industrial centre with five miles of quays and at the height of its power could count twenty-thousand inhabitants.

Only some of the four hundred villages in the province of Holland included in a 1660 census constituted small agricultural communities. These latter increased considerably in the eastern provinces but became fewer once again in the north of the country. These villages were smart and neat and had their own traditional local styles of living, determined by the nature of the ground and the character of the regional economy. The fishermen of Marken built their houses of tarred wood on artificial mounds or on high pilings; they comprised a single room in the centre of which a fire was kindled on a sheet of iron at floor-level. In the districts of Twente and Veluwe, the farmhouses were not partitioned inside and man and beast shared the same vast space; the floors were of beaten earth or rough paving, the roof-beams of plain oak, the walls made of mud. The main frontage, preceded by its well fitted with a bucket-chain, faced the opposite direction from the roadway; a large doorway gave onto the street itself and was used for the cattle and carts. In the wretched Drenthe the woodcutters lived in cabins made of peat blocks, practically windowless and half underground. The plains of Groningen were dotted with immense fortress-like farms divided into three main buildings.[3] In the Limburg region, constructions were of similar design to that prevalent in France at the time—living quarters, stables and barn surrounded a square courtyard closed by a large gateway.[4] A ditch surmounted by a removable bridge usually encircled these houses. The frontage was shaded by a curtain of trees and there would often be a vine planted near the door and growing as high as the roof, with its spreading branches supported by poles. The roofs were usually thatched, which was no doubt the reason why these houses had no chimneys; the smoke escaped through the door, or through a special trap-door.

Although they were sometimes isolated, farms tended more to be grouped irregularly around those specifically public establishments, the church, the smithy and the inn, whose picturesque appearance inspired so many painters. The fields were unenclosed, except in Friesland. Dogs were sometimes used to tow flat-bottomed boats along the ditches, and in the evenings the peasants went by boat to milk their cows in the pastures.

This tranquil atmosphere inspired wealthy townspeople to build elegant villas in the country, places where the great merchants could take their leisure, away from the bustle of the city, and where they stayed on Sundays and during the summer months. Favourite places for these country retreats were Betuwe, Veluwe, the regions around Delft and, above all, along river banks. These rural palaces were built on grassy slopes and half-hidden by a profusion of greenery; they were far the most extravagant luxury of the wealthy classes. Most of the great bourgeois families of Amsterdam had such properties along the Vecht or the Amstel. The magnificent appearance and interior comfort of these houses contrasted with a parsimonious attitude towards the gardens; the limited space available was devoted to a few fenced walks arranged around a lawn and sometimes a small pond, but there was neither decorative stone-work nor trimmed hedging. French and Italian influences gradually made themselves felt in garden design and there appeared miniature waterfalls, fountains, artificial grottoes, bowers of greenery, little islands, little bridges over tiny lakes. But the space available remained as limited as ever and the gardens sometimes became cluttered with an accumulation of ornamentations in dubious taste. A fashion of literary origin decreed that these pleasure-grounds should be transformed into Arcadias, and indeed a few people tried to recreate meticulously the gardens of Armida with the help of engravings and idyllic paintings! At another time a maze would be the fashionable thing to have, and people spent their time stumbling along twisting pathways between clipped hedges. This particular horticultural curiosity was so popular that in 1613 the city of Amsterdam had a maze designed and built on the edge of the Princes' Canal.

Castles in the real sense of the word were relatively scarce in the Union during the seventeenth century. The one exception was Gelderland, a land of minor squires. Elsewhere, some more or less modernised medieval structures still survived here and there. One of the most impressive was Muiden Castle, dating from the thirteenth century, on the bank of the Zuider Zee twelve miles from Amsterdam.

Provincial individualism, illustrated by the extreme diversity of landscapes, activities and ways of living, easily engendered a sort of chauvinism. Men of Holland, Zeeland and Groningen held jealously to the particularities of their local costume. It seemed that the patriotism aroused by the war of liberation had crystallised at a local level. The age was still close enough to its medieval origins for the ordinary people to visualise their country in terms of the town and, to an even greater extent, the village (since the city-dweller had more contact with the outside world). What could there possibly be in common, during the course of public life, between a shepherd from Drenthe, imprisoned in his heather-covered moors with its black peat soil, and a fisherman of Zeeland? The men of Gelderland were known to be unparalleled as warriors, yet the province of Holland recruited mercenaries in Germany and Scandinavia. From town to town, and from village to village, costumes, housing arrangements, the conduct of private or public feasts, the shapes of tools, the local dialect all varied in some detail; and this detail was of immense importance. Each district had its own special songs, deriving from folklore or literature, often printed in collections in the neighbourhood. There were pious songs and love songs and also innumerable patriotic songs turned out by local poets in praise of their little country. Within a few miles of each other, Hoorn, Alkmaar and Enkhuizen rivalled each other in versification. Each of these towns claimed to be the most ancient, the most beautiful, the most prosperous. In the taverns where these songs were sung the recitations often ended in brawls, usually when an outsider countered with a paean of praise for his own town and got soundly thrashed for his pains. Local legends nurtured this collective consciousness. In the village of Loosduijn two copper fonts in the church were displayed as being those in which had been baptised the 364 children born to the countess Machtilde in a single day. In Edam it was related that a mermaid had been captured and domesticated once upon a time. The sandbank obstructing the Stavoren channel was said to have originated as a cargo of wheat, dumped overboard long ago in spite by a rich widow whose sailors had refused to obey her orders.

The megaliths which were common in the north-east were thought there to be the work of gigantic demons.

HIGHWAYS AND CANALS

The network of internal lines of communication was developed to a remarkable degree, and the organisation of public transport was more advanced in Holland than in any other country of Europe during the era with which we are concerned. The ease with which one could get from one place to another in this flat country, criss-crossed with waterways, was an important factor in the establishment of commercial activity; and commerce in its turn provided the means for improving the conditions of the roads and canals and multiplying the possible means of transport. Between Delft and The Hague the traveller could choose between two itineraries, a tree-lined highway or a canal also shaded by trees. Between Leyden and Amsterdam he had a choice of four regular routes: by boat, either across the lake of Haarlem or through the canal which was dug about the middle of the century, or by the nightly public ferry across the lake of Braassemer, or by carriage or on horseback by the road leading through the marshes. Except in the east of the country, where the waterways were less frequent, there always existed two separate means of transport for any one journey. In general, the public preferred the canals and rivers to the roads.

But the technique of road construction left much to be desired. Earth paths running along the dikes and the sea-walls were sufficient for local traffic. A few excellent carriage-ways were constructed during the course of the century, as, for instance, the one connecting The Hague with Scheveningen, which Temple described as being 'worthy of the Romans'.[1] But more often than not the road was just a sandy track with neither embankments nor footpaths. They were only readily identifiable to the eye by the marks left by the carriage-wheels. And these ruts became gradually deeper and wider, so that in time the continuous traffic widened the road surface to such an extent that it began to encroach on the bordering fields. The very ancient road from Arnhem to Harderwijk, traversing a region without waterways capable of limiting its meanderings, achieved in places a width of over half a mile. The long autumn and spring rains turned these roads into bogs into which the carriages sank; the winter frost made death-traps out of the hardened ruts; and the heat of summer turned the surface into a dust that coated the traveller thickly. It was considered an important step forward at the beginning of the century when the States of Holland and of Utrecht decreed a standard axle width for carriages of both provinces. This helped to prevent the ruts from spreading too far afield and reduced the jolting slightly. But the unfortunate traveller using a vehicle from Gelderland or Overijssel to get to Amsterdam was simply shaken up worse than ever!

Yet this state of affairs was not as shocking to foreigners as one might imagine; the truth being that almost the entire European network of highways in the seventeenth century was lamentable. The one comparative advantage of the Dutch roads was that they offered rather more security than those of other countries, as a result of the enactment of appropriate penal legislation. During the first years after the army had been disbanded, gangs of discharged soldiers scoured the country, attacking stage-coaches and people travelling alone. But these gangs were gradually dispersed and brigandage soon became far less common.

Without doubt, the next clump of bushes might still conceal a band of thieves, but the magistrates kept a careful watch on the situation and miscreants were rapidly brought to justice: for example, arrested highwaymen were hanged at the spot where they had performed their final exploit. When Huyghens left for Italy in 1620 he counted no less than fifty gibbets along the 120 miles of the Rhine road.

Originally, traffic was limited to pedestrians, horsemen and private or hired carriages. Around the middle of the century there appeared stage-coaches, public vehicles organised into regular lines with a fixed time-table. These were long, open carts without springs, with high wheels, covered by a waxed cloth stretched over iron hoops, and driven by two or four horses. Small leather sails were hoisted, and furled or unfurled according to the wind; they helped the vehicle achieve remarkable speeds for this period (at the price of the passengers' extreme discomfort). Barring accidents, such as broken axles or wheels, over-turning into a ditch or a hold-up, the stage-coaches averaged fifty to sixty miles a day, even taking into account the time required for changes of horses and the postillion's stops at taverns on the way!

Departure, transit and arrival points in the towns, to be found either near one of the gates or in a square, constituted real highway stations. The Hague line left Korsjespoort for Amsterdam twice a day, in the morning (except during the summer, when the court was out of town) between six and seven, and every afternoon at one o'clock. The Arnhem stage-coach left Amsterdam each Monday at dawn, passed through the little villages of the Gooi, discharged those passengers wanting to go north at Amers-foort, and continued its voyage eastward. It reached Arnhem on Tuesday at ten o'clock, connecting with another coach leaving for Cologne. A stage-coach left Groningen at three in the morning, stopped at Beilen at eleven for lunch, and reached Kampen in the evening; here a night con-nection took travellers on to Amersfoort, and from there connections were available for Utrecht and Amsterdam. So the trip from Groningen to Amsterdam lasted forty-two hours.[2] Prices were extremely high, and the three outside seats were assigned different tariffs according to their relative degree of 'comfort'.[3]

The first public transport by water had originated during the fifteenth and sixteenth centuries between a few towns in the province of Holland. This initial system spread gradually until in the seventeenth century it embraced the entire country. At first, rivers and lakes were used, since they were easy to navigate by sail. Then canals were dug to connect these bodies of water, and the boats were towed from one to the other natural waterway. During the twenty years between 1610 and 1630 great constructional plans were put into action, all designed to speed up communications and accelerate traffic. Canals were dug between Rotterdam and Delft, Amsterdam and Haarlem, Amsterdam and Gouda, Haarlem and Leyden and Haarlem and Delft. The cost of these works was very small, since water was abundant everywhere and it sufficed sometimes to clear a channel between the marshes and lay out a rough tow-path along one bank. The construction and upkeep of the lock-gates was a more costly item than the digging and banking of the canals; in addition, each new waterway required the construction of numerous bridges, preferably wooden ones since it was necessary that the superstructure could be raised to allow boats to pass through. Even so, the prime cost of water transportation remained a quarter of the cost of road transportation.

In 1630 the economic importance of the canals was greatly increased by the invention of the 'water-coach', a boat towed by a horse. Up till then boats without sails had been towed by manpower, five men harnessed to a rope and plodding breathlessly along the tow-path. But from now on the boat's payload could be considerably increased and costs proportionately lowered. It was explained to William Temple that, with the same force being exerted in each instance, a horse was capable of drawing along a surface of water a load fifty times heavier than the contents of a carriage along a road.[4]

The passenger vessel was a long boat with a deck,

containing a public saloon and a cabin above deck, and could accommodate about fifty passengers with their baggage. The interior was scrupulously clean, and fitted with comfortable rows of benches; one could read and write there and sleep sitting up, and the passengers ate and drank there as well. The merchant on a business trip prepared his documents and so on. In fact, it was a sort of Noah's Ark, and foreigners were astonished by the mixture of different classes of the population, rich merchants, officials, peasants, sailors, prostitutes, sitting together in noisy and colourful proximity. Gossip flourished, political discussions became heated, romances developed. Song-books were produced specially for the use of the canal-boat passengers.[5] The boatman, sometimes a young lad, guided the craft from the bank, astride the horse. He was usually quarrelsome, vulgar and unruly, and it became necessary to pass a special statute forbidding him to brandish a knife during discussions with his customers.

These passenger-boats were run on the same kind of schedules as the stage-coaches, with the advantages over the stage-coach that they kept to their schedule with remarkable efficiency. At the appointed hour a bell was rung on the quayside to collect the travellers together. At the last stroke the vessel cast off, without waiting for latecomers. The cost of the voyage was calculated according to the distance involved, and even the smallest towns were served by this passenger-boat system throughout the Union. On each line a boat left more or less every hour from sunrise to sunset. Some lines, such as that from Amsterdam to Gouda, even kept up a night service.

The various advantages compensated the users for the slowness of this form of transport, which was three or four times slower than the stage-coach. This fact resulted mainly from the artificial obstacles which barred the way to the boat at regular intervals. Fixed bridges and dikes demanded frequent transhipments; this was the case, for instance, at Halfweg on the important Amsterdam-Haarlem canal. It would have been simple and inexpensive to create detours, but there were too many vested interests opposed to any change, especially if the presence of the obstacle involved some fiscal advantage in the way of tolls or taxes. Overtoom was the administrative headquarters of two water services, and although it lay just outside Amsterdam its canal installations were the responsibility of the Haarlem corporation; a small wooden dike cut the canal and boats had to be hoisted over with the aid of winding-gear, while large vessels had no choice but to make a detour by way of Haarlem where they had to pay a toll!

Such absurdities resulted from jurisdictions inherited from the Middle Ages, and their continued maintenance was justified by the differences existing between the level of the waters in the territories of the various municipalities. Certain localities possessed ancient privileges requiring that all traffic within a given radius must go by way of their urban waterways, so ensuring the imposition of a toll. This state of affairs was particularly irritating at Gouda where the toll-house was established on the town's extremely narrow central canal, and when traffic was dense, boats had to queue up for hours on end. Yet, a few hundred yards away, a broad canal skirted the suburbs. But the town corporation forbade access to it for any vessels other than warships!

The highways were by no means exempt from this kind of servitude, and in some regions a toll-gate barred the road at intervals. A notice-board indicating the amount of the toll had a box attached underneath, and the required sum was deposited therein. Every two or three days an official called by and emptied the box.

The legal status of the boatmen complicated the workings of the boat services in yet another manner. On each line the boatmen were appointed by the burgermaster: but which burgermaster? That of the town of departure or the town of arrival? Custom was the deciding factor, but gave rise to endless conflicts. One day the Haarlem passenger-boat tied up in the centre of Amsterdam, but the police forbade the passengers to disembark and arrested the boatman for verification of his identity. This was sheer harassment, and Haarlem lodged a complaint with the court of

Holland which judged in its favour. Feeling ran high in Amsterdam, and each arrival of a boat from Haarlem gave rise to disorders and brawls. Traffic became paralysed. Finally a contract was duly sealed which stipulated that a boatman from Haarlem and one from Amsterdam should operate alternative trips on this line. Along the highways, at road-posts, in the towns and hamlets, and in many of the villages the traveller could find any number of common inns, taverns equipped with a few bedrooms or simply a straw-covered floor, rowdy and often sordid. The great towns possessed more comfortable establishments, comparable to the hotels of today: *The Emperor* and *The Goose* at 's Hertogenbosch, *The Pelican* and *The Lion* at Haarlem. By 1680 The Hague possessed nine such hostelries, Rotterdam six and Amsterdam at least a hundred. In some places, such as 's Hertogenbosch, Dordrecht, Utrecht and Amsterdam, the old indoor archery ranges had been converted into municipal hostelries.[6] Lastly, there were official institutions called 'Gentlemen's lodgings' in the most important centres, offering hospitality to distinguished visitors. Where such lodgings did not exist the guest was placed in the hands of a prominent local citizen.

In 1689 an Amsterdam bookseller published a 'Traveller's Guide' giving detailed information about the means of transportation throughout the Republic's territory. It included maps of the land and water routes; time-tables; lists of fairs and markets, inns and churches; conversion tables for money and units of measure; texts of prayers appropriate to various stages of the journey; hymns suitable for singing in the morning and the evening at the inn. There followed advice of a hygienic and moral nature: beware of the pleurisy which menaces you in the humidity of the canal-boat; beware of the promiscuity of the prostitute; drink neither wine nor beer, since the subsequent evacuation may pose awkward problems. . . .

CHAPTER TWO

THE DUTCH INTERIOR

The House: Arrangement and Furnishing, Gardens and Flowers—The Toilet: Waking, Washing and Hair-styling, Ways of Dressing—Food: Setting the Table, Dutch Cooking—The Evening at Home.

THE HOUSE: *Arrangement and furnishing*

If we were to stop in front of some middle-class house overlooking one of the town's canals, we should find ourselves confronted by a heavy oak door, waxed or painted green and carrying a metal knocker, iron in the case of a modest establishment, heavy silver if the owner were wealthy. It would be considered good manners not to knock too loudly. In any case, if our voyage had led us to some small town in the province of Holland, we should rather have knocked at the small door of the 'vault', or entered by way of the courtyard, for in such houses the principal entrance was reserved by tradition for marriages and funerals.

A key would turn in the key-hole ornamented with copper plaques, a servant would open the door, and we should find ourselves in a room which we might hesitate to call an entrance-hall – the *voorhuis*, centre of domestic activity, often large and well lit by the front windows. Around and beneath this room a complicated system of short stairways, flights of steps and doors connected the rooms at street-level with those of the 'vault', the latter containing the cellars and domestic offices. In a typical Dutch house of this period no two rooms were at the same level, and going from one room to another involved climbing up or down stairs.

The nucleus around which the typical house was planned

consisted of the two rooms which originally constituted the entire dwelling, the 'front room' and the 'back room'. In the seventeenth century only the humblest town dwellings retained this simplicity. The two traditional rooms still remained, separated by a wooden partition-wall, sometimes with windows set into it, or by a corridor opening onto several small anterooms and divided half-way down by a few steps and an arched wooden framework. Through an open door we might have seen a room full of light and shade with an added splash of colour provided by a young woman's dress, and we might also have caught a glimpse of the reflections from a spring garden. A scene such as this often provided inspiration for Jan Steen, Vermeer, Pieter de Hoogh and Metsu. From this corridor, or directly from the entrance-hall, a spiral staircase would lead to a mezzanine room known as a 'suspended room', then to the upper storey. The way the rooms were divided up was sometimes strange, with the partition wall going up to the centre of a window so that the room on each side received light through half of it. Another staircase, so narrow that it was hardly more than a ladder, led to the loft and to the attics under their framework of huge black crossbeams and rafters.

The houses of simple folk were sparsely furnished, but during the course of the century wealthier families tended to accumulate increasing quantities of furniture. Local fashions were perceptible in the choice of all this furniture: Dordrecht still clung to traditional Dutch simplicity while Amsterdam, Rotterdam and Delft were busy imitating The Hague, where English and French styles reigned successively. On the whole, furniture was still heavy and massive at the beginning of the century and most pieces were made of oak or walnut, but dimensions gradually became lighter. By the end of the century lines had become more supple and graceful under the influence of the French cabinet-makers.

Three pieces comprised the basic units of furniture: the table, the chair and the cupboard. They were to be found in all the rooms, and were the pride of the housewife and the object of the carpenter's principal decorative efforts. In 1600 the table was still a thick rectangular platform resting on bulbous legs, sometimes covered with a serge tablecloth, or damask in a wealthy home. Later, various types introduced from abroad became popular: Italian-style tables with two flaps supported by vertical ledges, folding tables, three-legged pedestal tables designed to be placed against the wall, and various other English and French styles. Chairs kept more of their traditional Dutch style, with their leg-rails, high backs and low leather-covered seats on which one or even two thick cushions were placed. The habit gradually spread of covering the chairs with moquette or velvet attached by copper nails. At the same time various designs were carved in the chair-backs and the whole framework became lighter.

The classic furniture in good Dutch society was the cupboard. Modest townfolk and peasants had old-fashioned medieval chests set flat on the floor, which opened with a lid and were painted in green and red and decorated with rudimentary drawings. But the cupboard was an expensive article at that time,[1] the basic luxury of the household, symbolising success, social ambition, wealth and comfort. During the course of the century the original square, deep, massive, clumsy cupboard carved in plain wood also became lighter and began to resemble the French type of 'cabinet', inlaid with decorative panels of mother-of-pearl or ivory. From 1670 onwards wealthy householders flanked their cupboards with real cabinets, valuable chests fitted with drawers and standing on long legs. A well-furnished house included at least two cupboards. First there was the sacrosanct linen-cupboard, perfumed with sweet woodruff, entirely under the control of the mistress of the house. The linen-cupboard in the home of the wealthy Vrouw Blijenborgh of Dordrecht, for example, contained the following treasures: sheets from the East Indies, from Haarlem, Flanders, Amsterdam, Alkmaar, Friesland and Emden, arranged according to their origin; bonnets, handkerchiefs and neckerchiefs dating back to her grandmother's childhood; twenty-four dozen shirts, forty dozen table-cloths and napkins set aside for her children's dowries. As another example, an Amsterdam bookseller of modest fortune managed to squeeze into his cupboard sixty sheets, thirty table-cloths and more than three hundred table-napkins. Some fashionable people replaced the linen-cupboard by an Indian chest veneered with copper or silver, or by a chest carved in Holland which they covered with blue cloth. The second indispensable cupboard was the china-cupboard, given the place of honour in the main reception-room, displaying on its shelves plates, pots, dishes painted with designs and sometimes musical instruments. Dressers were also in use, with pyramidal rows of shelves. And many people, even in the country, possessed also a cupboard with glazed doors in which they displayed precious objects. Here the mistress of the house often kept the presents she had received at her baptism and her marriage souvenirs.

The general appearance of the Dutch interior, as outlined above, was often charmingly intimate, but most French visitors of the period found it lacking in comfort. Whatever the social class of its occupant the structure of his house remained essentially identical. In the poorer streets the façades would be even narrower, the windows scarcer and the main corridor wound its way under low ceilings. In the dim light the furniture would be reduced to a few in-dispensable pieces in the heavy, solid traditional native style. Poor workmen and apprentices crammed into the 'vaults' and the lofts.

Each room in the house had a particular character of its own, depending on the use to which it was put. The 'entrance-hall' was the successor to the old 'front room' which had once served as shop or workshop. In the case of small tradesmen and the humblest craftsmen it still retained this function, and they worked there with the door wide open and the merchandise displayed outside under the canopy. The teacher usually held his classes in the entrance-hall, and the inn-keeper used it for his tavern or his smoking-saloon. The petty bourgeois made it his main living-room, decorating it with plaques of painted porcelain and furnish-ing it with a table, a few chairs, his china-cupboard, a mirror and his set of copper cauldrons. Against a wall, in one corner, he would place a carved wooden bench. In wealthy homes the entrance-hall became a drawing-room. The bench would be marble, the walls would be covered with pictures and hunting trophies. The decorative function of this room in prosperous families inspired such wholesome respect that the mistress of the house, her daughters and her servant were careful not to use it for fear of disturbing its perfect order. They installed themselves in a small adjacent room (which, in the homes of plain people was sometimes confused with the old 'back room') and here the greater part of their domestic life took place. Here they sewed, knitted and served the daily meals. This 'living-room' was usually in the front of the house and had a small window giving a view of the street but letting in little light. It was simply furnished. A rich timber merchant of Dordrecht might have an oak table in this room and a few chairs with leather cushions, plaques of white porcelain and pictures on the walls, a lectern in one corner with a Bible lying on it and, finally, two heavy cupboards, one of which, under its green curtains, might be used as a bookcase.

The number of rooms on the ground floor varied enormously according to the wealth of the owner. But in every house there was either a kitchen, a recess, or some kind of space in which meals were prepared. In poor people's homes it was an alcove from which smoke, reeking with cooking odours, filled every corner of the house whenever the chimney was blocked or the wind was in the wrong direction. But in bourgeois residences, on the contrary, the kitchen was promoted to a position of fantastic dignity and became something between a temple and a museum. Copper and pewter kitchen utensils shone all along the walls, the table might be painted pink and sometimes the floor would be tiled with marble. A glass-fronted cupboard contained the crockery, while another cupboard, called the 'treasury', held provisions, the table linen in use at the time, sauce-boats and trenchers. An enormous chimney-piece dominated one side of the room; the hearth, with its tarred rear wall, contained the 'fire-pot', a kind of primitive stove open at the top and, on either side, the stew-pan and the peat-box. A small copper sink could be filled from a tap fed by a pump connected to a cistern. The kitchen of a wealthy bourgeois visited by Monconys in 1663 had a marble sink, a bronze pump and, as a final technical marvel, a copper tank concealed in the wall in which water heated continuously and invisibly.[2] But nothing in all this magnificence gave the slightest hint of gastronomic activity.

According to the abbé Sartre, 'they would prefer to die of hunger surrounded by their shining cauldrons and sparkling crockery rather than prepare any dish which might conceivably disarrange this perfect symmetry. They showed me proudly the cleanliness of their kitchen, which was as cold two hours before dinner as it might have been after dinner.'[3] Indeed, the mistress of the house often prepared the meals in some neighbouring recess and contented herself, in the kitchen itself, with boiling a kettle of water.

The staircase leading to the first floor in prosperous houses gave yet another opportunity for decoration. Usually made of wood, though sometimes of marble, its banisters were carved with figures, lions, plants or the arms of the master of the house. But this was becoming rarer, and the more typical staircase of the period was dangerously precipitous, winding in the older buildings and straight in the more modern ones, as narrow as it was steep. It opened on a corridor, with rooms leading off on each side, usually no more than two or three altogether. These were usually the family's bedrooms. But in some large houses the bedrooms were situated on the ground floor or relegated to the second floor, while the first floor was reserved for formal rooms. In addition, the idea of a bedroom, properly so-called, was new and by no means widespread during the seventeenth century. In modest establishments the beds were set up in the living-room: not set up so much as constructed, since they were built into the wall like wall-cupboards and were so short that one had to sleep sitting up. In their lower section these 'sleeping cupboards' had a drawer in which the small children slept. If the family was too large for everyone to find a berth in the available beds, some of the children went up to the loft to sleep.

If we should open one of these plain oak doors decorated by some painted or carved mythological scene and go in, we should find ourselves in a bedroom belonging, perhaps, to a prosperous merchant. Here, too, squares of porcelain would decorate the walls; a mirror would reflect the sparse light; there would be a few pictures. Some family souvenirs on the chimney canopy, two low chairs with very high backs, a table, the great linen-cupboard, a wash-stand consisting of a basin and jug on a flat slab, would constitute the room's entire furnishing, apart from the bed. A quarter of the room was taken up by the bed with its bed-posts and tester, square in shape and with a green damask curtain running around it. The finely embroidered top sheet was folded back over the damask bed-spread. This would be considered a 'modern' bed for the period, when the 'sleeping-cupboard' was just beginning to lose favour in the towns, though not yet in the country. But it still retained many features of the old-style bed, especially in the homes of the petty bourgeoisie; it was so high that a set of steps was needed to climb into it and the children's sleeping-compartments were arranged underneath – a custom which inspired a good deal of ribaldry among foreigners. In wealthy houses the bed was placed in the centre of the room, sometimes on a plinth, and the tester was decorated with garlands and festoons and had the owner's arms carved into its top. Sprays of feathers were attached to its four corners and the four posts supporting it and the curtains were carved in the shape of caryatids, satyrs and angels. It must be said that this decorative extravagance did not compensate for the unsatisfactory nature of the bed-clothes; one slept on a thick feather-bag, the bed-frame had no cross-bars, one's body was kept in a slightly raised position by piles of soft pillows and one was covered by a second feather-bag similar to the first one. The heat soon became intolerable between so many feathers.

At the beginning of the century, the floors of elegant houses were paved in the Italian manner with coloured tiling, formed, for example, from alternating square white and blue tiles. The formal reception-rooms might be paved in marble. Later, the French fashion of parquet flooring was introduced, but most interiors remained loyal to the traditional, more or less rough, native floor-planks. The flooring was rarely left bare. If it was tiled it would probably be partly covered by Spanish matting in black and yellow stripes with multi-coloured edging. Yet carpets were very little used; occasionally one very small carpet might be laid down in the centre of the room in honour of an important guest, but it would be rolled up again as soon as the guest had departed. If the floor was of wood it would be sprinkled with fine coloured sand; on special occasions flowers or other patterns were traced in this surface of sand.

The ceiling was made of open beams joined by cross-slats. The wealthy had their ceilings plastered and then adorned with romantic, mythological or allegorical paintings. In certain rooms little wooden or metal knick-knacks representing boats, coaches, fish, coats of arms and war-flags were hung from the beams. And one might see, swaying at the end of a chain or ribbon, the paper crown worn by the mistress of the house on the day of her betrothal.

The impecunious petty bourgeois contented himself with whitewashing the walls of his room. His more prosperous colleague would cover his with squares of glazed tile in contrasting colours. However, a panel of wood was generally placed behind cupboards and beds. In well-to-do households at the beginning of the century the walls were plastered; then the height of the plasterwork gradually diminished, and the upper surface of the wall was sometimes lined with gilt leather on which were hung pictures in carved wood frames. It is against this sort of warm but sober background that one should envisage Vermeer's yellows and blues and Frans Hals's blazing colours. But after 1660 leather passed out of fashion, to be replaced in favour by painted murals, spread out in large hunting scenes, complicated allegories or biblical allusions, similar to the themes of the tapestries which some people stretch over the walls of their reception-rooms. However, the favourite wall-covering remained porcelain, in the shape of soft-hued tiles – blues, yellows, oranges, mauves, delicate greens, against a white background, featuring stylised bouquets, or idyllic visions, showing the owner's arms, or quoting proverbs. These tiles became a national product, the object of a flourishing industry at Gouda, Haarlem, Delft and Rotterdam. Bare wood became less and less popular, and wherever it was still allowed, in window-sills and in doors, it was gilt or painted. Fashionable people called their various rooms after their style of decoration, as, for instance, 'the gilt leather room', 'the damask room' or 'the Adam and Eve room'.

The sash-windows were often fitted with coloured glass through whose fine leaded panes a subdued daylight filtered, spreading an atmosphere of silence and secrecy throughout the dwelling. Only the very poor did not have at least one window of this type in the façade of their house; at the very least there would be a circle of multi-coloured painted glass set into the centre of a casement-window.

Middle-class people in easy circumstances hung mirrors more or less everywhere in the house. At first they were mostly small Venetian mirrors framed in crystal and a border of glass roses; in the latter half of the century these were occasionally replaced by large French standing mirrors.

Clusters of small attic rooms were sometimes to be found under the eaves, around the loft used by merchants for storage purposes; these were servants' rooms and tiny compartments for various other purposes such as storing wood and peat.

Houses were heated by means of the chimneys and even the humblest dwelling possessed at least one. The chimney-flue was very wide under its square mantelpiece (so that it could easily be swept with a length of plaited straw), and the hearth was decorated with iron plaques sometimes bearing engraved designs (here large porcelain vases were displayed during the summer). In fact, the chimney had become an element of family luxury in bourgeois circles, its canopy was carefully carved and the ledge carried rows of porcelain and lacquered curios. It was kept in a state of perfect cleanliness, and cinders were never to be seen, for they dropped into a specially designed hole under the grate. Beech logs were sometimes burnt, but peat was the normal fuel and was used everywhere, in town as much as in the country. It had to be ventilated in a special way for it to burn properly and so the sods of peat were either put in the 'fire-pot' stove under the mantelpiece, or they were stacked over the grate in such a way as to form thin round towers, hollow in the centre and with small gaps at various points through which coloured flames licked. The effect was attractive and there was no disagreeable odour, but on the other hand its heating properties were low and a Dutch house gave foreign visitors the impression of being hardly heated at all. People with sedentary occupations passed the winter at home in dressing-gowns. And the women, who scarcely ever left the house, always had a footwarmer under their feet. Even in factories the workmen were provided with footwarmers. It was a box about six inches square, of hard wood or metal, pierced with several holes and containing a slowly-burning cake of peat.

The cheapest and most widespread method of lighting was the oil-lamp, a poor dim little light in the form of a spout through which a pale tremulous flame emerged. Tallow candles were expensive and the more effective wax candles even more so. In the formal reception rooms of prosperous households, candles were stuck on a copper or glass frame-work forming a chandelier, hung from the ceiling by a gilt, metal or wood rod. Several bracketed candle-holders were fixed to the walls and to the rim of the mantelpiece.

Peasant houses were quite differently planned, in general, from those in the towns, consisting of one large central room at ground level, sometimes surrounded by tiny recesses, but with no second storey. But houses built during the seventeenth century in villages near large towns began to show some urban influences, being planned in depth, with occasionally an added storey or at least a few little rooms grouped around the loft. Furniture was more basic than in town and retained archaic features. A few chairs, a table, some chests and a spinning-wheel would be considered sufficient furnishing. Painted or carved ornamentation perpetuated ancient native traditions. The use of the chimney was unknown and fires were laid on the ground itself. Interior shutters of plain wood closed the few windows.

The 'sleeping cupboards' were ranged around the central room (unless they had been constructed in adjoining alcoves), hidden during the day by doors or curtains. The wall surfaces remained bare, except perhaps in the case of prosperous peasants who would nail up small shelves on which they would display a few painted dishes, some pots and pewter measuring-vessels.

Whatever his social status, the Dutchman cherished a genuine love for his house. For the man, whose sense of economy sometimes reached a point of avarice, the furnishing and decoration of his house presented the only valid excuse for financial expenditure on a large scale. As for the woman, she devoted her entire life to the workings of the house. The house was the temple of the family, and the family in its turn constituted the centre of social existence. They liked to shut themselves up in their own homes and sit in their well-scrubbed and polished rooms, surrounded by well-waxed furniture and ornaments shining with cleanliness. As a result, foreigners living in the country found it extremely difficult to establish or keep up social relationships. Le Labourer in 1642, and Beyle in 1684, both deplored this situation which they attributed to a dull and surly temperament.[4] From mid-century onwards, the wealthiest merchants and some of the gentry emulated each other in an ever-increasing refinement in the interior decoration of their houses. Furniture, lighting-fixtures, fabrics and precious objects were accumulated at great expense and presented a spectacle which was opulent rather than in good taste. This display of luxury not only satisfied the individual's pride but fulfilled an economic function, since it was viewed as an investment absorbing surplus revenue difficult to dispose of otherwise. But this kind of sterile investment ended up by draining the country's economic resources, as a few prudent observers began to point out towards the end of the century. They blamed French influence. It was rumoured that Madame de Maintenon had persuaded Louis XIV that the best way to lure the Dutch away from the virtues which constituted their strength was to spread Paris fashions among them!

Gardens and flowers

From the 'back room' or from the end of the corridor a few steps led down to the yard surrounded by a fence, painted green or red-brown. Some artisans made their yard into an extension of their workshop and tradesmen might use it as a store-yard. But most citizens, even in modest circumstances, arranged their yard as a garden, however small it might be (and sometimes it measured only a few square yards). At least a grass lawn would be grown, a flower-bed and a few patches of moss. If the space available was sufficient, an elder tree or laburnum would be trained against the wall and two or three fruit-trees would be planted. The higher the family stood in the social scale the larger became the space devoted to the garden, although this never assumed really large proportions – land was scarce and valuable in the city. For this reason people of independent means began, during the second half of the century, to buy a second garden just outside the town limits, where they took the whole family on Sundays and holidays during the summer months.

The typical arrangement of a Dutch garden consisted of four square lawns separated by crossing pathways. There were flower-beds in the lawns and trees all around them and, in the centre crossing, a wooden (or, later, stone) pavilion with a domed roof; or, instead of a pavilion, an arbour under which the family ate meals and, when it became fashionable, took tea. The entire garden was neat, trim, geometric and Lilliputian – a doll's garden.

Everyone set his heart on having an annual crop of fruits. The apple-tree was the most popular and about twenty varieties were known (the favourite was the *goud-pipping*); fifteen varieties of pear-tree were grown, as well as cherry-trees and plum-trees. Melons and strawberries were cultivated, and mulberries, raspberries and medlars (the poor man's fruit) ripened alongside the fences. Many amateur gardeners had wooden-framed greenhouses in which they endeavoured to make apricots and peaches grow and even grape-vines – the latter formed excellent fruits but gave no alcohol. For men of letters, a love of plants often accom-

panied an innate taste for observing nature, and consequently
garden owners had a whole literature of manuals or learned
studies at their disposal – for example, Joan van der Meurs's
Arboretum sacrum, whose three volumes appeared in 1643.

Much to the disgust of a few arbiters of morals, the entire
nation nourished a passion for flowers. These were very
little used in the interior decoration of houses and were
left to provide a mass of colour in the garden. They were
arranged in separate beds according to species: roses here,
irises there, lilies elsewhere; hyacinths farther down the
garden and wild roses along the back; yellows on one side
and reds on the other. Flowers were planted without the
slightest creative imagination but in a way which reflected the
methodical spirit of their growers. At least, the scents of
the flowers were allowed to intermingle! And, in the tiny
gardens in the centre of large towns, their scent was also
mingled with the odours rising from the canals and, on hot
days, stifled by them.

Each town had florists' shops, where the owner sold the
produce of his own gardens or from some other garden
rented and cultivated by him in the neighbouring countryside. If his volume of business warranted it, he would order
additional stock from a Haarlem horticulturist. The soil of
Haarlem and its neighbourhood was so well adapted to
flower-growing that the gardens in that area had ultimately
lost their decorative function and been transformed into
a complete industry. All sorts of flowers were grown for
resale: narcissi, crocuses, aconite, delphiniums, sweet peas
and many other species, some of which were still unknown
in the rest of Europe. Flowers were imported, experiments
were made, new shapes and colours were created, plants such
as *apocynum canadense* (a kind of periwinkle) were presented
for the first time.

Until 1615 the queen of all the flowers was the rose. But
in a short space of time public opinion dethroned it in favour
of the tulip. Tulips had first been imported into Germany
from Turkey in 1559 and were first brought into the Netherlands in 1593 by the naturalist Clusius as an exotic curiosity.
Soon afterwards they began to appear here and there in

49

gardens, but the general public only began to take an interest in this new flower as the result of a sudden fashion for tulips in Paris at the beginning of the reign of Louis XIII. Suddenly the tulip found itself considered an elegant flower and a symbol of aristocratic delicacy. At that very moment, the sudden spread of a plant disease in Dutch gardens produced several strange changes in its corolla, and the horticulturists took advantage of the new craze to reap advantage from this plant disease by producing many curious varieties of tulip.

The French fashion for tulips had now spread throughout Europe, and the Netherlands became the principal supplier. In 1625 the bulb of a particularly sought-after tulip, *Semper Augustus*, was already worth its weight in gold; its large calyx was pure white, lightly touched with blue at its base and streaked with flaming red vertical stripes. The experts created pink, mauve, yellow tulips, and others combining all these colours in various ways, such as the *Laprock* which was as gay as a harlequin's jacket. Thirty, and soon a hundred, different kinds were produced. The bailiff of Kennemeerland named the variation he had developed *Admiral*. Immediately fifty other amateurs followed his example, and an entire onamastic group came into being, including *Admiral van Enckuysen* and *Admiral Pottebacker*. A group of *Generals* sprang up in its turn, including *General van Eyck*, and a publicity-seeking Gouda gardener launched the *General of Generals*. Simpler distinctions were made by calling a new variety – for instance – *Catolejn's red and yellow*. There were six different *Marvels*, four *Morillons*, seven *Tournais*, thirty *Paragons*. This inflation of varieties had its profiteers; the bulbs sold for high prices and it was easy to grow them in the smallest garden. Adventure suddenly beckoned for a number of sedentary citizens and sober-minded shopkeepers.

The weavers of Haarlem, who formed an important guild in this town, threw themselves into this speculative activity despite their entire ignorance of horticulture. The fever mounted, and this 'tulipomania' achieved its paroxysm in the winter of 1636, ending in catastrophe a few months later. It was an attack of gambling madness, an epidemic. The contagion had infected the entire population – butchers, porters, errand-boys, inn-keepers, students, barbers, chimney-sweeps, tax-collectors, turf-diggers, not one social category was spared; every sect and association was stricken by the same fever – Arminians and Papists, Lutherans, Mennonites, night watchmen and rhetoricians! The most affected regions were Amsterdam, Haarlem, Alkmaar, Hoorn, Enkhuizen, Utrecht and Rotterdam. The few citizens who kept their heads called the rest 'the hooded ones' (*kappisten*) in allusion to the hoods worn by madmen; they brought out pamphlets and satirical songs whose humour became increasingly bitter.

At Hoorn a house was bought for the price of three tulip bulbs. A single *Admiral Liefkens* was worth 4,400 florins and the price of a *Semper Augustus* ranged from 4,000 to 5,500 florins! When several buyers were after the same bulb they did not hesitate to offer the seller fantastic bribes – a coach, for instance, and a fine team of horses. In Amsterdam one citizen made a profit of 60,000 florins from his garden in four months in this way. People stayed awake all night to guard their flower-beds, or fixed to their beds alarm bells, connected to cords, surrounding the precious clumps. Buyers and sellers met, two or three evenings each week, in taverns where their discussions lasted late into the night. Children were positively encouraged to attend these business conferences, since it was considered advisable to teach them early in life how to make money! Even some predicants joined in this mad throng from which a few new rich men would emerge at dawn only to find themselves penniless again, perhaps a day later. The same bulb might be sold and resold ten times in a single day. Experts organised information services to keep track of the most interesting transactions; since most of these transactions took place in winter, the speculators relied on illustrations of the flowers in question, and catalogues of tulips were in circulation, sometimes beautifully illustrated, like those painted by Franz Hals's pupil Judith Leyster.

Many gullible individuals who had bought on credit and

failed to negotiate a resale found themselves unable to meet their obligations. Law suits piled up and hundreds of bourgeois families lost every penny they had. Suddenly the municipal corporations became scared; after all, the country's prosperity resulted from a commercial system based entirely on credit. This disquiet spread through the ranks of the speculators themselves, and the first indication was provided on 3rd February 1637 when a florist bought a bulb for 1,250 florins which he was unable to resell. The professionals panicked. On 24th February a general assembly of florists met in Amsterdam and decided upon a radical measure: from that date only contracts drawn up before 30th November 1636 were payable. Subsequent agreements were annulled and the buyer could free himself of his contract by paying an indemnity of 10 per cent to the seller and returning the bulb to him. On 27th April the States of Holland ratified this decision, and on the following day the price for the most expensive bulbs dropped from five thousand to fifty florins! Sanity had returned – at the price of many individual tragedies. Those who were financially ruined included the painter Jan van Goyen, the teacher of Jan Steen.

THE TOILET: *Waking, Washing and Hair Styling*
From one half-hour to another, since the beginning of their rounds, the night-watchmen had whirled their rattles and had announced successively, in a sing-song voice, midnight, one o'clock, two o'clock and so on. Each time they chanted the hour a trumpet blast echoed from the watchtower and the clock above the main gateway boomed out its strokes. During these few minutes the night reverberated with noise, then the town sank into silence once again.

In this way the town councils were fulfilling their duty of measuring the progress of the night. It was left to the private individual to measure the progress of the day. This he did, above all, with a sandglass, and it was to be found everywhere; it was an essential unit in a businessman's office and was equally to be found on the student's desk and in the kitchen. Large sandglasses were made with graduated surfaces which could measure time for twelve hours before the sand ran out – the period of a good day's work. Pocket watches, hunters and watches worn by ladies in high society on little chains around their necks together with their mirror, were all rare and costly luxuries. The principle of the pendulum, applied to clocks by Huyghens in 1657, led to the construction of wall-clocks, although it was 1680 before these began to come into general use. Travellers in stage-coaches and canal-boats improvised a makeshift sun-dial with a straw held upright in the palm of the hand.

When the night round was over, several trades had already started their day's work. Municipal decrees were necessary to forbid fullers to open their workshops before two in the morning, hat-makers before four in the morning; black-smiths were forbidden to start work, because of the din from their forges, until the bell sounded daybreak and informed the whole population that it was time to get up.

The master of the house was the first to get out of bed. In his nightcap and slippers, muffled up in his dressing-gown, he threw open the shutters, then opened the front door, stepped forward a pace and studied the weather. Neighbours greeted each other and exchanged a few words about local affairs or business matters. Then, the servant was called. Inside the house, floorboards creaked under footsteps and children's voices were to be heard. Doors began to open and close. People kissed each other. In the Netherlands everyone exchanged kisses: friends, visitors, travellers passing through town all received an embrace. Meanwhile, the street was beginning to stir. The milkman and the baker had already started their rounds, carrying their pail or dragging their hand-cart noisily behind them. The women waited for them on their thresholds. 'Beautiful milk! Warm milk! Sweet milk!' cried the milkman. The baker blew a horn and shouted, 'Hot white bread! Rye bread-rolls! Barley biscuits! All hot! All hot! Fresh bread-rolls!'

While the servant laid the table the members of the family proceeded, in their own rooms, to their 'toilet', a word which covered very little actual activity. The evidence of foreigners was almost unanimous: the Dutch were dirty. An English

53

visitor wrote: 'They keep their houses cleaner than their bodies' and added, no doubt with some exaggeration, 'and their bodies cleaner than their souls.'[1] In the seventeenth century Europeans on the whole paid remarkably little attention to their personal cleanliness. Even as late as 1660 people in the Netherlands sat down to table without washing their hands, no matter what job they had just been doing. The French openly expressed their disgust at this shamelessness.[2] Contemporary painters have depicted for us rich women standing over ewers made of precious metal and engaging in the most parsimonious ablution of the hand and foot, with the garment never exposing more than wrist and ankle. At some distance, under the bed, the chamber-pot would be waiting for a servant to come and fetch it and empty it into the canal. After 1672 a toilet table of French origin, called a *bouquet de nuit*, made its appearance in elegant society. This was a pretty little chest containing looking-glass and candle-holder, powder box, hair-brush and clothes-brush, a case for needles and a pair of snuffers; but nothing whatsoever for cleaning the skin. Public baths were almost unknown and in 1735 Amsterdam still had only a single such establishment. Sailors and fishermen stank abominably of fish and sea-water.

Personal toilet had a purely decorative function. Even young women from the least privileged social classes wore patches on their cheeks. Hair was always meticulously dressed. Until 1610 men mostly wore their hair short; later they let it grow to ear-level, rolling it into ringlets on the forehead, and from then on short hair marked a man as a peasant. Wigs were introduced from France in 1640 and soon became fashionable among the leisured classes, despite the protests of the predicants who, at the end of the century, still insisted on wearing their hair lank and straight. Blonde wigs were in particular demand and consisted of natural fair hair attached to a silk hair-net.[3] The longer became the hair of men of fashion, the shorter became their beards. At the beginning of the century old men displayed luxuriant growths of beard, but younger men cut theirs to a short triangle. Thirty years later nothing remained on the chin but a tuft of hair, though the moustache was still retained. By 1650 the face was entirely bare and the beard became a professional badge of professors and predicants.

As far as women were concerned, it was only in 1600 that their hair began gradually to play some part in their personal adornment. Until then their hair had been concealed beneath a head-dress. Then, under Italian influence, a few bolder young women allowed a curl or a fringe to protrude, then more and more hair. The whole head of hair emerged progressively from its covering and was allowed to show itself at the front of the crown and the temples and at the neck, where it was coiled up. From then on, hair styling developed very quickly and followed French fashion at some distance. In 1610 elegant coiffures were tall and very ornate; in 1620 hair was worn straight and drawn towards the back; in 1635 curls hung down on either side of the face as far as the shoulders, and a fringe, separated by a parting, covered the upper forehead with a row of tight ringlets. After 1650 the fringe became rarer, and hair was no longer curled except perhaps for the ends. With the peasants, the local costume was set off by coiffures with fringes, the hair usually drawn straight back and falling in a single tress or in a low coil. A few small towns, where the women did not wear caps, had their own extremely complicated traditional hair styles, with interwoven tresses and curls forming a kind of helmet. This was the case in Zijp and Alkmaar. In the villages of the province of Holland the hair was nearly always ringed by a gilt metal band set across the upper forehead.

Ways of Dressing

Men, women and children all got dressed the moment they were out of bed, and when breakfast brought the family together a few minutes later they were all fully dressed.

There was little variation in costume. At the beginning of the seventeenth century any display of elegance was viewed with suspicion, and it took fifty years for this obstinate prejudice to diminish to any extent. Differences in clothing lay more in the choice of material than in the style, and in added ornamentation rather than in the cut. Fashion progressed extremely slowly. Noblemen and army officers adopted the successive fashions of Paris, London and Germany, but the gentry and the bourgeoisie remained far more conservative; after the disappearance, about 1600, of the so-called 'Spanish' style, it was the latter group which provided the characteristics of Dutch costume during the century. Styles changed little. The few fashions borrowed from the Parisian tailors and dressmakers arrived ten or even twenty years late. But it is difficult to generalise; after 1630, differences in taste began to show themselves between the generations in a single family. The long cape known as the *vlieger* was worn by all the women in 1600, but by 1640 only the matrons wore it. In the lower classes the style of clothing hardly changed at all; the labourer, peasant and sailor bought a new costume when the old one was worn out (sometimes after two or three generations!) rather than when its style went out of fashion.

As we have seen, the heating in Dutch houses was quite inadequate, and the Dutch people's defence against the rigours of winter consisted in bundling themselves up in layers of garments. This habit became a remarkable national characteristic, especially among people of small means. Oliver Goldsmith remarked that 'the true Dutchman cuts the strangest figure in the world. . . . He wears no coat but seven waistcoats and nine pairs of trousers, so that his haunches start somewhere under his armpits. . . . The Dutchwoman wears as many petticoats as her husband does trousers.'[4]

The outline of the human body more or less disappeared under this weight of clothing. But at least the garments were well looked after; linen and costumes were kept as immaculate as the house itself, compensating to some extent for the dirtiness of the body they covered.

Despite the reservations we have made, it is possible to distinguish three periods in the history of seventeenth-century clothing in the Netherlands. At first, costumes were distinguished by the number of visible components, the richness of colouring, and the broken lines setting off the different limbs. In the second quarter-century, on the contrary, the various elements of the costume blended in a vague unity which blurred shapes and colours. In the third quarter-century garments regained a quality of stark simplicity contrasting with the richness of the accessories; new types of male clothing were either loose and flowing in line, like the 'rhinegrave' (a kind of petticoat-breeches named after the Rhinegrave of Salm), or narrow like the tight-fitting jerkin first introduced in 1660. Dutch clothing was drab compared with French garments of the same period. Van der Helst's *Marksmen's Banquet*, painted in 1648, shows an undifferentiated mass of greys, blacks, brownish yellows and whites, set off by a few orange-brown or dark blue accessories. Red was rarely seen. Ladies and gentlemen dressed in sombre colours, such as black or violet. Dull-surfaced materials were preferred for principal articles of clothing and glossy materials for secondary articles.

Masculine clothing comprised two principal articles, the doublet, more or less resembling our present-day waistcoat, and trousers. The doublet was worn under a kind of jacket known as a 'cassock', either with or without sleeves, sometimes cut like a chasuble and usually worn open. Its sleeves assumed a decorative function when worn by men of fashion and were adorned with rosettes, or epaulettes, or were slashed to allow a glimpse of the under-linen. Several different styles of trousers were current at the start of the century, either very baggy from waist to knee, or short and close-fitting, or a mixture of these two opposite types, with or without pockets. Eventually, until the introduction of the 'rhinegrave', tight-fitting trousers predominated – long breeches decorated with ribbons and knots, of French inspiration. The breeches were worn with stockings, usually of knitted wool, secured beneath the knee by garters. Often two pairs of stockings were worn, or ornamental rolls of material called canions were wound around the legs over the stockings. Shoes were tight and fastened by two cross-strips or by a rosette; they were usually encased in large mules to preserve them from dust and mud. Boots were little used at first in everyday life, although they became more widespread during the first half of the century. In

1650 they were made with very wide tops which were folded down, showing the lace edging of the tops of the canions.

Around 1600 men wore enormous conical hats with wide floppy brims turned up in front; twenty years later they were wearing something resembling a top-hat with a straight brim. Then wide brims came into fashion again, but cut in irregular lines this time. Male costume did not include a proper overcoat. The nearest approach to this garment was a short tunic, sometimes with a hood, split halfway up the back in the case of those who wore rapiers. On the other hand, the dressing-gown – that traditional Dutch garment which had long defied the dictates of fashion – scarcely left the shoulders of the Dutch bourgeois during the entire cold season. It was put on over the doublet and worn to the office, to the workshop, to the store. Sometimes lined with velvet or fur, it descended to the feet. Often the sleeve was slashed at the elbow, providing an opening for the arm, and the lower part of the sleeve hung loose.

The bodice was the part of a woman's dress in which most variety was to be met with. Bodices with sleeves, severe in style, were often decorated with vertical bands, thus giving an illusion of added height to the wearer. Or they were known as 'sleeveless' bodices, cut in a low triangular shape in front and decorated on the shoulders and the upper arms with false sleeves of different shades, pads and epaulettes standing out against the whiteness of the shift. The dress was worn over one or more petticoats and usually presented a contrast of colour and material with the bodice. It hung straight and fell to the feet; very occasionally it was lengthened at the back by a small train. A few ladies of fashion raised the front above the hem of the petticoat so as to form a fold of material around the hips. Most often the Dutchwoman wore over her dress an apron which might be white, black or violet, was sometimes trimmed with lace, and was in everyday use in all walks of life; so much so that it came to be regarded as a national emblem. It was fastened to the bottom of the bodice, by its corners if it was wide or by strings if it was narrow.

A sort of female dressing-gown called a *vlieger* ('flyer') developed from the robe worn as an outer garment during the sixteenth century; it was nearly always black, was sometimes fur-lined, and existed with or without sleeves. Broadened towards the bottom, it gave a conical outline to the wearer. After 1620 it was generally worn open, showing the whole of the front of the dress and bodice, and some elegant women then fixed a little cushion over their stomach so that their dress would puff out through the gap.

Even more than the *vlieger*, the characteristic garment of the Dutch was the *huik* or cloak, a long coat of sturdy material falling about the body from a tall hood kept upright by a stiff rod bent into a semi-circle. Sometimes this hood took the form of a little conical hat. After 1650 the *huik* was no longer used in bourgeois families, but it survived for a long time with working-class women, who used it as a raincoat. Dutchwomen seldom wore hats. During the first third of the century the hats sported by fashionable women scarcely differed from those worn by men, being tall and conical; this kind of headgear was eventually adopted by ordinary people and remained long in favour, as did the sunhat with large wings, which had also originated as a fashionable headpiece. Small feathered toques with bandeaux were also to be seen, imitations of a French fashion of forty or fifty years before. After about 1640–50 women no longer wore hats at all in bourgeois or upper-class society; a scarf knotted under the chin provided the only headcover. Stockings and shoes were exactly the same as those worn by men, during the entire century. Slippers, in the form of leather-soled mules, were worn by women of all classes; middle-class women wore them mostly indoors, but working-class women made them their regular footgear.

Under-linen consisted of two kinds of garment, those that were unseen and those that were seen. The first group included shifts, for women, covering either the bare skin or a camisole, and drawers for men; many women also wore boned corsets. The second group comprised decorative linen added to garments, mainly collars and cuffs and, for women, the ever-popular cap.

In the first half of the century the flat collar and the ruff were both in vogue. The collar could be soft or starched, open or closed, and was worn largely by young women. Older people preferred the ruff, which existed in various styles, differing in height and in the arrangement of the folds. In 1610 ruffs could be more than three inches high, but this was modest compared with the proportions fashionable during the same period in Spanish Belgium. After 1646 the ruff gradually fell into disuse, and the flat collar triumphed. The silk neckerchief also became popular with women, sometimes starched and worn like a second collar over the first one, or used as a fichu. From 1620 onwards the ruffles covering the wrists became voluminous, lace-trimmed, sometimes starched, and matched the collar. The starch used at that time gave the linen a slightly blue tint which became, later, a mark of supreme elegance when improved techniques no longer produced the same effect!

Apart from society women, and peasant women in a few villages, all Dutchwomen wore caps. These constituted the sole head-dress for women, indoors or outdoors, and were a survival of a tradition, once widespread in Europe, which hardly existed any longer except in the Netherlands. In 1600 the cap was made of two pieces of material superimposed and variously embroidered, tightly enclosing the skull, and hiding the ears and nape of the neck. Then it was reduced in size and became a narrow, dark-coloured bag, holding the back coil of hair and ending in three points above the ears and the centre of the forehead. At the same time a headgear for indoor wear became popular, consisting of a mob-cap in the French style – a big, floppy white cap covering the head entirely, with starched points reaching the shoulders.

The dress of prosperous men and women of the middle classes might well include various accessories which were more or less luxuries: leather or silk gloves; embroidered handkerchiefs, which remained rare objects until the end of the eighteenth century; and for men, at the beginning of the century, leather belts with daggers usually dangling from them. Women sometimes bound a coloured scarf around their waists. During the first half of the century, every middle-class woman carried, as a badge of domestic office, a long chain or strap attached to her petticoat by a hook, from which hung bunches of keys, a knife, scissors, a needle-case. After 1650 only elderly ladies still made use of this apparatus.

Fans, of multicoloured feathers stuck on a circle of hard paper painted or decorated with pearls, were known only to women of fashion. When these ladies left their houses, they preserved their complexions by wearing masks consisting of a piece of straight material cut in an oval, pierced with two holes for the eyes and leaving the mouth free. Alternatively, they affected a sort of eye-shade pointing downwards from above the forehead, rather like the eye-shades occasionally worn by tennis-players today.

A few figures may give some idea of the importance of the wardrobe in upper middle-class families. A girl from a wealthy Amsterdam family might easily have as many as a hundred and fifty chemises and fifty scarves in her dowry.[5] In 1620 the widow of a gentleman possessed thirty-two ruffs of various shapes. The inventory of the burgermaster van Beveren showed forty pairs of drawers, 150 shirts, as many collars, 154 pairs of ruffled cuffs and as many handkerchiefs, sixty hats (plus ninety-two night-caps), twenty dressing-gowns, a dozen nightgowns, thirty-five pairs of gloves, and so on. Among other items, the inventory states that twice a year Mijnheer van Beveren had had to summon the blacksmith to make repairs to his cupboard which seems to have been constantly on the verge of collapse under its weight of linen.[6]

The dress of poorer urban families was distinguishable only by its greater simplicity and old-fashioned appearance: woollen shirt; doublet of rough cloth, tight-sleeved, coloured black, blue, grey or brown and protected by a leather apron. The women wore a short jacket over their bodice, and for housework protective cuffs reaching from elbow to wrist. In bad weather the usual footwear was the peasant's clog.

The usual costume of sailors – trousers billowing around the legs, very short doublet, felt or fur cap – was almost identical with the local dress of maritime villages such as Volendam, and of the country districts of Friesland. All seven provinces possessed their own variations of these traditional peasant costumes, and they did not by any means present the immutable character which we have today incorporated into a fictitious folk-lore. They were influenced by city fashions, but this influence was greatly limited by the toughness of the materials from which they were made and by the gregariousness natural to peasants. Throughout the Dutch countryside female costumes had in common a long robe of coarse woolly material and a very close-fitting bodice. Bright-coloured stockings – red, yellow, flesh-coloured – were worn, and a blue or green apron with wide stripes. In every region the distinction lay in the ornamentation, the play of colours and the combination of accessories. Around Rotterdam and along the Rhine the peasant woman wore over her tunic a long frilled jacket, and a small serge coat with a collar standing up at the back of the neck. In Purmerend, a starched collar surrounded the back of the head and closed tightly over the chest, enveloped by a bodice-front whose lower tips descended to hip-level at the back. In the central and southern provinces it was normal to decry the skirts of women from northern Holland for being so disgracefully short that it was possible to glimpse the ankle, if not more! On the other hand, the women of Friesland left the upper bust uncovered. On the banks of the Zuider Zee, a rigid corselet crushed and flattened the chest. Almost everywhere, a hood covered the head closely and concealed the hair. In certain fishing-villages, the women covered their heads with large black hats whose brims were tilted up at the back and down in front. During the course of the century, a fashion became established in Zeeland and in the region of the Zuider Zee for large 'ear-rings' in the form of plaques of gold or gilt metal, fixed closely by a mount on each side of the cap.

The male peasant's costume of doublet and breeches was completed by a sort of frock-coat known as a *paltrock*. The general effect was drab, and the only occasional highlight was provided by a belt or by a few rows of coloured piping.

In some villages the doublet extended at the back into coat-tails, raised and fastened by large buttons. The short, wide breeches decorated with fringes or gilt buttons were some-times replaced by long trousers, more appropriate in muddy districts. Headgear consisted either of a very tall hat with a fringed brim, or a small flat cap, or a vizored cap.

The only footgear used in the countryside was the wooden clog, long and pointed, and painted black or yellow. Shoes were luxuries which rich farmers might, at most, allow themselves on Sundays. In 1600 the village of Lange Dijk possessed three pairs of shoes in all, and these were kept specifically for the local magistrates, for the days when they had to present themselves in The Hague.

The members of certain public bodies and the representa-tives of certain professions wore a costume which would indicate their particular status by its form or colour. We shall encounter several examples during the course of this book: the guilds' gala uniforms, the rhetoricians' fancy dress, the 'publicity' costumes of doctors, surgeons and apothecaries, the eccentricities of dress of fairground mountebanks. Predicants, professors and jurists wore – as a symbol of dignity and moral rectitude – a toga or *tabart*, a formal variation of the dressing-gown. This garment was black, fell as far as the feet, and was gathered at the back into one or several long vertical folds; a square collar covered the shoulders and the outfit was completed by a black cap.

FOOD: *Setting the Table*

The father presided over meals like the high-priest of a cult. No member of a bourgeois family would dream of being absent on these occasions without a very good reason. The entire tribe sat down together, with the maid-servant at the bottom end, and the small children at some distance from the adults, either sitting in chairs or on the floor. Meals were generally taken in the 'living-room', or else in a pantry at the back of the house, the 'best rooms' being reserved for feast-day banquets.

Each meal started and ended with a prayer. Everyone stood up in front of his place (or, more rarely, remained seated), the men bareheaded, while the father recited the morning prayer; all accompanied him in low voices, with clasped hands, and repeated 'Amen' at the end. The men then replaced their hats and everyone sat down. After the meal everyone arose and prayed once again or sang a grace. In many families, at the end of the main meal the prayer was followed by the meditation of a Bible passage; then the father or one of his sons would read aloud a few pages from some edifying book. During the meal the adults talked little or not at all, and the children had to remain absolutely silent.

The table was covered with a cloth which was sometimes finely embroidered, though some families were content to remove the cloth before meals and eat on the bare wood. Along the table were ranged goblets of plain or cut glass, dishes and pots of pewter or silver, earthenware plates and a wooden trencher on which bread or meat was carved. In rich families a small bell was placed in the centre of the table to call the servants. Table-knives had been in use for almost a century, but spoons were rarer, and in many petty bourgeois families were treated as precious articles, the objects of formal gifts, and carefully hoarded in the cupboard or chest. People ate with their fingers, aided by a knife. The fork appeared only in 1700 and, even then, remained a luxury for a long time. So the table-napkin was an absolute necessity, and before the meal was over it looked more like a greasy rag. In fact, some fastidious middle-class families preferred to wipe their fingers on a small piece of material concealed underneath an immaculate napkin!

A table laid out ready for a meal had a heavy but improvised appearance, abundant yet impersonal. It was difficult to distinguish any individual place-setting for each guest among the accumulation of table equipment. Nevertheless, the richness, variety, practicality and beauty of the plates and dishes, even among the poorest people, seemed to foreigners to represent one of the outstanding features of Dutch culture. Not only plates, pots, dishes and ewers, but also sugar-bowls, butter-dishes, sauce-boats, soup-tureens, egg-cups, brandy carafes, glasses and tall mugs with lids

were all made, most often, from pewter, the most usual
metal for domestic use since the sixteenth century; silver
remained a rare luxury. Only the very poor, and some
peasants, still followed medieval tradition in using wooden
plates and dishes. Pewter was considered an attractive
material, and people liked to treat it as a precious metal; it
was often engraved with ornamental motives or the family
arms. If they possessed no other objects of art the petty
bourgeoisie would display specimens of their table-ware in
the entrance-hall. Pewter had the practical advantage of
melting at F.530°, a temperature easy to obtain. On the
other hand, it was fragile and utensils made from it had to be
replaced frequently. Itinerant pewter metal-founders used
to go from door to door, and at their cry the women would
come running, their aprons bulging with worn dishes, leaky
pots and twisted ladles. The founder would take the lot
to his workshop at the street-corner and throw his harvest of
metal into the crucible of the brick furnace; then he would
pour the molten metal into one of the bronze or iron moulds
lined up on wooden boards, and the new pot, dish or ladle
would boast the traditional rosette or figure of an angel,
with his own special mark stamped on afterwards. Many
a mistress of the house knew, to her cost, that it was well
to avoid the clandestine founders who abounded in the
large towns – they charged less than members of the guild,
but robbed their customers freely by adding base metals
and cheating on the weights.

Drinking-vessels were made in glass as well as pewter:[1]
round goblets with wide stems, of Rhenish origin, or tall,
narrow flute glasses, both types usually decorated with
painted scenes or texts – Latin or Dutch proverbs, biblical
or historical scenes, coats of arms, landscapes. The products
of the Zutphen glassworks, founded by a Frenchman from
Tournai, became famous. In regard to tableware, the
wealthiest members of the bourgeoisie began to favour
porcelain over pewter, towards the century's end. The
former had the prestige of being an exotic and expensive
product, whose importation had become big business.[2] It
came directly from China, either in the native forms which

65

it assumed there or, more often, as 'China to order'. In fact, the art of the far eastern potters was not much appreciated in the Netherlands, and importers insisted on exercising control over the designs. To achieve this, orders were sent to the Chinese potters through the Cantonese agent of the East India Company, who specified precisely what shape the merchandise was to have and the designs it was to carry. The Chinese were constantly exhorted to 'paint no dragons or other animals' and 'to avoid your Chinese fantasies'. What was wanted was pretty flowers, if possible Dutch flowers, carefully painted against a pure white background; and the family arms, with the initials between trumpet-blowing angels. Sentences and proverbs were also in favour, for the Dutch liked to decorate plates and dishes as well as table-linen, silver and walls with words. And historical and religious scenes were popular, featuring someone such as Luther or William the Silent. But, alas, the angels were slit-eyed, and the mythological heroes wore silk robes and Chinese hats! There was constant astonishment at the peculiar way those far-off people interpreted perfectly simple orders. One mistress of a household, wishing to replace and match the remains of a favourite table-service, sent to China a slightly chipped cup as a model. When the new service was delivered after a few months she discovered with stupefaction that every single piece had a small triangular chip in the rim. Sometimes Dutch artists provided sketches; Pronk, for example, drew for a Chinese manufacturer a series of thirty dishes illustrating scenes of Amsterdam. The rims sometimes retained flowers or birds of eastern in-spiration; or a plate might have a small inset portrait of a female figure with parasol while, in the centre, a Dutchwoman picked her cherries.

The use of porcelain remained the prerogative of the nobility and gentry, decorating their tables and cupboards and embellishing their banquets. In the kitchen and pantry, pewter shared the stage with copper, crockery and earthen-ware. Most towns had pottery workshops, large sheds open onto the street, from where one could see jars and jugs drying on rows of shelves; against one of the walls, a massive brick kiln with a mouth like a room door belched flames and an apprentice would be working the treadle which set the potter's wheel spinning. Articles worked in copper and brass were made locally or imported from Germany,[3] but they were expensive and, therefore, the pride of every bourgeois housewife who possessed any.

The Dutch were huge eaters. Their reputation for frugality had to be interpreted qualitatively, since most of them absorbed abundant quantities of food. Four meals were taken during the course of the day. Breakfast was eaten in the small hours of the morning – at five or six o'clock in summer – the moment that the toilet had been rushed through and clothes thrown on. Even among the rich, this meal long remained very simple, being composed mainly, or entirely, of bread, butter and cheese accompanied by milk or beer. After 1670 tea or chocolate was drunk, and the left-overs from the previous evening's dinner were sometimes added to the usual fare. Only the quality of the bread varied according to the family's social standing. However, during the second half of the century, people in high society acquired the habit of eating game, meat-pies and fried fish first thing in the morning.

The principal meal took place at the end of the morning; it was commonly known as 'the midday' (de noen) and usually comprised two or three courses (soup and meat; or soup, fish and meat), concluded by a salad or fruit. Sometimes this menu would be completed by a dessert: pancakes, waffles or, most often, rice pudding. The soup consisted generally of vegetables and bacon cooked in milk. Simple people contented themselves, on several days of the week, with cold meat.

About three in the afternoon, if professional activities permitted, a snack was enjoyed: bread and cheese, accompanied by almonds, raisins, or other delicacies, and by either hot or cold beer sometimes diluted with water. By the end of the century tea had replaced beer.

At eight or nine in the evening dinner was served. In wealthy bourgeois families it was similar to the 'midday' and included several courses. But in general it consisted

67

simply of the remains of the day's previous meals, completed, if necessary, by butter, cheese or a porridge of stale bread soaked in milk.

Dutch Cooking

The ingredients may be summed up as being varied, solid, nourishing, and carelessly prepared. In the words of the abbé Sartre: 'Butter, cheese and salt meat are not foods which demand a great deal of attention. . . . Their meat-broth is nothing more than water full of salt or nutmeg, with sweet-breads and minced meat added, having not the slightest flavour of meat and showing quite clearly that it has not taken more than an hour to prepare.'[4]

The suggestion that it had taken as long as an hour was probably over-generous; a Parisian cook of the same period would spend at least half a day preparing a broth. And one would have been unlikely to find nutmeg on any but the most sumptuous tables, since spices remained very expensive despite the considerable trade in them.[5]

Whatever social level she belonged to, the Dutch mistress of the house took it for granted that she was to take charge of the cooking herself; yet she had little taste or aptitude for the art. In many families the operation of cooking was performed only once a week, and they contented themselves during the ensuing six days with reheating these previously prepared dishes. Only a few very great ladies had a butler and cook, in the second half of the century, who might even be French. Wealthy persons of refinement consulted cookery books such as *The skilful cook or the attentive housewife, describing the best way to prepare, cook and roast all kinds of dishes,*[6] published in 1668 in Amsterdam. A few works of Parisian origin were in circulation: La Varenne's *Le cuisinier français* (*The French cook*), for instance, and *L'école parfait des officiers de bouche* (*The perfect school for officers of the mouth*). These books made available some good French recipes, but the Dutch seldom risked making use of them, and, when they did so so, they did not follow them very closely. However, from 1660 onwards, such books did play some part in diversifying slightly the upper classes' diet.

One day a Spanish ambassador came across a group of deputies to the States-General, sitting on a public bench in The Hague, breaking their hunks of bread and gnawing their cheese while waiting for the session to open. 'Such a people is invincible!' exclaimed the Spaniard. Similar anecdotes are numerous. The scene which gave rise to this particular story occurred in 1610. Fifty years later the leisure classes lived better, but the peasants continued to nourish themselves almost exclusively with vegetables and dairy produce, while sailors lived on fish, gruel and cheese. The tables of the urban lower middle classes were hardly more varied. The poorest people ate turnips, fried onions, dry or even mouldy bread and drank beer. Social distinctions, so marked in habitat and furnishing, and less noticeable in clothing, hardly existed in the matter of nourishment. The national dish was the *hutsepot*, and it frequently turned up as the main course at the midday meal. According to a contemporary recipe, it was made of finely chopped mutton or beef, green vegetables, parsnips or prunes, sprinkled with lemon or orange juice, moistened with strong vinegar, well mixed and boiled for a long time with fat and ginger. Other variations existed, for example with onions. A more spicy dish of Spanish origin, olla-podrida (called *olipotrigo* by the Dutch), sometimes replaced the *hutsepot* on feast-days. It was prepared by boiling for three and a half hours pieces of capon, lamb, veal, beef, sausage, pig's trotter and sheep's trotter, pig's head, chicory, artichokes and various spices; the juice was drained off, four or five egg-yolks beaten into it, and sour wine and melted butter added. This sauce was heated separately and then poured over the meat and vegetables; it was served with chestnuts.[7]

At the college of the States in Leyden, in 1631, the students were served for their Sunday 'midday' with soup and bread, hot meat and *hutsepot;* during the week, the same soup with bread, followed by hashed meat with cabbage or a *hutsepot*, or haricot beans, or perhaps fresh or smoked fish, with bread, butter and cheese and beer to drink. Breakfast consisted of bread and butter: a quarter of a pound of butter and a wheaten loaf between four people. For dinner there was bread, butter and cow's cheese. This more or less represented a typical middle class diet.

Milk, the principal drink for children and the basis of numerous dishes, came into town from the immediately surrounding countryside. Through a curious circumstance,[8] no control was exercised to ensure the quality of this perishable commodity, and the city-dweller had to trust to the presumed honesty of the peasant delivering it to him. On the other hand, butter was distributed through tradesmen and its quality was therefore supervised. It was eaten spread on bread, and it also constituted the fat usually used in cooking. The quality of Dutch butter (especially from Delft and Leyden) was famous. For this reason, the Dutch preferred to export their butter, which fetched a high price on the international market, and buy English and Irish butter cheaply for their own domestic consumption.

Their German neighbours gave the Dutch the ironic nickname of 'cheese-eaters'. They did, indeed, consume very considerable quantities of this foodstuff, but not enough to absorb the entire national product, and cheese was one of the very few commodities exported by the Dutch which they had manufactured themselves; the commercial importance assumed by such a volume of trade contributed largely to the perfectioning of cheese-making techniques. Some makes were particularly sought after, especially those of Texel and Gouda. Leyden cheese was flavoured with cummin. Edam cheese, aged, was considered better than Parmesan.

Being poor in cereals, the Netherlands produced a bread which the French declared unanimously to be inedible.[9] Ordinary bread was made of the flour of rye, barley, buckwheat, oats, or even beans, and was black, soft, sticky, dense and indigestible. Fine wheaten bread was very dear and considered a delicacy to be relished on Sundays and holidays; only the rich ate it every day. The bakers took full advantage of this popular attitude of respect towards white bread and created innumerable variations of fancy breads differing in shape and composition. In addition, ancient traditions prescribed the consumption of special breads, probably of symbolic origin, during certain religious celebrations – Christmas, Epiphany, Easter, Pentecost and, in some districts, during the kermis. Innumerable guild regulations determined and controlled the appearance, contents, weight and price of these luxury products.

The Dutchman was the biggest consumer of vegetables in the whole of Europe. The soil throughout the country districts lent itself well to market-gardening, and although the crops were not very variegated they played an important part in the country's agricultural economy. Peas, haricots, white cabbages, carrots, turnips, cucumbers formed, together with dairy produce, the basis of popular sustenance. Savoy cabbage, cauliflower and salsify appeared daily at the tables of the wealthy. Artichokes and asparagus grown in Zeeland and Holland enjoyed an international reputation and were exported to England. Scallions were used for seasoning. On the other hand, the potato, which had been introduced into the Leyden botanical gardens by Clusius at the end of the sixteenth century, was generally considered to be poisonous; wealthy amateurs grew it, as well as the tomato, in their gardens as an ornamental plant.

The towns swarmed with vegetable sellers: peasants at the market, itinerant sellers pushing their barrows or carrying their baskets, stall-holders under their awnings between piles of cabbage and strings of onions. All these people sold fruit too. Fruit was not always eaten raw; often – especially the prune – it was cooked with vegetables. There was pea and prune soup flavoured with ginger; white haricots in prune syrup; roast pork with prunes and raisins; mutton with prunes and mint; hashed meat with prunes, grapes and treacle; minced ox-tongue with green apples. Fruit was also used to make jams, sometimes according to strange and complicated recipes, such as the one using fruit blended with white of egg and diluted with rainwater, or the jam made from nuts.

Eggs were used for a great number of desserts, especially the many kinds of pancake which were so popular. Eggs were fried in oil rather than in butter. In the words of a proverb of the day: 'A fried egg is the consolation of the poor man.'[10] Holland and Gelderland had large chicken-farms, and the egg was one of the cheapest foodstuffs available.

Fish completed this essentially vegetarian diet. Every kind of fish was eaten: sea fish and river fish, eaten fresh, smoked or salted, with or without sauce; carp, bream, roach, perch and dozens more species. The herring achieved the status of a national symbol. During the weeks following the annual fishing expedition, at the end of summer, raw herring-fillets were eaten as a delicacy. Later in the season, red herrings took their place. Dried or salted cod was just as popular. Sea-food such as mussels, oysters and crabs were consumed boiled or fried, accompanied by a sweet sauce.

Meat was rarely seen, and ordinary people ate it only once a week – except during November, at the time of the cattle-slaughtering festivals which will be described in a later chapter. Even the small amount of meat that was eaten – beef, mutton and pork – was not always fresh, and part of the population knew only salted and smoked meat. If a piece of fresh meat did appear on the family table it was most likely to be in the form of a mince. As for poultry and game, they were the food of peasant or nobleman.

Drinking-water did not exist in its natural state in Holland, so reservoirs were established and wells dug; in case of dire necessity, even canal water was used. In fact, very little water was drunk, and even the poorest people disdained it and used it, if at all, to dilute other liquids such as milk and beer.

Beer was the national drink. Even after a taste for wine had become widespread among wealthier people, beer remained the sole beverage of the greater part of the population. It was drunk at every meal, between meals, at home and at the tavern. There were two kinds, known as 'simple' and 'double' according to the alcoholic content; double beer was very strong, intoxicated quickly and with lasting effect, and was responsible for much ruffianism. The national consumption of beer was enormous. In 1600 it reached the equivalent of more than five and a half million gallons[11] just for the customers of the Haarlem taverns. But most towns had their brewers' guilds, and even English and German beer was imported to satisfy the national thirst.

Various delicacies supplemented the Dutch diet. Apothecaries held the privilege of selling tarts of all kinds; fruit tarts, similar to those of today, and tarts filled with cheese, fish or meat, or flavoured with wine or marzipan. Pastrycooks, grouped in certain towns in separate guilds from those of the bakers and biscuit-makers, sold 'pies', by which was meant not only pies as we know them but almost every kind of fancy pastry. They also prepared dessert creams made of milk, sugar, cinnamon, eggs beaten with chopped parsley and apples. The Dutch, especially in the province of Holland, adored cakes. Pies, often of cheese or poultry, and tarts were the prerogative of wealthier gluttons, as were *marrons glacés* imported from France. Plain folk were content with biscuits of innumerable shapes, sizes and contents; biscuits made with either aniseed, butter, fat, sugar, treacle, dried fruits, cherries, raisins or some other filling. Franken[12] lists forty-one different kinds of biscuit, and even they represent only a small sample.

Marzipan was made at home and had a place of honour on the table at all feasts. The traditional recipe called for the almonds to be soaked for a day and a night; they were then pressed to extract their oil, an equal quantity of sugar was added, the whole was mixed and crushed, then thinned with rosewater. It was cooked over the fire, the mixture being sprinkled with sweetened rosewater during cooking.

Sweetened drinks were popular: sweetened wine, sweetened brandy, even sweetened beer in the inns on Twelfth day (Epiphany). For special occasions, such as marriages, hippocras was brewed. There were various recipes for this spiced wine; a typical one blended sweetened Rhine wine, slightly diluted with water, with cinnamon, ginger and cloves. A simplified variation was the caudle, made of sweetened white wine with a stick of cinnamon floating in it.

THE EVENING AT HOME

Artisans, peasants and small business men worked right up to dinner-time, but during the course of the century the wealthy bourgeois developed the habit of completing his business by late afternoon. A few idlers could be seen from midday onwards, mainly old people who liked to take a siesta until three o'clock, women of the leisured classes and young men from high society. As soon as his work-day ended, the Dutchman devoted himself to the pleasures of social life. But until 1670 these pleasures were enjoyed almost entirely in the family circle.

The upper middle classes liked to pay each other visits at the hour of the 'afternoon snack', and this occasion then assumed a greater importance, with the host offering fish, cold meats and sweets. If the weather allowed, this meal took place in the garden. Once the drinking of tea had become widespread it became fashionable to invite friends to 'take tea' (with biscuits or other delicacies) at two or three in the afternoon.

Between five and seven in the evening the town's activity began to calm down, traffic became less frenzied, and the bourgeois would leave his office, descend from his warehouse or return from the port. Once home he put on his cap, donned his dressing-gown and, if it was not too cold, sat on the bench in front of his house, under the canopy. Here he was joined by his wife and daughters. Before the house next door an identical group would form itself. The small children ran here and there, scuffled together or floated a sabot on the canal. The mother of the family would have brought the last-born child out on the porch in its cradle. The father read the gazettes. From their respective benches the men discussed the latest events, raised questions of politics and deplored the decadence of the world.

They often expressed their wisdom in proverbs; Dutch tradition was rich in adages such as: 'Cards, tankards and petticoats have ruined more than one young man,' and, 'Opportunity makes the thief.'[1] The women, with foot-warmers under their slippers, enveloped in their *huik* or *vlieger*, knitted or mended linen and gossiped about house-cleaning and the servant problem. This outdoor relaxation lasted until dusk and dinner-time. At this hour, too, the rich citizens who owned a garden outside the town returned home after having spent an hour or two among their lawns and flowers. At The Hague, the bourgeoisie would stroll along the Wood to admire the fine coaches and horses; they were informally dressed: the men in dressing-gowns, the women in dishabille. The sound of musical instruments echoed from nearby taverns.

In bad weather the pre-dinner family gathering took place in the 'living-room'. Round the table, the mother and the elder daughters sewed or embroidered; in a corner, the servant turned the spinning-wheel; the sons did odd jobs, carved a piece of wood or wove a net; sitting upright in his chair, the father read aloud from the Bible or a history book. The peat-oven would be alight, and the candles lit. Sometimes friends knocked at the door, extinguishing their lanterns as they entered. These would be young people of both sexes, for middle-aged people hardly ever went out. At Dordrecht and The Hague, a young girl among these groups of visitors might be carrying a small wooden bucket as a handbag, containing perhaps a collection of songs – mostly love-songs written and illustrated for her by young men of her acquaintance, or else some tiny printed book. If no such 'young lady's book' was available among the guests, the mistress of the house would extract from her cupboard *The super-admiral of Holland*, or *Apollo among the goddesses of song*, or *The delights of piety*, works to be found in every Dutch home, among hundreds of similar collections. Some were specially designed for particular social categories: there were anthologies of sea-shanties (*Neptune's chariot*), songs for merchants (*The new Amsterdam Mercury*), for peasants (*The Jolly singing countryman*), for shepherds, and even for florists![2]

The material included in these collections was very varied. Some of the works were purely edifying, even going as far as a rather confused mysticism; others were entirely profane. Most of them blended these rival inspirations and contained not only double meanings but also openly suggestive references. But at least there existed, during the first half of the century, a certain freshness, naïvety and even wit, which gave to these innumerable song-books a happy and spontaneous character that they lost after 1650, when they began to record fairly faithful imitations of French and Italian words and melodies.

They sang duets, or in chorus, accompanied by flute, violin and lute, or, in wealthy families, by spinet or harpsichord. So the winter gatherings of well-to-do families were mainly enlivened by song and music. The level of these performances was usually reasonably high, and occasionally brilliant. By the middle of the century, indeed, the musical education of the young was well looked after. A fashion originating in England had led to a great number of music-teachers giving private lessons at home, and teaching singing, and the flute and harpsichord, had become an established profession. Besides the usual mediocre teachers there were a few excellent ones who have left us original compositions in the form of books of musical studies composed for their pupils. Although the Church was hostile to the arts in general, it accepted music and even encouraged its practice. The schools instituted singing classes, and several towns established public lecture courses on music.

On evenings when the family did not hold a sing-song and in those rare families which did not practise music, the visitors would be invited to join in some parlour game. Games of chance were in great favour. The Dutchman was an inveterate gambler; in wartime, he used to go so far as to bet on the outcome of a battle in progress. Only the opposition of the Church and the judiciary restrained this natural tendency. Yet Parival found that little gambling went on in the Netherlands, compared with the habits of French high society.[3] The ancient game of dice had long passed out of fashion in the homes of the rich, but remained popular with the common people despite official interdictions. Several variations existed, included one of French origin called 'pass-ten', in which each player threw in turn, using a glass as a shaker: if the player was a man, he had immediately to down as many drinks as the total number he had thrown; if a woman, she had to give her fellow-players an equal number of kisses.

Dice were used in the ever-popular game of goose, and in several variations of hopscotch. People played at knuckle-bones. But, above all, people played cards; they played cards everywhere – at home, in the taverns, in their gardens, in the street. Card-playing became so widespread that the more conservative gentry banned cards from their houses as being both vulgar and a blameworthy dissipation. The predicants thundered against this passion. From the height of his pulpit in Middelburg, Henri de Frein made a moving evocation of these groups of gamblers huddled over the table-cloth: 'Young girls got up like dolls, with shameful hair-styles, their necks, shoulders and bosom bare, offering to young men a spectacle of sinful flesh which tempts them to stray in the paths of their own hearts and amid the impure visions of their eyes, contaminated by disgusting pleasures, forgetful that one day they will have to appear before their judge. . . .'[4] This lament was echoed by predicants every-where, who complained that some families devoted even Sunday afternoons to card-playing! The government imposed a heavy tax on cards. All to no avail.

At least twenty different card games were played. *Roemsteken* was played with thirty-six cards divided between any number of players from two to six; ombre (*omberen*) was played with forty cards by three players; faro, piquet, lansquenet were other popular games. Some packs included emblematic cards, the master-cards being Death, Life and the King.

The nobility had retained the medieval tradition of chess-playing, but it was not until 1700 that the game was taken up by the middle classes whose preferred game hitherto had been draughts.

After 1650 the increasing influence of French manners and the multiplication of coffee-houses led to a profound change in the traditions that had reigned over the family evening at home. Thenceforward, once or twice a week

77

or even more often, the bourgeois would return home as late as possible, just in time for dinner. For their part, his own wife and daughters began to go out, and the younger children soon followed this example. Serious-minded people became alarmed. This gadding about, these hours of promiscuity in smoking-saloons and coffee-houses must inevitably break down social barriers, and thus bring about the ruin of religion and respect. The old bourgeois austerity, the strict economy of time and money, the pious conservatism and everything else that went to make up the strength of the Dutch people would vanish or degenerate. The family was no longer really a family; the house was no longer really a home.

Nevertheless, at 10 o'clock the bell sounded and the guard's drum beat out its rhythm, and everyone returned home. The Dutch were great sleepers and mostly went to bed early. After ten o'clock the streets were empty except for the night watch, malefactors lurking in the shadows and a few more or less clandestine revellers. The bourgeois banked his fire. Everyone knelt down for the evening prayer. The father blessed his children, then everyone kissed good night. The candles were blown out, and they all went to bed. The town slept.

CHAPTER THREE

THE COURSE OF LIFE

Religion—Children—Education: The Junior Schools, Higher Education and the Sciences—Love Life—Domestic Existence— The Guilds—Sickness and Death: Patients and Doctors, The Art of Medicine, Surgery, From Death-bed to Cemetery.

RELIGION

The Netherlands were steeped in a religious atmosphere that impregnated their entire national existence. Temple observed that 'this people's religion resides in the heart and draws its strength therefrom'. Its strength, not its passion.[1] Violence between members of opposing faiths became rare after 1620; disputations between the sects were conducted without excessive animosity, and any agreement that might result did not necessarily imply an alliance. A profound faith, attending carefully to its outer manifestations, totally devoid of mysticism, often niggling and meddlesome in its most sincere proponents, it nourished itself on the Bible, whose vivid style furnished the speech of the epoch with its pious rhetoric and sometimes determined its very processes of thought. People prayed a great deal, on getting up, before and after each meal, at the end of the day. Sometimes the evening would have been occupied by the reading of works of piety. If one passed beneath the windows of the devout during the morning or evening one would hear voices singing psalms. On all such occasions the father presided, one might almost say officiated. Dutch religion had a family character; the family constituted the natural frame for all religious activity, and this fact explains to some extent the tolerance which reigned at institutional level.

The mother taught her child to pray, and gave it its first elements of religious instruction. Young Anna-Maria

Schuurman knew her catechism by heart at the age of three
– though it is true that she was an infant genius. In any case,
by the time a child was old enough to go to school its little
soul was already thoroughly impregnated with religion. The
authorities made sure that, from infant school onwards,
religious instruction received a central place in the curriculum, and usually Wednesday afternoons and Saturday
mornings were set aside for it. Each lesson began and ended
with a prayer or the reading of a passage from the Bible. On
the eve of the great feast-days the children were made to
learn by heart the entire text for the following day's office.
As a general rule, schoolmasters used the Heidelberg
catechism, which had become the official instrument of
religious instruction since the synod of Dordrecht in 1618.
But this catechism was a dogmatic definition of the reformed
faith and was ill-suited to the needs of primary schools.
Some abridgements were in circulation in manuscript form
and a few had been published; but even these were clumsily
worded, encumbered with abstract terms and useless polemics, and misstated the arguments without really simplify-
ing them. As a result the teaching of religion still remained
lamentable by mid-century. The schoolmasters compounded
their lack of pedagogic instinct and their small-mindedness
with sheer negligence. In the country districts they
suspended religious lessons during the summer months.
Elsewhere, they too often devoted them to absurd discussions (Did Eve eat an apple or a pear?) or to simple
recitations of precepts. The predicants themselves never
gave lessons except to the faithful who were preparing
themselves for their Confession of Faith, a ceremony which
gave the right to attend Holy Communion. The first
Communion was one of the great dates in a person's lifetime:
it was the threshold to maturity, and bore witness to the fact
that the man was thenceforward competent to assume public
responsibilities, and the woman to manage a household.

Dutch Calvinism appears to have originated in France
about the middle of the sixteenth century, by way of Belgium
where the first ecclesiastical organisation of the reformed
religion of the Netherlands was set up. It was not until

1571 that the first specifically Dutch council was held. But during the war of liberation Calvinism acted as a powerful inspiration and was an important factor in the final success. Yet it was never able to achieve its original ideal of some kind of theocracy; the newly acquired political liberties and the sudden economic development were equally opposed to such a concept, and a great many individuals found the idea repugnant.

Until 1612 the aristocrats who held power in the State showed themselves indifferent if not hostile, and favoured a more liberal conception of religious faith. The clash came in 1618, and the Calvinist Church immediately summoned the secular arm – the might of the Prince of Orange. The death-sentence on Oldenbarnevelt marked its triumph. However, tensions remained high for another decade and retained a certain social coloration;[2] Gomar's strict Calvinism recruited the majority of its adherents from among the least privileged classes of the population, while Arminius's more liberal Protestantism attracted the upper classes. This opposition was also noticeable culturally and psychologically. Dutch Calvinism was hostile to the basic tenets of humanism; it extolled sobriety of expression and reserve, and condemned all exuberant forms of spontaneity, any idea of art for art's sake, and, in particular, the irrational element in inspiration. In its humourlessness and its attachment to the earth (which was all the stronger for being allied to the feeling that all was ephemeral), Calvinism represented a return to medieval Christianity, and the humanist opposition represented modernism.

It was only after the 'Great Assembly' of 1651 that the Reformed Calvinist Church (*Hervormde Kerk*) achieved the status and power of a State Church. It then became the only church to possess public places of worship and have the right to teach religion. Its catechism was taught compulsorily in all the schools, and its ministers and professors received a civil servant's salary. But by the same token the State limited its liberty, administering its ecclesiastical estates and benefits, and intervening in the nomination of individuals to the chairs of theology. The Reformed Church had no clergy in the real sense of the word; at the top of the hierarchy it had its synods, and it had its secular 'Church Councils' (*Kerkeraden*). It had not inherited the former estates of the Catholic Church, for these had nearly all been sequestered during the war by the State. In Utrecht certain benefices had been appropriated by private persons. The Catholic convents now sheltered colleges, administrative institutions and hospitals. The means the Reformed Church used to exercise its authority over the people were, above all, moral in character, and extraordinarily discreet compared with what was going on elsewhere during this era.

Since 1637 the Church had possessed its official translation of the Holy Scriptures: the 'Bible of the States', established by order of the Dordrecht synod. Its liturgy was conducted in a church stripped bare of any ornamentation reminiscent of Catholic luxury, where even music intruded only gradually during the course of the century, where the congregation remained seated, head covered, motionless. Only psalms were sung, and all hymns were rigorously excluded despite their established place in the people's affections. The emotion which Catholic worship excited through the senses was provoked in the Calvinist liturgy through the intelligence alone, by means of preaching. The ceremony of Holy Communion (for which the communicants gathered standing around a table brought along specially for the purpose) was celebrated only rarely. The greater part of these two or three hour-long Sunday services was devoted to the sermon.

A few collections of sermons from this epoch have survived; set compositions in which literary inflation is blended with erudition and scholasticism. But the general tone of the Dutch predicants was rather one of familiarity, often violent in tone and of a complete simplicity of expression, whence the popularity of certain preachers among the common people. When the celebrated Borstius of Dordrecht announced a sermon for nine o'clock, a queue had already started to form outside the church at five.

After a passage from the Bible had been read from the lectern, the predicant mounted the pulpit and began by reading out various announcements, often of the most com-

pletely profane nature – sales by local merchants, neighbourhood events and so on. Then he preached. Starting with a
biblical text, the orator moralised in a highly coloured
language, making use of puns and quoting proverbs. Simon
Stevinus remarked unkindly that 'the preachers' words cling
to the heart like ringworm to a sheep.'[3]

These sermons dealt not only with individual conduct but
also with public life (with the exception of politics), and
the preachers did not hesitate to criticise people of the highest
standing. No doubt their display of dogmatic certainty was
sometimes of the highest standard; nevertheless, a censor-
ious tendency led the popular predicants to condemn every
possible manifestation of luxury and love of pleasure in a
manner which often seems puerile to our eyes. In 1640 the
pulpits echoed with vehement protests against the wearing of
long hair by men. The scandal reached such proportions that
the Brielle synod of 1643 was obliged to devote its attention
to the capillary problem. The illustrious Poliander delivered
a learned disquisition in Latin on this occasion.

This holy wrath was also directed against slightly less futile
objectives, and the wearing of jewellery was for a time stigma-
tised as shameful. Throughout the century the Reformed
Church continued obstinately to legislate in the field of
morals and customs, through the words of its predicants, the
writings of its theologians and the recommendations of its
synods and Councils. The effects of these admonitions
appear to have been minimal outside a small circle of strict
believers. Their one effect, perhaps, was to give Dutch
society until about 1660 a relatively austere appearance.
Some of the condemnations were based on a literal interpretation of the Bible. Measures against epidemics were
opposed by virtue of the saying: 'God shall deliver you from
the peril of pestilence.' As a consequence, peasants were
known to refuse medical remedies offered to them, as being
an insult towards Providence. Other condemnations were
justified by a patriarchal conception of morality and heaped
anathema on all kinds of recreation and amusement.

The Church never abandoned its onslaught on the theatre.
Even the religious dramas played in the colleges aroused

protests. A clique of ecclesiastical origin succeeded in banning Vondel's admirable play *Lucifer* from the stage after two performances. The town administrations did not always share the consistory's prejudices; but the necessity of maintaining a good relationship with the Church occasionally forced some interdiction from them or a vexatious measure. When, in October 1668, the Queen of France's players asked the Prince of Orange for permission to perform at The Hague, the consistory dispatched a delegation to the future William III requesting him to refuse. The Prince resisted their demands. Finally a compromise was arranged: the French actors would not present farces or scandalous plays, they would not perform on Sundays or holy days – and the prices for the seats would be doubled!

Dancing was viewed with equal disfavour. Before a marriage it was known for the Church Council to appoint one of its members to visit the betrothed to persuade them to renounce this pleasure on their wedding-day. When the University of Franeker engaged a dancing-master for its students, the predicants raised such an outcry that the States had to take the matter up. In July 1640 the synod of southern Holland decided not to admit to communion people guilty of having attended a ball or worn fancy dress.

The predicants railed against tobacco and coffee. They decried too, not without some reason, the persistent custom of celebrating popular festivals in which some vestiges of Catholic traditions survived: Saint Nicholas, Saint Martin, Twelfth Night, Shrove Tuesday. The Church applied pressure to the municipalities, with occasional success: in 1607 Delft forbade the sale of gingerbread and pastries shaped like human heads which were traditional at the feast of Saint Nicholas; in 1657 Dordrecht quite simply proscribed the celebration of this festival. Even the kermises appeared in the eyes of certain predicants as a detestable survival of papal idolatry: did they not derive originally, in fact, from the old patron-saints' days? In various communities the incumbent delivered special sermons on the days preceding this festival to remind the congregation of the sins to which Christians were about to

84

be exposed. The election of the Queen of the May was viewed with grave suspicion.

If life in general was affected by the Church's strictures, Sunday in particular, the day of the Lord and the faith, was singled out for attention. The predicants condemned even the taking of walks in the country, because 'the sabbath was not established for the pleasure of sinful flesh'.[4] As a result, Sundays were unspeakably tedious. All commerce was interrupted; no payments might be made, and no credits were valid on that day. The theatres were closed; the streets were deserted except for the few minutes preceding the hour of worship. The only people to be seen were those going to church; in the morning at eight o'clock and again soon after midday the school-children paraded under the eye of their teacher or school-mistress, who interrogated them after the service to make sure that they had paid attention to the sermon. In Amsterdam the town gates were closed during the church services. But this did not prevent the wealthy citizens, who were seldom possessed by such excessive zeal, from leaving very early for their country estates from which they would return only on Monday, in time for the opening of the money market.

Despite the pressure it exercised upon public and private life, the body of predicants did not constitute a priestly caste. In the whole country it amounted perhaps to two thousand members.[5] Of modest social origins, the predicants remained attached to their background by custom and by spiritual sympathy, and often had a feeling of inferiority towards the gentry and nobility. At first the Reform had suffered from an extreme shortage of ministers. It had been necessary to recruit predicants and catechists almost at random; one-time monks, or well-disposed laymen, completely lacking in adequate training or sense of vocation, were still to be seen here and there as late as 1650, and the intellectual level remained very low for a long time. When the Leyden Theological Faculty was created in 1575 it had been necessary to import professors. For many years most villages remained without a pastor. The studies demanded of prospective predicants were long and fairly expensive to complete; the young man began with 'Latin school', usually by private instruction in the home of an officiating predicant, for whom such lessons were an important source of income. Many predicants lodged six, eight or ten pupils whom they prepared for their entry into the faculty. In order to facilitate the provision of a constant flow of pastoral candidates at this level, the central government founded in 1592 the 'College of the States', at Leyden, where poor students were admitted, fed and instructed in theology at the expense of the state or the cities. This 'College', to which was attached a corps of lecturers, constituted a centre of preliminary studies and training which became the seminary of the Reformed Church. Subsequently, several other theological faculties were established throughout the country. After completing his studies, the new predicant registered himself with the church council of his home town and, after an examination, received the right to officiate. He then usually offered a banquet, which in the villages could reach the proportions of a popular festival and often plunged the unfortunate man into debt. The councils protested in vain against this custom.

Most of the predicants lived in circumstances not far off poverty, enjoying neither benefices nor tithes, and belonging to the category of the averagely or poorly paid. The church council fixed the salary, which varied considerably. In the country districts of Groningen, for instance, whose inhabitants were shrewd and business-like, the salary was more than adequate – nearly twenty bushels of rye and about seventy-five florins in cash a year; but in Drenthe it was possible for the salary to be entirely in kind. They had to live, and life was not easy, especially if they had several children – for all the predicants were married. Often the wife had to keep shop, and the predicant himself officiated as a public scribe, or even became a medicine man or inn-keeper. On top of all these indispensable activities he had to find time to officiate, preach, visit the sick and perform the rest of his appointed task.[6] In the towns, the council appointed a paid assistant to the predicant, a sacristan who relieved him of some of the routine functions, such as opening and closing the doors, ringing the bells, keeping the clock wound up, cleaning the church and chasing out the dogs and children who misbehaved.

But the predicant's social position did not correspond to his economic insecurity; on the contrary, he was honoured, treated with particular respect by the political authorities, and at banquets took precedence over the doctor. In the large towns, relates the abbé Sartre, he could be seen striding along in his black robe, keeping to the right and the inside of the pavement, leaving his wife the left and the outside.[7] This was a genuine privilege in a country where the custom was the opposite.

The descendants of the Protestant refugees who had come from Hainault and French Flanders in the sixteenth century remained grouped in the powerful 'Walloon Church'. The originality of this Church, which was not in any dogmatic conflict with the Reformed Church, lay in its liturgical tradition: the services were conducted in French, and most of the pastors were French, Belgian or Swiss. From 1609 to 1699 the Walloon Church administered a college in Leyden, similar to the College of the States, from which scholars were sent to the Theological Faculty. The church's fashionable status allowed it to recruit part of its faithful from among the ranks of the aristocracy, whose members gladly intrigued for posts in its governing organisms, the College of Elders and the College of Deacons.

On the fringe of these two official churches, a number of small reformed sects existed in an atmosphere of considerable tolerance. They were ignored by the State, supported their ministers and meeting-houses at their own expense, and were excluded from all branches of local government, but at least these dissident sects enjoyed complete religious freedom in private. Any group wanting to hold public assemblies, or engage a pastor or professor, simply made an application to the municipal council which granted it freedom of worship after payment of a tax, having made sure that nothing in the new faith was contrary to the constitution. Here and there free worship was limited by a refusal to allow the construction of proper churches, and, in addition, the administration demanded free access for its delegates to all assemblies. This obliging attitude on the part of the authorities led to an expansion of religious communities that greatly astonished foreigners and contributed enormously to the liberal reputation of the Dutch régime.

The Remonstrants, who had sprung from the liberal Calvinist party of Arminius (which had been rejected by the Dordrecht synod of the Reformed Church) had been faced with great difficulties to start with. The persecution to which they had been subjected in 1620 and 1621 had concealed political motives. Then the situation had become stabilised, and Temple remarked that the Arminians constituted 'a party within the State rather than a sect within the Church'.[8] By 1660 it was even possible to find an occasional Remonstrant in some of the municipal magistratures.

The origins of the Anabaptists and Mennonites – two branches of the same stem – were steeped in the blood of a long line of martyrs. The Anabaptists were numerous among the common people and mariners, very powerful in Friesland and northern Holland, and were distinguished by a strong collective conscience. Tolerant, eschewing all violence, avoiding the excesses of literalism, they wore a kind of uniform which was entirely black and was composed of a long jacket, baggy breeches fringed at the knee and a tall round velvet hat.

Almost everywhere, ordinary-looking town houses, isolated farms and the manors of sympathetic nobles harboured more or less heretical groups, such as the Rijnsburg sect where any believer took over the service when the Spirit moved him. The whole country was in a religious ferment. There were a number of fellowships which brought together at regular intervals the devotees of the Reformed Church or the various sects, and these meetings easily slipped into a kind of illuminism. They called their assemblies 'exercises', and there they read the Bible and discussed the last sermon or some pious work. Sometimes the 'exercise' brought together young people of both sexes who were taught by an expert to read the biblical languages – Latin, Greek and Hebrew. Often the conversation took on a polemical tone. Certain 'exercises' were frequented by 'pietists' who had a generally unfortunate public reputation. These were naïve or unlettered mystics, known by all sorts of contemptuous nicknames, using a sickly jargon full of 'little brother', 'little sister' and 'my little soul'. They would open the Bible, read out a few verses and indulge in their prophetic gift of interpretation, prognosticating and falling into trances. Theologians such as Brakel and Hellebroek condemned them. Although illuminism was fairly uncommon it made frequent reappearances; first Amsterdam, then Franeker sheltered the Frenchwoman Antoinette Bourignon, who expressed contempt for all forms of open communal worship. In 1625 the Haarlem authorities denounced the collusion between the Rosicrucians of France and Holland. At Leyden, Nicolas Barnaud demanded that theosophists and cabbalists should unite with a view to discovering the universal panacea.

A French official estimated in 1672[9] that a third of the Dutch population was attached to the Reformed Church, another third supported the various dissident Protestant sects and the remaining third were Catholics.

This last category was in a very peculiar position. Numerically in the majority until the end of the sixteenth century,[10] the Catholic Church had seen its estates sequestered and its hierarchy abolished at the very moment when the Counter-Reformation was embarking on a purge of its own inner structure; in 1592 the ancient bishoprics had been replaced by an apostolic vicariate of the Netherlands. However, the triumph of the party of strict Calvinism in 1618 and the installation of the patrician régime checked what might have been a profound renewal. Catholics were gradually removed from important offices and positions of responsibility. The profession of schoolmaster was specifically forbidden to them since it required adherence to the reformed faith. The celebration of mass was permitted only in private, so churches were set up in private houses whose interiors were sometimes entirely reconstructed for this purpose, the upper floors and inside walls being removed altogether. Elsewhere, wealthy merchants and owners of mansions would set up chapels on their own estates. These places of worship were indistinguishable from the outside, yet they were far from being clandestine, and during services the voices of the choir and the sound of the organ could be heard. The church-house sometimes belonged to the priest, or else to a group of prosperous supporters; or it was simply rented from a Protestant owner. Its upkeep was assured by the congregation, who had even been given the right by a papal indulgence to serve mass. In 1700 Amsterdam counted twenty such parishes. The governments did not interfere. They contented themselves with prohibiting any public manifestation such as assemblies or processions, and with imposing a heavy tax on church buildings, individuals or families. Police regulations limited the number of people authorised to attend a mass, though the number was often exceeded. But both sides were accommodating; the priest offered his 'compliments' to the bailiff, and the latter passed by from time to time to collect the legal fine.

The clergy depended entirely upon the liberality of the faithful, and was attached to them by close ties. The priests could be recognised in town by the particular costume they wore, consisting of black clothes, cravat, cane and a voluminous wig. The Jesuits were proscribed in the province of Holland, but were tolerated in Utrecht where they ministered to several parishes. About the middle of the century two French Carmelites remained unmolested when they arrived to make a tour of inspection of the missions in Leyden and The Hague. But, during the same period, several defrocked French priests were warmly welcomed into the Reformed Church and given material and moral assistance; such was the case with the ex-Jesuit Pierre Jarrige in 1648.

In the countries of the States-General, the Catholics formed a strong majority; the peasants near the frontier defied governmental interdictions by sending their children to school in Belgium in order to avoid their being taught by reformed masters. In the Provinces the Catholics were numerous in the country but less so in the towns; however, they were well-organised, and since they enjoyed complete economic freedom they accepted loyally their status as second-class citizens. No tension was apparent on the political plane. The people's state of feeling towards the papists varied according to the place; Leyden was hostile, Rotterdam benevolent.[11]

Catholics were to be met with at all social levels. They formed an important group among the textile workers of Leyden, and, on the other hand, noble families such as the van Forests, with whom Descartes lived, had remained Catholics. Even a priest like Jan-Albert Bau was admitted to the exclusive Muiden circle because of his talents as a composer. Vondel became converted to Catholicism. In Amsterdam, in 1650, of the hundred odd bookshops and publishing houses six were in Catholic hands. The Vulgate version of the Bible was published there four times between 1646 and 1690.[12]

Convents survived here and there (including one in the very centre of Amsterdam), in the form of walled enclosures containing a church around which were clustered small houses inhabitated by nuns who lived alone or in small groups. These remained celibate, spent their days in prayer and manual work, and covered their faces with a black veil when outside the limits of the convent. The convent had a mother superior who made sure that the entrance-door was locked at nine o'clock each evening. Some time towards the end of the century a Protestant who had bought a house within the boundaries of the Amsterdam convent found the door locked the first time he arrived home rather late; he took legal action against the mother superior but lost the case.

Amsterdam possessed a church of the Armenian rite, which was attended by Christians of the western Asian community, and even by a few Dutch Catholics. A monk of the order of Saint Basil was attached to it as priest in charge. One day his congregation found him dead drunk and, on their own authority, banned him from officiating for three months, during which period they attended the services of the Catholic Church.

By the end of the century Amsterdam numbered more than twenty thousand Jews among its population. The Hague, Rotterdam and a few other towns also had smaller Jewish colonies. The social and ethical situation of these groups was by no means identical everywhere. Being barred from public functions and excluded from the guilds, the Jews engaged chiefly in trade; and when, as in Amsterdam, a few of them were brilliantly successful their prestige, if not their influence, could become considerable. But the Jewish community lacked unity, being divided into two clans distinct both by geographical origin and by the date of their entry into the Netherlands. The Portuguese and Spanish Sephardim, who had arrived freely and in large numbers at the end of the sixteenth century, had been in the process of establishing themselves, since 1600 in Amsterdam, in several important branches of foreign trade. Their power was such that they had been able, in 1612, to build a large synagogue without permission of the authorities, who promptly accepted the accomplished fact. Later there was an influx of German Jews, pathetic creatures uselessly proud of a synagogal tradition they claimed was more ancient than the Sephardic. They led a separate, more or less impoverished existence.

The Jewish population of Amsterdam was concentrated in one district of the town, but it was in no sense a ghetto. Yiddish, Judeo-Spanish and Portuguese might be the languages most often heard in the streets, but many beautiful houses stood out among the obscure shops and stalls of the small artisans and second-hand dealers. Facing the Montelbaan tower arose the great synagogue, built in the shape and size of the temple of Solomon following Leon's reconstruction, a high, square building with a triple nave surrounded by galleries. On Saturdays, from eight o'clock in the morning onwards, five or six thousand people would cram inside for the Sabbath service. And each evening, at six, pious Jews would assemble for prayer. The 'German' community had its own synagogue, smaller and simpler but modelled after the bigger one. Attached to these places of worship were rabbinical schools, where the children were taught the Law, the liturgy and the chants. In other towns the Jewish colony was less well provided for; in Rotterdam, it owed everything to the influence and fortune of the fabulously wealthy Abraham de Pinto, who had established a synagogue in his own loft, then in a specially rented house. He had also organised a school under his own roof, giving accommodation to its pupils, and paid a stipend to the chief rabbi.

Under these ethically favourable conditions an intense cultural life developed among the Jews. Men like Grotius and van Baerle conducted fruitful relationships with the Amsterdam rabbis, one of whom, Menasseh ben Israel – scholar, writer, and founder of the Netherlands' first Hebrew printing shop – was spiritually quite close to certain reformed theologians. A group of Jews collaborated with the Protestant Surenhuijs in a Latin translation of part of the Talmud. On the other hand, it would be wrong to exaggerate the importance of the Jewish colony in the Dutch economy during the seventeenth century. Among the fifteen hundred biggest tax-payers in Amsterdam in 1631 only six were Jews, all businessmen.

At mid-century The Hague possessed, beside its official churches, one belonging to the Remonstrants, one to the Lutherans, three Catholic churches and three synagogues. The diversity of these 'houses of prayer' presented a striking image of tolerance. But the ecclesiastical authorities in each religious community were quick to act against those they considered to be lost sheep. For living as a husband with his maid-servant when he was a widower, Rembrandt was summoned before the Church Council; and his mistress was barred from communion. The Jewish community of Amsterdam declared Spinoza an outcast. The more aggressive forms of unbelief were also severely dealt with; in Amsterdam, in 1642, Francis van den Meurs was thrown into prison for denying the immortality of the soul and Christ's divinity. But he was set free again after seven months.

In this country permeated by a religious mentality there stood out, nevertheless, a certain number of individuals – aristocrats, scholars, writers – who were called 'free-thinkers'.

The word was vague, and free-thinking never adopted a dogma; it embraced a very wide spiritual field, ranging from philosophic scepticism to an emotional rejection of all intolerance. The one common denominator was the humanist opposition which the free-thinkers presented in regard to the Church. This opposition, whether in the form of rationalist criticism or simply of a deep-felt emotional attitude, was to be found as much in the heart of the Church as outside it, and derived more or less from the Erasmian tradition. But it remained the viewpoint of a small minority, powerless against a collective evolution which, as the century progressed, increasingly hardened social structures and emphasised rigidity of mind and spirit.

CHILDREN

In a prosperous middle-class home a child was about to be born. A few months before the young woman had felt indisposed. A smouldering cord had been held under her nose, and she had felt ill as a result, a sure proof that she was pregnant. From the seventh month the mother-to-be had fasted for six weeks. Now she was lying on the conjugal bed; a feeble light filtered through the curtains drawn over the narrow windows. In the centre of the room the couch on which the delivery was to take place was already prepared, and the other indispensable pieces of furniture were also there. The linen-warmer, made of wood or wicker-work, was positioned behind the fire-screen which was providing a shield against the heat from the fireplace; or there might have been a layette, adorned perhaps with precious fabrics. The cradle was also of wood or wicker-work, shaped like a boat and surmounted by a hood; it rested on two rockers and its bed-clothes were covered by a satin quilt with embroidered edges. At the foot of the bed the garments for the expected baby were folded in baskets; on one side the magnificent baptism costume, on the other, the everyday clothes and linen. Various instruments had been laid out on a table, and under the chimney-canopy were ranged a selection of mugs and pots, the spice-box, the gruel-cup with its little spoon, and the bowl for spiced wine. At intervals a female neighbour would enter and verify at a glance that everything was in order. All this coming and going had created an extraordinary confusion in the household. Neighbouring housewives would join in the family meal at midday or in the evening, and the evening would be passed in gossiping, drinking and eating cakes.

All the women of the neighbourhood had been collaborating with the family for several months in preparation for the great event. As soon as the first labour-pains had started, some of them had hurried off to fetch the midwife, while others had undertaken to make the rounds of grandparents, uncles and cousins, in the exact order of their relationship, to invite them to the festivities; any delay, or an error in the order of precedence, might result in an interminable quarrel.

Those keeping vigil around the woman in labour made sure that the candles burnt with a blue flame, a sign that no evil spirit was hovering near. Before long the after-birth had been buried in the courtyard. The child was born. The midwife wrapped it in a warm blanket and presented it to its grandmother or else to its godmother, at which point she received a tip. Then she tended the woman in child-bed, dressed the baby, and placed it in the arms of its father, pronouncing the traditional words: 'Here is your child. May Our Lord grant you much happiness through him, else may He call him back to Him soon.' Here she received a second tip.

The new-born baby entered immediately into social life. Parents and neighbours surrounded it, praised its beauty and strength and looked for resemblances. Meanwhile, the midwife's assistant had prepared the caudle and was stirring it with a long stick of cinnamon adorned with ribbons. The colour of the ribbons and the length of the stick varied according to the child's sex. The father had donned a feathered cap of quilted satin, symbol of the husband of a woman who has just given birth. While the new mother restored her energies with buttered bread and ewe's milk cheese, the caudle was still being busily stirred in an adjoining room where visitors had begun to arrive in some numbers. Sometimes brandy was drunk instead of the spiced wine, and sugared almonds were eaten, but poor people contented themselves with sweetened hollands gin. These celebrations usually became wild and noisy, and the Church finally succeeded in abolishing the old tradition of parties for the newborn. Thereafter, families in good society offered at least a party on the day of birth or shortly afterwards to the children of the neighbourhood. They were shown the baby: if it was a boy, they were told that he had been found under a palm-tree or on a cabbage-leaf; if a girl, that she had been discovered in a clump of rosemary. Then they shared a traditional circular or crescent-shaped cake.

If, unhappily, the young mother did not survive her confinement, this day of rejoicing became a death-vigil; the dead woman was laid out on the bed and the child placed in the lifeless arms.

In Amsterdam, Haarlem, Dordrecht and a few other towns the family hung on the door of the house, soon after the birth, a small placard made of wood covered by red silk and trimmed with lace. If the child was a girl, the centre of the board would be hidden by a square of white paper. This placard was a real family treasure which the parents often had possessed ever since their marriage. If twins had been born, two placards were hung out; if the infant was stillborn the silk was black instead of red. Certain rich families used two placards, one for weekdays the other for Sundays, and occasionally even three – the third being a less ornate one for rainy days! Poor people substituted linen for the silk. In the country districts, the same symbolism was obtained with branches attached to the door handle. In some places baskets of flowers were displayed, or festoons of shells. They were the equivalent of our public announcements of birth, and attracted much attention from passers-by who would stop to examine them while groups of neighbours gathered around for a gossip about the event. It was known for the midwife's assistant to be sent around the locality to listen in on these conversations and bring back a report.

On that particular day the midwife had reigned supreme over the family. These superstitious but self-confident matrons enjoyed a prestige with their clients which they easily abused. To have delivered the wife of a regent or a rich bourgeois could give her a genuine power over the humble folk with whom she usually dealt. Even the doctors respected and feared her. Blending a rudimentary knowledge of medicine with a store of obscure peasant traditions, the midwife's prescriptions were much sought after, and it was often she who was consulted first in case of sickness. Socially, she enjoyed valuable privileges, and in many districts she was exempt from taxes on beer, tea, coffee and even brandy. Local administrations attached great importance to her functions, and, as a result, all the towns and some of the villages engaged municipal midwives; when one of these practitioners made a reputation for herself anywhere, rival offers would pour in from all parts of the country. If she accepted one of these offers she swore an oath of allegiance to the corporation for which she was to work, and in return the local council provided her with a regular salary and free accommodation; the sign over her door depicted a cross, in the centre of which lay a baby with some pious text encircling it. When the midwife was forced to retire through old age, the corporation presented her with a small house in which she could end her days peacefully.

Various parties and ceremonies marked the first weeks of the child's existence. Following an ancient tradition, the ninth day after the birth was devoted to a general reception. For this occasion the father donned his feathered cap for the last time; and the midwife, in her finest gown, made an official presentation of the infant, dressed in its ceremonial costume of dark material – garnet-red or green, carefully embroidered. In wealthy households a banquet was held, but a meal of some kind was provided even in the most modest establishments. And, in any event, tongues wagged and the married women retraced the history of the particular confinement with a wealth of appropriate details.

The Church desired that baptism should be carried out as soon as possible after birth, and among the lower classes this was, in fact, the rule; but the upper classes preferred to wait until the mother was able to leave the house. The ceremony took place in church, usually in the afternoon, before or after the regular sermon – but never without it. The presence of the father was considered indispensable, and sponsors of the child, together with its brothers and sisters, were required to attend so long as they were members of the Reformed Church. Everyone was dressed in his best clothes, and those who were unable to afford a special ceremonial costume wore their marriage outfits. The baby was swathed in a ceremonial robe and draped with symbolic accessories: for example, a boy's cap was composed of six panels and a girl's of three. If the mother had died in childbirth, the infant was dressed entirely in white with a black border to its robe. To stop the child crying during the ceremony it was given a milk-soaked sugar-stick to suck. The procession returned from church on foot or by carriage, according to individual circumstances, the father blessed his son, a banquet followed, songs were sung and the guests presented gifts.

Even in prosperous families the mother nearly always looked after the babies herself, and if a nurse was necessary for medical reasons she always left the house as soon as the child was weaned. On the other hand, an old female servant, who had been with the family a long time and was on intimate terms with its members, would often look after the slightly older children. She dressed them, washed them and, making use of her repertoire of children's folk-lore, sang them lullabies and told them fairy-stories.

Babies were protected by every possible means against fresh air. They were so tightly swaddled that they could not move their limbs, bundled into head-dresses, sleeved vests and jackets, enveloped in a woollen robe and shut up in a room with closed windows, tucked under the covers of the cradle with a hot-water bottle alongside. Despite the advice of certain doctors, many people administered soporific medicines to their babies. As soon as the infant could stand upright it was placed in a wheel-chair shaped like the bottom part of a pyramid, made of wooden bars, resting on big casters and enclosing the chest tightly;

or the chair was shaped like a table and the child was held upright in it by a high back. To teach it to walk, it was supported by reins, a cord, or leading-strings attached to its body. It was soon old enough to receive its first plaything, a wooden hobby-horse crudely carved and painted.

Until the young child could walk with ease it continued to be burdened by a mass of clothes; in addition, it had to suffer a barbarous equipment designed to save it from knocks and from bone deformations, including a leather cap, a tightly laced whalebone corset with iron and lead inserts to make it narrower, and a dress over the whole contraption. From 1620 onwards protests were raised against such a harsh régime, but it took more than a century to conquer these ingrained and antiquated ideas. When it was a little older the child was suddenly put into adult clothes: stockings, breeches, miniature doublet for the boys; jacket, bodice, long robe for the girls. They were allowed absolutely no intermediate costume, and indeed there existed nothing suited to their age. In some villages the boys wore feminine garb until they were seven.

Until they were old enough to go to school the children mostly played in the street; if the family was rich the children were sent outdoors, unless the weather made this absolutely impossible, so that they should not disturb the house's perfect cleanliness; if the family was poor the street was the only place for them to go. So the Dutch town swarmed from morning onwards with children from three to six years old, of all classes of society, mixed into a playing, yelling, fighting mass on the pavements, under the house-canopies, along the streets. After the schools closed in the afternoons they were joined by the older ones. This open-air education was an extraordinary phenomenon for the time in Europe. It astonished all visitors from other countries, more especially since it went hand in hand with an indiscipline and rowdyism about which everyone complained. The urchins were disrespectful towards adults, and people whose clothes seemed strange to the juvenile mob could expect to be jeered at in the street if, indeed, they were lucky enough not to have stones thrown at them. The mob would attack passers-by, hurl lumps of earth at them and scream insults. This state of things became so widespread that it verged on public scandal; in Zaandam in 1642, for instance, the Church Council complained to the local magistrates who resuscitated an old police regulation. But all to no avail. The trouble had its roots in the actual relations between parents and children. The worship of the head of the family, and the polite phrases with which parents, brothers and sisters addressed each other in bourgeois society (the equivalents in English would be 'Sir my father', 'Madam my mother', 'Young lady my sister' and so on) were not founded on a genuine authority. Children were adored and spoilt, and lived under conditions of almost total liberty. Excessive tenderness made the parents incurably weak. If a visitor were to suggest to them that it might be appropriate to combat certain faults, he would be answered with a pessimistic dictum such as: 'Cutting off the nose spoils the face'.

Under this permissive régime children acquired a capricious and unstable nature and exerted an influence over their parents which did them no ultimate good. The girls in bourgeois families, treated as equals by their mothers, often became intolerably pretentious. Parival wrote: 'It is partly from this excessive indulgence towards their children that there results the disorder which is often to be seen in their conduct. It is nevertheless surprising that there is not more disorder than there is, and there is perhaps no better proof of the natural goodness of the inhabitants of this country and the excellence of their disposition.'[1]

The municipal corporations took care of the orphans whose families were unable to look after them. Small towns entrusted them to citizens known for their respectability, but the big towns possessed hostels designed to accommodate them and bring them up in the Reformed Church, together with children found abandoned. A chamber of guardianship administered the estates of wealthy orphans; the less fortunate were taught a trade. The principal orphanage of Amsterdam lodged as many as one thousand two hundred children. These houses were dismal abodes. The children were packed into vast barrack-rooms supervised by their masters, subjected to a régime of harsh corporal punishment, and often exploited savagely under the guise of professional instruction. To take one example, even at the end of the century the regents did not hesitate to go to the rescue of the near-bankrupt Amsterdam woollen and silk mill founded by the Huguenot Pierre Baille, by delivering two hundred and forty orphans to the manager as unpaid and undemanding labour.

In the next chapter we shall consider the child of school-going age and follow him in his studies. But it may be said at this juncture that these years of adolescence presented parents and local administrations with worries which only ceased when the individual reached adulthood and abandoned the turbulence of his youth. Drunkenness, in particular, had never been so widespread among young people in any previous period of Dutch history, and this despite the most stringent police measures which were renewed at regular intervals. It is true that girls were strictly supervised in respectable bourgeois society, and never left home without being accompanied by their mother, even when going to church. In more modest circles they were kept at home by household duties. But as soon as the school or the work-shop closed its doors, the boys had nowhere to go except the house, which was either too small or too austere, the street, or the tavern. Their youthful passions were assuaged by drinking and dice-playing, an endemic disease which affected even university students. Only the influence of exceptionally strong family ties was capable of modifying these habits.

Among the aristocracy it was customary to send the young men abroad as soon as their studies were completed; the voyage provided them with a pleasant change of atmosphere and scenery, and gave them experience which would prove valuable in the magistratures they would eventually occupy. They were usually sent on visits to England and France, more rarely to Italy, but had no opportunity to see Spain or Scandinavia unless they were attached to some embassy.

Serious conflicts between parents and adolescents seem to have been frequent, and the young firebrands presented a problem to families in good society which was insoluble in the current state of manners and morals. Or rather, there did exist a radical solution, and one that was regularly employed: banishment to the East Indies, 'a real sewer of a country into which flows all the garbage of Holland' in Parival's words.[2] The crews of ships sailing for the Cape or Java often included a group of rebellious sons signed on by their fathers by virtue of their legal authority. In the most stubborn cases, when the child – son or daughter – appeared incorrigibly wicked, there remained one more solution open to the father: to have him put in prison.

EDUCATION

A few wealthy families engaged a 'pedagogue' to direct their children's studies, a private tutor who often retained his post with the family over a long period of time. Herman Bruno, for instance, was engaged to teach the children of Constantin Huyghens and remained many years. The tutor gave his pupils instruction at what we would call primary and secondary level. Later, he would accompany them to the university and even on their educational voyages abroad. But these arrangements applied only to a small privileged minority; normally, children were submitted to school discipline from an early age.

The Junior Schools

The Netherlands possessed no central organism responsible for administering and controlling education. The creation and upkeep of the 'junior schools', equivalent to our infant and primary schools, was left to the initiative of individuals or private associations, subject to the approval of the municipal authorities. These authorities limited themselves to operating an occasional and rather vague control which they placed in the hands of the local Church Council. In a few places corps of 'inspectors of the teaching body' had been brought into being, responsible to the governors of the local 'Latin' (secondary) school. In those towns where a guild of schoolmasters existed the guild itself supervised its members; they were known to dismiss incompetent masters engaged by the corporation. These various in-spectors exercised their authority in regard to the school-masters and schoolmistresses rather than to the schools as such. The master or mistress of the school was obliged to sign a declaration of support of the reformed faith, and swear an oath of loyalty; this was sufficient to ensure the handing over of a certificate which had to be fixed to the main door. Yet neither the applicant's degree of learning nor his morals were made the object of a genuine examina-tion. Church sessions raised fruitless protests; a report in 1611 stated that there were schoolmasters incapable of reciting the letters of the alphabet correctly or of teaching children correct pronunciation.[1]

On all sides families complained; but a real scandal was needed – such as a master's open drunkenness during the exercise of his functions – before the inspection committee could be induced to intervene and, in such a case, deliver a judgement not subject to appeal. Some rural districts were even worse served. In Brabant, for instance, it was quite usual to engage young cripples of good family as teachers, or men-servants no longer able to follow their calling. In the villages, where the school was usually an annexe of the church, the sexton was put in charge.

The women in charge of the infant schools were often worse than their male colleagues. These poor creatures were sometimes recruited from the town's slums, over-whelmed by their responsibilities and combining their profession with that of dressmaker, knitter or lacemaker. They were not even required to know how to read or write. In class they limited themselves to teaching by heart the Lord's prayer, the Ten Commandments, the formula of Confession and the names of the letters of the alphabet. It was in 1655 that an edict finally required that candidates for the post of teacher should be able to write, read printed and manuscript characters, perform the four basic mathe-matical calculations, know hymn tunes and – possess a sound method of teaching!

Despite the gross deficiencies of the system, and the fact that schoolmasters constituted one of the poorest professional categories, a certain basic education was spread fairly widely and the proportion of illiterates was far smaller in the Union than anywhere else in Europe. School fees were paid partly in cash (a nominal amount) and partly in kind: for instance, one sod of peat a day and one candle a week during the winter, an expense beyond the means of only the most impoverished.

Children between the age of three and seven attended infant school; this was situated in some house in the neighbourhood, its identity revealed by a signboard in the name of the teacher or the building, for example, 'Grietje's school above the fish market' or 'School of the Apple'. The 'classes' were usually held in the 'back room' which would be partly occupied by the teacher's bed or by the fireplace where she did her cooking. The walls were white-washed, the floor of bare bricks. The children settled themselves as they pleased, squatting, lying down, sitting on the ground, playing, boys and girls together, among the messes made by the youngest ones – a swarming, stinking throng in an ill-lit room full of smoke and the smell of tallow. The mistress's voice raised in anger or her hand wielding a ruler constituted the only instruments of a very approximate discipline. The older ones droned out the ABC or the Lord's prayer, swaying to and fro. Two or three times a week in the afternoons the girls learnt the rudiments of dressmaking and knitting.

In the prosperous districts of the big towns, the infant schools offered a less disheartening spectacle and even achieved a certain decorum. The mistress presided from behind a desk, and the children sat in rows on benches. As a supreme luxury, a bucket in a corner of the room served as a urinal.

At the age of seven the child passed into the hands of a teacher conducting an establishment distantly comparable to our present-day primary school. He stayed there for five years.

A signboard drew attention to the school's existence, and its proprietor: 'Adriaen Wouterszoom Cuyper. Here, children are taught', for example. Sometimes the inscription had a more literary flavour. One Rotterdam teacher drew attention to himself by a couplet:

Vomited by the whale, Jonah visited Nineveh, knowledge to impart.
Here, prayer is taught, and recitation of the Catechism by heart.

Elsewhere, a picture might represent the teacher surrounded by his pupils. Or the sign might be designed to arouse curiosity by appealing to thrifty parents with a slogan such as 'Knowledge at bargain prices'.

The school's premises would be found either on the ground floor of the house, where the most space was available, or, on the contrary, on the cramped upper storey, according to the social level of the clientele. They consisted usually of two rooms, allowing the pupils to be divided up into two groups according to various criteria – the big and the small, or simply the rich and the poor. Whichever was the less fortunate of the two groups was entrusted to the care of the teacher's wife or even his man-servant. In each room the children were seated according to sex and sometimes according to age. But there was no equivalent to our present-day division into classes.

In the countryside matters were simpler. In Friesland and Gelderland the village schools occupied a stable or barn, or occasionally even a mud-walled hut, freezing cold in winter, suffocating in summer.

With a large cap on his head, and his open robe exposing his breeches and waistcoat, the master sat enthroned in a heavy chair. Close by, on a lectern or a row of shelves, he had arrayed a Bible, a Psalter, an hour-glass, a few manuals, a supply of quills, an abacus, a bottle of ink and the sandbox for blotting purposes. Beside these professional instruments was to be found an iron haircomb, used for straightening the tousled locks of the more dishevelled pupils; its vigorous application constituted a much-feared punishment. On the walls hung spelling-charts, word-tables, the Ten Commandments, the Lord's prayer, the Confession of faith and, most important of all, the 'Statute', a list of regulations which every teacher had to display prominently and which dealt with correct behaviour in class, in church and in the street.

Each day, class commenced with the recitation of a prayer and the reading of a chapter from the Scriptures. Then followed the singing of a psalm. After that each child worked individually. The pupil approached the teacher's chair in turn, removed his hat, and received his task or recited his lesson by heart. Then he put his hat on again and returned to his bench (which was provided in different heights, with or without desks attached) or to one of the tables provided instead. So it went on throughout a long day, repeated more than three hundred and thirty times a year! In 1600 school opened at six in the morning in summer and seven in winter, and closed at seven in the evening. Two breaks were allowed, from eleven till one and from four till five, when children could return home for meals, or eat the food they had brought with them in the classroom. Gradually during the century this time-table was reduced, and hours of attendance became eight till eleven in the morning and one till four or five in the afternoon. Once a week, on Wednesdays or Thursdays, lessons ended an hour earlier, and were abolished entirely on Saturday afternoons; but these 'holidays' were occupied by singing practice and catechism rehearsals. During the dogdays the town schools closed for two weeks or so. The law also allowed the masters to award additional holidays so long as they did not coincide with papist festivals. This permission was invoked by most of the schools during the annual cattle fairs. Families often asked leave for their child to be absent so that he might attend an anniversary or some domestic celebration, and the master usually granted these requests. But woe betide the pupil who played truant: his reward would be a sound caning.

Indeed, the teacher had a wide range of punishments at his disposal. Whip, cane or strap was applied to the child, either clothed or on his bare behind. In some schools, especially those attended by poor children or orphans, the pillory was used; or a perforated block of wood was attached to the child's leg for a specific period, sometimes several days, so that the victim had to drag this weight around with him in the street and at church. The dunce's cap was a positive treat in comparison; it was worn hung round the neck, and the victim had to kneel on a chair in this garb, with a placard spelling out his misdeed.

The programme of studies at these institutions was limited essentially to sacred history, reading, writing and arithmetic. The girls' education was even less demanding than the boys', and a slight knowledge of needlework was considered sufficient to launch them in life. The children were taught to read the letters from A to Z in their alphabetical order but without any attempt to demonstrate the various ways they could be grouped into words; the letters were simply pronounced in sequence by the master, and repeated (and distorted) untiringly by the children in a sing-song voice. If it was a large class, the din was loud enough to annoy passers-by in the street outside. There was a saying that it was better to pass by a blacksmith's shop than a school!

Because of its commercial importance elementary mathematics was taught with some care by most masters, who often held the additional post of municipal accountant. Their teaching remained practical rather than theoretical, and the pupils were liable to be faced with problems such as: 'Two people have together bought eight pints of malmsey wine, which they want to divide up into two equal quantities. But to accomplish this they have available as measures only a five-pint bottle and a three-pint bottle. How are they to achieve their aim?'[2]

Handwriting was considered the first of all the useful arts and so enjoyed an enormous prestige. Some practitioners made a positive aesthetic out of calligraphy, and wrote as carefully as though they were engravers. The fame of the handwriting masters from Holland and Zeeland had spread beyond the country's frontiers. A fine hand sufficed to guarantee a teacher a choice clientele, however incompetent he might otherwise be or however deficient his character. Pens were fashioned from quills or reeds, and a black ink was made by steeping soot in oil. Children were initiated into the mysteries of Roman and Gothic scripts, and of sloping and upright letters. Each year the municipal corporations organised a handwriting contest for their town's schoolchildren, and the winners received a silver pen, a writing-desk, a book or had their names inscribed on a roll of honour.

For public officials, businessmen and jurists proficiency in calligraphy was an indispensable attainment. The habit of writing letters and messages had already become widespread, and men and women in the upper and lower middle classes wrote a great deal. At school the teaching of writing was accompanied by instruction in the rudiments of a basic rhetoric. If the pupil grew up with an insufficient command of the subject he could buy and study didactic works on rhetoric, and even collections of letter models, including love letters.[3] In special circumstances, people had recourse to public scribes specialising in ornate prose and versification, expert at formulating a marriage proposal, an announcement of birth or death, a formal invitation and so on.

The school curriculum (based inefficiently on a few mediocre text-books[4]) did not lead very far. In addition, the masters complained that many children were withdrawn from school prematurely by parents anxious to see them earning a wage as soon as possible. The situation was considered generally disturbing. Besides the usual 'little schools' several towns boasted other schools, which were really almost indistinguishable but claimed to provide a more specialised training for commercial careers.

Huguenot refugees had founded 'French schools' which were financially supported by the municipalities from the middle of the century onwards. These schools added to arithmetic and calligraphy the study of French, considered to be the language of international relations. Some of these French schools, directed by more or less incompetent women, had made a speciality of instructing young ladies of good family, who, in particular, were taught letter-writing style appropriate to ladies; unfortunately, the teachers often lacked any knowledge of syntax or orthography.

The French schools became increasingly fashionable during the century, despite their mediocrity. However, if the French language occupied a privileged position in the Netherlands during the seventeenth century, it was not so much due to these schools as to family and political traditions. The families of French refugees of the cultured classes jealously maintained the purity of their maternal language, and were aided in this by the fact that the preaching in Walloon churches was in French. In Dutch high society the education of young people (who were often already very frenchified) was completed by long voyages throughout France or French Switzerland.

At government level French was the language of foreign relations, and also served as the common tongue with the many foreigners employed in various capacities by the Republic. It was only in 1609 that the army stopped using French for words of command. Prince Frederick Henry, the son of Louise de Coligny, wrote his *Memoirs* in French; William II was bilingual.

But, in fact, the popularity of the French language did not extend further than aristocratic circles and the prosperous commercial classes. Even during the last quarter of the century, when French influence was at its height, René Le Pays needed an interpreter for his journeys through the Dutch provinces. And then, most of the Dutch who did speak French murdered it. Even the French refugees themselves, except those with a distinguished cultural background, soon succumbed to the influence of their surroundings and came to use a debased jargon.

English was taught in a few schools, though neither this language nor German was very widespread. Italian and Spanish enjoyed a certain favour in fashionable circles, but Portuguese was considered the most useful acquisition, especially for those in the merchant marine trading in the Far East, who used it extensively for communicating with the Javanese.

Dutch was, in fact, the one language that was not taught at all as such, despite the fact that it was during this century that the language became stabilised and produced its first literary classics. As used orally by ordinary people it presented a number of extremely varied dialects. In the northern provinces these dialects formed actual languages with an original structure quite distinct from Dutch, though springing from the same basic roots: that is to say, the 'low Saxon' of the Groningen region and, above all, Frisian, which in the Middle Ages had transmitted a deeply original culture of its own.[5] But, in this field, the Reformation and the War of Independence had been accompanied by a consciousness of identity and efforts to normalise usage; three generations of writers and humanist scholars, the influence of the States' Bible and of the preachers combined to produce a common national idiom and to lead it to its maturity during the seventeenth century.

Higher Education and the Sciences

If a child's parents wanted him to acquire a classical education (considered necessary for exercising important public functions) he went from the 'junior school' or the French school to the 'Latin school'. By the terms of a 1625 decree a knowledge of reading and writing was a sufficient qualification for entry, a modest demand which said much for the contempt in which these 'junior schools' were held by those in authority. Before 1625 many of the 'Latin schools' had to devote a first, and even a second, year to completing their new pupils' elementary studies; Gelderland and Groningen introduced local legislation which expressly forbade entry to illiterate adolescents.[6]

Until the start of the seventeenth century complete anarchy reigned in the organisation of this secondary education, and there was no uniformity whatsoever of curriculum methods or textbooks. Since these 'Latin schools' trained the élite of the nation and so had the status of important public institutions, the Church synods expressed concern at regular intervals at this state of affairs. At least twenty synods between 1570 and 1620 tackled this problem, and the edict prepared in 1625 at the demand of the States of Holland and adopted gradually in all the provinces created at last a relative (and, for the era, remarkable) unity.

Thenceforward the Latin school was divided into six classes – sometimes four – through which the pupil was supposed to progress between the age of twelve and sixteen or sometimes eighteen.[7] Girls were not admitted, and young women from the upper classes who might wish to pursue classical studies had recourse to a tutor. The administrative responsibility of the Latin school was vested in a college of 'curators', formed of members of the local government administration and of predicants; its authority extended to the nomination of professors, control of the pupils' promotion from one class to another, award of prizes and allocation of penalties. The direction of teaching was in the hands of a rector.[8]

Discipline was severe and corporal punishment formed an essential part of the system. The schools were usually established on the premises of one-time convents, and comprised living quarters for the rector and rooms for those pupils who were boarders. The cloister was cut in two by a fence, providing a private garden for the rector on one side and an exercise-yard for the pupils on the other. The buildings were usually hideous: depressing, sparsely furnished with a few benches and heavy tables, badly lit by tall narrow windows, reeking of peat-smoke in winter.

The bell over the entrance-door tolled each morning, at eight in the summer, at nine in the winter, to announce the start of lessons. Work finished at eleven, then recommenced at one or two in the afternoon and went on till four or five. Apart from three weeks in August, holidays were provided by a series of individual free days distributed fairly generously throughout the year: public feast-days, the rector's birthday, special book-sales, public executions and similar occasions.

Latin was the principal subject taught: out of a weekly total of thirty-two or thirty-four hours of class, it occupied between twenty and thirty hours during the first three years, and between ten and eighteen hours during the three final years. The rest of the time was divided equally between religious instruction and calligraphy and, in the senior classes, by Greek and the elements of rhetoric and logic.

Teaching methods were based mainly on memorisation and on rather naïve principles of emulation such as the distribution of prizes following the biannual examinations. The results remained mediocre and complaints were made of the young people's lack of enthusiasm for their studies. By the end of the century the Latin schools were thoroughly discredited, at least in the small towns.[9] In addition, the French language and French culture was beginning to supplant Latin and classical culture among the privileged classes, who tended to avoid the official Latin schools in favour of private high schools directed by French refugees; or, if they could afford it, they engaged a Swiss tutor.

After Latin school the youth was ready to begin specialised studies, classed traditionally in four faculties: 'arts' (that is to say, science and letters), theology, law and medicine. These studies lasted four or five years, and the young man then found himself, at some age between twenty and twenty-five,[10] considered competent to exercise a profession.

There were two sorts of establishment offering instruction at this level, the universities and the 'illustrious schools', identical apart from historical and juridical distinctions. The universities had been created originally to provide pastors for the Reformed Church and dated from the first days of the Republic: Leyden was founded in 1575, Franeker in 1585 and Groningen and Harderwijk at the very beginning of the seventeenth century. Then, after 1630, a spirit of emulation induced other towns to found their own higher educational institutions; but the title and privileges of a 'university', so jealously guarded by the original foundations, was denied to the new-comers. For this reason, Dordrecht, Middelburg, Breda, 's Hertogenbosch, Nijmegen, Deventer, Rotterdam and even Amsterdam had to be satisfied with the title of 'illustrious school', limit themselves to three faculties, and agree not to confer doctorates. The 'illustrious school' of Utrecht, which achieved university status in 1636, two years after its foundation, was a quite remarkable exception.

The level of teaching at most of the universities and 'illustrious schools' during the seventeenth century was extremely high, and achieved for the Netherlands an international scientific reputation. The greatest centre of learning was the University of Leyden. When it was founded by the States of Holland, it had immediately engaged nine scholars representing the various human and natural sciences, in addition to the theologian whose presence justified its existence officially. The original nucleus expanded during the course of the century and served as a model for all the other Dutch universities.

As an institution with a public charter Leyden University was administered by curators, while the teaching side was managed by a rector assisted by a senate composed of the entire faculty. Its first site was the former convent of Saint Barbara; later it established itself in the convent of the White Sisters, which burnt down in 1616, was reconstructed and then altered several times during the course of the century. The university impressed visitors, both by its austere appearance and by the excellence of its equipment. With its dependent institutions, the College of the States, the students' lodgings, the premises of the great convent (whose rooms were leased by the municipal corporation to the professors 'for an honest sum'), the university was truly a city of Science.

The teaching faculty included a certain proportion of foreigners: as early as 1575 there were two Frenchmen and a German. Then the number of Frenchmen and Belgians increased rapidly, only to diminish again after 1609. Anxious to attract Europe's most celebrated scholars to Leyden, the curators (who, at one point, had the temerity to pen an invitation to Galileo), sometimes made them very tempting financial offers; they even sent envoys who were promised a bonus in case of success – as was done in the case of the negotiations with Joseph Justus Scaliger. In 1578 the senate sent the physician Ratloo to Germany on a tour of recruitment.

The student body likewise contained a considerable number of foreigners. Parival met, in Leyden's various schools, Germans, Frenchmen, Danes, Swedes, Poles, Hungarians and Englishmen, and, 'among these national groups even princes are often to be met with'.[11] The French complement reached a figure of fifty in 1621,[12] but was usually more in the region of ten to twenty. Guez de Balzac, Théophile de Viau and Descartes all studied at Leyden. The other universities and the 'illustrious schools' could not all compete with Leyden in scientific excellence or in fame. The senate of Harderwijk was suspected of selling their doctors' diplomas, and Nijmegen with its three professors seemed like a poor relative. On the other hand, Franeker presented sufficient attractions, despite its geographical remoteness, for Descartes to enrol there in 1629.

A real advantage possessed by the Dutch institutions of higher education in comparison with nearly all those in the rest of Europe was their newness. Having been created from nothing they were not bound by a strongly entrenched medieval tradition; they were, on the contrary, permeated by a spirit of innovation. Certainly the Church had every intention of maintaining the supremacy of theology, but although it remained at the centre, it was by no means dominant. The sciences in which the Dutch faculties excelled represented rather the mind's most recent conquests: Greco-Latin philology, the study of eastern languages, anatomy, astronomy, botany, and the first beginnings of chemistry; all those branches of a modern humanism founded on linguistics, history and the natural sciences.

As a new-born state, the Union felt an organic need to create a culture of its own that would parallel its political and economic originality. The fundamental qualities of the Dutch intellect expressed themselves in a liking for the concrete, a preoccupation with experimentation and practical applications and realism. All the evidence of the period bears witness to the Dutch middle class's touching attachment to science, combined with an avid and sometimes naïve curiosity. They remained undismayed by even the most basic revaluations of ideas; in 1630, for instance, Descartes observed that the Dutch scholars had all been won over to the theories of Copernicus. Almost complete religious tolerance contributed greatly to the lively atmosphere in the faculties, which did not even require the students to swear the confession of faith.

Certainly a more conservative outlook still existed in places, and some teaching was more or less delusory. Nevertheless, the hegemony of traditional science had been broken; optics and meteorology were formulated, and the different branches of mathematics asserted their independence. Medicine discovered its affinity with physics, and students often worked for a doctorate in the two subjects combined. Since the universities only taught theoretical medicine, their doctors were considered publicly to be entirely inexperienced, and many people preferred older practitioners who had had no theoretical training; still, there was at least a general tendency now to consider medical problems from a scientific angle.

In 1587 the 'Frenchman from Lécluse' known as Clusius had established, on ground just behind Leyden University, a botanical garden designed to initiate medical students into the knowledge of medicinal herbs, and this institution soon became a research centre, with expanded facilities including hot-houses where tropical plants were grown. In 1631 Franeker created its own botanical garden and Utrecht, Harderwijk and Groningen followed suit.

In 1632 an astronomical observatory was constructed among the buildings of Leyden University. Utrecht used one of the town's towers for the same purpose. Anatomical collections, consisting of skeletons, mummies and stuffed animals, provided practical examples in the medical classes, and there were also collections of apparatus used currently in physics and mathematics. A gallery leading off Leyden's botanical garden housed a museum of antiquities and 'rarities'. Since the start of the century the Dutch had turned into passionate collectors. All sorts of amateurs built up collections of minerals, shells, plant-life, reptiles, winged creatures and embryos. Fredrik Ruysch collected corpses; a sea-captain set up a museum of navigation in his house in Edam in 1600; the medical authority Paludanus, after long voyages through Europe and the Near East, had established a museum of rare curiosities at Enkhuizen: birds of paradise, poisoned arrows, Indian gold, Chinese porcelain, ancient coins and even a bit of the red earth of Damascus from which God is supposed to have fashioned Adam.

Leyden University possessed an important library rich in rare manuscripts, many of them taken over from the old convents. This basic stock was added to regularly by gifts and legacies, and also by purchases; on several occasions the curators bought valuable lots – in 1629 a collection of oriental works for four thousand five hundred florins, and in 1690 the late Isaac Vossius's library for thirty-three thousand florins.[13]

The full professors and lecturers of the faculties enjoyed great moral authority with the public courts and, generally speaking, their work was not hampered by any extra-academic control. Occasionally a dispute on a matter of dogma might lead the municipal magistrate to intervene in a personal capacity, but such intervention rarely assumed an official character.[14] On the other hand, those professors who did not boast private means were not particularly well-off. Individual salaries were fixed by contract but without any general guiding rules. The average figure was modest (about a thousand florins a year), but in exceptional cases there could be wide differences; for example, Amsterdam offered Vossius two thousand five hundred florins a year and a house worth nine hundred a year in rent. These sums were often augmented by various additional allowances such as travelling expenses and personal bonuses. In addition, the teaching body shared with the students the benefit of exemption from liquor taxes on a maximum of six barrels of beer and forty-five gallons of wine a year.

Teaching was divided into two parts, lectures and 'disputations'. Each professor gave between two and five hours of lessons a week, devised by himself and delivered in Latin (except for some scientific subjects), and interspersed these with directed discussions (*disputationes*). The professors of the natural sciences also organised sessions of observation in the botanical garden or the museum.

Examinations for the Degree of Doctor took the form of a debate or 'dispute' on a theme proposed by the candidate. This ceremony usually took place in June or July, in public, and in the presence of the local magistrates. They were sometimes announced in the town by trumpets. Afterwards, there would be a parade and a banquet which Parival assures us often lasted two days.[15]

It was rare for a young man of aristocratic family not to pursue any higher studies at all. So a certain number of rich students formed a group of a superior social class in the universities, providing a strong contrast to the Theological Faculty's modest scholarship-holders and the floating mass of poor students whose existence is vouched for by entries in the academic registers. These mention exemption from enrolment fees 'because of indigence', fines 'devoted to the benefit of impecunious students', interventions by the senate in cases of insolvency. Some students exercised a trade, such as that of barber.

The student entering a faculty registered himself with the *pedel*, the university's factotum, a powerful official who combined the functions of beadle, bailiff, mace-bearer and secretary. Apart from academic privileges, an enrolment at Leyden conferred the right to walk in the streets in dressing-gown and slippers so long as wig and hat were worn! If he did not live at home the young man would look for a room in town. He had several alternatives: to take lodgings with one of the professors, who were only too glad to supplement their income in this way, to enter a boarding-house run by some elderly spinster prepared to overlook minor disorders, to stay at a local inn, or to rent one of the private rooms which were always available in university towns. The landlords were not always of blameless respectability; while Tristan the Hermit was studying at Amsterdam he was robbed one evening, when drunk, by his own landlady, in the loft he had rented from her.

Students from outside the town and the province tended to group themselves by 'nations', while the 'natives', on their side, set up 'national colleges'; relations were cordial between these various associations. Student life was lively enough, and a good deal of fairly harmless horseplay was indulged in, including the sport of ragging teachers in class, interrupting solemn 'disputes', and noisy heckling of unpopular professors. On the other hand the bullying of 'new boys' reached such a degree of cruelty at some universities that in 1606, for instance, the States had to forbid the practice at Franeker. Drinking sessions were frequent and easily led to trouble; in Leyden students and professors drank together at the *Fir-cone* and the *Fighting Lion* and often became involved in brawls and in acts of violence against townspeople. Drunkenness at the universities, abetted by the tax concessions, became a public scourge. On several occasions the wearing of arms had to be forbidden; duelling between students was prohibited in 1600 but was never entirely eliminated. The university did exercise rights of civil and criminal procedure against those under its jurisdiction, and the rector and his assessors formed an academic tribunal with the addition of the burgermaster and a group of municipal magistrates. The tribunal was competent to hand down penalties ranging from fines to expulsion and even banishment, as well as imprisonment with bread and water. Even these strong measures did not prevent trouble from breaking out among the students from time to time and leading occasionally to actual riots and violent clashes with the authorities; riots occurred at Leyden in 1594, 1608, 1632 and 1682, at Franeker in 1623, at Groningen in 1629 and 1652.

Dutch science was directed towards practical experimentation and went beyond the limits imposed at the universities. Outside the faculties, and beyond the scope of authoritative teaching, science concerned itself with technical considerations. Inventions of capital importance in the history of European civilisation, such as the telescope, microscope, pendulum-clock, logarithmic, integral and differential calculus were all due to seventeenth-century Dutchmen; and to these must be added a long list of attainments in the fields of anatomy, biology, cosmography and geography. Most of these discoveries were the fruit of an inventive imagination as much as of patient observation, deduction and systematic research. The glass lens was born in a humble spectacle-maker's shop. Antony van Leeuwenhoek of Delft, the inventor of the microscope, showed his instrument at country fairs before a Leyden doctor discovered him and launched it in the international scientific world. The telescope, invented by a vagrant, bohemian scholar, Cornelis Drebbel, permitted Christiaan Huyghens to explain the composition of the ring of Saturn in 1655 and that of the nebula of Orion at a later date. Huyghens himself was a high-ranking government official, a wealthy enlightened 'amateur', inventor of the pendulum-clock, author of the first theory of light. The physician Swammerdam used the microscope to examine tiny insects. These rapid advances in science were given added impetus by research accomplished during long commercial or diplomatic journeys.

The botanist Bontius accompanied Coen to Java in 1627, and the physician Piso went with Prince John Maurice to Brazil. 'Indian' fauna and flora now came within the scope of science. Ever since the end of the sixteenth century the East had held the attention of Dutch linguists and historians. Leyden had created a chair of Arabic which one of its holders, Erpenius, strengthened by the addition of a printing-plant equipped to set up type in the semitic languages, Ethiopian and Turkish. His successor, Golius, had himself sent on a mission by the curators, furnished with two thousand florins in funds; he spent three years in the Ottoman Empire and brought back the most important collection of oriental manuscripts that Europe had yet seen, some three hundred volumes. On his return he undertook the composition of an Arabic-Latin dictionary, for which he engaged several oriental collaborators, including a deacon from Aleppo, a Persian scholar and an Armenian. By 1660 Holland had become the world centre of oriental studies.

LOVE LIFE

William Temple remarked, using the medical terminology he affected, that the constitution of the Dutch was basically 'temperate', neither sufficiently 'volatile' to allow the most spiritual revelations of joy nor sufficiently 'warm' for love. It was true, he continued, that the young people sometimes discussed their feelings, 'but as though it were all something they had heard about rather than experienced, and as an unavoidable rather than fascinating subject of conversation. . . . One meets pleasant young gallants, but no mad lovers.'[1] The evidence of most foreigners agrees on this point. The men in the Netherlands were mostly big, strong and robust, plump, well-built, with white skins and high colouring. But no sexual passions animated them; business affairs seemed more important to them than love-affairs, and for their diversion alcohol was preferred to women as being simpler. For their part, the women refused to allow themselves any signs of flirtatiousness, partly because of a very strong attachment to their independence but also because the men's coldness very soon cured them of any inclination to indulge in amorous wiles. They gained thereby an extraordinary freedom of action with regard to the opposite sex, and were outspoken on erotic matters to a degree which astonished the French of the time. In Paris, about 1660, there was a pleasantly allusive saying: 'To make love like a Dutchwoman.' René Le Pays, visiting the Netherlands during this period, remarked ironically that the Dutchwomen did from stupidity what the girls in Paris did through licentiousness: 'At the climax of pleasure they start eating an apple, or break nuts with their teeth.'[2] Apart from such pleasantries, there was a more subtle analysis by Saint-Evremond in his statement that, once they had reached adulthood, Dutch men and women tended to become generally cold and aloof, presumably as a result of marriage and maturity, whereas young bachelors were radically different.[3]

It is certainly quite true that the relative strictness of Dutch morals contrasted strongly with the licence reigning elsewhere. Every kind of obstacle was set in the path of unauthorised associations and, consequently, unofficial traditions became established. In the island of Texel the young men made up a group two or three times a week to pass the evening with one or other of the local girls; there they ate, drank sweetened wine, made a lot of noise, beat out rhythms with keys, sprawled around and got acquainted.

The preaching services were much in favour for meeting new people or making rendezvous. A pastor of The Hague, Eleazar Lotius, condemned this habit in violent terms, claiming that people only went to church with this aim in mind. But there were other possible meeting places: the theatre, for example, where young people could kiss and cuddle in the dark, or the skating rink where couples could skate with an arm around each other's waist. In the summer months excursions were very popular. On holidays bands of young people in carriages or on horseback invaded the countryside, far from prying eyes, heading for the peasant inns, the woods or the beaches. When the carriage jolted its way across a bridge over a ditch, custom allowed the youth holding the reins to call out: *Heul! Heul!*, entitling him to a kiss from the girl by his side.

If the trip led to the seaside, it was customary to play a bolder game, in which each boy scooped up a kicking, screaming girl and ran with her into the sea until he was knee-deep in water. Then he would turn round and, still clutching his precious burden, run back up the beach and to the top of the nearest sand-dune, from which they would roll down to the bottom again in a chorus of screams and laughter and with the inevitable display of female legs and underwear. This tradition, probably of ancient origin, was considered as a test, and the girl who submitted bravely to it would make a good wife. But accidents were frequent.

On 1st May, an official holiday, young people exchanged presents, and met together in the evening to sing songs. The usual gallantries sometimes went so far that municipal corporations periodically banned the celebrations of the subsequent 1st May as a punishment. In the countryside many customs dating back to distant springtime folklore were observed, most of them more or less erotic in significance. In Texel, on the night of 30th April, the young people of both sexes danced round bonfires lit in the fields. In Lage Zwaluwe, at dawn on 1st May, the boys climbed up on the roofs of girls they were courting or hoping to court and attached a green branch to the ridge-beam. All the girls in the village, still half asleep, rushed to look out of the window to make sure they had been honoured in this way. Elsewhere, the boys might remove the scarecrows from the gardens during the night and stick them up on the roofs of those girls they considered too disdainful.

However, outside these rare occasions, the rigid structure of Dutch family life imposed its restrictions on the arrangements young people could make to meet, and matrimonial intentions were usually advanced as a pretext for such meetings. Dutch mothers began thinking very early on about their daughters' eventual marriages. The baby would still be in her cradle when the mother set to work on her future trousseau, and began to save up the sum of money that would be needed to cover the wedding expenses. Occasionally two young people would be betrothed before they had even reached puberty, if the families could draw some particular advantage from a premature agreement. But in general a complete freedom, which astonished foreigners, attended the first plighting of troths. With the unselfconsciousness so typical of the Dutch, the mothers would often give themselves the task of initiating their daughters into the art of 'honest' flirting, that is to say the kind of flirting likely to find a husband. A copious literature in prose and verse popularised the 'art of love' in forms imitated from Ovid. It was firmly believed that marriages were made in heaven and that in this world it was sufficient to encourage the realisation of divine intentions.

The young man who wished to make approaches to a girl and had honourable intentions would tie a flower or a wreath of greenery to the knocker of her door one evening. If he found on the following day that the flower or wreath had been thrown on the ground, he would not despair; he would replace it by a bouquet tied with a ribbon. The suitor might need to be insistent. Perhaps the fourth or fifth bouquet would carry a card giving his name.

The girl would react in one way or another. If she accepted his preliminary advances she would find the means to place a little basket full of sweets or flowers on her window-sill at some appropriate moment. These stratagems were allowed to drag on for a considerable time. The choice

of flowers on either side constituted a symbolic language;
if the young girl was bold enough to pin to her bodice a
white sprig offered by the young man, it was a declaration of
true love. Or a discreet note concealed among the flowers on
the window-sill would express appropriate sentiments,
either composed specially for the occasion or copied out of a
book. Meanwhile the young man had engraved his sweet-
heart's name on the trunk of a tree, or written it in the sand.
In the villages of northern Holland the procedure was
simpler: two evenings running, the boy scratched at the
girl's door, and on the third evening he knocked. If he heard
knocking from the inside in reply, he knew he had won his
cause.

The moment had then arrived for the first conversations at
the window or on the threshold. Sometimes one or two
musicians would accompany the young man and call the girl
with a rustic serenade. Her father and mother would await
the suitor's first visit, but when he arrived they did no more
than greet him; it was up to him to discuss matters with
their daughter alone. In fact they were so obliging as to
retire, leaving the young people the freedom of the darkest
corner of the room. In some districts the girl's first gesture
at the entry of her suitor had a special meaning: if she got up
and readjusted her shawl or bonnet she accepted his advances
but if, on the other hand, she reached down for the fire-tongs,
it meant that she had thought about it and refused them.

In the first case the boy would make himself comfortable
and a tête à tête would begin that might last five or six
hours without a break, or even the entire night, usually
conducted in complete silence so that no word or gesture
might compromise the fair one's virtue. After that the lover
would return each evening. In Texel he came through the
window, lifting the latch by breaking a window-pane and
passing his hand through; very few houses in this island had
any windows intact. The visit took place – in the girl's bed,
but with the best and most honourable intentions. The girl
lay under the sheet and the boy between the sheet and the
cover. Within reach was an iron cauldron, and at the first
over-bold gesture the girl would strike it with the fire-tongs

and the parents came running in. This custom, known as the *queesten*, was practised also in the Frisian islands, in Wieringen, in Overijssel, and elsewhere. The parents encouraged it, considering it an honour for their daughter, but it was forbidden to boys from outside the village. Things sometimes went very far, and though the girls were usually reluctant to give in completely there was still a large incidence of pregnancy before marriage, especially in the fishing villages. A child born before the wedding took part in the ceremony, officially in secret but, in fact, clearly visible beneath the mother's cloak. Here and there actual trial marriages were permitted, the girl 'trying' several boys until she finally became pregnant, when she would remain faithful to the father of her child and marry him.

At Schermerhorn, on the contrary, preliminary associations were avoided. Young men wanting to get married clubbed together from time to time and hired a crier, who would announce that all girls in search of a husband could go at a particular hour of a particular day to a particular inn, where they would be served with beer and brandy; the youths arrived a little later and made their choice. At Schagen a 'market for girls' was held each year just before the kermis. One afternoon the young women in their Sunday best would meet in an enclosure behind the cemetery after paying a fee of two stuivers to a door-keeper who would also keep out female visitors he considered too young or too old. One hour later the boys appeared and opened discussions with the girl of their choice. Agreements entered into were only supposed to last for the duration of the kermis, but in fact marriage usually followed.

Bachelors over a certain age were viewed with disapproval, and in several parts of the country their forty-fifth birthday would be celebrated by an improvised concert in which metal plates were beaten with tongs and cows' horns were blown. As for girls difficult to marry off, their parents tried to find them husbands through an 'agency', if they lived in a district where such go-betweens existed. They consulted a specialised intermediary who would summon a few young men one Sunday and furnish them with a list of the eligible females. Each made his choice and at nine o'clock that same evening knocked at the door of the chosen one; if he arrived late it was taken that he had already been elsewhere and had just been turned down. The girl opened the door and the conversation began on the threshold. If the first impression was favourable he was asked to come in, whereupon the youth would doff his hat, say a few words and run off to tell the good news to his friends. Good manners required him to return on three consecutive Sundays before demanding her hand.

Engagements were celebrated solemnly. In Broek the engaged couple sat side by side on a bed in the presence of both families and exchanged their first public kiss. The exchange of rings (only the poorest people did not wear them) constituted a formal engagement; the rings were massive, made sometimes of two parallel circles or engraved with conjugal allegories. In some districts the solemnity of the occasion was marked by a symbolic act: the betrothed both cut themselves slightly and offered the blood from the wound to the other to drink; or they would share a coin cut in two; or, again, they might sign with a drop of blood a written promise of fidelity. In Friesland the young man gave his fiancée a sum of money, sometimes a large sum, wrapped up in a fine linen cloth embroidered in red with their initials and the date of their engagement. In rich families the future father-in-law made a gift to the fiancée of a portable workbox in silver or gold, containing scissors, knife, needles and mirror.

Breaking off an engagement constituted a legal offence within the jurisdiction of the civil courts. The contract,[4] or simply the ring, provided proof; in default of these, the love-letters were exhibited to the court.

The period between engagement and marriage was often brief, but marked by invitations, excursions and banquets. Friends of the betrothed were chosen as 'playfellows', entrusted with helping them prepare the wedding festivities. The best room in the house was decorated, the bride's wreath and robe made up and displayed in two richly ornamented reed baskets, and the pipe that the bridegroom would smoke on the wedding-day was adorned with leaves.

Municipal officials in charge of conjugal affairs kept a registry of engagements, and supervised the regularity of the future marriage and the publication of banns. Three successive announcements were required, either at the Reformed Church or at the town hall.

Immediately after the engagement the mothers had fixed the date of the wedding and started issuing invitations. They would avoid choosing a Sunday because of the impossibility of having any kind of gay celebration on that day, and the month of May was also avoided because of the tradition that it brought bad luck. Meanwhile the bride and groom had drawn up their list of pages and bridesmaids, and of the children selected to strew flowers in front of the wedding procession.

The official ceremony took place either at the Reformed Church before a predicant or at the town hall before a local magistrate. In either case the marriage had to be registered, and since the registrar's office was only open for business on certain days, most marriages were conducted in series. However, important people loath to rub shoulders with the masses could persuade the official, by means of a sufficiently substantial tip, to open up specially. The church ceremony sometimes took place at night so that the procession could be made more impressive by the addition of torches, but in general it was held at midday. The building was decorated with carpets and flowers, and the young couple's seats with garlands of greenery. After having pronounced his 'yes' the groom placed his own ring on the finger of his bride who thenceforward wore two, one above the other, on the second finger (or sometimes even the thumb) of the right hand. Catholics had a different custom: the bride and groom wore a ring on their left hand during their engagement and both kept the rings after marriage, but the wife transferred hers to her right hand.

The procession formed up to return to the house where the married couple were to live (though the common people sometimes held the wedding-feast in an inn). It advanced under a rain of flowers, on foot or by carriage, the married couple at the head and everyone else crowding behind.

When the husband belonged to the magistrature the town delegated halberdiers to escort him. Among the nobility these processions gave rise to such a display of luxury – as many as fourteen carriages, the two leading ones drawn by six horses – that sumptuary laws had to be passed, imposing heavy taxes on these displays so as to limit their extravagance.

The married couple and their guests were received with due solemnity at the threshold, and then invited into the rooms prepared for the festivities – ponderously furnished rooms decorated touchingly in the worst possible taste, garlands of flowers mixed with silver or gold leaf hanging everywhere, the walls covered by all the mirrors in the house, collected for the occasion and embellished with devices and enigmas. The entrance-hall was a jungle of greenery fashioned into bowers. Wreaths and wax cupids and angels hung everywhere from the ceilings. If the house boasted a garden, a temple of foliage was built in which the representation of a burning heart stood between two candlesticks, or a statuette of Venus arose from the centre of a circular candelabra. In the centre of the reception room two chairs were decorated with coloured paper and so converted into thrones, and on these the married couple took their places. The bride's robe in all its splendour was now the centre of attention. Wealthy people liked to have it fashioned from heavy materials in contrasting colours, violet and white, light green and garnet-red, or sometimes in cloth of gold and silver. Simpler folk preferred a black material so that the gown could be used again for the mournings to come. Poor people contented themselves with white.

A floral-patterned cloth or a carpet was hung up behind the young couple, or their chairs might be surmounted by a canopy. Pages and bridesmaids gathered around them, and then parents and friends approached, offering congratulations and gifts of furniture, silverware or kitchen equipment. The newly-weds were served with a cup of *hippocras* (or brandy, in simpler households) and the husband was handed his decorated pipe. In the province of Groningen two people offered them a salted cream heaped with sugar, inedible but symbolic of the bitter aspects of married life. In a neighbouring room the older men drank and smoked. Pedestal tables carried assortments of biscuits and jams.

In the evening everyone sat down to table for the nuptial banquet, an occasion more solemn than really joyous. The attendance was huge at these affairs, and police regulations were made at intervals (for instance, at Amsterdam in 1665) limiting the number of guests and even the number of dishes, since menus sometimes included as many as fifty courses. Even the least prosperous families considered it a matter of honour to offer their neighbours a feast.

During the meal someone recited a poem in honour of the married couple. However unlettered the family might be, this poem was an original composition and was often made to sound more impressive, at least in theory, by being written in French or Italian, or even in Latin, Greek or Arabic! The author offered his opus on parchment emblazoned with heraldic bearings. For those completely devoid of poetic inspiration there existed printed collections of nuptial poems. Between two of the courses the basket full of song-books was drawn from under the table, where the husband's mother had placed it, and the repertoire was executed in chorus. A small orchestra (police regulations forbade a total of more than three musicians) played during part of the meal, on instruments which might include harpsichord, viol da gamba, lute, hautboy, guitar, 'cello, harp or cithern. In the country, bagpipes and shepherd's pipes were played, and everyone drank as much as he could hold. Finally, there was dancing.

The festivities ended with a piece of traditional stage business, in which the 'playfellows' tried to smuggle the young couple out of the room without the knowledge of the guests, who, for their part, tried to prevent this departure or at least accompanied it with an uproar. They kidnapped the bride, hid her somewhere in the house, and would only restore her to her husband after he had promised, willingly or unwillingly, to organise a few days later some excursion, banquet or other diversion. Or someone would declare that the groom's shoes needed repairing, whereupon they were torn off his feet and the whole company took turns in gripping the shoes like hammers, squatting down, and beating out a rhythm on the floor-tiles or floorboards. When the din had lasted long enough, everyone got up and formed a circle round the bride's wreath, then unhooked the garlands and went off.

In some districts the young men seized the bride just as she was about to retire, and blindfolded her; she then placed her wreath at random on someone's head and the lucky recipient would be the first to get married after her. Elsewhere, the entire wedding-party danced behind the bride all the way to her marriage-bed, by the side of which her mother was waiting to say farewell. The young woman lifted her skirts, undid her garter and gave it to a guest of her choice or even permitted him to take it off himself. The favoured person attached this trophy to the lapel of his doublet. Eventually the party broke up, after many hours of rowdy merriment.

The prospect of being exposed to all this was so unnerving for some engaged couples that they borrowed from some neighbour a room in which they could spend their first night in secret. But woe betide them if a guest detected this deception! Then the entire company streamed out into the street, holding candles, and clanging together noisily the pieces of metal equipment they had seized from the kitchen. They lit a bonfire in front of the house where the newlyweds had taken refuge, and kept up the banging and shouting until the bride and groom could stand it no longer and came out; then they were drawn into the circle dancing round the fire and were only set free when the last spark had died down.

Husband and wife often preserved reverently the shirts they had worn during their wedding-night (no one in those days would have dared go to bed naked); and they were only made use of once again – to dress their corpses on their death-bed. In northern Holland the wedding-bed itself was used only three times: for the first night of marriage, and later for the lying in state of each spouse.

The morning after the wedding the husband offered his wife a present, after which the day was spent in celebrations.

The previous evening's guests returned to finish up the remains of the feast, and, among the leisured classes, this 'repeat wedding party' lasted for several days. Then, for several weeks more, visits, games and various outings combined to delay the return to serious life.[5]

With this beautiful memory in their hearts, and the bride's wreath and bridegroom's pipe safely stowed in the treasure-cupboard, the young couple embarked upon the austerities of conjugal existence. Dutch households generally gave foreigners the impression of a solidly established union without prudery (wife and husband kissed openly in public), governed by a rigorous fidelity. This last element occasioned much surprise to foreigners, some of whom attributed it to the influence of Calvinism and others to the national temperament. The fact remains that unhappy or broken households were rare. Police regulations provided for severe punishments in the case of violence exercised by either husband or wife on the other; some municipalities fined a brutal husband a sum equivalent to the value of a leg of ham, and a cruel wife double that amount. Adultery was pitilessly repressed by the law, and a married woman found *in flagrante delicto* was handed over to the vengeance of husband or father.

One morning during the summer of 1656 a peasant of Voorschoten discovered a young woman lying in her bed with her throat cut. The husband admitted the deed and was arrested, but released the following day; his wife's transgression was proved and so he was within his rights. Such harsh legislation, together with the structure of the Dutch family, made female adultery very rare, except perhaps in the seaports where sailors' wives were numerous. A man could hardly risk a liaison except with an unmarried woman, and even then, if he were married himself, the adventure would expose him to certain risks: if he were surprised in 'amorous conversation' he would have to pay a heavy fine and his partner would be sent off to a house of correction. The application of this law gave rise to a widespread form of blackmail, in which police agents got in touch with prostitutes and provided them with accommodation and protection on condition that they lured in some wealthy citizen – who was promptly seized and fined; the girl received a handsome percentage.

Even so, many amorous escapades managed to pass through the meshes of the police net. The theologian Pineau, sending a report to Rivet of the debates of a synod in 1645, informed him that 'they have just unfrocked a minister for adultery with a widow in his diocese, despite the fact that he has a wife of his own whom he has cuckolded without scruple. She is not in a position to render him the same service, from what one hears. I cannot imagine what he wants with two women, since so many other colleagues of his find a single one trial enough.'[6]

Grosley reported an eloquently laconic conversation:

'Good day, neighbour.'

'I wish thee the same, neighbour.'

'I wonder if I may speak my mind?'

'Speak thy mind in all frankness.'

'They say, neighbour, that thy maidservant is with child.'

'What care I?'

'But, neighbour, they add it is by thee.'

'What matter to thee?' Whereupon each doffed his cap courteously, and so they parted.[7]

The tenth month after a kermis always produced a rash of illegitimate births in the neighbourhood. While Descartes was living in Amsterdam he had a daughter by his maidservant; he named the child Francine and brought her up himself. Nicolas Heinsius seduced a young girl by a promise of marriage and left her with two children; he was taken to court by his mistress and found guilty. Midwives were placed under oath by the Church to report all illegitimate births to the Council. But many natural children were simply abandoned by their mothers, who would wrap them in a blanket and deposit them in a public place in the early hours of the morning when no one was about. This constituted a misdemeanour, punishable by a spell in the pillory, but most of the time the mother escaped detection and the child was placed in an orphanage.

During the era when the passion for tea spread like an epidemic, the girls from the low quarters of town would sell themselves for a handful of tea-leaves to sailors back from the East. Prostitution thrived in the seaports, where a heterogeneous and professionally roving population swarmed. In Amsterdam entire streets were devoted to this industry, near the docks. The girls frequented the neighbourhood taverns, especially the low-class *cafés-chantants*, picked their clients up there and took them home with them so that the establishment's reputation should remain unblemished. At The Hague in 1670 street-walkers solicited openly in the Wood. A number of lodging-houses existed in Amsterdam in 1680 whose proprietors had the services of a certain number of girls. Each one had her own room leading off a corridor, and the client studied the portrait of the occupant which hung on each door. After making his choice, he paid and entered the room. It seems that the customer frequently discovered that the portrait was over-flattering.[8] Licentiousness did not spread far afield in this form, for urban prostitution had become the object of an embryonic organisation: that is to say, police sergeants had the privilege of managing brothels in specified areas of town.

The law provided for the crime of rape, and for that of homosexuality. The latter remains covered by the veil of decency cast over it at the time, but it appears to have been practised mainly by sailors. It was proceeded against with the utmost severity; the guilty parties were sewn in sacks and thrown into the sea, or condemned to solitary confinement for life.

DOMESTIC EXISTENCE

The Old Testament taught womankind that man was her master and that he, in return, would honour his spouse who, after bearing children in suffering, was destined to support the burden of the family. It mattered little that a wife should remain pretty and amiable; her husband expected her to be robust, reasonable, peaceable, conscientious in her tasks and fecund. The ideal wife was faithful to her husband, devoted to her children, an efficient mistress of the house, able to cope with the various practical problems of life. If one is to believe the 'free-thinker' de Hooft, young men put up with a certain amount of frivolity in their wives, but the general austerity of manners and morals sprang from a profound tendency in the national character. Erasmus, in his *Anti-barbarus*, had already noted the almost absolute moral domination exercised by the Dutchwoman in her own home; a domination justified by her skill and diligence and facilitated by the men's easy-going nature. It was an authority that easily turned into tyranny.

Calvinism had added a moral note to this long-standing tradition. At a wedding ceremony the minister's peroration was full of exhortations reminding the woman of the necessity of the humblest virtues and advising her that she would put into the world 'children of fear'. This moralising was sometimes expressed in fairly crude language. Jacob Cats, the supreme poetic representative of the Dutch petty bourgeoisie, wrote of married life rather as though it were a stock-breeding enterprise.

The Dutchwoman's appearance was doubtless influenced by the prevailing style of feminine existence. As a girl she gave foreigners the impression of fresh beauty: usually tall, blonde, fair-skinned, attractive. There were regional differences, and it was said that the ideal woman would combine 'a face from Amsterdam, gait from Delft, bearing from Leyden, voice from Gouda, stature from Dordrecht and complexion from Haarlem'.[1] The girls of Dordrecht were considered particularly beautiful. But everywhere marriage produced the same effects: waist and features thickened, surplus fat accumulated. According to Grosley,[2] many women, especially in the country, were stoop-shouldered and broad-rumped, walked awkwardly and allowed their bosoms to sag dreadfully. As soon as they had lost the freshness of youth they assumed the appearance of heavy and sometimes shapeless matrons, with characters occasionally resembling their physique only too closely.

Their extremely sedentary life made them subject to unjust accusations of idleness. But it is true that the average bourgeois wife spent five or six hours a day sitting down with her feet on her footwarmer, and hardly ever

133

went out except for a little cursory shopping or to go to church, eyes lowered, a heavy, velvet-bound, silver-cornered book held tightly under her arm. Very occasionally she went into the country alone, 'without scandal or peril' remarked the French in stupefaction, so sacred was the married woman in the eyes of the Dutch.[3]

From the top to the bottom of the social scale the mistress of the house made meticulousness in managing the household the supreme virtue. Only women who had no maid-servant, and were thus deprived of the pleasure of gossiping with her, bothered to spend time with their neighbours.

'Ah, what cares are those of a woman! Her children cling to her; it is an uproar from morning until late evening. Washing, scrubbing, polishing; errands, house-cleaning, laundering: nightmare and torment that make her life a hell.'[4]

If hardly a hell, at least a dreary succession of duties; indeed, Temple wondered whether this monotony was not in fact the essential cause of their lack of imagination, and thence of their much-vaunted chastity.[5]

A small élite of women (which became more numerous during the course of the century) in the nobility and upper middle classes took pride in being elegantly dressed, at least outside the privacy of their homes. And a few intelligent women were the equals of their friends and husbands in the sciences and arts. Huyghens carried on a correspondence with several of these female scholars affected by French 'preciosity'. In 1647 he dedicated his *Pathodia sacra et profana* to Utricia Ole, the wife of Count Swann.

Music became a passion with these intellectuals. Francisca Duarte, named 'the French nightingale', enjoyed a tremendous success, while Suzanna van Baerle, Maria Pelt and Anna Engels were all praised by Huyghens, de Hooft and Vondel. Maria Tesselschade Visscher occupied an important place in Amsterdam literary and musical circles. Anna Maria Schuurman of Utrecht was both painter, illuminator and engraver, as well as being a skilled student of oriental languages, and figures under the name of Statira in Somaize's *Dictionnaire des Précieuses*. With her face

veiled, she took part in the university's lectures and 'disputations'. When Descartes visited her he found her reading
the Bible in Hebrew, and maliciously expressed his astonishment at 'seeing a person of such distinction wasting her time
in so trivial an occupation'. This remark wounded her deeply
and she immediately noted in her diary: 'God has dismissed
this profane man from my heart.'[6] But Anna Maria Schuurman and her emulators remained exceptions, and their very
existence remained unknown to the vast majority of Dutchmen during the seventeenth century. On the other hand,
widowhood or the prolonged absence of their husbands
induced many women to take up shopkeeping or other
commercial activities with a vigour and efficiency equal to
that of men.

In the Netherlands servants were used far less frequently
than in the surrounding nations. The girls and men-servants
who in other countries were attached to the personal service
of their master were scarce here, in wealthy families, because
of the general preoccupation with individual independence.
The State disapproved of the employment of male servants
and placed a heavy tax on the employer for each one in
service; consequently, even the greatest houses never had
more than three male staff: a coachman and either one or
two footmen. There were no porters, or any of those flunkeys
stationed in front of the main door as proofs of the owner's
importance. The domestic arrangements of a solid bourgeois
family called for only a very small number of servants and
most often just one maid, who slept in an alcove off the
kitchen. Her rights and duties were laid down in various
official regulations. The newly engaged servant had to
report on an agreed day, modestly clothed and carrying a
permit; she was forbidden to be coarse or uncivil, or to
indulge in calumnious gossip. For their part, her employers
were prohibited from inflicting corporal punishments, and
any case of physical violence could be adjudicated by a
civil court and might result in the imposition of a fine equal
to a year's wages, however short a time the plaintiff had
been in service. Only theft was a permitted ground for
dismissal, yet the servant could give in her notice whenever

she chose.[7] In the eyes of a Frenchman like Parival such a situation was little short of scandalous: 'this kind of person' took advantage of the situation insolently, and it was impossible to get oneself served decently in Holland, he complained.[8]

Well paid, cared for during illness, often mentioned in their master's will, treated as members of the family, most servants had every reason to remain permanently with one employer. The result was an inevitable and thoroughgoing familiarity. De La Barre, visiting a bourgeois of Edam, recorded the following scene with astonishment: 'The hostess seated herself first without any ceremony; the servant sat down familiarly next to her mistress; the master uncomplainingly took one of the two remaining places, and the man-servant seized the other. The mistress and maid-servant served themselves first, and took the choicest portions too. However, we felt that long-standing habit had arranged the order of seating in this household, and all went well until the master was rash enough to tell the maid-servant to go and get something for him. The mistress thereupon told her husband to go himself, and that she wanted her servant to rest. Then harsh words started to fly. The servant supported her complaisant mistress enthusiastically, and husband and wife glared at each other until the husband, finally convinced of his error, apologised to his wife and stole a kiss from her.' The wife justified her conduct, afterwards, to their guest by saying that this servant was 'affectionate and hard-working', took great care of the dishes and looked after the chimneys.[9]

Domestic contracts usually ran from Saint Michael's day, 29th September. But once she had gone into service with a family the servant often stayed there until the end of her days. Quite often, when the daughter whom she had known since birth got married, she would join the new household. When age reduced her activities she was given a young maid as an assistant. From then on she lorded it in the entrance-hall or courtyard and ruled over her world. Only rich people concerned with propriety made the servant eat in the kitchen and used a bell to summon her. In many prosperous families the one servant acted as a 'cook-general', helped occasionally by a seamstress, a laundress and a woman in charge of heavy cleaning.

The legal archives of Amsterdam testify to the fact that this idyllic scene had a few gaps. A certain Trijntje Abrams, a sixteen-year-old servant-girl, in revenge for some scolding, succeeded in convincing her employers that their house was haunted. She shook their bed-curtains at night and wandered through the corridors under a white sheet. This comedy finished for her by two weeks in prison and a spell in the pillory. A twelve-year-old girl, Weijntje Ockersdochter, hard-worked by demanding employers, gave way to a fit of hysterical mania and poisoned the soup one day. She was condemned to a whipping and seventy years' imprisonment.

One of the advantages of being a domestic worker was the multiplicity of tips which, following Dutch custom, could be extracted. When a guest took his leave the servant was waiting on the threshold with her hand out. Some servants hired themselves out entirely for tips, which they considered their due for any errand or commission that they were not commercially or legally bound to perform. All such services were rewarded with tips.

The reputation for cleanliness of the mistresses of Dutch households was well established, though certain paintings by Jan Steen suggest that it was not always fully justified.[10] Even so, among all social classes and in the country as well as in town, it was a source of amazement to foreigners. In the words of Parival: 'Dutchwomen pride themselves on the cleanliness of their house and furniture to an un-believable degree. They never seem to stop washing and scrubbing all the wooden furniture and fittings, even the benches and floorboards, as well as the stairs; and most of them take off their shoes at the foot of the stairs before going up to any of the first-floor rooms. When they are obliged to allow a foreigner into the house they usually provide straw slippers in which they encase his feet, shoes and all; or else there are mats, on which he has to wipe his feet carefully, and cloths to remove the last vestige of dust from the shoes. No one would dare to spit in any of the rooms; even spitting into a handkerchief is frowned upon,[11] so that it seems that those who are phlegmatic must be in great discomfort.'[12]

Temple had this very experience one day. Invited to an all-male luncheon party by a high Dutch official while suffering from a bad cold, he was seized by a fit of coughing and spat on the floor. A servant immediately rushed up and removed the offending sputum with a clean cloth. 'Is the Ambassador ill?' he was asked with concern. 'It is lucky,' said the host, 'that my wife is not here, for had she been she would have shown you the door, ambassador or not, for fear of contagion.' Temple showed his astonishment, and his host continued: 'Let me tell you that there are two rooms in my own house that I have never even entered, and I doubt whether she opens them up more than twice a year – and that for cleaning purposes.' Reacting to the Englishman's expressions of ironic admiration, the host insisted that he was perfectly content with this arrangement and blessed his lucky stars for having such a model wife, the ' gentle mistress' of whom everyone dreams.

During that same afternoon Temple visited another Amsterdam family and related the earlier incident as a curious anecdote. The mistress of the house assured him that it was entirely normal, and proceeded to tell him the following story. It appears that one day a burgermaster knocked at the door of a bourgeois house, and told the servant who appeared (a sturdy Frisian peasant-woman) that he wished to speak to her mistress. He made a move to enter the house, but the servant had noticed that a little mud was clinging to the soles of his shoes. Without saying a word, she seized him by the wrists, hoisted him on her back like a sack, carried him in this way across two rooms, stopped at the foot of the stairs, dumped the burgermaster down on one of the steps, took off his shoes, fitted him with a pair of slippers, and stood up. Only then did she say, quite politely: 'But of course, the mistress will be delighted to receive you.'[13]

In some households the entire family confined itself to the kitchen so as not to dirty the 'staterooms', which were used only for great occasions. These rooms were cleaned each week nonetheless, and a conscientious housewife would make herself responsible for this task rather than entrust it to her servant. In every social circle washing and cleaning constituted these ladies' favourite subject of conversation. There were two categories of house cleaning, the regular weekly operation and the annual spring cleaning. The weekly cleanings took place on Fridays, the eve of the Sabbath, in Jewish families, and on Saturdays in the case of Christians; the latter often cleaned house twice a week, and in some towns every day except Sunday. The house was stripped of its furniture, and things were scrubbed with copious applications of water, or scoured with sand, or polished. Throughout the town, buxom women servants with their sleeves rolled up made vigorous attacks, under the canopies, on articles of furniture. People hardly took the time to eat; after swallowing a few hunks of buttered bread standing up, they rushed back to work. The façades were washed by sprays of water from special syringes whose jets could reach the roof of a house.

Some households used thirty or forty buckets of water a day simply for cleaning purposes, and in some families a servant was employed specifically to do nothing but cleaning jobs from morning till evening. As a result, the interiors of Dutch houses were constantly damp and a source of rheumatism. The annual cleanings, carried out in the spring, or in the spring and autumn, unleashed even worse upheavals in the house and in the lives of its male inhabitants. Some men named this period 'Hell' and referred to the cleaners as 'female Satans'. Poets and actors poked fun at this furious obsession with hygiene, but no mockery ever had the slightest effect on these women in the throes of their passion for cleanliness.

Each day the mistress of the house performed her other ritual task, shopping. Even the wife of Admiral de Ruyter, one of the leaders of the Republic, went shopping alone, on foot, with a basket on her arm, in the streets of Amsterdam. It is true that Vrouw de Ruyter incarnated the ancient virtues of Dutch simplicity. The day after the Admiral's death, when a special envoy arrived with a message of condolence from the Prince of Orange, she excused herself for not being able to receive him: it seems that, that very morning, she had fallen while hanging out the washing and suffered some slight injury.

Most women of good bourgeois families were accompanied on their shopping expeditions by their daughters or servant, carrying the basket or wooden provision bucket. Soon after breakfast the women in the town were making their way to market, which was held in a central square usually dominated by the building housing the offices of the municipal inspector of weights and measures; this building was always the pride of the district and the symbol of its commercial prosperity, a large square house combining elegance with solidity, designed in Renaissance style as at Amsterdam, or in classical style as at Gouda, or occasionally crowned by a belfry as at Alkmaar.

All around, butchers' stalls, benches and barrows cluttered up the square, amid the cacophony of sellers crying their wares. 'Fine brandy! Hey, aniseed, aniseed-liqueur for your stomach ailments! Choice cinnamon-water! See our bread-rolls, our cakes, our rye and barley! Fresh herrings! All fresh, sweet as sugar, herrings! Keep your spirits high with raisins and prunes that smell good! My pears! My carrots! Fresh radishes! Green herbs! Show me any better ones and I'll give them to you free! . . .'[14] Quacks, pedlars of almanacs and gipsies mingled with the throngs of peasants laden with fruits, vegetables and dairy produce, and with buyers and sightseers. The municipal corporation hired out a bench to every stall-holder, or in special cases granted free usage.

The large towns established a certain rotation between the various commodities. The Hague held a general market every day; Leyden had one only, on Saturdays, but held special vegetable markets on Mondays and Fridays. Most often, markets were devoted specially to butter, to cheese, to vegetables, to meat or to fish. Sometimes the meat market was held in a special building where the produce was subject to control. Alkmaar has remained famous to this day for its cheese market, preceded ritually by the weighing of the huge balls brought along on wooden stretchers by members of a special guild. Amsterdam possessed a biscuit market, which served as an outlet for the factories at Wormer and Jisp, and was most profitable to the town since the traders paid a tax of eight stuivers per ton of merchandise.

The cattle market, held at regular intervals, created a tremendous stir in town. On that day, as soon as the town gates were opened, a bleating, bellowing herd filled the streets as they were urged forward with loud cries to the central square. A gay disorder filled the districts through which the procession passed. Schools were let out for the day, and children mixed with the women and bourgeois citizens moving about among the animals chained to the trunks of the linden trees or tied to stone posts. Prosperous-looking, fat gentlemen, accompanied by a master-butcher, made their choice on his advice and led the animal away after taking a drink with the seller. On that evening or the following day it was slaughtered in the courtyard and its quarters hung up under the canopy like trophies.

THE GUILDS

The professional existence of artisans, workmen and small businessmen in the Netherlands was governed by guilds. These guilds had emerged from the old medieval 'fraternities' and had the function of exercising a complete control over the production of manufactured goods and the distribution of merchandise. Their power was based on a conception of group ethics which was intended to protect the members of a particular guild. Based upon ancient privileges, and complicated by a multitude of more recent regulations, the system laid the ground for a struggle between licensed professionals and outsiders and between tradition and individual initiative. Starting work before the prescribed hour or selling below the agreed price were misdemeanours that the guild's executive committee was authorised to investigate and punish.

The division of jurisdiction between the various guilds and the extent of their powers varied from town to town and were a disruptive factor in the country's developing economy. Utrecht had twenty-one guilds, including five for the garment industry alone: tailors, fur-lining makers, glovers, shoemakers and cobblers. Psychological and social differences were at the root of these arbitrary distinctions; the guild of curriers, working fine leather, considered itself superior to the guild of saddlers working coarse leather. On the other hand, some specialised activities existed side by side in the same guild; the guild of carpenters also included the cabinet-makers and turners, the bakers' guild included the millers, and the shoemakers' included the tanners. All these divisions resulted in harsh regulations by which, for example, a certain workman had the right to sew a new sleeve on to an old doublet but not to make a new doublet. The guild of pewter founders protested against the fact that booksellers were selling ink in pewter inkwells.

A guild member was not permitted to open more than one shop or have more than one market-stall; people were allowed to hawk goods only if their stock was worth less than a certain sum. Certain guilds forbade their members to sell in the markets for fear that they might undercut their fellow-members; weavers were not permitted to weave or card wool during the summer, or to possess more than three looms; brewers could brew only once a week; pastrycooks were prohibited from baking cakes in any but officially sanctioned shapes. All products were stamped, and anything not bearing the appropriate seal was confiscated and destroyed if found. Thirty regulations governed the preparation of herrings. To some extent this niggling legislation did enhance the quality of products, but at the cost of slowing down the rhythm of production.

A guild's governing body was composed of one or several 'doyens', assisted by a few 'jurymen' and sometimes inspectors. These officials were appointed by the municipal corporation, and the board personnel was partially changed each year.[1] The board met once a week on the same premises, which would be either a house belonging to the guild, or a designated room in the Clocktower, or a tavern chosen for its comfort and elegance, or perhaps the building of the inspector of weights and measures. These meetings usually developed into boisterous parties. The guilds had their own suites of furniture, and their own table-ware and glass-ware, all bearing the arms of the guild; each guild possessed its own seal and banner as well.

Workers were subject to guild control from their earliest years, since an apprenticeship could be served only with a guild master. Apprenticeships generally lasted two years, but with surgeons the period was three years, and with the hatters of Amsterdam four; on the other hand, the wood-sawyers only required a six months' apprenticeship. No master was entitled to accept more than two apprentices, and these entered into his service very young, usually at the age of twelve, after having paid an enrolment fee which the master sometimes advanced them against their future wages. In this way they lost all freedom of action: they lodged in their master's house, and if they left him they had to repay him for their board and lodging. They also ran the risk of not being able to find another master to accept them. The choice of one's master was more or less the choice of one's fate; conditions of apprenticeship were not strictly regulated, and some apprentices spent years cleaning the workshop and looking after the tools and equipment before they really had a chance to prepare themselves for their final apprentice's examination.

After passing this examination the apprentice became a journeyman and had to find a new master. Armed with his diploma, he often had to go from town to town in search of employment. This roving existence, which was even more developed in France than in the Netherlands, constituted a period of institutional unemployment in his working life. When a master finally accepted him, the journeyman registered himself with the appropriate guild. Then, after a fairly long period, he could, in most guilds, present a so-called 'masterpiece' for examination and judgement, and, if successful, was entitled to call himself a 'master' and had the right to keep a shop or open a workshop in his own name. Even so, he had to be in a position to pay his dues and to offer a banquet or at least a toast-drinking reception to his examiners. Many journeymen could not do so and remained salaried workmen for the rest of their lives.

The members of a guild paid a regular subscription to an official whose duties consisted not only in collecting dues but also in performing various secretarial functions, such as sending notifications to attend meetings, arranging the funeral ceremonies of those who had been members, and looking after the upkeep of the guild's place of assembly. This employee's fixed salary was augmented by a percentage of the fines imposed by the doyens. Each year, on the feast-day of its patron saint, the guild gave its official banquet, a celebration that sometimes lasted two days and occasionally led to such excesses that the authorities attempted to ban the tradition outright or at least limit its duration. The wealthier guilds also organised expeditions, to which the ladies were invited, and private parties. A guild's entertainment and recreation fund was always substantial.

But the country's economic development threatened to sweep away the ancient guild structure, despite the support of the dignitaries with life tenure who formed the urban administrations. So long as these gentlemen controlled the guilds they dominated the local economy and were safe from any outside competition; nevertheless, signs of progress became more and more frequent. During the first half of the century the creation of new industries led to the constitution of hitherto non-existent guilds: linen-weavers in 1614, timber-merchants in 1615, and makers of fustian in 1631. But this development of new guilds was only super-ficial. Branches of industry in full expansion, such as the textile trade, began to establish factories outside the juris-diction of the towns, in villages where no guilds operated, with the consequent advantage of cheap manpower. And big contractors took full advantage of the opportunity to exploit the blind rivalry which set at odds identical guilds in different towns. In Amsterdam urban extension played its part in breaking the guilds' influence. Big business, as well as most of the new industries, escaped their domination. The guilds defended themselves by means which inevitably rebounded on them eventually, that is to say, a multiplication of controls and obstacles which finished by making them into exclusive castes barring practically everyone except the sons of deceased members. As a result the volume of 'illicit' work increased rapidly despite the most vexatious measures. Within the framework of the guilds the crafts remained predominant, and the regulation of wages placed fairly strict limits on the possibilities of additional payments. The development of large-scale capitalist business enterprises worked doubly against this archaic structure; guilds were either suppressed entirely, as happened to the hatters in 1680, or they became mere insurance agencies in many towns after 1660. Each guild possessed an assistance fund earmarked for the relief of old, sick or needy members. The practice grew, in some places, of selling guild diplomas to people outside the profession; in this way the fund acquired a new subscription and the pseudo-member gained the right to its assistance. Traditionally the guilds imposed certain reciprocal duties on its members, such as looking after the sick and officiating at burials, but this custom of mutual aid had fallen into such neglect that by mid-century fines had to be imposed for failure to perform these duties.

In every town guild members formed a citizens' militia which was originally entrusted with defensive military duties, but during the seventeenth century no longer played any real military role. At the most it gave assistance to the police during civil disturbances or outbreaks of fire. It had really become a friendly society, with its own uniform, parading on major occasions and organising archery competitions. In 1672 the Amsterdam militia numbered at least ten thousand men.

In theory dealers were organised in a 'merchants' guild', but in fact only small shopkeepers were dependent on this association. The more a merchant's affairs prospered (especially when he began to deal in international markets, and transit and cash shipments) the less need he had of the guild's controls and assistance. A big merchant's way of life distinguished him immediately from the host of small merchants; he was often a well-educated man, and Sorbière recorded in mid-century that he knew many merchants who spent their evenings in instructive reading.[2] Some of them had been to a university, but they had little opportunity there to learn the elements of their profession; the future merchant spent his apprenticeship as an office-boy in his father's establishment or that of one of his father's colleagues. After spending some months sweeping out the office, replacing the candles and keeping the fire going, he graduated to the position of clerk, sharpening quills, running errands, making book-entries, learning accountancy and familiarising himself with the use of almanacs.

These almanacs, published annually, gave lists of fairs and markets, time-tables of passenger barges and ships and details of high and low tides, and served as the main instrument of commercial 'culture'. They were produced in great numbers, some being more comprehensive than others and often dealing with a specific town. One of the Dordrecht almanacs even supplied information about the competence of the various town officials. Sometimes, too, the authors supplemented all this information with doctrinal instruction: Gaspar Coolhaas, in his 1606 'Businessmen's Almanac', provided a refutation of the errors of the Catholic Church.

The businessman's office was usually situated in the basement of his house, or occasionally in the loft next to his warehouse, where it would not disturb domestic harmony. He called it his *Kantoor* (a corruption of the French *comptoir*), and the choice of site was dictated less by considerations of comfort than by the wife's refusal to allow the living-rooms to be used for business purposes. So that although a Dutch businessman had his living quarters and his offices under the same roof they were kept rigorously separate, and when the volume of business demanded expanded accommodation, interior walls were put up forming corridors that gave access to the premises, and a special entrance door was let into one of the outside walls – all this to avoid creating any disturbance in the living-rooms!

The merchant's working day started at about ten in the morning. Actual trading activities were only conducted during four hours of a single day. From ten until midday the merchant presided over his office and the apprentices and clerks who had arisen earlier from the attics where they slept and were waiting to start work. Offices were furnished with utmost simplicity: a few sturdy desks, with lead inkwells nailed to them, chairs with leather seats, bookshelves laden with registers, a sand-glass. The boss sat at a raised desk, wearing a night-cap; the clerks sat two by two beneath him, wearing protective oversleeves.

At midday the Stock Exchange opened and was soon crowded with the town's merchants, plus a good number of onlookers and idlers. All important business was conducted here. Brokers hurried to and fro inside the building, carrying a portable writing-desk, and prepared contracts; when two merchants had struck a bargain – perhaps one of them had assigned a cargo of copper still in transit on the high seas at the time, in exchange for a cargo of precious wood plus a cash sum – they signed a contract, went straight off to the bank where their funds were deposited and arranged the transfer of this sum from one account to the other. They had perhaps completed a deal involving thousands of florins, without having had to handle a single coin. All business had to be completed by two o'clock when the Stock Exchange closed. If urgent business demanded a return to the building a little after that time, a fine was levied. This arrangement permitted an advantageous centralisation of major commerce, helped speed up its operations and consequently facilitated credit.

From the sixteenth century onwards each large town involved in trade had its own Exchange; a few had possessed Exchanges since the fifteenth century. They were originally held in the open air, in a square, a street or any other convenient location. The first building designed specifically for the purpose was constructed in Amsterdam in 1611: a huge two-storeyed square edifice in the very centre of town, with a central courtyard measuring nearly five hundred and fifty square yards surrounded by arcades in which the stalls were set up. Free access was provided by a large open porch at each end of the building. Built above a canal, the Exchange served also as a port, and large ships could sail in under its vault after lowering their masts.[3]

Dutch commerce acquired such flexibility under this system, and the credit system became so widespread, especially after 1650, that the Amsterdam Exchange was thenceforward the centre of world trade. When the 1672 crisis occurred, the Austrian ambassador sent his monarch a daily report of exchange quotations.

SICKNESS AND DEATH: *Patients and Doctors*

Temple attributed the frequency of epidemics in the Netherlands to the climate, claiming it to be humid throughout the year and unhealthily warm in summer.[1] Leyden's lack of flowing water and Amsterdam's sheer size made these cities particularly susceptible, and an outbreak occurred at least once every three years. Epidemics were of various types, one of which was described at the time as a high fever affecting the brain, contagious and sometimes fatal. The seventeenth century followed the example of the Middle Ages in classifying as 'plagues' a number of different infectious diseases, all of which were endemic and deadly.

These diseases struck hardest at the underprivileged, those who were undernourished and living in hovels. In a single year thirteen thousand unfortunates perished in Leyden – a quarter, or perhaps a third, of the entire population, and eighteen thousand in Amsterdam, though these figures are the highest recorded. The century was landmarked by tragic dates, beginning with 1597, 1601, 1602, 1604, 1617, 1624, 1635, 1636, 1639. . . . Almost always, only the towns were affected. In Amsterdam in 1601, in Zwolle in 1602 and in Leyden in 1635 and then in 1639, the cemeteries were not big enough to hold all the corpses and many bodies had to be buried on the ramparts. The municipal administrations avoided compiling exact records of the death-rate, but nevertheless business always suffered and values tumbled on the local Exchange. The 1636 plague ruined for ever Helmond's local weaving industry.

Despite a blind faith in Providence which tended to militate against the taking of common-sense precautions, local administrations did, nevertheless, employ special 'plague doctors' as soon as an epidemic broke out, recruiting them from among surgeons, physicians and healers. They were provided with special clothing which they put on when entering the sick man's home and removed on departing, placing the garments eventually on a chair in their own house. Later, both chair and clothes were burnt. Some of these 'specialists' concerned themselves with particular diseases whose contemporary names leave us in some doubt as to their real nature: smallpox, 'scrofula' and 'canker', for example.[2] In all these cases treatment was limited to a few elementary hygienic precautions, to controlling the disease from spreading and to removing the corpse. In 1655 the Zwolle town council was so alarmed by the epidemic's ravages that it created a 'plague advisory body' which had a special hospital opened. During that crisis so many people died, even among the middle classes, that it became necessary to modify the law governing the making of wills. Those of hardy constitution who survived the epidemic were mostly scarred for life.

Malaria was a recurrent scourge in marshy regions; and scurvy and gout were considered typically Dutch maladies.[3] Foreigners living in the Netherlands complained constantly of 'melancholia', probably a bilious condition resulting from the diet. According to Temple,[4] the Dutch aged quickly; he claimed that a healthy septuagenarian was a rare phenomenon, especially in the towns.

Popular tradition offered an immense store of empiric medical treatments, some of which derived more or less directly from medieval sorcery. Most households had a special shelf in the kitchen displaying a multitude of small pots, containing preparations such as cinchona wine, tincture of aloes, myrrh, saffron, gentian solution and an unguent composed of three parts olive oil and one part yellow soap tinted with red lead or white lead.

Juniper oil was used as a remedy for toothache; skin irritations were treated with a compress of herbs and rye flour diluted in milk; a compound of aniseed water was considered the best cure for chills; hot carrot or turnip juice was prescribed in cases of quinsy; to stop nose-bleeding, a few drops of blood were allowed to fall onto a red-hot iron. Cow's urine and dung formed an essential ingredient of many country remedies. Spiders' heads inside a nut-shell were worn on the chest to guard against fever, although some fastidious people replaced the spiders by a verse from the Bible.

The most popular salve was one whose basic ingredient was froth, produced preferably by soaping the skull of a hanged man or one who had died a violent death, mixed with two ounces of human blood, a little lard, linseed oil and a few spices. It must be admitted that, in that age, the general mental climate was not conducive to an appreciation of the scientific, theoretical aspects of medicine. Despite the enlightenment of a small minority, and the Reformed Church's war against superstition, many traces of medieval animism still survived in the Netherlands. Church authorities had finally succeeded in preventing boats from being named after saints, and in substituting designations drawn from geography, recent history or even zoology; but that was almost the sole province in which their reforming zeal bore fruit, and even that progress was not extensive. A ship might well be named *The Rose*, *The Seven Provinces* or *The Elephant*, but there could still be no question of its setting sail on Midsummer Eve or Christmas Eve, simply because the crew would have refused to work. As for landlubbers, no one would think of starting a journey on a Friday, especially Good Friday. And a spilt salt-cellar, a dropped knife, a loaf placed upside down on the table was a sure harbinger of bad luck.

Breaking a mirror, hearing the tick of a clock in the next room, or having three candles alight, were all signs of approaching death. Everything was an omen: the way a flame flickered, a dog's bark, a cock's crow, the croaking of a raven or hooting of an owl. The crucial year in a human life was supposed to be the sixty-third, and once that was successfully negotiated a long future existence was assured. When travelling by stage-coach it was well to study the hair of one's fellow-travellers – if anyone had dyed or false hair you could be sure that highwaymen would attack.

On Christmas Eve the bees sang a psalm in their hive. Storks were considered sacred birds and police regulations prohibited the destruction of their nests; in town, any house on whose roof they nested doubled immediately in value. Whenever circumstances demanded a difficult decision, the Bible would be opened at random and a verse touched with the end of a key in order to produce a providential message. The future could be interpreted in the skies: a comet or eclipse presaged a war or a public disaster. Casters of horoscopes, fortune-tellers by cards, palmists and clairvoyants included the highest State dignitaries among their clients. There was a brisk traffic in such literature as 'The wheel of fortune', 'The prophetic and astrological guide to the planets' and all kinds of dream-books. No one dared enter a cemetery at night, and it was well known that the devil sometimes appeared in person to carry off the first corpse interred in a new cemetery. The entire country was dotted with haunted houses.

The belief in witchcraft was so widespread that a catechism published in 1662 devoted an entire chapter to a demonstration that its practice constituted a sin. Even good Christians avoided the malefactions of witches by simply placing their shoes upside down at the foot of the bed at night. And then there existed two infallible means of unmasking adepts of the diabolical sciences: first, the verification of an abnormal blemish on the body, which was a sure trace of the Evil One's claw, and secondly, the weighing of the suspect. The second method was based on the idea that sorcerers and witches always weighed less than their height and size warranted, and this somewhat vague criterion was freely applied until about 1610. The municipal weighing office was used for the test, the suspect being brought along dressed in an undershirt and with hair let down in the case of a woman; the physical examination and weighing was undertaken by the town crier or the midwife, according to the individual's sex. If the suspect's weight was finally considered normal he was released after paying a fine;

otherwise he was convicted of witchcraft and burned alive. The weighers in the village of Oudewater had such a reputation for leniency that people flocked there from all over Europe to submit themselves to their judgement, knowing that the weighers in question had never been known to find anyone guilty. Here and there, local authorities had recourse to the water test, in which the victim's thumbs were tied to his big toes and he was thrown into deep water that had previously been exorcised: if he floated, his guilt was proved, but if he drowned he was considered innocent. An alternative procedure involved dragging the suspect into a church and there making him plunge his arm up to the elbow in boiling water. Small stature, thinness, darkness of complexion or hair were often taken to be suspicious signs, and all these considerations were invoked, for instance, in the apprehension of Claes Arienszen and his wife Neeltje in Oudewater at the beginning of the century. At about this time trials for witchcraft were still taking place in Schiedam and on the island of Goeree, but enlightened opinion was already making itself heard in protest. Jacob Cats took up the defence of supposed witches. In practice, none of them was executed after 1595, and from 1610 the holding of such trials was gradually abandoned in the Netherlands. This fact by no means signified that people had stopped believing in witchcraft; far from it. But at least the Netherlands was the first country in Europe to abolish this shocking form of traditional criminal law.[5]

Charlatans of all sorts overran the country, offering supposedly miraculous powders, salves and herbs. The authorities were cautious enough to tolerate their activities while attempting, at the same time, to regulate them, and they were allowed to set up their stands at markets, fairgrounds and kermises after paying a fee to the medical guild. The costumes and sales-patter of these individuals attracted considerable attention: the quack was often wrapped in a voluminous doctor's cape, complete with collar-bands and wig, or else dressed as Harlequin, or even got up in some fantastic pseudo-oriental costume, and in all this finery he would extract teeth, give the recipe for the philosopher's stone and brag about his particular panacea. He was often an Italian, a German or a Pole, and his exotic features would add to the mystery; sometimes, too, he was entirely ignorant of the Dutch language and contented himself with gesticulations while his Dutch crony harangued the crowd. In the countryside the quack's recommended remedies were more popular than those prescribed by the physician and prepared by the apothecary. Soldiers were excellent customers of 'love-powders',[6] perhaps the biggest seller in this whole illegal pharmacopoeia. Most villages had a bone-setter, a female healer acquainted with the secrets of purifying the blood and setting fractures, or able to cure maladies by touching or breathing on the patient.

The Art of Medicine

Despite such superstitions, the Netherlands remained in the forefront of European medical progress, and modern scientific medicine can be said to have originated there. It is equally true that the official body of physicians lacked a sense of unity, and that the average intellectual level remained fairly low despite the creation of faculties of medicine. The physician in the Netherlands was just as much a figure of fun as in Molière's France, but, even so, a few research workers and practitioners were aware of this state of affairs and denounced it. The rival theories of Hippocrates, Galen, Paracelsus and Sylvius battled for supremacy, while in Amsterdam the strongest influence was that of Vesalius, the first of the 'moderns' and the opponent of authoritative principles. Van Helmont condemned blood-letting because God had forbidden the spilling of human blood, and his disciples went so far as to condemn purges on the grounds that they impoverished the blood.

Nevertheless, a general tendency was perceptible in medical circles, and at the same time as people were beginning to abandon theoretical speculations, the investigation of the natural sciences was opening new horizons. Experimental methods were based mainly on a study of human anatomy. Ever since Swammerdam had obtained authority from the Amsterdam municipal council to dissect corpses in the hospital, the ancient prejudices, still deep-rooted in the rest of Europe, had collapsed in the Netherlands. No matter how much reactionaries and simple folk mocked, nor what ridiculous epithets they heaped on the physicians who practised dissection, the principle had become firmly established in the curriculum of the faculties, and the better-educated sections of the public showed great interest in the new science. In fact, the study of anatomy became quite fashionable, and non-university towns such as Dordrecht and The Hague instituted public lectures which attracted huge attendances despite the fact that they were really intended for the training of surgeons. The universities, for their part, advertised their anatomy lectures and opened their doors to the public on those days, so that the genuine students were submerged under the waves of eager amateurs. Rembrandt's *Anatomy Lesson*, painted in 1632, represented Doctor Tulp delivering a lecture in Amsterdam, and bore witness to the new craze. At this time Amsterdam was the centre of anatomical studies, and the new theory of the circulation of blood had just gained ascendancy there over all objections. Anatomical studies had been paralleled by the development of the technique of preserving dead organs, and the dissection classes provided a valuable source of supply for subsequent specialised research. Animal anatomy was also studied, and sailors made a good business out of selling monsters of the deep to the scientists.

Physicians enjoyed considerable moral and social eminence; most of them came from the aristocracy or from the most prosperous merchant classes, and often exercised important public functions in addition to their profession. Nicolas Tulp, famous in his lifetime for his *Observationes medicae*, was four times burgermaster of Amsterdam; he showed a rare originality for the age in visiting his patients by carriage, since most physicians preserved a tradition of great simplicity until the end of the century. Doctor van Hogeland, considered something of a miracle-worker by his contemporaries, mixed his potions and received his patients each day punctually from eight to nine a.m. and from one to two p.m. clad in slippers and night-cap. Consultation fees varied according to the client's social class, rising from four stuivers for a small businessman to as much as a florin for wealthy people; but predicants, lawyers and apothecaries were entitled to free treatment.

Physicians belonged to the same guild as surgeons, but constituted a sort of aristocracy at its heart. Their university degrees gave them the right, in fact, to hold examinations of their surgeon colleagues and to supervise their more delicate operations, such as excision of stone or of cataract, and the setting of fractures. This partnership was not entirely harmonious, and in 1635 Amsterdam followed Tulp's advice and established a separate college for physicians and apothecaries.

The towns selected one or more members of the local medical body to serve as municipal doctors. Enkhuizen employed two, and Amsterdam boasted a fairly large staff – two ordinary physicians, two deputies, a professor of anatomy, a surgeon, an 'operator' and a 'plague doctor'. These functionaries all received a salary, but were permitted to retain a private clientèle, and, in fact, their official status was of some publicity value to them. Their duties consisted in providing assistance and exercising public control; that is to say, treating paupers rescued by charitable institutions, and supervising surgeons and midwives.

Every town of any importance maintained one or several hospitals and a leper-house. Amsterdam also possessed a lazaretto for the 'plague-stricken' and a lunatic asylum; Leyden had a house of refuge for the aged infirm. These institutions all suffered from the same institutional disadvantage in that they provided shelter for the needy as well as hospitalisation; consequently, prejudice prevented many people from taking advantage of their services, and to enter a hospital was considered a mark of social disgrace.[7] In 1623 out of seven hundred patients in the Amsterdam hospital only one was a bourgeois citizen.

Surgery

By virtue of an ancient tradition, 'surgeons' were also barbers. Their authority, during the seventeenth century, extended to the treatment of wounds and fractures, and blood-letting, in addition to beard-trimming and haircutting. But these last two offices passed increasingly into the hands of a specialised hairdresser who was often the surgeon's assistant, and by the end of the century most surgeons had entirely abandoned their shaving-bowl and scissors. At the same time, French-style hairdressing shops were set up in the towns. During this entire epoch the political authorities joined the guild's officials in making every effort to give surgery the status of a science by allowing it to benefit from the advances achieved in the field of medicine. Courses of lectures in anatomy were instituted specifically for this purpose, and at The Hague the city's surgeons established a *Theatrum anatomicum* out of their own funds.

Although the surgeons' guild was legally on the same footing as those grouping artisans, it differed from them in that mastership was achieved through examination rather than the submission of a 'masterpiece'. A panel of physicians and master surgeons interrogated the candidate on anatomical theory, and made him perform various manual tests such as applying a cautery, bandaging, using a lancet and performing blood-letting.[8] Less expertise was demanded of naval surgeons, who were required only to know how to treat the ordinary ailments of sea-going folk: musket wounds, bruises, burns, fractures and gangrenes. But the simplified nature of their examination also served to keep them attached to their ships since it did not give them the right to open a shop.

The others, so-called 'house-surgeons', installed their surgery in some room of their house, and displayed their instruments. Many of these instruments were recent inventions. They were made from iron, copper or bone, and the most commonly used were straight and curved lancets, surgical knives, a blood-letting gauge, and forceps for pulling teeth. The room's decoration was completed by a skull, some phials and the master's diploma. But a high stool served as the operating-table, and the assistant's strong grip took the place of anaesthetics in keeping the patient still.

Playwrights enjoyed poking fun at the profession, and the surgeons, for their part, were resentful of the public's obstinate tendency to treat them as barbers. They did not pass through university, and two years of apprenticeship was their sole training. And, unlike physicians, they wore no distinctive costume. Nevertheless, the guild numbered some distinguished individuals among their members, including public office-holders. Several towns engaged municipal surgeons as sworn officials; they had the privilege of supervising every operation performed within municipal limits by surgeons out of town.

Roving surgeons did indeed exist. They were mostly poor devils, expelled from the guild, doing the small tedious jobs that the local man could not be bothered with, but also performing risky or painful operations which the resident practitioner was reluctant to undertake in case he harmed his reputation. Finally, the guild included secondary members who were exempted from paying dues but were forbidden to perform operations without the governing body's authorisation and except in the presence of the municipal physician; these were mostly oculists, bone-setters and stone-extractors.

At the start of the century the apothecaries formed part of the grocers' guild, but they were subsequently regrouped with the physicians. This professional upgrading affected their commercial privileges adversely, since the drysalters had remained in the grocers' guild and were able to sell some medicaments which were, thus, not subject to pharmaceutical control. Moreover, the physicians detested the apothecaries, considering them disloyal colleagues, for not only did both groups wear the same costume (black robe and coat, pointed hat, collar-bands) but also, the apothecaries gave clandestine medical consultations in their shops, seated beneath the stuffed crocodile that was their traditional sign. It is true that they had some competence in this field, since the examination preceding their entry into the guild ensured that they possessed good theoretical knowledge. Certain apothecaries engaged in scientific studies, as, for example, did Jacob Le Mort, who taught chemistry and pharmacy at Leyden University; the physicians, however, made his life such a misery that, for the sake of peace, he finally underwent examination for a doctorate in medicine.

From Death-bed to Cemetery

Sickness or old age asserted its sovereignty sooner or later. When a man or woman was on the point of death the family notified the neighbours and called in the predicant. The latter stood by the bed and recited prayers for the dying, joined in chorus by those present.

When the dying man had breathed his last, his eyes were first closed and then his face was covered with the top bed-sheet, and the bed-curtains were drawn. Condolences were exchanged, then the deceased's next of kin washed the body, dressed it, and arranged it on the bed with the head raised. Mirrors and pictures were turned with their faces to the wall. A host of local customs regulated the way of closing the windows and dictated the arrangement of the room (usually the entrance-hall or a room leading off it) in which the vigil was to take place. Usually all furniture was removed, apart from the bed, and those taking part in the vigil remained standing. If the dead person was a child, it was shown to its playfellows who were afterwards given a sweet rice-pudding to eat, the survival of an ancient pagan custom. The lying in state lasted several days, both before and after the placing of the body in its coffin. This last ceremony, in Leyden, had to take place in the presence of two witnesses unacquainted with the family. The coffin was placed on a trestle, with the dead man's feet pointing in the direction of the door. Only suicides and criminals were borne to burial head first.

Meanwhile the sacristan tolled the bell, and the family composed, or had written by a public scribe, the text of the announcement of death that they intended to send out. Here is a sample:

It has pleased the eternal and immutable Wisdom of Almighty God to call to His bosom from this sinful world to the blessed joy of His eternal Kingdom, on the eleventh day of this month at the fifth hour of the morning, my beloved wife, Mrs X, after the noble lady had been confined to her bed for ten days with a serious illness which yet, on several occasions, seemed to allow us to glimpse a glimmer of hope of the possibility of an eventual recovery.[9]

Some even went so far as to have this announcement composed in verse. Others did not make use of written announcements at all, but hired 'public priors',[10] specialised messengers who formed a guild of their own and wore a costume similar to that of the predicants. They transmitted the news of the bereavement orally, and the family's wealth and social station was judged by the number of priors they had engaged.

Most funeral arrangements were put in the hands of a benevolent association, some of which were those established by the various guilds and others were 'neighbourhood societies'; the latter existed in many districts and were designed to ensure each member a dignified burial, with a large cortège and voluntary pall-bearers. These associations all had funds derived from the members' subscriptions, and if it was a prosperous organisation these funds would cover not only the expenses of the ceremony but also those of the subsequent banquet.

At the appointed time all the participants congregated in the bereaved family's house. The predicant read a few verses from the Bible, then the coffin-lid was screwed down, and the coffin was draped in a black cloth embroidered with the arms of the guild of which the deceased had been a member; if it was a young person who had died flowers were heaped on it. As the church bell began tolling, the six pall-bearers lifted the coffin and placed it on a hand-bier. The cortège formed up behind them in a specific order determined by local tradition. Then the procession moved off slowly, in twos, without giving any particular outward signs of grief. Grosley noted[11] that their tears flowed 'quietly'. The mourners all wore long black coats, going down to their feet, usually hired for the occasion.

A catafalque covered the coffin during the church service. It was here, inside the church, that rich people arranged to have themselves buried, after payment of a tax, in one of the side-aisles or chapels. Often they purchased their tomb during their lifetime, and decorated its ledger-stone with their arms and family motto, engraving the stone itself or affixing a plaque. But most burials, of course, took place in the cemetery which often surrounded the church. The graves were dug so that the dead man's head pointed towards the east. The cortège circled the open grave a few times, then grouped itself around it. After the coffin had been lowered, everyone present approached in his turn to give the deceased one last look. The pall-bearers were all given tips, and the ceremony was over. Occasionally the bereaved family had special medals struck carrying the deceased's name or bust, and these were distributed to all the participants.

The funeral ceremony was just as important as the marriage ceremony in asserting family ties and enhancing the clan's social prestige. Consequently, it gave rise to the same display of clumsy vanity to which the rich added extravagant trappings; the house was draped all over with black cloths, the cortège seemed endless, and there was a parade of carriages. About mid-century special hearses became fashionable. The supreme luxury was the celebration of the obsequies at night, by torch-light. Such goings on scandalised people of sober disposition, and local administrations intervened on several occasions to limit such ostentation or at least to derive some profit from it. In 1661 the Amsterdam authorities forbade nocturnal burials; the following year they were authorised once again, but only on payment of a special tax rising to as much as one hundred and fifty florins. In Dordrecht, at the end of the century, the taxes imposed on carriages in funeral processions reached the sum of one hundred and twenty-five florins for a cortège of six carriages bearing the deceased's coat of arms.

On leaving the cemetery the family returned home and spent the rest of the day receiving visitors' condolences. During this ritual drinks were offered and consumed. Even among poor people, thirty, sixty or a hundred people might well enter the house during a few hours; in fact, the entire population of the street or district would come to pay their respects, and two or three toasts were drunk with each one of them. Afterwards came the tradesmen who had supplied the deceased during his lifetime, and they were offered beer with white bread or rice-pudding.

By evening the quantity of liquid refreshment which had been absorbed in this way had begun to drown all sorrows. A few friends were asked to stay behind and treated to a lavish meal, to be followed by more drinking and a sing-song. This funeral banquet, prohibited by both Church and State, nevertheless remained a very widely held occasion until mid-century, and was still observed long after this date in the northern provinces. After 1650 those who no longer invited their friends to a meal simply offered them even more to drink, and the house would echo with the uproar of coarse drunkenness. In order to avoid the presence of so many drinkers, wealthy people distributed silver coins to the pall-bearers, neighbours and less exalted mourners, inviting these people to go and have a drink in a tavern.

CHAPTER FOUR

RECREATIONS

Sports and Games—Banquets and Drinking-bouts: Traditional Guzzling, Fashionable Beverages, Tobacco—Feast-Days and Holidays: Traditional Celebrations, Kermises.

SPORTS AND GAMES

Hunting had been the pre-eminent sport in Europe since the very beginning of the Middle Ages, but as far as the Netherlands were concerned its part in the country's social life seems to have been very much diminished by the time the seventeenth century was under way. The feudal rights of hunting deer and boar had been abolished, and the forests were now administered by a master of the hunt in command of a corps of gamekeepers. Rabbiting was specifically forbidden,[1] but the peasants continued this practice illicitly as a means of supplementing their diet. Their method was to put a few cabbages in their cellar, with the outside trap-door wide open; hungry rabbits would jump down through this opening and be unable to get out again. The owner simply went into his cellar from time to time and killed the animals he found there, without fear of being caught.

But there was no restriction on the hunting of birds in the dune country that followed the coast from Helder to The Hague, and this fact probably explains why it is almost exclusively winged game which is to be seen in hunting pictures painted by artists of that period. The dunes, the Frisian islands and the marshy regions of northern Holland were used as a resting place by migratory birds such as heron, woodcock, wild goose and duck, and students from Leyden used to organise hunting expeditions in wintertime. In other seasons thrushes, partridges and swallows abounded. Colonies of lapwings nested all along the lakes and canals of

Friesland, and this bird was adopted as the emblem of the province.

The Dutch preferred line-fishing to hunting. The lakes and rivers, and even the canals, were well-stocked with fish: the maritime provinces provided pike, perch, carp and loach; in the rivers salmon made their annual pilgrimage upstream, and eels performed their mass migrations.

In summertime the national sport was to go on outings. Every Sunday and holiday entire populations of towns streamed out on the roads, footpaths and canals, all making for the countryside or the coast. The Netherlands swarmed with a host of people, of every class and kind, all eager for green fields and the open air, so that, in the words of Parival, 'wherever one goes here one finds as many people as one would see elsewhere in public processions'.[2]

Some walked, but most used a kind of wagon called a 'sporting cart', which was little more than a wooden tub set on wheels, jolting, creaking and groaning, making conversation impossible, and which was driven as fast as possible over the ruts and the bridges' wooden planks. Foreigners were indignant at the discomfort of this means of transport, but the Dutch became used to it from an early age: there were similar carts for children, drawn by goats or dogs. Less hardy spirits preferred travelling by boat. Sailing boats went up the Amstel, the Vecht and the Rhine, and navigated between lakes and canals. At this more leisurely pace people were better able to enjoy the beauties of the countryside and the pleasures of company. Sorbière relates that, in 1640, 'it was a favourite pastime among ladies of the nobility to go by boat from The Hague to Delft or Leyden, in bourgeois dress, mixing with the common people, to listen to their gossip about the aristocracy. . . . And since these ladies were extremely daring they never failed to make the return journey without acquiring some gallant, who offered them his services and was inevitably disabused at the end of the voyage of any small hope he might have had that they were courtesans, by the sight of the carriage which always awaited them.'[3]

The youth of Leyden liked to make trips in springtime

to the forest of Zevenhuyzen, just over twelve miles from the town, where they devoted themselves to the pleasures of destroying the herons' nests; in the summer they preferred the dunes of Katwijk and enjoyed the sea-food served in the pleasure gardens there. Scheveningen and its beach attracted the inhabitants of The Hague, who had easy access by a charming, shaded, straight road three miles long. The people of Amsterdam were less well placed, having to travel about twenty miles to the east or west to find pleasant country greenery.

These outings started early in the morning. Often the party would stop at an inn for a breakfast of sour cream, cherries, strawberries, wholemeal bread, butter, cheese and biscuits, washed down with wine, before setting off again. The various members picked flowers in the meadows, organised games or sang in chorus. A bucket full of provisions was brought along for the midday picnic, or else a visit was paid to a second inn. Freshly caught fish were bought at some point along the river, and on their return in the evening they would have another banquet before parting. Parival's style becomes lyrical when he evokes these 'innocent pleasures' nostalgically and at length: 'All these excursions finish up at one of the inns which are to be found everywhere. . . . And everywhere there are green arbours where the sun cannot penetrate; the trees are sometimes pruned and the branches trained to form cool canopies or simply to give pleasure by the admirable art with which they are shaped. . . . There are all sorts of machines in these pleasure gardens, some for suspending people in mid-air, others for whirling them around, and still others that make dolls move like puppets. . . . These inns are always packed with visitors, and the confused murmur of many voices is like the sound in a city square. These are inexpensive pleasures which all, even the humblest labourer, can share.'[4]

But sometimes these parties ended up with dangerous games. On some public holidays bands of a dozen or more young men would jump yelling into their wagons and hurtle towards a nearby tavern. There they would laugh and shout, eat pancakes and gulp down glasses of hollands gin. Then

suddenly some lad would draw his knife, brandish it above
his head and make to stick the blade in the ceiling. The
others would immediately hurl themselves at him, each trying
to tear the knife from his grasp. The first player would try
to prevent them. More knives emerged from pockets and a
free-for-all developed. The one rule was that eyes were not
to be touched. Blood streamed down slashed faces until the
spectators decided to call a halt to the exhibition by crying
'Enough! Enough!', after which the player with the best
technique was adjudged winner.

The favourite winter sport, so often illustrated in paintings,
was ice-skating. At this time of year business slowed down
and everyone had more leisure. During the few days or few
weeks in which the lakes and canals were frozen over, people
practically never took their skates off. Everyone lived on the
ice – young and old, men and women, predicants, magistrates
and princes. Each year an ephemeral unity of classes was
thus re-established through the excitement of sport. Skating
provoked passionate enthusiasm, and partisanship was shown
for one or other of the champions; among the most celebrated
were Cornelis le Fleur, Judith Johannes and Marie Scholtus.
The skates worn were wooden, with metal blades curved
upwards in front like the prow of a ship, and were twice the
length of the foot; the skaters glided past, hands clasped
behind their backs and body bent slightly forward, or in
couples with an arm around each other's waist, or long snake-
formations in which everyone clutched the hips of the person
in front and the entire column of skaters leaned to the right
and then to the left, very quickly, in perfect unison. Instead
of wearing overcoats or furs, people skated in their ordinary
indoor clothes supplemented by extra layers of wool underneath, so adding colour to the scene. Among the throng on
the ice tinkled the bells of caparisoned horses, their headgear
crowned by a plume, drawing sleighs of painted wood. Small
children and old folk were pushed along in armchairs on
runners, while the elder children went tobogganing, propel-
ling their vehicles with poles, or practised skating by pushing
a chair along in front of them on the ice. Inn-keepers set up
tents on the edge of the ice and lit fires; here the skaters came

to take a rest, have a drink and warm their hands at the fire before darting off again.

The prowess of the Dutch at this sport was such that it was common to see peasants skating along carrying a basket of eggs. Accidents, especially to children, were frequent, but nothing could curb their audacity. Some skaters went out in the pitch dark onto unlit canals. When travelling on skates peasants sometimes strapped a long pole across their shoulders to hold them up if they fell through a hole in the ice. If the ice was in good condition it was possible to skate from Amsterdam to Leyden in an hour and a quarter. A nineteen-year-old peasant boasted of being able to cover eighteen miles in an hour. One man, the father of a family, is reputed to have skated a hundred and twenty miles in a single day to be at the bedside of his sick child. Competitions were organised, the most important being the famous Circuit of the eleven towns which in favourable years could extend to more than a hundred and twenty-five miles. On one occasion, Saturday, 19th December 1676, half a dozen racers set off from Zaandam at four in the morning, traversed Amsterdam, Naarden and Muiden over the icy surface of the canals, and from there set off across the frozen Zuider Zee towards Monnikendam, Medemblik and Alkmaar; by half past eight that evening they were back in Zaandam, having made only one halt, at midday. In The Hague, young nobles organised sleigh-races on the canals near the palace; these sometimes took place at night by torchlight, and ended with a ball.

Every Martinmas (11th November) Amsterdam held boat-races on the Ij. From four to five hundred light craft, both rowing-boats and sailboats, used to take part under the eyes of a vast and totally impassive crowd massed on the banks.

In such competitions, sporting rivalry was a more important element than the lure of victory. The loser stood the winner a drink and was considered quits. The Dutch preferred those recreations in which they could display skill, strength and endurance, and make full use of their muscles.[5] On the ice in wintertime, and on the beaches in summer, bourgeois and peasant alike played at rolling the disk, in which a sort of wheel had to be sent as far as possible with the smallest possible movement of the hand. There were more than fifteen varieties of ball-game; the most popular was called *kaatsen*, the 'open-air tennis game' (a forerunner of lawn-tennis), and took place on a wooden or brick track divided up into several areas by painted lines. Two teams took part, using a very hard leather ball which alternated between each team according to fairly simple rules. This game became so popular during the course of the century that many inn-keepers had a covered *kaatsen* track built alongside their establishments, next to the traditional skittle-alley.

The 'game of hoops' (*klosspel*) was an ancestor of croquet, but the ball was launched by hand and the game demanded considerable muscular strength. There were several different versions. In one of them, 'mall', the ball was propelled with the aid of a hammer whose handle was about the length of a walking-stick. This game was played on a very extensive course which in most towns was beautifully laid out, as we have already seen in a previous chapter. 'Grosse' (*kolf*) analogous to modern hockey, was played on the ice in winter and on level ground in summer. Small wooden balls were sent towards a goal-post by striking them with sticks curved at the end. The entire population from the old people downwards took part enthusiastically in this game. Whereas mall primarily demanded strength on the part of the player, *kolf* required above all an accurate aim.

The citizens' militias formed by the guilds (reduced, as we have seen, to a purely decorative function) maintained the tradition of the medieval martial sport of archery. They practised it in public on Sunday mornings and on the guild's special feast-days, accompanying the display with warlike parades – the artisans in multicoloured uniforms and armed to the teeth, the officers helmeted, drummers at the head of the column. On the morning of the opening of a kermis, the militia would march around the town in all this finery until it reached an open space where a post had been set up, surmounted by a wooden bird known as the 'parrot'. They aimed at this target, and the first one to knock it off with an arrow was proclaimed master marksman, crowned with a symbolic hat, and awarded the right to choose a female companion for the duration of the kermis from among the town's prettiest girls. Between ceremonies of this nature, the members of the militia practised their art in often splendidly equipped shooting-ranges (*doelen*) which, in the large towns, had become centres of bourgeois merrymaking. The Hague possessed two *doelen*, considered to be annexes of the town hall.

Each region had its special traditions: in Friesland, ring-catching races, elsewhere foot-races or horse-racing. In the island of Terschelling, which lay on the route of the seals' seasonal migration, disguised peasants joined in the frolics of these trusting animals, lured them away from the shore, then threw themselves on them and captured them.

Several popular amusements involved a quite barbarous cruelty towards animals. 'Goose-shooting' consisted in hanging a live goose, whose neck had been thickly greased, by its feet from a cord stretched horizontally at a certain height. The young men raced along in a carriage or on foot, at full speed, until they were underneath the animal when they tried to remove it by getting hold of its head. Sometimes the cord was stretched over a canal, and the players passed underneath, standing half-naked in the stern of a boat. If they missed their attempt to grab the goose's neck they fell into the water. In 'cut the bird', the players were blindfolded and armed with a knife, and had to sever the neck of a duck or cock, also blindfolded and suspended by its feet from a cord. In the taverns they played at 'cat'. A cat was shut up in a wooden keg slung between two pillars by a cord. Each player put down a certain sum, the total of which made up the winner's prize. Everyone in turn gave the keg a heavy blow with a cudgel. The wood began to crack, and the cat went wild with terror. Finally a stave broke, the animal fell out in a more or less injured state and the cudgels continued to rain blows upon it until it died. This repulsive practice enjoyed such favour that, towards the end of the century, it was known for upper-class devotees of the 'sport' to add a note of elegance by replacing the cat in the barrel by a peacock.

Children joined in all these games, and their sensibility was hardly enhanced as a result. Bands of urchins amused themselves by capturing stray dogs and submitting them to the strappado, in imitation of a punishment in use in the navy which consisted in hoisting the victim to the top of a gibbet, letting him fall to the length of the rope, hauling him up again and repeating the process several times. Even children from the best families took pleasure in such games. Complete military panoplies were manufactured for children from cardboard, wood and tinplate, together with swords, pikes, drums and trumpets. But they preferred to make their own pea-shooters and catapults, and these weapons in the hands of an accurate shot were the cause of frequent accidents. In Brabant, teams mounted on stilts, accompanied by drummers, took part in pitched battles, imitating army tactics. Sometimes the great political crises were reflected in the children's games. During the events of 1619 the bourgeois citizens of The Hague discovered five life-size snowmen on the Voorhout one morning, representing Oldenbarnevelt and the leaders of the Arminian faction; a gang of urchins was busy bombarding these effigies while singing at the top of their voices: 'An Arminian is the plague of the land, his house is a nest of salamanders. . . . The Arminians to the gallows.'[6]

A catalogue of games, drawn up in French at the end of the century, included a list of children's games played in the Netherlands: the big ball, I spy, flick-fingers, hunt-the-slipper, quoits, clappers, knuckle-bones, little windmill, prisoners' base, slabs, equal-or-not, conkers, marble-pits and hey-cockalorum.[7]

One may add blind-man's buff, paper windmills, leap-frog, spinning-tops, bow and arrow, and marbles, played in the cemeteries on the tombstones or even in the church itself, since the road surface was neither hard nor straight enough; girls danced rounds and played with dolls. Dolls were made from wood, cloth, paper or even of silver, in every possible shape and form, sometimes with eyes that moved, or in various provincial costumes. Little girls in rich families owned sets of doll's furniture and miniature cooking utensils in porcelain, copper, iron or silver; doll's houses had up to eight rooms, furnished with pieces made of wood or precious metal. Games changed with the seasons: in the spring the girls skipped while the boys jumped ditches; in autumn they all flew kites. A number of counting-out rhymes have survived, together with the names of the games (often unidentifiable by now) for which they served.[8] Each province and island had its own, differing both in name and detail, though doubtless basically identical and deriving from child folk-lore common to the whole of Europe.

Despite ecclesiastical condemnations, dancing remained popular throughout the century. Dancing schools and dancing masters flourished. No public holiday or private celebration was complete without a ball. There were two distinct styles of dancing, the rhythm and steps being inspired either by ancient folk-lore traditions or by recent importations. In the countryside and among the urban petty bourgeoisie, dances included 'raise-the-foot', the 'hat-dance,' 'seven jumps', 'Jimmy-be-still', the 'clog-dance' and many others, some of purely local usage. On the other hand, the gentry and aristocracy danced the minuet, the coranto, the scaramouch, the galliard, the beautiful bride, the *farlane*, the *alcide*, the kind victor, and so on; these dances were all known by French names, a sufficient indication of their national origin. But however elegant the ball, it would nearly always end with a round-dance.

BANQUETS AND DRINKING-BOUTS: *Traditional guzzling*
Although his daily diet was relatively frugal, the seventeenth-century Dutchman used any special occasion as an excuse to gulp down incredible quantities of food and drink. A rather parsimonious household economy inevitably invited these compensations, the cost of which more than absorbed the accumulated savings of thriftiness. Whatever the pretext, the banquet and drinking-bout served to break down momentarily the solid barriers of family exclusiveness, and thus constituted fundamental manifestations of social relationship. Banquets were organised to celebrate the birth of a child, its baptism, its weaning, the mother's churching,

family anniversaries, Shrove Tuesday, a forthcoming journey, a return home, an election to some post or an acceptance into an official organisation, engagements, weddings, funerals. The Church protested in vain against this exaggerated attachment to earthly goods, and the State against such improvidence; the tradition remained intact throughout the century, especially among the bourgeoisie and the peasantry. Humble folk, too poor to provide much food during their reunions, simply drank more. Banquets were sometimes designed to bring together families connected by marriage, or neighbourhood groups; but many were arranged by various public and private associations.

The burgomaster entertained the town council, the university rector entertained the faculty. At the banquets organised by the 'chambers of rhetoric' each member had the right to bring a guest who was allowed three drinks at the expense of his hosts.

The members of the Musical Association of Arnhem stood host to their colleagues once a month, in turn. The statutes obliged them to serve a leg of mutton, a haddock, two salads, butter, cheese, pears, either apples or plums and wine. This restrictive list was designed to avoid excesses unworthy of the art cultivated by Society. In contrast, the banquets given by the guilds were proverbial for their extravagance, and the carousal sometimes lasted two days or more. The guild of surgeons in Enkhuizen had to promulgate an edict forbidding its colleagues to become indecently drunk and ordering them to carry back home anyone who fell under the table.

In Amsterdam the wealthy guild of merchants known as the Guild of Saint Martin served the following menu for one of its banquets: on the morning of the first day, calvesfoot and tripe with green peas, a fatty *hutspot* and roast meat with butter and cheese; in the evening the left-overs were eaten, supplemented by salt meat and rice; on the following day, meat-pies, rabbit, chicken and goose. The sheer quantity made up for any lack of quality. The bill of fare of some banquets consisted entirely of meat, various pies, and fruits in syrup, all in unlimited quantities. The formal meal offered by Nicolas Tulp on the occasion of his jubilee lasted from two in the afternoon until eleven at night, during which period courses were served in a never-ending succession.

The 'neighbourhood associations' which were sufficiently prosperous sent out an annual invitation to the local fathers of families and their wives; widows were allowed to bring a female companion of their choice. These feasts were usually held during the autumn, the season when foodstuffs were cheapest. On these occasions the participants' enjoyment showed itself exuberantly in ludicrous gaiety, rowdiness and practical jokes. The reveller elected 'glutton of the assembly' climbed on the table, crowned with a cooking-pot, holding a serving-spoon as a sceptre. These antics were observed through the window by passers-by.

Banquets were often held in taverns. If they were given at home, the main dishes were ordered from a pastry-cook specialising in public catering. Whenever a municipality received a prince or a foreign ambassador it authorised the burgomaster to draw up a menu and establish the order of precedence at table.

This protocol followed complex rules which varied according to the circumstances, but which were rigorously observed by Dutchmen at all social levels. In winter the men were placed closest to the fire, and the women farthest away with their footwarmers as compensation. The meal was preceded by a speech of welcome, delivered by the master of the house, during which as many toasts were drunk as there were guests. Tradition dictated the order in which these toasts were proposed, the choice of glass and the quantity of liquid poured into it. Everyone drank enormously. Large glasses were used, with wide or flute-shaped bowls, the capacity of which astonished foreigners. The Dutch bourgeois distrusted anyone who drank less than he did, and would have reproached himself for rudeness if he had not got all his guests drunk.

In 1681 Lemaitre took part in an extremely 'respectable' engagement banquet attended also by a certain number of elderly couples, the local divines and two monks. For the whole five hours that the meal lasted those present drank Rhine wine without a pause, shouting out toasts, arm in arm, smashing glasses, spilling drinks on the table. In this way some downed as many as fifty glasses, and at the end the diners' faces were flushed purple, though no one seemed actually to be drunk.[1] The guilds ordered wine by the barrel for their banquets. In Temple's view: 'The qualities in their air may incline them to drinking. For though the use or excess of drinking may destroy men's abilities who live in better climates, yet on the other side, it may improve men's parts and abilities in dull air; and may be necessary to thaw and move the frozen or unactive spirits of the brain.'[2] Temple commented further that although it was true that the upper classes hardly drank at all except at banquets, still there was not a single Dutchman who had not got drunk at least once during his life.[3] And he maintained finally that the austere existence of this people knew only one joy and one real luxury, alcohol, without which they 'would otherwise seem poor and wretched in their real wealth'.[4]

The women drank as much as the men. Even young girls began drinking in the morning, and some of them absorbed such regular quantities of beer that their inflated appearance was matched by a look of helpless stupidity that never left them. What struck foreigners was the systematic, organised character which this drunkenness assumed in bourgeois traditions. 'All these gentlemen of the Netherlands,' wrote Théophile de Viau, 'have so many rules and ceremonies for getting drunk that I am repelled as much by the discipline as by the excess.'[5] Poor people drank nothing but beer and cheap spirits; the bourgeoisie also drank wine, and the consumption of wine increased in proportion to the consumer's social eminence. In the Dutch economy of the seventeenth century, based almost entirely on transit trade, wine constituted one of the very few imported commodities of which large quantities were reserved for internal consumption.

Apart from the Rhineland, the principal supplier was France, more especially Anjou and Bordeaux. The wine was consigned to the ports of Nantes and, after 1630, Bordeaux, whence it was transhipped by Dutch boats to Rotterdam. By 1618 the wine trade had become Rotterdam's most profitable activity. During the autumn, after the wine-harvest, traffic became so heavy that their own fleet could no longer handle such a volume of cargo and the Rotterdam contractors had to hire additional ships from Zeeland. Dutch merchants were based in the departments of Loire and Gironde to supervise the production of many of the vineyards. In Ponts-de-Cé, Dutchmen were in charge of the selection and apportionment of the vintage, setting aside the inferior quality for Paris and reserving the best for Rotterdam.[6] Wine was imported also from Spain and the Rhineland. Cretan malmsey was bought from the Portuguese, and since this wine was supposed to be improved by sea-travel it was shipped from Candia to the Indies by the Portuguese merchants and reshipped from there to Europe, where the Dutch took delivery at prices as high as two hundred ducats for a hundred-gallon cask.

Wine was subject to high import duties and was sold retail in the apothecaries' shops. It was kept in barrels, in stone jugs or in leather bottles. Inn-keepers served it in pewter pitchers ranging in capacity from two pints to one and a half gallons. It was only towards the end of the century that elegant cafés and wealthy individuals began to use special bins in which the wine bottles were kept on ice.

Grape brandy imported from France competed with the native grain alcohols. Rotterdam and Weesp had been operating large-scale distilleries since the beginning of the century, and this profitable industry was often coupled with pig-breeding, the animals being fed on the waste products. Spirits distilled from barley, arak, and ratafia liqueur were the most popular strong alcoholic drinks of the time. Although hollands gin had been known since the sixteenth century its consumption seems to have been restricted to court circles during the seventeenth century, and even in the eighteenth century it remained the privilege of the rich. But by 1660 the Schiedam distilleries were producing considerable quantities of hollands.[7]

The one word 'tavern' covered very different types of establishment. There was the peasant pub where the customers drank small beer in the corner of a cellar or a gloomy kitchen; the small urban inn set up in the proprietor's entrance-hall; a vast marble-flagged hall with stained-glass windows like that owned by the painter-brewer Jan Steen; country establishments for wealthy gourmets, such as the *Learned Man* in Bennebroek, famous for its speciality of salmon with *sauce verte*; elegant taverns with luxurious furnishings and splendid glassware, frequented by magistrates, professors, guild masters, and providing the site for official banquets. Whatever the category of the establishment, people seldom drank alone – they either came in company or joined some group of previous arrivals. Toasts were drunk, with each one offering a round in turn. Everyone sang. The owner and his barmen darted to and fro; the barmaids flirted with the customers. The establishment's personnel was generally considered, rightly or wrongly, to be essentially dishonest. There is no doubt that the more drunk a customer became the greater was the chance of cheating him, and there were constant accusations of diluting the wine and colouring it with sunflower, of stuffing a cloth into the bottom of the beer-pitcher, of snatching away the bottle before it was empty, of increasing prices arbitrarily, of writing the figure 2 for 1 on the account 'by mistake' and so on.

Nevertheless, the entire male population and many women of the lower classes frequented the taverns assiduously. Even adolescents and children were to be seen there. During the course of the century a whole series of edicts attempted to place some kind of restriction on these premises, which were seen increasingly by the government as a public calamity; one such edict, issued by the States of Holland in 1631, ordered the closing of all taverns and inns during hours of worship and after nine in the evening, and prohibited the serving of spirits to young people.

Taverns employing an orchestra were called *musicos*. Some of these were designed for a wealthy clientèle and possessed an impressive hall in which concerts (that sometimes reached a high standard of excellence) were listened to by the customers while they drank. But most of them were shady joints frequented by sailors and girls, where a few poor devils scraped away at their instruments, producing more noise than music. The 'orchestra' played from four or six in the afternoon until nine or ten in the evening. There was no entry fee, but the proprietor served nothing but wine, and that was expensive and often adulterated. In an atmosphere made foul by pipe-smoke, rows of stout girls sat on wooden benches ranged around a low-ceilinged room, waiting for customers to ask them to dance. The violins sawed and screeched to a chorus of wine-sodden voices. The drinkers set their empty glasses down on the wooden shelf running along the wall, gripped their chosen dancing-partner by the wrist, shoved her into the thick of the throng which entirely filled the centre of the room, and started dancing. If they agreed on a price they soon disappeared in the direction of the girl's nearby lodgings. And it was not long before they were back again.

Fashionable Beverages
During the second half of the century the Netherlands first sampled three new products whose use eventually made a profound impact on the social manners of the population – tea, coffee and chocolate.

In 1640 certain herbal doctors began to prescribe, as a remedy for fevers or as a stimulant, the infusion of a rare and costly herb imported from China, tea.[8] By this time the high society of The Hague had already taken a liking to it and was partaking of it even without medical prescription; these elegant people bought it at the apothecary's, a few of the dried leaves costing a fortune, and sampled the brew at home in the company of a few friends, as an aristocratic pleasure. It suddenly became fashionable, and by 1660 wealthy families throughout the country were drinking it regularly. Ten years later the bourgeoisie adopted the habit.

By 1700 tea from China and India had become one of the chief commodities imported by Dutch traders. But it still remained expensive. The price gradually fell from a hundred florins a pound to ten, but even this latter price was still exorbitant and served to class tea among the appurtenances of bourgeois extravagance, making it the object of a snobbish cult. Enthusiasts discussed it like vine-growers discussing their crop, comparing the various types, analysing sowing and picking methods, and holding learned dissertations on the influence exercised by the nature of the terrain on the quality of the crop. For a guest to refuse the cup of tea offered him would have been as great an insult as to refuse a glass of wine. An addict easily swallowed twenty to twenty-five small cupfuls during the course of an evening, and some managed to absorb as much as fifty. In fact, by the end of the century physicians had changed their mind and had begun denouncing the harm this beverage did to the constitution, especially to women's nervous systems.

Originally tea had been drunk on the premises of the merchant who sold it. But, soon, families in easy circumstances set aside a particular room in their house for the purpose, usually one of the small rooms adjoining the entrance-hall. People met there at more or less fixed hours during the afternoon and evening, though in fine weather the tea-drinking ceremony took place in the garden. A positive ritual surrounded the instruments of the cult; the tea-tables and special sideboard were sometimes worth their weight in gold (they were, indeed, sometimes made of gold studded with pearls), and the cups and other accessories were copied from Chinese or Japanese models. Hermetically sealed boxes contained five or six different varieties of tea. The teapot was a vast container with an opening on each side; the water was poured into one, and the infusion emerged from the other. A small lump of sugar was placed in the mouth and the scalding liquid gulped down through the gradually dissolving sugar-lump. Between cups everyone munched one of those 'tea biscuits' which the bakers were beginning to manufacture, or marzipan, or jams and waffles. Before leaving the 'tea room' the company drank a glass of sweet liqueur or a dry white wine.

Coffee had been known to Dutch botanists since the end of the sixteenth century, but it only passed into general use after 1665. Although recommended by physicians as a stimulant and astringent, it does not really seem to have become popular before the closing years of the century, and at the beginning of the eighteenth century the peasantry was still unaware of its existence. During this period, Dutch planters had succeeded in cultivating the Arabian coffee-shrub in the East Indies, and in 1711 the first shipment of Java coffee arrived in the port of Amsterdam.

Meanwhile, fashionable people had adopted the habit of enjoying their coffee at one particular moment of the day, towards midday. A porcelain bowl was placed upon a table together with some small cups; the bowl contained cold water into which the cups could be dipped to cool or rinse them. In the centre a tall coffee-pot of copper or silver, with three feet, contained the powdered coffee (sometimes mixed with cinnamon, ginger or cloves) upon which boiling water was poured. Three small taps at the base of the apparatus allowed the beverage to be poured into cups, where it was sugared, sometimes with honey. Some added milk as well. The resulting brew was no more than a 'tincture' of coffee, of which the French made great fun.[9]

At the end of the century tea and coffee were often served at the same time during afternoon or evening gatherings. 'Associations of tea- and coffee-drinkers' had been set up in several towns, condemned by orthodox opinion because they were considered over-bold in bringing together people of both sexes united by nothing more than the passion they shared for these stimulants. These associations held their sessions in 'coffee-houses' or simply 'cafés', which were distinguishable from the taverns only by the fact that the servers were all female. These establishments opened originally from nine to eleven in the morning, and their clients smoked and read the papers while sipping their chosen brew; gradually, they became evening meeting places as well, mainly for gambling. Wine was also served, and in the eighteenth century chocolate was added to the menu. Chocolate had been drunk at court in The Hague since the end of the seventeenth century, but it does not seem to have become really popular before 1750. The abbé Sartre drank some in 1719 at the home of a distinguished citizen, and commented that it was as delicious as their coffee was dreadful.[10]

Tobacco

'Nicot's herb' was known in the Netherlands, under the guise of a medicinal plant, from the beginning of the sixteenth century, but during the truce years the habit of taking it as snuff and of smoking the leaves spread astonishingly quickly, and by 1625 the entire population was involved in this new pleasure. The language of the time associated smokers with drinkers of alcohol and spoke of 'drinking a pipeful of smoke'. Poets composed hymns in praise of tobacco, and songs were composed on the subject. An entire medical literature concerned itself with the problem. In fact, tobacco had become a centre of national interest.

Everyone took snuff. By the end of the century even the beggars had their own snuff-box and dipped their fingers into it before extending their hand for an offering. Tobacco was at first sold by the apothecaries, but soon became the object of a specialised trading enterprise.[11] Inn-keepers kept stocks for their clients. Leaves intended for pipe-tobacco could be bought dried but uncut, and were kept in pots at home or carried around in pouches; the pipes were made of clay, with long, straight stems. Attempts had been made to produce pipes from silver, but the metal imparted too much acidity to the smoke. A dozen towns in the Netherlands possessed pipe factories, the best-known being Gouda, and the pipe-making industry expanded so rapidly that by 1720 it employed fifteen thousand people. Smoking, like drinking, demanded time, concentration and a certain ceremonial: the well-mannered smoker sat down at a table, brought out his tobacco, chopped it finely with the aid of a special knife, filled his pipe, and lit it at a candle or at a specially designed brazier.

Tobacco was the cheapest of all pleasures, and it was common to smoke four or five pipes one after the other. People smoked everywhere, at home, at the office, in the shops and inns, in the stage-coaches and barges—even in church, sometimes. The entire Netherlands stank of tobacco. Grosley related that on opening the door of a small coffee-house in Rotterdam he was blinded by the thick clouds emanating from three hundred smokers seated inside![12]

The provincial governments became uneasy at this profligacy and imposed heavy taxes on tobacco, as well as posting notices warning the people against its harmful effects. Prince Maurice forbade pipe-smoking to the soldiers in his armies, and Piet Hein issued a similar edict to the sailors in his fleet, while the synods launched a constant stream of anathemas. But all in vain. Only the Anabaptists succeeded in resisting this poison which had so baneful an influence on human dignity. Working-class women and peasant women smoked almost as much as their menfolk. On the other hand, ladies in polite society resisted this passion and suffered all the more in their mania for cleanliness. They had to make prodigious efforts in order to keep their apartments spotless, and their last resort was to sacrifice one room to the un-hygienic outrages of the smokers in the family. Some women even inserted a clause in their marriage contract forbidding their husband to smoke at home. This feminine campaign contributed, in fact, to the success of the 'smoking-saloons', and wives were soon complaining that their husbands had found a new excuse for wasting money and a permanent temptation towards drunkenness and immorality. These smoking-saloons sprang up in great numbers during the century and were really only glorified taverns in which the customers drank and gambled while smoking a communal pipe that passed from hand to hand.

The fears of the married women were fully justified. The multiplication of smoking-saloons and tea- and coffee-houses completely transformed family traditions during the second half of the century, because the men adopted the habit more and more of going out in the evening and even of spending an entire feast-day in these establishments.

FEAST-DAYS AND HOLIDAYS: *Traditional Celebrations*
From birth to death the great events of life punctuated the family life of the Dutch with festivities, as we have already noticed, and these occasions constituted a kind of periodical renewal of communal awareness. The number of such celebrations increased as the family grew and became older, since in addition to feast-days and public holidays the Dutch

were passionately attached to birthday parties. Distant rela-
tives, neighbours and colleagues all took part, bringing congratulations and presents, and joining in the merrymaking.
At these reunions all sorts of ancient customs whose original
significance had long been forgotten were perpetuated. A
favourite diversion at these gatherings was to produce a range
of ear-shattering shrieks and groans by an expert manipulation of the foot-operated bellows which every well-organised
household possessed. Banquets and, to an even greater
extent, the giving of presents on the occasion of a birth, an
engagement, a marriage or a birthday had an institutional
character, and organised authority may be said to have
given tradition official recognition. When members of the
municipal administration celebrated silver or golden wedding
anniversaries, baptisms, or their children's weddings, the
town would present them with a goblet engraved with their
coat of arms. At the birth of a prince or other distinguished
scion whom they wanted to honour or flatter, municipalities
or States would offer a life annuity bond, enclosed in a
precious casket, whose presentation was surrounded by great
ceremony. The future Stadtholder William II, while still
in his cradle, received three such bonds of an annual value
of thirteen thousand six hundred florins, while to mark the
same occasion the government distributed two hundred and
twenty-five florins to the poor of The Hague! William III
was presented with an annuity of eighteen thousand florins.
The authorities responsible for the gift were designated
collectively as godfather, and sent a delegation to participate
in the baptismal ceremonies, thus enhancing the occasion
with their prestige and adorning it with their embassy's
display of finery.

The month of November was enlivened by a traditional
family festival which had originally an economic purpose:
this was the so-called 'butchery'. At this time most bourgeois
families laid in a supply of meat to last the winter or even the
entire year. The master of the house went to the cattle-fair
and bought a pig and a cow, either on his own account or in
combination with neighbours, depending upon his family's
importance and wealth. The animal was slaughtered in the

courtyard or in front of the house, and the quarters hung from hooks fixed into a beam for the purpose. Then began the salting or smoking operations. These lasted some time, and the two or three days in question provided an excuse for a real popular festival. During the day everyone worked hard, downing a glass of hollands from time to time and, at lunchtime, snatching a quick meal of bread and beer, while the mistress of the house presided over the operations from the back of her kitchen. Then, in the evening, there were invitations from one house to another to share lengthy meals of roast meat and fresh pork, washed down with a great deal of beer and accompanied by bacon omelettes. For many modest households these were the only meals during the whole year in which they ate fresh meat, and for the other eleven months they simply carved pieces from the salt meat they had stored up.

From about 1635 the bourgeoisie developed a hitherto unknown or at least repressed taste for diversions outside the family circle, and so-called 'colleges' of amusement (*collegien*) sprang up throughout the country. These institutions were provided with their own sets of statutes, and served to bring together people of both sexes who shared a common interest or were united by profession or age. The members called each other 'colleague', drank, sang and played cards. The 'colleges' were to be found at every social level, and ranged from the elegant to the sordid. Parival was invited, in 1660, to a meeting of one of the 'colleges' and described it in the following terms: 'Six or seven distinguished personalities divide up the days of the week among themselves so that each one plays host on a particular day. They meet at six or seven in the evening and spend the time gambling or conversing, until ten o'clock when they all return home for supper. . . . Similar soirées are organised by young ladies: . . . they do not play for such high stakes, but in compensation one often finds among the group such charming and intelligent creatures that one has no occasion to regret the time one has spent in their company.'[1]

When the first 'coffee-houses' appeared, the 'colleges' held their sessions there, and provided the bourgeois citizens who also frequented these newfangled establishments with the social justification which their passion for coffee required.

Despite the recriminations of the Reformed Church, a number of the old Catholic feasts survived in popular tradition, though in secularised form. A deep-rooted folk-lore still attached itself to the celebration of Twelfth Night, Shrove Tuesday, Martinmas, the feast of Saint Nicholas, and even Whitsuntide, all of which remained both family and social occasions, though varying considerably from one region to another. These were all public feasts in which the entire nation participated, except for a few puritans. In the opinion of Temple they constituted one of the charms of Dutch existence.[2]

On 6th January, Twelfth Day, each family chose a 'king' during breakfast, by means of a bean or a silver coin hidden in the loaf which was to be broken that morning, or by drawing lots. In some districts three kings were chosen, two of them dressed up in white robes, the third with his face daubed black and wearing a black robe. All three, candle in hand and carrying stars made from paper, left the house followed by a procession of children with baskets on their heads, and figures representing the Fool and the Glutton in grotesque costumes, all singing traditional songs on the theme of Herod and the Three Magi. They ended up inevitably in some tavern, where they were offered Twelfth-cakes.

In some towns, including Amersfoort, the most distinguished citizens drew lots for the 'kings' at the town-hall. And in certain villages, until the beginning of the eighteenth century, the rhetoricians acted out on that day the old medieval pageant of the Three Wise Kings. Elsewhere, ancient custom prescribed that a line of lighted candles should be placed on the floor of a room and that all the small children should leap over them. At Noordwijk, the celebrations began on Twelfth Night, at five in the evening, when a procession of children went from door to door, carrying bags and soliciting bread, cheese and money.

The first Monday after Epiphany was marked by festivities originating in the ancient feast of the Innocents. Printers

made this date the occasion for solemn professional ceremonies, the various guilds organised processions, the rhetoricians presented the *Pageant of the Innocents*, the wealthy held
banquets, and the municipal administrations offered presents
of wine, poultry, clothes or money to their employees.

The provincial governments had succeeded in forbidding
the wearing of fancy-dress on Shrove Tuesday (*mardi gras*),
and only the rhetoricians in a few villages, and some nobles
at the court at The Hague still wore masks for the occasion.
Consequently, the celebration of the feast was confined to
the ritual of eating pancakes, often in some tavern, where a
special annual repertoire of more or less obscene popular
songs was bawled out for the occasion. In Dordrecht, special
dances were held on this day. In certain villages, the children
made a tremendous uproar, running through the streets
brandishing a 'musical instrument' consisting of a pot with
a bladder stretched over its mouth whirled around on the
end of a stick.

Whitsuntide was marked by pigeon-shooting expeditions,
dances and communal singing. A procession of young people
crowned with flowers and foliage and adorned with emblems
made from gilt or silver paper followed the 'Whitsun bride'
through the town, singing songs. The 'bride' was chosen as
a beauty queen from among the local girls, dressed at public
expense in a white robe adorned with flowers, and proceeded
on her way surrounded by maids of honour in similar garb.
Along the procession's route a collection was taken, and the
proceeds were used for a drinking session. This custom
resulted in such excesses, and the traditional songs shocked
the more straitlaced citizens so deeply, that at one point or
another most towns prohibited the Whitsuntide procession.

Martinmas[3] was celebrated in every Dutch home during
the evening of 11th November, when the family was united
for a meal around a brilliantly lit table. The company ate
pancakes, medlars and a roast goose, drank new wine and
sang the old refrain:

> *Saint Martin! Saint Martin!*
> *New wine today, old wine tomorrow!*

Then the young people spread through the streets, singing, carrying paper lanterns, and knocking at the doors of rich people to ask for firewood with which they made a bonfire. The children threw baskets of medlars and chestnuts or other nuts into the flames.

Saint Nicholas's day was the children's feast-day. The tradition went back at least as far as the thirteenth century, and drew upon an ancient magic symbolised by the appearance of presents in shoes left under the chimney. Since the previous evening the children from the neighbourhood had gathered at the baker's shop to decorate the traditional gingerbread with silver paper. They ate, drank and danced. They sang:

> *Saint Nicholas, good holy man,*
> *Put on your best coat,*
> *Then gallop to Amsterdam . . .*
> *Apples from Orange!*
> *Apples from trees!*
> *Rich men live down there,*
> *Rich ladies live down there,*
> *Who are broad-minded as well as broad-sleeved.*
> *Sweetheart, let's get married!*[4]

These celebrations were sometimes so noisy that, here and there, the authorities had to put pressure on the parents to prevent their offspring from taking part. In Rijnsburg the peasants went and milked the cows in the meadow, in the presence of the local inhabitants, and distributed fresh milk and biscuits. In Rhijnsaterwoude, a crier assembled all the children under fourteen and the old people over seventy, and sent them on to the dike of the Wassenaar polder, where they found seven great pails of warm milk and fifteen dozen biscuits waiting for them. Throughout the country the inmates of old people's homes and orphanages were entitled on that day to a few delicacies such as white bread and sugar-candy.

Mayday celebrations went back to even more ancient pagan customs. During the evening of 30th April a maypole was set up in the marketplace, decorated with wreaths, paper streamers, gilded brushwood and mottoes. On the morning of 1st May the town's youth, dressed all in green, danced and sang around it, and a drinking-session followed. Young people in good families sent each other presents and good wishes. A great deal of singing went on, and the bookshops sold compendiums of special 'May songs'. In the evening the town was lit up, the entire population streamed into the streets, and the festivities ended very late, usually in chaos. In The Hague its celebration assumed an official character. The Stadtholder's household walked in procession, and three maypoles were set up, dedicated respectively to the States of Holland, the Union government and the various princes of the family of Orange.

Most of the towns had particular customs, giving rise to local festivals. In Amsterdam and the surrounding district the *luylak* was such an occasion. Troops of children ran through the streets at dawn on the Saturday preceding Whitsunday, carrying a wreath of greenery, creating an uproar so as to awake respectable people from their sleep, knocking at doors, throwing stones at windows and singing more or less insulting songs, such as:

> *Luylak!*
> *Sleeping-bag,*
> *Bed-cover,*
> *Fairground doll*
> *Lying in bed till nine!*

Sometimes gangs of young ruffians got completely out of control and roved the countryside, either fighting with rival gangs or else combining with them to attack the wooden windmills which were plentiful in the area, damaging their equipment. The Amsterdam municipal administration had to order that all doors should remain locked on this day until six in the evening. Repeated interventions by the police finally succeeded in limiting this rowdy tradition to the singing of songs.

In Amsterdam, also, the Stock Exchange building was

opened to the children during the first week of the September kermis. Small boys went there in the mornings in procession, with drums and flutes, and were allowed to spend the entire day playing there except for the two hours during which business was conducted. On Saint Job's day, the youth of Rotterdam made an expedition to the village of Schoonderlo, famous for the number of its taverns, and created a fantastic uproar. In 1625 an edict put an end to this habit. In Friesland, on New Year's Eve, the young people ran around the streets in bands, seizing any movable object they could find, such as implements and vehicles, and switching or hiding them in a general shuffle.

On 3rd October Leyden commemorated the anniversary of its liberation, as it still does today. 'Gastronomic' rituals (consisting of *hutspot* and herrings) marked this patriotic festival, the only one in the whole country to be celebrated on a fixed date. On the other hand, great events in national history and certain diplomatic triumphs were recognised, during the course of the century, by a series of special celebrations, some magnificently impressive like the welcome arranged in 1638 in Amsterdam for the queen-mother Marie de Médicis. On that occasion the guilds paraded, troops were deployed, buildings festooned with bunting, and banquets organised. This was the first time that the town had had the opportunity of receiving a 'real queen', and the Amsterdam newly-rich prided themselves that this visit put a seal on their own recently acquired prosperity. They became dizzy with success. The citizens' militia commissioned a huge mural for the wall of their meeting-place, depicting their procession on that day. During most of the century Amsterdam took charge of the Republic's ceremonial responsibilities towards the various European courts, and it was that city which welcomed the Queen of England when she came to present her daughter as bride to William II, and which organised the celebration in 1869 of the stadholder William III's crowning as King of England.

When Maurice of Nassau visited Amsterdam in 1618, after the arrest of Oldenbarnevelt, the local rhetoricians staged a series of allegorical mimes commemorating the Prince's titles to fame, followed by a procession of chariots picturing the seven provinces rendering homage to him, and finally, a series of *tableaux vivants* representing some of the great events in recent national history. The Westphalia peace treaty was celebrated throughout the Union by tremendous festivities, including the public recital of poems, historical narrations, the decorating of house fronts, flags, trumpets, peals of bells, banquets, prayer-sessions and the firing of salutes. In Amsterdam's Damplein, an allegorical mime represented the Prince surrounded by Wisdom, Prudence, Justice and Courage; Maurice of Nassau was symbolised in the figure of Numa Pompilius, Frederick Henry in that of Hannibal, and William II in that of Augustus. Everywhere there were public illuminations, and this became a regular feature of all such festivities. Each victory reported by the Prince's armies called for the illumination of streets and public buildings by means of braziers of wood-logs, pitch, or even tar, the latter being a notorious fire hazard. Sometimes wealthy families organised illuminations and firework displays in their own gardens.

Kermises
Of all the ancient traditions, that of kermises had the deepest roots in Dutch character and temperament. After William III had become King of England, he admitted in confidence to friends in London one day that he would willingly give two hundred thousand florins to possess wings and be able to fly to the kermis at The Hague. In previous years he used to attend, accompanied by his entire court. Princes and princesses, high magistrates and government officials, all mingled with the crowd in the same explosion of joy. In 1654, during the worst point of the Anglo-Dutch crisis, Johan De Witt, who was burdened by heavy responsibilities of state at the time, was to be seen discussing politics at the kermis, in front of a waffle-seller's stall.

In the good old days people talked about 'Saint Kermis' in the same way that they would refer to 'Saint Nicholas'. The kermis was more than a festival and holiday; it was a periodical expression of collective instincts, a fleeting

communion of liberty and fraternity. It originated as a
'church mass', a local feast-day held in connection with
a particular chapel or convent, but had become secularised with the Reformation. High-principled predicants
denounced it in vain as a relic of papism. During the
seventeenth century, every town and village of any importance had its annual – and sometimes bi-annual – kermis.
The local population mingled with the inhabitants of
neighbouring communities and people coming from more
distant regions. Buying and selling was originally as important a function of the kermis as amusement, so that it
helped to strengthen the country's economic ties as much as
its cultural ties. But the atmosphere degenerated gradually
during the century, and the kermis turned into a drunken
spree serving to liberate all the vulgar passions normally
held in check. At the same time, a certain social cleavage
became apparent, and 'respectable' folk tended more and
more to come as spectators rather than to mingle with the
crowd. Although the nobility was more free-thinking by
nature, it allowed itself to be influenced by the puritanism of
some of the important bourgeois families in this respect.

The kermis usually lasted a week, sometimes two weeks,
and occasionally even three weeks, as at Haarlem. In The
Hague the May kermis lasted two weeks and the September
kermis one week, but the latter was abolished by a 1643
decree. In this city the festival's organisation was in the
hands of the court itself and of the government, who took a
share of the profits; and, as a result, it had a special character,
relatively more official and more sumptuous than elsewhere.
It took place inside and outside the huge quadrilateral
formed by the royal palaces in the centre of the town. It
began on 3rd May, at exactly half an hour after midday,
heralded by a peal of bells from the clocktower of the town
hall lasting until one o'clock.

Tents were set up in the square and the surrounding
streets, and the tradesmen and entertainers were able to
enlist the aid of the crowd in establishing their temporary
quarters, either gratis or at the price of a free ticket. By now
the entire town was out of doors and milling around in a

state of excitement, while the great coming event was announced by gatekeepers, drummers and private publicity agents touting their masters' wares in rhyming verse. The affair always started off with a parade by the guilds, followed by an archery competition. The crowd thickened. Rows of shops, stalls and booths cluttered up the public thorough-fares. The bakers all had their special kermis cakes on sale, flat, oval girdle-cakes with pink sugar icing on which were written in white letters surrounded by preserved fruit some such encouraging message as 'For your Kermis', 'With my Love', and 'With all my Heart'. These cakes served as go-betweens; young men offered one of them to some pretty girl who would then keep it until the second Sunday after the Kermis, when the suitor would come round to see if a slice of the cake had been specially put aside for him.

The taverns were jammed. For many peasants the kermis in the neighbouring town was essentially an occasion to drink in unaccustomed surroundings. Long tables were placed out of doors, and people sat on benches, barrels or on the ground. The adults danced; the children yelled, chased each other and played the tambourine and penny-whistle; fiddlers scraped away among the goods displayed on the stalls. Passers-by were sometimes seized by the scruff of the neck, and a glass of beer poured down their shirt, or their faces smeared with flour and wax. The kermis began to turn into an orgy. In some villages, a 'kermis ox' was solemnly paraded, wreathed with flowers, and then slaughtered in the market-place, roasted, and eaten by the population on payment of a contribution. 'Kermis singers' paraded through the streets, carrying a sign that gave the words of the songs they sang. Everybody sang. Women's yells mingled with the creaking and groaning of the merry-go-rounds. The atmosphere in the tents soon became unbreathable, and the odour suffocating. Ladies fainted. Stall-holders sold cakes, pottery, cloth, glass or silver trinkets, souvenirs and pictures. Acrobats and tight-rope walkers competed with troupes of gymnasts performing Egyptian pyramids. Talking dogs and sum-adding horses were on show. Fairground attractions came to the most important kermises from all over Europe, and introduced some of the great foreign clowns with names such as Jean Potage, Punch and Hanswurst. Holland had its own favourite clown, nicknamed Pekelharing. These individuals performed slapstick comedies, sharing the stage with the rhetoricians' satirical farces. Occasionally, the theatrical productions at the kermises were of a rather higher standard; the Amsterdam theatre company performed at the Haarlem kermis, as did the Prince of Orange's troupe in 1640. 'Mechanical theatres' showed puppets, worked by clockwork, which played the drum or the bugle.[5] Foreign 'artistes' supplemented the usual crowds of gipsies and local circus-folk at the principal kermises. There were Swedes who plunged their hand into a crucible full of molten lead. The Englishman Richardson swallowed liquid sulphur and molten glass, and ate lumps of coal.

Among the charlatans, healers and fortune-tellers, there would usually be a 'rat-catcher' shouting the virtues of his arsenic-cake and exhibiting his most recent victims on a line. Craftsmen created the marvels of their art for the public's amusement, while self-styled Bohemians blew glass. Exotic animals such as camels and elephants were rare, but every kermis had its quota of horses, cows, dogs and pigs with either two heads or three or six feet, or of an unusual colour. A bee-keeper would demonstrate how the bees returned to their hive at his command. Or there might be a limbless man who could sew, weave or fire a pistol by using his mouth alone. Occasionally the 'rarity' existed only in the fairground barker's impassioned description – a wild woman in chains, for instance, or a man bound hand and foot who was supposed to have been a slave in Turkey for seven years.

One of these monsters has left some trace in popular history. This was a fisherman known as 'Long Gerrit', eleven feet nine inches tall, and reputedly as strong as a horse. No doubt his glory aroused jealousies, for the poor devil appears to have perished in 1668 during some brawl at the kermis where he was on show.

In fact the kermises, especially in the country, rarely finished without disorders of some kind. After a few days, when people had got excited enough and absorbed sufficient alcohol, an unguarded word, a bold gesture towards a woman, a single glance was sufficient to release all this pent-up energy. Then fists would fly, and sticks descend on heads, if nothing worse. There were traditions in this field, too. Potential combatants gripped an earthenware pipe in their fist to provide greater impact; or kept a pile of sand in reserve in one pocket to hurl in an opponent's eyes at the right moment; or filed their finger-nails so as to produce jagged points with which sharper wounds could be inflicted when it became time to settle scores. In some villages, brawls were officially integrated into the celebrations; tournaments were organised in which the combatants were armed with blunted knives, so that the spectators could see the blood flow but no one actually got killed. The revellers waded ankle-deep in filth and rubbish.

CHAPTER FIVE

ARTS AND LETTERS

Fine Arts: Painters, Musicians—Belles-lettres: The 'Rhetoricians', The Theatre and its Actors, Men and Women of Letters, Books and Publishing.

FINE ARTS

The militant Calvinism of Holland's martial epoch, bitterly opposed to humanism yet influenced by it, held the seeds of an original intellectual culture whose first fruits became visible shortly before 1600. This culture was based on religious exigencies and on the necessity of capturing the allegiance of the ordinary man – the soldier, the simple peasant, the small workman; during the entire century it retained its essentially religious, popular, nationalistic character. Even when the ideas and styles of French classicism began to penetrate into the Netherlands, about 1660, they remained importations, decorative, episodic veneers. Puritanism exercised an indirect influence on the whole, in the sense that it promoted an interiorisation of feeling. As a result, the gap gradually widened between the popular, savage, energetic tendencies of the Dutch temperament and its formalistic, pompous, orthodox tendencies. The first set of instincts corresponded to what the country's bourgeoisie had been, and the second to what it dreamed of being in its new-found prosperity. Or, again, the first corresponded to baroque style, and the second to Louis XIV tastes. But even in the context of puritan classicism, the Dutch upper middle class conceived of itself less in terms of royalty exalted by French art as in terms of the ancient heroics of the *civis romanus*.

Perhaps these contradictions explain the absence of 'style', in the strongest sense of the word, which is so marked in seventeenth-century Dutch society, and the lack of which prevented the nation from expressing itself validly in the arts based on solid media – sculpture and architecture.[1] The arts in which the country excelled, and which gave genuine expression to its deepest feelings, were exactly those which gave direct access to the interior life, to the life *of the interior*, that of the family hearth: in other words, poetry, music and painting.

Painters

'There can surely be no other country in the world,' wrote Parival, 'where there are so many, and such excellent, paintings.'[2] History offers few examples of generations as richly endowed with great painters as that which sprang up in the Netherlands between the years 1595 and 1625. Van Goyen was born in 1596, Aelbert Cuyp in 1605, Rembrandt in 1606, van Ostade in 1610, the Both brothers in 1608, van der Helst in 1613, Metsu in 1615, Ferdinand Bol in 1616, Terborch in 1617, Wouwermans in 1619, Potter in 1625, Jan Steen in 1626. And this extraordinary flowering of talent was almost entirely concentrated in the province of Holland; Leyden was the birthplace of Rembrandt, van Mieris, Jan Steen; The Hague of Potter, van Ravesteyn and van Goyen; Delft of de Hoogh and Vermeer; Dordrecht of Cuyp; Haarlem of van Ostade, Brouwer and Wouwermans.[3] Amsterdam was a painters' colony.

Despite all differences in inspiration and style, these artists offer us an extraordinarily homogeneous body of work, whose essential characteristics developed as a result of the social function it fulfilled. The rising bourgeoisie liked to surround itself with the signs of luxury which had once been the prerogative of the nobility and the Church. The merchant was driven by economic necessity, the need (to which we have already alluded) to be able to invest his commercial profits. This desire to acquire objects determined largely the character and development of the nation's cultural existence during the seventeenth century, and over a period of several generations provoked a considerable demand for consumer goods. But the structure and morality of Dutch society limited the choice of these principally to things which could add to the comfort of the house or enhance its appearance.

For the Dutch bourgeois of that epoch a painting was a piece of furniture, and a piece of furniture that had an essential function, that of covering bare surfaces. He was only happy when every inch of space was fully utilised. At the same time, the picture had to flatter the rather simple vanity of the newly-rich, especially if it was a portrait or represented an interior. The proprietor of the 'nobles' residential chambers' at Edam commissioned a painting in 1633, specifying that the portrait should emphasize the corpulence which was his glory and pride; at the age of forty-two he weighed over thirty stone! J. Molenaer depicted a shipowner surrounded by his entire family, and pointing with his finger to the ninety-two ships he owned. A well-to-do Amsterdam bookseller in 1675 had no less than forty-one paintings in his house; and he was by no means exceptional, although it is true that by this date tapestry workers were providing the painters with keen competition.

Until about 1660 the most modest shopkeeper had his collection of pictures, and hung them in every room. Peasants were known to pay as much as two or three thousand florins for a painting. And yet none of these people had the least idea of being patrons of the arts; in fact the vast majority of collectors had no conception of the state of perfection which the Dutch school had attained. Muiden's affected but shrewd circle of art-lovers were contemptuous of Rembrandt's abilities; their hero was the Fleming, Rubens.

In the eyes of the aristocracy and the wealthy bourgeoisie the painter was a supplier of goods like any other. They were not interested in becoming patrons; they simply commissioned a work and paid for it. It is probable that all the forty canvases by Vermeer which constitute his known output were painted to order. At the very most, clients agreed to lend money to an artist whose idleness or extravagance had impoverished him, and even then the terms of the loan were very harsh. Rembrandt had this experience on several occasions, and at one time he owed Cornelis Witsen four thousand florins. A failure to repay a debt meant bankruptcy and seizure of goods, even if the artist was ruined thereby. It was not so much the picture-dealers' terms that ruined Rembrandt and hastened his end as the demands of his creditors, all Amsterdam aristocrats. Pieter van Laar took one way out: suicide. Hercules Seghers drowned his miseries in alcohol. Frans Hals, Ruysdael and Hobbema all ended up sooner or later in charitable institutions. Despite the five hundred canvases he painted, Jan Steen remained poor; and when Vermeer died he owed his baker six hundred florins.

On the other hand, the painter could integrate himself into the social scheme without any essential conflicts. Nothing was farther from the manners and morals of the era than any revolt by misunderstood individuals or a frantic desire for originality. The artist simply strove to make full use of a technique and a craftsmanship which he had learnt as an apprentice, never questioning himself about its profound complexities. Painters had their own guild, and membership was acquired by the usual process: the apprentice cleaned the master's brushes and swept his studio; as a journeyman he had the chance to sketch in the backgrounds of the master's canvases, to paint subsidiary figures and to execute work on the basis of the master's sketches. When he at last became a master he was subject to the usual laws of supply and demand, and his work as such was not deemed worthy of any particular consideration or honour.

The painters' guild was a modest guild. Although the artist was considered by his compatriots to be a fairly worthless fellow, his membership of an organisation allowed him to feel involved in society and escape that sensation of being apart, of being 'different', which would have made any Dutchman of the time uncomfortable. The artist's own taste was largely determined by the prevailing taste of his fellow countrymen, which loved harmony of design and richness of colour and abhorred sentimentality and mysticism. What we consider today to be the 'realism' of the great Dutch painters is, in fact, a direct reflection of this strict unity between the artist and the society he lived in.

Picture-dealers did exist in that era, in the shape of shop-owners who acted as intermediaries between the artist and his clients. But pictures were sold also at the fairs and kermises, and the cheapness of the wares attracted customers. Although the prices may seem fairly high when translated into present-day currencies, they were nevertheless far less than those prevailing in Spanish-dominated Belgium, and this economic factor certainly encouraged the development of the Dutch school. Six hundred florins seems to have been considered a reasonable price for a medium-sized picture, and van Mieris, for instance, demanded one thousand two hundred for a *Woman at her Window*. But no doubt bargains were also struck at far more modest figures.[4]

The plasticity and shading of the nude body were considered of no interest. The sole human type to merit any attention was the citizen, man in his true costume, his daily aspect. On this point there was a total break with the Renaissance and especially with Italy, although Dutch painters had learned much from that country. Many of them, in fact, still visited Rome, but rather to study the art of landscape painting. They fought shy of all heroic themes, and the canvases they brought back from Italy would feature a peasant-woman with a pitcher, a pedlar, a herdsman, a herd of cattle – living embodiments of everyday existence illuminated by the warmth of a sun lacking in Holland. Allegory, mythology, symbolism and so-called academic processes played little or no part in Dutch painting. The landscape itself had lost the sense of cosmic seething which Brueghel had portrayed, and in van Ostade's work, for instance, the landscape surrounding one of his peasant figures was nothing more than a discreet invitation to investigate the personality of the man it framed. In 1600 the main interest lay in the elaboration of forms and colours, and in the decorative division of surfaces. Thirty years later, contours lost their hard outline and use was made of monochromatic effects; the underlying tension was accentuated. But by 1650 a certain theatricalism had intruded itself, and artists began to concern themselves once again with classical themes. From that point onwards the heart began to go out

197

of Dutch painting, although the artist's vision had become even more refined, with an acute perception of surface reflections and the fall and spread of rich materials. The essential was evoked in the iridescence of background objects, and the effect was dramatically impressive. After Rembrandt's death, a technical tradition survived, but the final quarter-century marked the decline of an art, and the success of Gerard de Lairesse was the first sign of degeneracy.

The forms taken by this art were fairly limited. Portrait painting was, socially, the most important category, and the demand was enormous. The studio of van Mierevelt alone turned out five thousand portraits. Clients sometimes commissioned several examples of the same portrait, rather like someone having a studio photograph taken today. It was exactly the same in France. The most genuinely lyrical form taken by Dutch painting of the era was the landscape, with the chiaroscuro inspired by the vast expanse of the Dutch sky. Subject pictures owed their existence, originally, to the Reform's condemnation of representations of religious themes, as a result of which scenes of interiors, kermises and still lives replaced the crucifixions which the churches no longer commissioned; and these new subjects corresponded to the deepest needs of a new society. Humour, irony and caricature formed an integral part of this new tendency, while pictures of towns, seaports, fleets and naval battles expressed this collective consciousness in a different way. It remained for Rembrandt to re-create, around biblical themes, a religious painting adapted to the Calvinist soul.

Engraving followed the same path. It has been considered with some justice to be the most typical art form of the Dutch seventeenth century, and it left a considerable body of work. We have portraits, series representing the kinds of work performed in different seasons, subject pictures, landscapes and, above all, pictures and cartoons representing contemporary scenes, all of these in the form of separate sheets, albums and illustrations for pamphlets or literary works. In the last category we have van der Venne's engravings for Jacob Cats's poems. Engraving mirrored all the aspects of national life, while drawing and painting drew out its tendencies and effects. In certain respects, the engravings of the epoch can be compared to present-day newspaper photography. They, too, represented the acts and fluctuations of political and military history, and provided a precise picture of a nation's self-awareness. At their best, they approached great art; at their worst, they were 'penny plain, tuppence coloured'. Popular engravers used the same plates as long as possible, simply altering the principal figure, a fact which explains the antiquated naïvety of many of the illustrations in contemporary pamphlets and cheap books.

Musicians

The Netherlands possessed long-established musical traditions. The 'Flemish' school of the fifteenth and sixteenth centuries exercised its influence not only in France, but also in Italy, where the work of composers such as 'Clemens non papa' made its mark on Palestrina and others close to that country's great upsurge of native music. The Reform dealt a death-blow to this tradition, and after 1600 there were no new great names in Dutch music. Even so, an intense collective musical life survived, a profound and mostly sure taste characteristic of this otherwise unartistic nation. The seventeenth-century bourgeois succeeded in integrating this particular penchant with the civilisation he had created.

Music, in the form of singing, was viewed first and foremost as a social bond. As we have already observed, every family celebration and every public ceremony was accompanied by singing. Snobs spoke disdainfully of these melodies, which had, in fact, very genuine qualities, but were derived from the old medieval traditions; their modest charm was not to the liking of lovers of the Italian or French styles.

> *Good evening, Joosje,*
> *My little box of sweetmeats,*
> *Kiss me, we are alone . . .*
> *. . . I call you my heart, my consolation, my treasure.*
> *I swear to you by the skin of Uncle Lubbert's cat,*
> *Oh! oh! how I've tricked you!*[5]

This kind of love-song was naïvely pretentious, sometimes moralising or, on the contrary, almost obscene, and could hardly be expected to please the members of the Muiden circle, whose own pastimes imitated the affectations of the Marquise de Rambouillet's salon. Huyghens composed several ballads for them, in French or Italian, which later formed part of his *Pathodia*. Here is a typical example:

> *Grave witnesses of my delight,*
> *Bushy oaks, lovely precipices,*
> *Since so many summers*
> *Jealous and proud of my happiness,*
> *Do not expect me any longer to go*
> *Anywhere except where love beckons me.* . . .

From the end of the sixteenth century musical societies were established in several towns and developed rapidly during the truce period. Their members were recruited from all social classes. The most distinguished of these *collegia musica* were the Arnhem society, founded in 1591, and the Saint Cecilia Society organised in 1631 by a group of distinguished citizens in Utrecht. Amsterdam acquired its musical society only in 1634.

These associations consisted of about fifteen or twenty members, and met at each participant's house in turn to practise singing, both sacred and secular songs, songs for a single voice and part-songs, or more rarely to practise instrumental music. Subsequently the municipalities took an interest in these meetings and often provided them with premises. The societies designed their own coats of arms, like the guilds, and drew up statutes prescribing a minimum standard of discipline and imposing a certain degree of regularity and dignity on the sessions. A discussion that became too heated, or a quarrel, was subject to a fine of from four to eight florins; a member unable to produce a good excuse for an absence had to make amends by contributing the best bottle from his cellar. The musical exercises ended with a party, but at eleven o'clock the man-servant collected the glasses and wiped off the tables, the signal for everyone to be off home after noting for future reference how much remained in his particular wine-bottle.

Sometimes the society gave a special performance, supplementing its choir with a small orchestra. Under the direction of the local choir-master, a few violins were used to accompany the high voices, and there would be a harpsichord-player. But it was not until the eighteenth century that the Netherlands instituted public concerts where tickets were sold to the audience (unless one counts the low-class *cafés-chantants* that had sprung up). On the other hand, some towns had set up a municipal band; Groningen had possessed one since 1617, equipped with its own uniform. In Utrecht and elsewhere the trumpeters of the guard performed for an hour each day in the main square.

The Reformed Church had originally banned everything except vocal music from its liturgy; but by the beginning of the seventeenth century such austerity was provoking protests, and by 1640 the pressure of public opinion had forced the reintroduction of organ music. The predicants soon discovered how useful the organ was. They invited their organists to give recitals, announced in advance, which were designed to lure the faithful away from the temptations of the *cafés-chantants*. Sometimes special concerts took place after church service or at important festivals, when the choir sang psalms, either in the traditional manner or by fitting the words to secular melodies.

The few musicians of any importance in Dutch music of this era were all organists: Willem, the organist of Amsterdam's New Church; Joan du Sart at Haarlem; Hedrrik Spaen at Dordrecht, so highly regarded that the town paid him a hundred florins for the music he had composed for a psalm. As for Swelinck, the organist of Amsterdam's Old Church, named 'the Phoenix of Music' by Vondel, a group of local notabilities decided to help him financially by making him a present of two hundred florins, but in share certificates, not in cash. The donors had simply invested the sum in their own businesses, in the name of the musician; and from then on they kept him informed as to the profits his capital had earned.

Small groups of strolling musicians played in the villages, at kermises, at weddings, hiring themselves to lovers in need of serenades. Many contemporary paintings delineated these picturesque groups in their habitual rags and tatters, or in fancy dress, and the strange instruments they played in addition to the lute and the penny-whistle: the *bombas*, a long single-stringed violin with a pig's bladder for a sound-box, and the *draailer*, a portable barrel-organ.

BELLES-LETTRES: *The 'Rhetoricians'*
The Dutch were enthusiastic versifiers. The writing of verses was a regular part of daily existence, whether it was a question of dedications, or the greetings inscribed in a friend's album, or the innumerable inscriptions – some ironical, some simply pompous – on public buildings. And people quoted verse at the first opportunity. Even among the petty bourgeoisie, the exchange of verses was an essential aspect of social courtesy. Each town had its poets with their own local reputation, and a few of them really were poets. Amsterdam could count most poets among its population, and Dordrecht came second. Professional rhymesters wrote to order for ungifted amateurs; educated people composed Latin verses, and the Amsterdam Academy awarded an annual Latin poetry prize.

These traditions were preserved by venerable institutions known as 'chambers of rhetoric'. Originally more or less religious medieval associations, these 'chambers' had become amateur literary associations whose members wrote poetry, organised writing contests and produced plays. The humanists despised these relics of a bygone age perpetuating outmoded fashions, and the clumsy versifications of well-meaning folk entirely lacking in literary culture. Even so, the 'chambers of rhetoric' were still very much alive in 1600, except for the north and east of the country, and fulfilled a real social function.

Every town and village had its own 'chamber', holding its meetings in the inn or on premises lent by the local administration. It had a patron and patroness, a motto, a seal, a standard, and a symbolic flower or tree from which it derived its name. The three 'chambers' in Leyden were called respectively the *White Columbine*, the *Orange Lily* and the *Palm-tree*; that in Alkmaar was entitled the *Green Laurel*; those in Schiedam were the *Red Rose* and the *Fig-tree*. A president and a board of elders directed the organisation, sent out notices for meetings, administered the funds, and levied fines. In quest of the approbation and support of the great, they often offered the honorary presidency to a noble or member of the local gentry who was then adorned with the title of 'Prince' or 'Emperor'. The group had its official poet, the *factor*, charged with the drafting of the prize-winners' diplomas and the composition of texts for certain ceremonial occasions. When the 'chamber' wanted to perform a play, the 'factor' allocated the parts and took charge of the production. This individual was also responsible for teaching 'rhetoric', that is to say the rules of versification, to the youngest members.[1] The 'chamber' also had its clown, the 'fool', dressed according to ancient custom in a yellow and green costume, or a blue and white one, with black stripes; his dubious antics were supposed to enliven the meetings. For public appearances the 'rhetoricians' wore a special uniform; in Middelburg, for instance, it was a red toga embroidered with the 'chamber's' arms and with mottoes in silver thread.

The meetings took place on Sundays, after church. Beer and wine were drunk, and everyone spoke in verse, even to call the barman; the eventual account was drawn up in verse. The rules forbade gambling, swearing, naming the devil (except in songs), dirtying the walls and bringing along prostitutes.

The actual 'poetical' activity consisted in the composition of rondeaux, ballads, songs, back-rhymes, verses with double meanings, and the whole of the rest of the bag of tricks from Matthys de Casteleyn's verse manual. Or else the participants got together a dramatic spectacle, in the form of a medievally inspired satirical farce, or an allegorical morality-play, often based on events of the day. Their aim was less to provoke a new emotion than to give the spectator the pleasure of the well-known. They seldom used more than four characters in these compositions, and the comedy resulted from mime rather than from any subtle display of temperament or language.[2] Later on, it became fashionable to produce modern-style tragedies and comedies, but the public continued to prefer the original manner.

At the kermis, at Easter and Whitsuntide, and at some special festivals, the 'rhetoricians' appeared in public. They had sent out invitations to take part to other local 'chambers' months in advance, setting out the chosen theme for the competition (for example, 'Love is the Basis of Everything'), and the number and kind of verses to be used in treating it. Prizes were also awarded for the best decorations, heraldic devices and even the fanfares produced by the competing 'chambers'; the prizes consisted of objects of gold, silver or pewter, goblets, candlesticks or pipes. Sometimes improvisation contests were held, with a member of the jury asking questions and the poets, seated with a sheet of paper on their knee, writing the replies in verse. The first person to finish won a prize. Such festivals attracted large crowds and involved some degree of display, in the form of processions, musical exhibitions, and elaborately prepared stages and rostrums. The local administration took care of the accommodation of the visiting 'rhetoricians' and shared the expenses involved.[3] An added attraction at these ceremonies was often a lottery, with the profits devoted to a cause such as the town's poor-houses.

During the first third of the century the importance of the 'chambers of rhetoric' diminished rapidly in the towns, and many of them disappeared altogether. By 1660 the only ones left were to be found in the villages, and even those were considered by a foreigner such as Parival to be antiquities in the process of dissolution.[4]

The history of Amsterdam's two 'chambers' is significant. The older of the two, the *Eglantine*, founded in 1517, competed with the *White Lavender*, created by Brabantine and Flemish immigrants. By 1614 their quarrels had become so acute that some members of the *Eglantine* withdrew. But this latter 'chamber' included several men of letters such as Hooft, Breero, Vondel and Samuel Coster, who were anxious to throw off traditional inertia and to open up their circle to the fresh breeze of humanism. Faced with these threats of schism, Coster took the initiative in 1617 and formed the liveliest group of the association into an 'Academy' which broke all ties with the 'chambers of rhetoric'.

Coster's Academy was set up in a wooden hut in the centre of town, on ground bought from the municipality, and was inaugurated in 1618 by a performance of the tragedy, *The Murder of William of Orange*. An agreement worked out with the regents of the municipal orphanage put the financial administration in their hands, and they were soon benefiting to the amount of a thousand florins a year. Coster was concerned to renew the rhetorical tradition rather than to abolish it, and his main purpose was to provide the Amsterdam bourgeoisie with a cultural institution worthy of it, one that provided immediate access to classical literary sources. With this aim in mind the Academy proposed originally to organise courses in history, philosophy and aesthetics. But the spirit of such an enterprise smacked of 'free-thinking' and the Church was soon up in arms. The municipal authorities intervened, and finally, in 1623, Coster gave up in disgust. But what he had created was in the process of becoming the Netherlands' first theatrical company. They performed plays by Coster, Vondel and Hoogendorp, the classical Dutch school (more baroque than classical in our sense of the word). The two 'chambers' were unable to compete with such an institution, and in 1635 they surrendered and joined the Academy.

The Theatre and its Actors

By this time Coster was dead and his wooden building was in a state of imminent collapse. The directors of the orphanage decided, in 1637, to invest twenty thousand florins in a new building, to be made of stone. This new theatre was built quickly, despite the machinations of the Church, and was inaugurated by a performance of Vondel's *Gijsbrecht van Aemstel*, a drama exalting the grandeur of Amsterdam. The building comprised a hall surrounded by two tiers of boxes which could be closed by drawing a curtain, an arrangement facilitating the pursuit of romance. A large stage without special lighting was bound on each side by walls symbolising two prisons, and its dimensions narrowed down towards the back, where a raised platform dominated the centre under the pillars of its canopy. On either side of this structure small square spaces framed by columns represented living-rooms. The main action took place on the huge apron-stage. An orchestra was stationed at the foot of the stage, consisting of trumpet, 'cello, violin and lute, whose duty was to provide incidental music and to play during the intervals. The general arrangement derived partly from the traditions of the late Middle Ages, but the building was renovated and modernised in 1664, by which time more modern ideas had come into vogue in the field of theatre design: the stage was deepened, perspectives introduced and mechanical apparatus installed.

This theatre became an important source of revenue for the orphanage, and soon came under the eye of the local administration as well. Although the municipality exercised a certain degree of censorship over the programmes, it also allowed the theatre a complete commercial monopoly, and for this reason Amsterdam rarely had the opportunity of seeing foreign touring companies.

Until 1658 Amsterdam remained the only town in the Netherlands to possess a permanent theatre. The first one in The Hague was built in that year, and in 1664 a prosperous timber-merchant of that town reconstructed a tennis-court to make an opera-house, 'of the usual length of thirty to thirty-two feet';[5] this establishment lasted for nearly forty years. In the absence of a permanent theatre, performances took place either in a tent, a rented hall, private premises, a shed, archery-range, riding-school or even a poor-house refectory; or for a few hundred florins a carpenter would set up a stage and some rows of benches. The show usually ran as long as the fair or kermis taking place at the time, although sometimes it lasted longer. By 1660 it was known for theatrical troupes in major cities to sign contracts for a six-week performance or even, occasionally, for as long as six months.

Even so, the country's theatrical life did not amount to much. Even in Amsterdam, the theatre was open only a few months a year, two days a week. The Church's opposition to this form of entertainment was never relaxed, and created a moral and intellectual climate that was hardly favourable to any development in dramatic art. The town administrations were under constant pressure and were forced into taking restrictive or harassing measures. Theatres were forbidden to give performances at Easter or Christmas, on holy days, on occasions of public mourning, during war-years or years of famine; any excuse was good enough. And the poor devils who were sufficiently in love with their profession to produce plays despite these vexations found themselves hard-pressed by the local tax office.

The members of the audience paid for their admission at the door, and proceeded to the seats marked on their tickets by a central or side aisle. Often the seat would be already occupied, since it was by no means unknown for the administration to increase its profits by selling the same seat twice over. The unlucky one would challenge the first arrival, and if there were not many spare seats left the argument quickly developed into a fist-fight. Once the audience had settled down, women would pass along the rows selling beer, holding a jug in one hand and glasses in the other, while programme-sellers cried their wares. People cracked nuts, munched apples, smoked pipes. Every class and walk of life was jumbled together in this throng. Young girls attended in hopes of a flirtation; beautiful women went there to be seen; pickpockets devoted themselves assiduously to their profession. In the boxes and in the stalls people laughed and fondled their partners, while the actors shouted at the tops of their voices so as to be heard above the din.

The success of the Amsterdam theatre was due in part to the forceful personality of a few actors such as Adam Karels Germes, who, from 1617 onwards, was one of the Coster Academy's leading actors and became a professor of elocution in his old age. Another notable performer was de Boer, the nephew of a governor-general of Java, who preferred the freedom of theatre life to the responsibilities of a high administrative position. And there was Cornelis Bor, who played Agamemnon in Racine's *Iphigenia*. But the general level remained low. For one thing, few of the actors were professionals, though the proportion increased gradually since the amateurs found it impossible to mount a different production each week, as was the habit in Amsterdam. There were very few theatrical companies before 1650, whether occasional or regular performers, settled or itinerant, and they recruited their members from every possible profession – sailors, stevedores, barbers and booksellers. The female roles were originally played by men, and the first actress, Ariane Noozeman, appeared in 1645 in a strolling company. It was not until 1655 that she was allowed to perform at the Amsterdam theatre. Despite the protests of conservatives, this novelty was so much appreciated that the actress was paid the unprecedented salary of four and a half florins a performance.[6] The company divided its profits into two equal portions, one for the communal fund, the other for the support of paupers. As for the author, no one gave him a thought. Vondel never made a penny from any of his plays.

The performances were characterised by grandiloquence and platitude. Until 1650 most of the actors were almost illiterate, and the lack of competent performers sometimes led to strange consequences. In 1670 Blasius translated a Latin comedy for the Amsterdam theatre, and replaced the character of an old father by an old mother, because the company had no one capable of playing the role of a father whereas the actor Baast had made a speciality of playing mothers' parts. The foreign touring companies were not much more competent. Saint-Evremond, attending a performance of *Tartuffe* in The Hague in 1669, adjudged the actors 'reasonably good in comedy, dreadfully bad in tragedy, except for one woman who was excellent in every respect'.[7] In 1687 Misson attended a French opera in Amsterdam which he reported to be poorly staged and badly acted, the least incompetent actress being a stout Dutch-woman playing a man's role, who spoke the French lines fairly well despite the fact that she did not understand a single word.

The first half of the seventeenth century was the golden age for the strolling players, ten or twelve strong, sometimes accompanied by a set-designer, who toured throughout western Europe. As early as 1598 an Italian troupe visited Leyden, but on the whole Italians remained rare until after 1670. On the other hand, a large number of English companies visited the northern and central provinces, and played in Leyden and The Hague on at least twenty occasions between 1590 and 1656. After 1660 the French were the only foreign actors to visit the United Provinces regularly. They had first performed in the country in 1605,[8] and were particularly fond of playing at The Hague, where the court welcomed their appearances and gave them financial support. Prince Maurice granted them safe-conducts; Frederick Henry distributed gratuities among them; William II paid the travelling expenses of troupes he liked. As a result the French placed themselves at the disposal of the court as soon as they arrived in the Netherlands, presenting themselves and requesting permission to play. After the inevitable delays caused by conflicts of jurisdiction, they would install themselves in their chosen premises, often the *Piquerie* riding-school, the largest hall in The Hague, measuring a hundred and twelve feet by thirty-two. A drummer paraded the town rounding up customers, who particularly appreciated the presence of actresses in the French companies. In 1622 a troupe featuring Charles le Noir, Charles Guérin and François Métivier obtained the title of 'The Prince of Orange's Players' and kept it throughout their European peregrinations, until 1655. Shortly afterwards, in 1658, the small tennis-court in The Hague was turned into a permanent French theatre.

At the theatre, the Dutch public demanded either escapist fantasy or, on the contrary, a more or less satirical commentary on contemporary events. When they first appeared, tragedies observing the 'three unities' and containing long harangues did not please the audiences, much to the disappointment of a few well-read people. At the beginning of the century political and other farces and cloak-and-dagger dramas dominated the scene. The great Dutch dramatists such as Coster and Vondel produced work in the classical tradition, but of English rather than French inspiration. Elizabethan dramas were imitated and translated. The most popular author was Jan Vos, a glassmaker by profession, whose terrifying *Arian and Titus* was a favourite choice of the 'rhetoricians' at kermises. A character would collapse on the stage and fake blood pour from a bladder concealed under his jacket. Jan Vos specialised in producing blood-and-thunder epics, was on intimate terms with the Amsterdam aristocracy and became the director of a theatre where he put on performances of Calderon and Lope de Vega, whose exuberant style suited the Dutch public's tastes perfectly.

In a serious vein, Dutch drama drew heavily on the Bible: Vondel's *John the Baptist* and *Lucifer*, Heinsius's *Slaughter of the Innocents*. In 1638 a French company played *The Cid* in The Hague; it created an immediate sensation, and van Heemskerck translated the tragedy into Dutch. It seemed that a movement had been launched. In 1639 Heerman translated one of Mairet's plays, while in 1647 the Grand Pensionary himself, Johan De Witt, translated *Horace*. But the nobleness and spareness of style then triumphing on the French stage hardly fitted into the framework of this bourgeois society, and the influence of such works on Dutch drama remained very small for a long time. Their chief support was provided by the *Nil volentibus arduum* society, founded in Amsterdam in 1669 to encourage the study and imitation of French classicism. The members of the 'Nil' published several theoretical and critical works, as well as translating or adapting Corneille, Racine, Quinault and Molière, and producing their work at the municipal theatre. Between 1680 and 1700 about fifty French tragedies and comedies were presented in this way. From then on the cause was won and the old Dutch drama disappeared completely; the francomania which was unleashed around 1670 triumphed on the stage as it had already triumphed in dress fashions and the use of coffee.

Some of the nobles at the court in The Hague, and a few members of the gentry, cultivated unobtrusively a fashionable theatrical activity involving performances given for their own entertainment or for their children's edification. For example, in 1605 the Huyghens children acted Bèze's *Abraham Sacrificing* at their own home before a fashionable audience. In 1641 the daughters of the widowed Queen of Bohemia, refugees in The Hague, presented Corneille's *Medea*.

In the 'Latin schools', an ancient tradition survived of using the theatre as a means of teaching languages. Particularly on the occasion of prize-giving ceremonies, classic Latin or Greek tragedies and comedies were acted before a chosen public; the municipality paid the expenses and rewarded the best actors. But the theologians questioned whether such a practice might not run counter to moral exigencies, and therefore the curators imposed a censorship on the material. In the schools where French was taught religious plays or moral tracts were occasionally played in that language.

Dramatic performances often ended with a ballet; or sometimes, this latter was staged during the interval. Dutch ballet derived from a native tradition which remained entirely free from foreign influences until the eighteenth century. Its basic inspiration was provided by the old kermis dances and the diversions carried out in the chambers of rhetoric, while the choreographic themes borrowed from peasant round-songs, popular songs and sailors' hornpipes.

As for opera, it was first brought to The Hague in mid-century by French companies, but never made any headway outside that city.

Men and Women of Letters

Poets, novelists and historians during this 'golden age' of Dutch civilisation were very conscious of belonging to a society in which they fulfilled their essential function by being officials or businessmen. They had no sense of being professional men of letters, and their verse or prose was nothing more than an adornment of their life or an instructive testimony. Even among the most cultured of them, the admiration of classic beauty had an essentially abstract quality about it; an ideal, heroic, sculpted world interposed itself, in their imagination, between reality and the act of writing. Hooft's *Account of Conflict* viewed recent Dutch history through the eyes of a Tacitus, and gave full weight to the self-satisfaction of the triumphant bourgeoisie of 1640-50, while ignoring the nation's complex vitality. Heinsius was a powerful and pompous individual, but basically just a poetaster despite the correspondence he carried on with various Parisian men of letters. The people's temperament during the epoch when the then impoverished Republic was founded had been better symbolised by the vulgarly moralising realism and the coarse gaiety of the old 'chambers of rhetoric' or by the zest of the sixteenth century's 'vagabond' poets.

The bourgeois citizen had not developed into a literary type. Literature had only been able to present him in the tawdry finery of ancient times, or in caricature. Literature was too bound up with ideas in an era when analytical thought was still undeveloped, and so failed to achieve what the pure art of painting succeeded in portraying magnificently. On the occasions when a writer attempted to grasp living reality, he only managed to achieve anecdote, and his incapacity was accentuated by the fact that, unlike the painters, the writers belonged mostly to the ruling classes and were strictly conservative in their political views. The popularity of the poet Cats was due less to literary than to religious and moral reasons.

The influence of English, Italian and even French baroque was very marked during the first half of the century. Sydney's *Arcadia* was translated and then rewritten. From *Astraea* to the works of La Calprenède and Madeleine de Scudéry, every successful French novel produced its Dutch imitation. A cloying style was decorated with the trappings of mythology and allegory, and the resulting preference for the romantically poetical soon emptied the 'chambers of rhetoric' of all those with any intellectual pretensions. The farther the century progressed, the more involuted literary form became and the more it tended towards solemnity, if not turgidity.

Nevertheless, several first-class authors emerged from this horde of amateurs, and their work represents the real worth of seventeenth-century Dutch literature. One of the most noteworthy was Gerbrand Adriaenszen Breero (1585-1618) of Amsterdam, the son of a wealthy shoemaker. Although he was accepted into the town's literary circles and enjoyed a considerable reputation in them, he had had no classical education. In fact, his ignorance of Latin probably helped to strengthen the bonds which attached him to his native language and to the living people who spoke it.

Breero drew his inspiration from these ordinary people, and the themes of his work from their seething, vital existence. Originally a painter, Breero was a man of powerful originality, and retained from his first profession an observant eye, an awareness of colour and shape, a sense of caricature and a vigorous nature. He possessed humour and eloquence, and embodied the spirit of the Renaissance without ever copying a formula. He died at the age of thirty-three, leaving a considerable body of work: love songs, folk songs, satirical songs, as well as several cloak-and-dagger dramas, and the plays and farces whose dramatic perfection ensured him a lasting success, first at the Chamber, then at the Academy.

Pieter Corneliszoon Hooft (1581–1647) formed a sharp contrast to Breero. The son of an Amsterdam burgomaster, Hooft belonged to the aristocracy of the 'regents' with their free-thinking, humanist inclinations. At the age of seventeen he left for France, Germany and, finally, Italy where he spent three years, won over by its art, its landscapes and its language. He read Petrarch, Tasso and Guarini. On his return he studied law and letters at Leyden, and in 1609 assumed the magistracy of Muiden. From then on he divided his time between his Muiden mansion, which he made his summer residence, and Amsterdam. He had sensitive tastes and a real love of beauty. He was also sociable and liked to surround himself with men whose talents blossomed forth under the influence of his scientific knowledge and worldly experience. Soon after his return from abroad he had his play *Granida* acted by the rhetoricians, but this pastoral of Italian inspiration proved unpopular with the public. In 1614 he presented *Geeraert van Velsen*, the first modern-style tragedy in Dutch, but it received a mixed reception. His comedy *Warenar* was more successful. Hooft was less good as a playwright than as a writer of historical works composed in a rich, pointed, almost obscurely laconic style, influenced by Latin models. These were really works of magnificent eloquence rather than history properly speaking. As a man of letters Hooft may be considered the Guez de Balzac of the Netherlands. But he was above all a poet, especially a writer of love poems, songs and sonnets in which the mannered style contrasted with a vigorous liveliness. The author was entranced by a vision of formal beauty deriving from his complete spiritual involvement in the Italian Renaissance in all its most exquisite refinements.

Constantin Huyghens (1596–1687) was close to Hooft in some respects, but less endowed with a sense of harmony and subtlety. The son of a wealthy family from The Hague, a doctor of law, he was to become the father of the scholar Christiaan Huyghens. In his youth he had been a member of embassies in England and Venice, and in 1626 he became secretary to the Stadtholder, a post he retained under three successive reigns. Although a high state dignitary surrounded by honours, Huyghens remained accessible and never abandoned his all-embracing interest in all the arts and sciences; a warm-hearted, easygoing man, he was as much at home among the bourgeoisie as at court. His poetry was certainly unequal in quality, but at its best was characterised by a richness of imagery which won the praise of Vondel, and by a constant search for rare expressions, obscure allusions, exotic combinations. Huyghens aimed at a maximum of expressiveness through a minimum number of words. The lines of his verses were crammed with words, explosively dense, their syntax bunched up or contorted, suddenly bursting out into *concetti*. He used no great themes, and most of his subjects were taken from everyday life. His poem *Batavian Tempe* described the Voorhout of The Hague during the four seasons. *The Precious Banquet* vituperated the futile love of fashion and the stupid kinds of luxury. His body of work included at least three thousand impromptus and epigrams.

This school of Amsterdam was dominated by the figure of Joost van den Vondel (1587–1679), 'the prince of Dutch poets', the Corneille, if not the Shakespeare, of the Netherlands. Vondel was born in Cologne, his father being an Anabaptist refugee from Antwerp who came to Amsterdam towards the end of the sixteenth century to found a stocking-making business. The son was trained to take over the business eventually, and so had little opportunity for a formal education. It was only as an adult that he learnt French, German, Latin and the Sciences. When he did inherit the business he put the shop into the hands of his wife, and devoted himself to the world of letters. He began to write in 1612. After being financially ruined later by the activities of his son, he became the accountant of the Loan bank, and passed the last twenty years of his life in very modest circumstances. His conversion to Catholicism in 1614 had alienated friends like Coster, van Baerle and de Groot, with whom he had shared the years of his youth.

Vondel was a man who typified his epoch; he was even-tempered and good-natured, a good citizen, a faithful friend, a model husband and father, keenly aware of all his century's happenings – in short, a paragon of Dutch virtue. His work seemed to give expression to something quite different from the tranquil life he led, being deeply introspective, enlightened by his acute perception of the world, enriched by a solid culture, enlivened by a great freedom of syntax and, at its best, achieving universal dimensions. The United Provinces' 'Golden Age' found its image reflected in his work, among other images of celestial or infernal forces going beyond its limits. His work included occasional verse, historical poems, social, political and religious satires, in addition to a series of dramas filled with lyricism and with a didactic quality that achieved occasionally a state of pure meditation. The great formal richness of the language was forged from a tremendously individual perception, obscure by reason of its very inventiveness; his work provided the culmination of the creative efforts of writers from the final war period, such as Marnix, Coornhert and Spieghel, and transcended their creative efforts.

The so-called Dordrecht school provided a complete contrast to that of Amsterdam; its traditionalism and its opposition to modern humanism was symbolised in its leader Jacob Cats (1577–1660). His triumphant success may well seem almost incredible to us today, yet the seventeenth century shows no career more brilliant than his, nor any more intimately bound up with the history of an entire people. Cats was a native of Zeeland, born in Brouwershaven in the island of Schouwen-Duiveland, brought up in Zierikzee, and a student at Leyden and then at Orleans. From 1626 he assumed high public offices: first he became pensionary of Middelburg, then of Dordrecht, then of the province of Holland; he was ambassador to England on several occasions, and ended his days peaceably in his country house at Scheveningen, leaving an enormous mass of writings. It was in vain that his more enlightened contemporaries poked fun at his platitudes, his monotony, his total ignorance of the ideals of brevity, allusion and humour. 'Father Cats', as he was known, possessed neither the vigour of Vondel, the harmoniousness of Hooft, nor the ebullience of Huyghens, but in the eyes of the Dutch bourgeoisie of the era he was 'the Poet'. After the Bible, his work was the nation's favourite reading matter. Cats was an integral part of the nation, sharing all its faults and virtues, and incarnating the Calvinist spirit of the times. His avowed aim was not the quest of beauty in its own right but the moral support of the average Dutchman's family life by genteel, edifying stories. His theme subject was daily life itself, with its small events and habits offering him familiar material for his didactically inclined homilies. He had an infallible instinct for striking exactly the right note in delineating the reader, recording his true face, his natural likes and dislikes, and the mentality which justified established custom and strengthened it. His greatness lay in the extraordinary degree in which he combined these facilities.

These five names could be supplemented by others. Literary circles had sprung to life throughout the country; it became fashionable to exchange visits and correspondence, to build a universe of words and beautiful thoughts.

Societies were set up in which sonnets and odes were written and then published in collections; the members held literary debates and critical discussions of each other's work. The society's headquarters were usually established in the home of one of its members, but rather than being a 'salon' in the Parisian sense it was more like one of those little 'academies' which were so common throughout the French countryside during the same era. Statutes were propounded and prizes awarded. Local notabilities made it a point of honour to join, and if they were not blessed with poetic gifts, at least they paid up. The chambers of rhetoric became more and more outmoded, retaining the affections only of the most vulgar spirits. By the end of the century the literary societies had superseded them entirely.[9]

Among the prosperous merchant-class of the big towns, a few literary circles had more liberal tendencies, being influenced by some strong personality who surrounded himself with a group of sophisticated, literary, artistically-minded people. Such a group existed in Amsterdam, under the aegis of Roemer Visscher, a shopkeeper's son who had become a wealthy grain-merchant, and was cultivated, jovial and an occasional writer of satirical poetry. His way of life was more like that of some Italian patrician. He belonged to the progressive faction of the *Eglantine*. Anna and Maria Tesselschade,[10] his two daughters, enlivened his beautiful house on the embankment; they were talented young women, whose father had given them a broad education including calligraphy, drawing, music, dancing and embroidery, as well as the applied arts of modelling in clay and glass-engraving, the sports of swimming and riding, and the study of languages and history. These two sensitive and charming personalities, devotees of poetry, painting, engraving and music, formed the nucleus of Amsterdam's most dazzling mid-century intellectual *salon*. Every worthwhile literary and philosophical achievement in this city originated in their house, and Vondel evoked the memory of 'Roemer's blessed house, where the floors and hearth-stones are worn smooth by the tread of painters, actors, singers and poets'.[11]

Nevertheless, the movement centring around the Visschers

remained somewhat artificial in this seething town dedicated to profit-making activities. The kind of poetry encouraged by these ladies was restricted to such things as madrigals. Anna, the more lively, and Maria, the more tender, were the *précieuses* of the Netherlands, the literary leaders of polite society. Maria reached the age of twenty-nine before she married, sharing with her French colleagues a profound distaste for all conjugal ties.

From 1609, when Hooft was appointed magistrate of Muiden, his mansion there housed the most active centre of Dutch literary preciosity. The house was about thirteen miles to the east of Amsterdam, on the bank of the Zuider Zee, a splendid Gothic fortress surrounded by pleasant gardens. Literary groups met there between 1609 and 1647, during almost exactly the same period as the Hôtel de Rambouillet held sway in Paris (1610–52).

Maria Visscher was the leading light of this circle, and continued to frequent it even after her marriage. It was she who introduced her young friend Francisca Duarte into the company. Vondel, Constantin Huyghens, the scholarly ex-governor of the Indies Reael, and the professors Vos and van Baerle were among the regular attendants at these soirées. Van Baerle held the chair of Latin oratory at the university, and was a typical personality of the Amsterdam literary world, an exuberant, carefree Renaissance man, fond of pretty women and always eager for opportunities, in conversation or poetry, to display his pointed wit and erudition. Like him, the other habitués of Muiden enjoyed exploring anything bizarre or complicated, devising parodies and puns. The composition of verses to set rhymes was a favourite diversion. Hooft once wrote Maria a long letter consisting entirely of mythological allusions, just to inform her that she had left her slippers at his house.

But the Muiden circle was something more than a mere symbol of literary preciosity, and Vondel firmly rejected such a definition.[12] Their aim was not so much to foster elegance of expression (indeed, they were remarkably outspoken in conversation) as to mould manners and emotions, in reaction to the prevailing uncouthness. The atmosphere of Muiden was one of stoicism, and the circle constituted the ultimate manifestation of the Renaissance on Dutch soil, an artistic Renaissance stripped of unnecessary luxury. Hooft and his guests were all prosperous people, but led an unpretentious and, in fact, very bourgeois existence. In the mansion's 'knights' hall', with its high ceiling of waxed beams and its walls hung with heavy draperies, they would gather around the vast medieval fireplace and read Lucian or Giambattista Marini, submit in turn their latest poem to the judgement of the assembly, or accompany Francisca Duarte on the lute or theorbo as she sang one of Huyghens's sonnets. Or they would spend the afternoon walking in the country, gossiping and playing pranks on each other; one day they raided the garden of a certain Heer Schaep for artichokes.

Books and Publishing

The Dutch were avid readers. Books were widely circulated, and their use was not reserved for a few privileged people as was the case in most other European countries at that time. The illustrated edition of the poems of Cats, a relatively expensive book, had sold fifty thousand copies by 1655, a fantastic figure for that era.[13] Reading aloud, usually accompanied by a commentary or discussion, was one of the regular features of family life. Books were bought, but each family also had its collection of books handed down from previous generations and read and reread with the same pleasure.

The predicants recommended the reading of the Bible and of various edifying works which formed the basic library of most bourgeois households: *The Threshold of Paradise, The Garden of the Heart*, collections of sermons, more or less allegorical catechisations that were to be found even in army tents and ships' cabins. Catholics were still reading *The Lives of the Saints*. But the taste for reading went far beyond these limits. Descriptive moral poetry was appreciated for its narrative rather than its form. One of the most widely read books in 1650 was Guevara's adaptation of Marcus Aurelius's *Meditations* translated from the Spanish. Collections of apophthegms drawn from the Bible or from Erasmus, or fashioned by some contemporary pen, catered for a national fondness for maxims and proverbs.

The old romances of chivalry remained popular. During a period of seven years, from 1644 to 1651, the Amsterdam bookseller Cool reprinted *The Knight of the Swan*, *Sir Frederick van Jennen*, *The Destruction of Jerusalem* and *The Seven Sages of Rome*, the final expressions of a literature going back to the thirteenth century. The story of *The Four Sonnes of Aymon* was still read in the schools. Modern taste preferred *Astraea* and its imitations such as *The History of Damon*, published in Hoorn in 1634, which developed one of the episodes from d'Urfé's romance. *Don Quixote* was read in translation. The classical authors were read, either in the original or in translation, according to the individual's cultural level; not only the great classics but such books as Apuleius's *Golden Ass* and *The Life of Aesop*. None of this reading matter was specifically designed for children, apart from a few collections of Bible stories and dismal moral tracts such as *The Ladder of Youth* and the *Children's Mirror of the Dutch Wars*.

Works of popular science sold well, but more popular still were travel books based on the diaries or reminiscences of navigators. Bontekoe's *Journal* of his voyage to the Far East, published in 1646, ran to fifty editions. The Amsterdam bookseller Commelin had tremendous success with a book he published in 1644 consisting of twenty-one accounts of voyages to the Indies. Carelessly written, and without any literary pretension, these books approached the heart of everyday life; the authors were chiefly concerned to furnish useful information for navigation and trade, though their prose showed unwittingly an occasional love of the marvellous and a biblical moralism. A few of these accounts had a genuine scientific character, such as the works in which the orientalist Cornelis de Bruyn described the two voyages he made in the Near East and then in Russia and Central Asia, financed by the burgermaster of Amsterdam.

The publishers of travel books also issued land-maps and sea-charts, atlases, and maps of towns, all printed most carefully and sometimes with consummate artistry. A classic in this field was Mercator's *Atlas*, published in 1604 in Amsterdam by the engraver Hondius. The productions of the Amsterdam geographer and publisher Blaeu were famous throughout Europe, and people came from Paris to consult him. The quality of book production in the Netherlands during the sixteenth century was very inferior, despite the fact that Haarlem could boast of having been the birthplace of Lourens Janszen Koster, the inventor of the printing-press. There was a shortage of books, and scholars had to order them from Germany, Switzerland, France and Italy – a risky business, since the lengthy process of transportation by stage-coach exposed them to dampness and consequent mildew. Apart from Leyden, no town possessed a public library, except perhaps for a motley collection of works of piety. But the book industry developed rapidly after 1580, and in 1584 the celebrated Plantin of Antwerp became printer to Leyden University. During the first half of the century two hundred and forty-four 'booksellers' were registered in the Amsterdam guild, while the number had grown to four hundred and seventy-six during the second half. The word 'bookseller' usually meant printer and publisher as well, the three functions being combined without any specialisation. At Blaeu's establishment ten presses were working full time. Professional translators such as Glaze-maker provided an endless flow of manuscripts, embracing every category from philosophy to history and music.

The development of this industry was bound up with the manufacture of paper. From the end of the sixteenth century Dordrecht, Utrecht and Alkmaar all had their own paper-mills, and during the first years of the seventeenth century mills were set up in Gelderland and the Zaandam area. After 1672 Zaandam became the principal centre. Although the Elzevirs continued to import French paper, Holland paper was at a premium on the market and was widely sold outside the country. Rags were accumulated by specialised buyers, ground between millstones, and disintegrated in a bath of very pure water, a process which restricted the locations suitable for the industry. The pulp was rolled out in long wooden troughs, during which process it acquired its water-mark depicting the manufacturer's arms, and was then laid on strips of felt to dry. After being exposed to the air under cover, the sheets underwent treatment in alum and size. These operations demanded great dexterity, and the members of the guild of paper-makers had tremendous pride in their profession: 'journeymen' in search of work carried a diploma couched in verse.

The printer had his own type-founder, corrector, typographers and binder. Bindings were made of glued or stapled leather. The general quality of Dutch book-making was famous throughout Europe, and in 1640 one of the Elzevir brothers made several trips between Leyden and Paris to obtain French commissions. A good deal of speculation was engaged in, especially when a particular edition was much in demand and copies became scarce, or when the condemnation or official disapproval of a book provided the opportunity to sell it clandestinely. Since book-printing was subject to regulations, the sale and distribution of books fell within the competence of the municipal councils. But since the legislation varied from one district to another, according to the interests of local trade, there was in fact a large measure of freedom of publication, despite the censorship; it was simply necessary to know the shady side of the business.

This situation proved most profitable to enterprising printers, and explains why a certain number of French works were published in Holland from the beginning of the seventeenth century onwards. After 1680, with the fresh outbreak of anti-Calvinism in France and the increase in non-conformist writings, the printing of French texts in Holland increased enormously. But as early as 1613 a Dutch editor had published, both in the original and in translation, the works of the dissident Calvinist Castellion, the apostle of tolerance.

In 1648 Elzevir published Balzac's *Selected Letters*, aided by the fact that the author had lived in Holland and had remained in touch with his acquaintances there. Books were often printed on the basis of a manuscript sent from France;

sometimes reproductions were simply made of French original editions which were out of print, or were confidential, or had been seized. Descartes was in Holland when he wrote his *Discourse on Method*, and the printing of the book was undertaken by the bookseller Jean Le Maire of Leyden; the contract between author and publisher, signed in the presence of a notary, is still in existence.[14] In it, the author undertakes to collaborate with the publisher in distributing the book in France; the publisher claims the right to arrange two impressions, of which one may be in a country other than Holland, these not to exceed three thousand copies. After the entire edition has been sold, or any unsold copies rebought by the author, the latter regains the copyright to his work. As payment Descartes receives two hundred personal copies.

CHAPTER SIX

DUTCH SOCIETY

---

*The Power of the Hierarchies: Class Distinctions, Social
Exclusiveness—The People: Bourgeoisie, Workers, Seamen,
Peasants—Paupers and Criminals—The Armed Forces—
Foreigners and Refugees.*

THE POWER OF THE HIERARCHIES: *Class Distinctions*
The first years of the seventeenth century saw the passions
of a rebellious people blunted not only by the weariness
engendered by a protracted war but also by the enormous
development in large-scale commerce. Yet the struggle
for freedom had altered the nation's social structures
radically, for the possession of wealth and political power
gave rise to social distinctions at the same time as it satisfied
people's acquisitive fervour. The new ruling classes were
generally tolerant and practised an oligarchic authoritarianism
whose preoccupations seldom went much further than local
economic interests. They were quick to resent any imagined
slight by a prince. But the classes that were destined to be
ruled retained all their old reflexes; their political enthus-
iasms were dominated by a strong emotional attachment to
the House of Orange, the descendants of the liberating hero.
The quarrels of the theologians often found their echoes in
the streets, with reactions leading sometimes to extreme
violence. This opposition of class interests was aggravated
by the fact that political and economic power was concentrated in the same hands; in a Republic where everyone
paid taxes and where everyone had an equal right to buy a
share in the East India Company, the actual privileges
enjoyed by the powerful without any legal basis appeared to
the masses as a brutal form of oppression.

Although, in this sense, Dutch society was two centuries in

advance of European evolution,[1] it remained archaic in many respects and deeply rooted in the Middle Ages; hence some of the contrasts it presented. The towns had bought their freedom dearly, through a long war, but their idea of freedom was similar to that of the old 'communes' ('free towns'). Although trade had been developed on a world scale through the energies of a few clever businessmen, commercial methods remained imprisoned within the ancient conventions of the guilds. Even among 'property-owners', the wealthiest financier and the most modest shopkeeper shared the customs, morals and ways of thinking of the bourgeoisie of previous ages – equally conservative, methodical, opinionated, law-abiding, distrustful of all innovations and, to some extent, proud of their narrowness of judgement.

The further Dutch activity extended in the world the more their habits were affected by foreign influences, but since these influences were felt closely by certain sections of the population and only remotely or not at all by others, they only served to accentuate social differences. After 1650 French customs and manners were increasingly adopted by the nobility, the officers of the army and a few rich bourgeois, but this influence never reached further than the villages close to The Hague; the southern region of the province of Holland was much affected by the French vogue, to the disgust of the rest of the country. By 1680 a shop-keeping petty bourgeoisie found itself facing an increasingly frenchified, wealthy exclusive caste on one side and, on the other, the poverty-stricken, unenlightened masses who remained almost impervious to outside influences right up to the end of the eighteenth century, while offering no more than a feeble image of the prodigious courage and resoluteness of the previous century's 'Sea Beggars'.

After 1610 the divisions between the social classes became more clearly defined with each succeeding generation. A pamphlet published in Amsterdam in 1665 deplored the fact that class-distinctions were becoming blurred in the large towns because of a general taste for sartorial elegance. 'I am disgusted,' cried the author, 'when I see a tailor's wife flouncing around in velvet. . . .'[2] His moral was that one should not be deceived by appearances, and his complaint at least showed that a certain equalisation was capable of imposing itself from above, at least between the upper and lower middle classes. The upper classes reacted quickly against this tendency by erecting barriers of etiquette around their caste. Human relations remained gentle, for violence of expression remained alien to the national temperament, and foreigners continued to marvel at the atmosphere of general good will. Nevertheless, the linguistic nuances of polite society maintained the necessary distances.

A complex system of titles and nomenclatures emphasised social distinctions. Some terms, such as *monsieur* and *seigneur* were borrowed from the French, others were supplied by national tradition. Members of the States-General were 'most mighty *seigneurs*', Admiralty officials were 'noble and austere *seigneurs*' and their wives were addressed as *madame*, the burgomaster was *monseigneur* and the surgeon, lawyer or guild president was *maître*. With this jargon, society raised a dividing wall which was not to be surmounted with impunity. A professor was a 'venerable and most learned *seigneur*', while merchants assumed different titles according to the extent and prosperity of their affairs. The veneration in which the idea of commerce was held is indicated by the fact that a man named de Vries, trading in edible fats, would be addressed as '*seigneur* de Vries in oil'. Small artisans contented themselves with the French title of *monsieur*. But these terms became gradually devalued and by the end of the century people were calling their barber *seigneur*, the word (which, in fact, had never had the aristocratic connotation it possessed in France) having lost all significance, to the indignation of those concerned with rank and precedence. It is true that familiar modes of address avoided these exaggerations, and at least the habit of emphasising the profession of the person addressed (*monsieur le docteur, monsieur le pasteur, monsieur mon maître* and so on) indicated his social function. Correct designation was considered so important that a magistrate, for example, was quite likely to return a communication whose heading omitted the mode of address to which he was entitled.

But in comparison with the France of that day, this apparently compartmentalised society hardly amounted to more than one of the 'orders' retained by the French from their old medieval traditions. In the Netherlands, only the 'third estate' really existed. The few remaining members of the nobility had outlived their day. The Catholic clergy had been driven into a semi-clandestine existence, and the Calvinist predicants hardly constituted a real 'corps'. For this reason, the social – and political – distinctions in the Netherlands differed from those prevailing in the rest of seventeenth-century Europe in that they were almost exclusively based on economic differences. These differences are difficult to calculate, even approximately. There is no lack of documents relative to the living standards of the upper classes, but it is not often possible to determine accurately what proportion of a merchant's fortune derived from business affairs and private income respectively. We possess some information on workmen's wages, thanks to guild contracts and regulations, but the incomes of other categories of the population are unknown to us today.[3] We can at least indicate the financial hierarchy.

At the top of the pyramid was a small group of financiers such as Lopez Suasso, of Portuguese origin, who in 1688 was able to lend William III the two million florins he needed for his English expedition. The biggest ratepayer in Amsterdam in 1624 possessed a fortune estimated at a million.[4] Although these figures were huge in terms of the nation's income, they remained very modest in comparison with the biggest fortunes of the land-owning nobility of adjoining countries.

In the Netherlands land owners constituted a far less prosperous class. There were few great properties, and land revenue seldom exceeded two and a half per cent, according to Temple.[5] The important State offices held by nobles and upper class citizens were unremunerative; the occupants of these offices were supposed to sacrifice themselves to the public good, and they could only afford to hold their rank by entering into commerce, buying shares in one of the companies or investing a family legacy. The admiral commanding the fleet received an honorarium of five thousand florins on the eve of the 1672 war; the Pensionary of Holland, who was then, in fact, the Republic's first magistrate, received two thousand.[6] A merchant of average importance could theoretically enjoy equal or superior buying power.

An Amsterdam bookseller with a flourishing business paid fifty florins in taxes at one-half per cent, implying a cash capital of ten thousand florins supplemented by letters of credit to a value of twelve thousand florins. This business-man lived well in an attractive house, possessed silverware and comfortable furniture, and had purchased in advance a tomb in the old Church for himself and his wife. One can only guess at his annual income: several thousand florins, certainly, and perhaps as many as ten thousand. Amster-dam's 1630 fiscal registers mention about fifteen hundred fortunes of from twenty-five to fifty thousand florins. Compensation awarded in that year to distinguished individuals whose estates had been destroyed by natural disaster amounted to as much as twenty and thirty thousand florins.[7] The nation's wealth was widely and fairly evenly distributed among the mass of the bourgeoisie, and a few dozen very wealthy families were more than balanced by a large leisured class. On the other hand, most wage-earners in commerce and industry enjoyed a far lower standard of living, although the wages in small businesses, controlled rigorously by the guilds, were generally higher than those in large-scale manufacture where the proprietor was able to lay down rates of pay.

The average wage remained extremely modest. A carpenter in a navy yard earned half a stuiver an hour in 1600, so that with a work-day of about twelve hours his annual income amounted to less than a hundred florins (even if fully employed throughout the year). In 1662 a mason working full-time earned a maximum of twenty-four stuivers a day, or about three hundred and sixty florins a year; but he had to provide and maintain his own tools.[8] It would be unwise to compare these two figures, since wages continued to rise during the entire century. Cloth shearers,

who in Amsterdam in 1607 received a daily wage of fourteen
stuivers, an amount considered 'reasonable', obtained a
series of rises during the ensuing years; by 1631 they were
getting eighteen stuivers a day, that is to say about two
hundred and seventy florins a year.[9]

However, this advance did not in general imply a higher
standard of living, since during the same period the price-
index had risen and outpaced wage increases.[10] Without
taking local variations into consideration, the price-index
for staple commodities had risen from 100 in 1580 to 166
in 1620 and 250 in 1650, and between 1650 and 1655 the
curve reached its peak.[11] Bad crops and wars made some
years, including 1623 and 1630, particularly difficult.
Throughout the century foreign travellers considered
Holland an expensive country to live in. In 1620 the wife
of the French professor Rivet objected to her husband
accepting the chair offered him at Leyden because she found
prices too high and salaries too low in this country. The
increasing cost of rentals aggravated this situation. An
averagely large house rented for one hundred and forty-five
florins a year in Leyden in 1631, while a luxurious house in
Amsterdam in 1675 cost seven hundred florins a year. The
revenue officials increased costs further by imposing a tax
of one-eighth on rentals. As the century advanced the
development of commerce widened the disparity between
living standards; large fortunes accumulated faster than
smaller ones, and in the larger towns the wage-earners
became proletarianised despite the fact that in 1690 wages
in the Dutch guilds were 16 per cent higher than in
England.[12] The more the gap widened, the more strained
became class relations, and among the most underprivileged
section of the population spiritual traditions atrophied. By
1700 all popular culture, in the sense of a collective
consciousness, had disappeared from the principal urban
centres.[13]

Social Exclusiveness
The word 'court', so full of glamour for a seventeenth-century
Frenchman, was not unknown in the Netherlands. It was

used (*het Hof*) but without undue significance. The Stadt-holder had no real political power, was an arbiter (within strict limits) rather than a depository of sovereignty, and could not possibly have fashioned a Versailles around him even if he had wanted to. His responsibilities were ill-defined and fitted awkwardly into the state structure. During fifteen years Frederick Henry exploited cleverly the reputation he enjoyed and achieved almost the status of a monarch. Then the stadtholdership was abolished in 1651, to be re-established in 1672, and so the vicissitudes of the royal house continued throughout the century.

The dominant influence of the bourgeoisie imposed a relatively simple style of life on the princes of Orange. Of the three palaces at The Hague, one was nothing more than a very imposing, fortress-like, baronial manor; the second was a luxurious patrician residence; as for the 'House in the Wood', the local Luxembourg, it was just a pleasant country estate. The Prince's income, derived from his personal estate and from the sums voted to him for his military offices, would not have sufficed to provide a royal retinue. In any case, with the exception of that great innovator Frederick Henry, no members of the House of Orange had any of the qualities likely to attract a brilliant society around them. None of the progenitors of this century of progress emerged from this milieu of officers, women of the nobility, minor courtiers and throngs of transient foreigners. Frederick Henry's bride, Amalia van Solms, made attempts during the second quarter of the century to create a court worthy of this great man and of a country at the height of its power, but she only succeeded in drawing the coterie of princes even more closely around her and estranging herself from the nation; the court was an isolated island, a French-inspired colony out of touch with the real Holland. The palace's population became swollen with a swarm of uniformed pages in Spanish-style breeches, and with young French and German nobles holding ranks in the Dutch army. Plays, concerts, masquerades, balls, horse-races, hunts and even tourneys created a simulacrum of Versailles' feverish activity, but the true soul was missing.

All this was merely a façade, and one that was a constant source of annoyance to rigid moralists among the bourgeoisie. The King of France addressed Frederick Henry as 'Your Highness', and the King of England offered the hand of his own daughter in marriage to the Stadtholder's son. No one spoke Dutch any longer at court; French was the only language heard, and everyone dressed in the French style and ate French dishes. A section of the middle classes aped these manners, but with completely sterile effect. William II, disdainful of politics, sophisticated, a woman-chaser, involved in a scandalous liaison with the French actress La Barre, was the supreme example of the court's isolation from popular feeling. During the twenty years when the stadtholdership was abolished the court survived in a diminished form, more than ever wrapped up in its own intrigues.

These things mattered little to the humble mass of peasants and labourers, who were still living mentally in the time of William the Silent. In a 1660 painting Jan Steen depicts for us these worthy folk celebrating the Prince's birthday in a tavern.[14] A pathetic prince, this future William III, dancing ballets in his palace at The Hague, during the course of ghastly parties like the one he gave to celebrate the 1668 peace treaty: the guests wedged tightly together throughout a long night, struggling towards ill-provided refreshment-tables, fainting away for want of air, while other unfortunates signalled wildly through the windows of the riding-arena which had been turned into a dance-hall for the occasion, pleading with servants to bring them glasses of beer or wine from outside.

The nobility, descended from enfeoffed families in the Middle Ages, was very unequally represented in the Netherlands during this period, being non-existent in the north and in Friesland, but relatively numerous and politically active in the rural areas of Gelderland and Overijssel. In the west, the war of liberation had decimated it, and in 1620 there were only thirty-five noble families left in the province of Holland. Thus, the nobility constituted a narrow social fringe, integrated into the new social order, whose members furnished the Union with a part of its administrative and military officer-class. But its real power was greatly reduced by the way it was represented in parliament; in the States of Holland, for instance, the corps of nobles possessed only one vote as opposed to the eighteen votes available to the urban bourgeoisie. No more titles of nobility were conferred, so that titles became extinct, or else the family would overcome its strong prejudices against misalliances and allow itself to be tainted with bourgeois blood. In reaction to this sad state of affairs, certain nobles affected an exaggerated pride in their exclusivity, sent their cook, tailor and architect to study in France and copied the manners of Versailles. But this was the privilege of a fortunate minority; many impoverished lordlings were difficult to distinguish from the peasants among whom they lived, and limited their ambitions to becoming village notables, while dreaming of a vanished past.

The nobility lived like exiles in the heart of a nation of traders and merchants, refusing absolutely to engage in trade of any kind. They stayed in their castles and manors, moving sometimes to a town-house during the winter. They engaged in the study of literature and mathematics, devoted themselves to hunting and agriculture, and offered their services to the State. They accomplished their responsibilities honestly and were generally highly thought of. Parival admired the courtesy, moderation and wisdom of these gentlemen. But he added: 'Any who are violent, arrogant or haughty find themselves held in contempt in their turn, since they have no rights of constraint or subjection to exercise, and therefore the commoners have no reason to do honour to any except those who merit it through their gentle and engaging manners.'[15] Whether it liked it or not, the Dutch nobility had become part of the bourgeois scene. It had accepted the latter's customs and, to a lesser extent, its utilitarian philosophy. It cherished the memory of its ancient rights but did not attempt to exploit them.

The 'patricians', derived from the wealthy bourgeoisie, provided the governing caste, concentrating all effective political power in their hands. They constituted a strict oligarchy jealous of its privileges and considering co-option to be the only possible means of access to any administrative post. They were sometimes known as 'regents' since, in addition to their political functions, they presided over numerous organisations dealing with public or private affairs, and their wives very often directed committees of public welfare and charitable institutions. Some foreign travellers during mid-century referred to them as *'rentiers'*.

Completely separated from the class of merchants during this era, the patricians existed on the income they derived from their investments in State bonds, company shares and recently purchased real estate. They had substituted the manipulation of capital for trading in merchandise, though until about 1650 their style of life was hardly distinguishable from that of the bourgeoisie. Thereafter, their social conventions gradually approached the exalted level of the top-ranking nobility, to a point where, around the turn of the century, the two classes had become so united through a series of intermarriages that they had more or less absorbed each other.

The patricians' opposition to Frederick Henry played a definite part in this evolution and was able to go as far as a certain display of power. Their class-consciousness developed and hardened, and was often symbolised by a deliberate austerity and simplicity that astonished foreigners, though there was doubtless an element of arrogance in their attitude. According to Temple, who knew him well, Johan De Witt, more or less dictator for twenty years, led the life of a medium-ranking civil servant. He dressed with taste but without pretension, and usually went on foot, reserving his carriage for official occasions. The fare he offered was exactly what one might expect in any bourgeois household. The State provided him with several servants, but in private he did not hesitate to help with domestic tasks, without apparent affectation but simply because such was the national custom.[16]

There were very few high functionaries whose style of living was any more impressive. The large towns furnished their burgomaster with a staff of servants intended exclusively to cope with official functions, and these took no part in his family life; hence the reputation for incorruptible honesty that the patriciate enjoyed, rightly or wrongly. This reputation was an indispensable factor in the country's political equilibrium, since the patriciate possessed a *de facto* rather than a *de jure* existence. Historically, it had emerged from families in the medieval 'communes' or 'free towns' who had taken advantage of the municipal charters to acquire illegal power. The war had provided them with an opportunity to extend their influence as far as the Union's government, which they ended up by controlling entirely while still making full use of the talents of the nobility and merchant class. The régime they had succeeded in imposing on the country had to struggle for its survival both against the influence of the petty bourgeoisie and that of the stadtholdership. This struggle sums up the political history of the Netherlands during the period under review.

The most powerful weapon at the disposal of the patriciate was the moral credit it had acquired. The business community deplored this situation. In 1652 the merchants of Amsterdam expressed their regret at being governed by magistrates who, having abandoned commerce, had lost touch with the realities of vital economic problems. Nevertheless, there were considerations which made the outbreak of open hostilities improbable. Chief among these was the fact that it was from among the wealthiest merchants that the patriciate gradually drew the fresh blood it needed, while still surrounding itself with endless social precautions. The passage from one milieu to the other was effected by marriage; this presupposed the renunciation of commerce – and an endless patience.

THE PEOPLE: *Bourgeoisie*
A few magnates of Dutch commerce, more or less closely associated with the patrician élite, achieved real world-wide power through their wealth, personal influence and extensive contacts; men of the stature of Moucheron, Isaac Lemaire or Louis de Geer (all three of whom were originally immigrants) dealt with kings and navigated the hazards of international politics. But such individuals remained exceptional products

of the bourgeoisie of commerce and crafts, the great proportion of whose members, whether draper, brewer, fashionable tailor or small grocer, shared a family atmosphere and common interests despite differences of fortune. Commercial specialisation was still relatively undeveloped, and the numerous strands of business activity were closely interwoven.

The bourgeois citizen's individualism was reinforced by the lack of political responsibilities, allowing him to devote himself exclusively to his commercial affairs, so that his sole preoccupations were trading and leisure activities, the latter often puerile or superficial. If he dreamt of anything at all, it was to marry off his daughter to someone richer than himself. Even if he achieved a certain prosperity and became the owner of several warehouses or ships, the rapier he would begin to wear in public was only for show; at home he still went around in dressing-gown and slippers. Yet he was by no means dull-witted, and his shrewdness and even guile more than compensated for any lack of subtlety. He was imitative and methodical, and in almost every sphere surpassed his models in effectiveness. To these qualities were added an absolute steadiness of purpose: a Dutch merchant never yielded his rights. If he was dealing with someone as man to man, he was the frankest and most loyal individual imaginable, but if he suspected that the person he was bargaining with was ignorant in any respect he did not hesitate to take advantage of the fact. His concept of justice derived less from high moral integrity than from a candid appraisal of circumstances.

For the great majority of these merchants, the general enrichment which characterised the Netherlands' 'golden age' had been the fruit of fierce tenacity, absolute thrift and carefully calculated ventures. As an example, the Witsen family of Amsterdam spent sixty years in achieving their ambitions; they were of peasant origin, and started their business career by signing on one of their sons in the merchant marine and finding a place for another as a worker in a fish-market. From that beginning the clan improved its lot gradually, until it was able to buy a small ship and launch out into the Baltic with a cargo of cheese, bringing back a shipment of wheat. Soon they were able to buy more ships. But success was not automatic, and bankruptcies were frequent. These failures were adjusted with a casualness that was almost dishonest, and creditors were sometimes paid at a rate of no more than 3 or 4 per cent. A settlement of 40 per cent was considered extraordinary.

The lower class of this bourgeoisie comprised a mass of small tradesmen, many of them impecunious, responsible for nearly the entire output of general equipment. These were tailors or dress-hirers, spectacle-makers and pewter-founders, knife-grinders, flower-sellers and all the other categories of those who kept shop or installed a workshop in the entrance-hall or courtyard of their house. The catering business was carried on in specialised shops: meat, bread, pies and cakes were sold by butchers, bakers and pastrycooks, spices and wines by the apothecary, and fruits and vegetables by the greengrocer. Shops similar to our grocers' shops sold salt, soap, dried vegetables, butter and cheese. The owners of all these establishments formed a settled group without much hope of social promotion.

The representatives of the liberal professions did not constitute a particular class as such. Predicants and professors, physicians, advocates and notaries distinguished themselves from the rest of the population more by their individual achievements than by their origin. Nevertheless, the mode of recruitment for these professions was not subject to purely intellectual criteria, since a general spirit of conservatism prevailed. As we have seen, physicians usually came from the upper middle classes, if not from the patrician class, while, in contrast, predicants belonged to the lower classes. On the whole, the Dutch 'intelligentsia' sprang from a bourgeois environment and retained many of its mental attitudes and social habits, embodying an uneven mixture of good nature and class-consciousness, scientific curiosity and narrow-mindedness, unconstraint and formality. Worthy citizens felt themselves united by common ancestry, diplomas and the knowledge of Latin into a body of people acutely conscious of their professional dignity; but they were torn by mutual jealousies and rivalries, and often, too, they were of humble origin, uncultured, lovers of banquets, easily led to drink, such as the notorious professor Baudius whose debauchery was the scandal of his colleagues at Leyden University. An empirical scholar like Leeuwenhoek, the inventor of the microscope, was never admitted to a university chair, for his ignorance of Latin and of foreign languages constituted an insurmountable obstacle for him. He was never able to raise himself above the rank of a minor functionary in the town of Delft.

Workers

Blending into the petty bourgeoisie, but separated from it by economic instability except at the highest level, stretched the great mass of those who lived almost permanently on the brink of penury through their dependence on others and the impossibility of saving money. At a time when the Netherlands were considered to be the richest nation in Europe, the 'populace' had almost no share whatsoever of the national capital. Although economic and social evolution had created divisions in its structure and dissipated its common interests, the working class remained characterised by one sociological feature: it was almost wholly unaffected by the puritanism of bourgeois morals. These workmen, servants and the whole host of the underprivileged struck foreigners by their extraordinary kindness and thoughtfulness.

If a stranger in a big town asked his way from some servant or pedlar, the local person would immediately leave his home or turn from his own route to accompany the visitor personally and put him on his right road. The plain man was often garrulous and nearly always fond of gossip and scandal. He was also terribly grasping, and the prospect of an immediate profit could set an entire working-class district in an uproar of excitement. Inn-keepers, coachmen, porters, hawkers all had a single instinct when confronted with an unknown customer – to fleece him as thoroughly as possible, without regard for established tariffs. The foreigner had to be constantly on guard, and this necessity for haggling annoyed many foreigners, despite the fact that exactly the same conditions prevailed throughout Europe. Nevertheless, the

Dutch were singled out as being stingy, greedy and inveterate money-grubbers; even their frugality and lack of ambition was decried as being merely the fruit of avarice.

In addition, the Dutch were inveterate brawlers. Not so much among the wealthy classes, where duelling had become rare except in the case of army officers and students, and was in any case illegal; but peasants, labourers and sailors joined battle on the slightest pretext and fought with great brutality. Knives were drawn and blood flowed, but the police usually turned a blind eye towards these affrays and the tribunals showed extreme leniency despite the prison sentences and heavy fines prescribed by law.

The chronic housing shortage which, as we have seen, afflicted Dutch urban areas throughout the century was the most important determining factor in working-class conditions. Of the twenty thousand workers employed in 1638 in Leyden's textile mills, the majority lodged in hovels devoid of any furniture except a straw litter. Gerrit Kist, the Zaandam carpenter whom Peter the Great visited, lived with his family in a single room. But miserable conditions had not succeeded in killing the old traditions of hospitality: an old woman of Zaandam, Marie Hitmans, the mother of a workman employed by Peter the Great, invited the Czar to join her in a glass of hollands gin, while the wife of another workman persuaded him to share her frugal meal.

Guild regulations governed the working hours in most trades, and thus the rhythm of working-class life. Only the municipal magistrates had the authority to modify these regulations, and even then procedures were slow. This resulted in a general stabilisation of living conditions, affected only by unemployment, except in certain industries particularly susceptible to disturbing outside influences. Firms engaged in shipping traffic and ship-building, depending entirely on the state of international trade, cut down their activities and dismissed part of their work force whenever a trade recession appeared, as when a war broke out, even if it was far away. And mills getting their power supply from windmills had the habit of extending the working day excessively whenever the wind was favourable.

Some ancient crafts, such as those involved in cloth production, had taken only a few years in the province of Holland to achieve the status of industries, and thus put themselves effectively out of reach of guild regulations. The rapid development of Leyden's manufacturing activities had attracted such a huge number of workers to the town that, in the seventeenth century, Leyden was second in importance only to Lyons among European industrial cities. The influx of refugees had made possible the replacement of the traditional female labour by male workers, and this suddenly increased volume of job-seekers enabled the employers to keep wages at the lowest level. Subsequently, the women were re-engaged at a mere pittance, and there was an increasing tendency to hire children (by interpreting perversely guild regulations concerning apprentices). The exploitation of these children, sometimes thrust into workshops at the age of six, from 1620 in Leyden and shortly thereafter in Amsterdam, Alkmaar, Utrecht and Groningen, foreshadowed in its shamelessness the use of child-labour in England at the beginning of the industrial revolution. Already in 1597 a decree had condemned the practices of certain employers who, under the pretext of apprenticeship, had reduced young children to a state of actual 'slavery'.[1] Cases were reported of children being sent out by their employers, after working hours, to beg in the streets. Occasionally the judiciary intervened, as in Delft in 1636, when particularly flagrant abuses could no longer be ignored.

The workers' children were also recruited, and their service thereby assumed a hereditary character. Touts procured stray children, most of them found begging on the highways, some having come all the way from Friesland, Flanders or Germany. Orphans in the official institutions were sometimes hired out by their guardians for miserable wages. When the textile boom was in full swing between 1638 and 1648, the Leyden employers imported four thousand children from Liège, obtained for them by a trafficker. The town councils did not dare forbid these practices but occasionally attempted to limit the consequences. Leyden established a board of work inspectors in

239

1641, charged with supervising the conditions of child-labour. In 1646 an edict limited the work period for children to fourteen hours a day! And in 1648 the town hired a teacher whose task was to give a little rudimentary education to the children working in the mills.

The lot of adult workers in those trades in process of industrialisation was hardly better than that of their children. The trades which still retained their original craft character could continue to offer some warmth in human relationships, but actual working conditions deteriorated as the century advanced. Colbert declared that a Dutchman worked harder in one day than a Frenchman in a week. Louis XIV's chief minister had every reason to envy the high output resulting from the Dutch worker's devotion to duty and his long working day. In fact, working hours and the number of working days a year had increased considerably since the Reform, mostly because of the suppression of the various saints' day celebrations previously prescribed by the Catholic church. Even the Sunday day of rest was no longer entirely safe. And in a few places night work was instituted.

Even so, one cannot really talk about 'labour unrest' or 'social problems' in the Netherlands of that age, because it seems that no one ever really became conscious of an injustice. At the very most, a certain disquiet became apparent, as when the 1619 synod in Dordrecht opined piously that wages should always be fair and that workers should be able to enjoy a Sunday rest, or when the town of Amsterdam forbade the pastrycooks in 1601 to over-decorate the cakes they displayed in their shop-windows 'for fear of saddening poor people in whose hearts the sight may arouse covetous instincts'![2] In fact, as we shall see in a later chapter, the social conscience of local government administrations limited itself to the organisation of various charitable institutions.

The social upheavals which occurred in the Netherlands during this era resulted from a more or less anarchic individual violence rather than from any preconceived plan initiated by some organised movement. It is also a fact that the demonstrations, strikes and conflicts that did occur originated more often in those trades that had remained strictly guild-controlled than in the big industrialised plants. Strikes are recorded as having taken place in Leyden in 1637, 1643 and 1648, and a 'rebellion' in 1638. Such incidents occurred periodically in all the main towns, but they led to nothing. Sweden's intervention in the Thirty Years War in 1629, cutting off supplies of Polish wheat, led to an increase in the price of bread, and a mob of poor people in Leyden attacked and looted a bakery. The local authorities called the police, who seized three or four ringleaders; these were given a public flogging, and things quietened down immediately. In 1672 the riff-raff of Hoorn, egged on by a woman, stormed the burgermaster's house, smashed the furniture and broke open wine barrels in the street; but by the time the militia had arrived she had already made her getaway.

The most frequent subject of dispute was the wage level, and protests quickly led guild masters and judicial authorities to denounce a 'plot' and invoke the full force of the law, including imprisonment, heavy fines and even banishment to the country which, in this overpopulated nation, might well mean a condemnation to starve. Very occasionally, however, wage increases were authorised. The real issue at stake in these struggles seems to have been less the worker's standard of living than the economic monopoly exercised by a few contractors whose main concern was to preserve public order at any price. As a result of the 1638 disturbances in Leyden, the States brought about the creation of an employers' association covering the ten towns engaged in the textile industry. This association's main achievement was the control of itinerant labour by forcing workers to possess a certificate of good conduct. Such measures were sometimes matched by official recommendations inspired by a genuine spirit of justice, but these invariably remained a dead letter.[3]

Seamen

Mariners formed a numerically important social group in the provinces of Holland, Zeeland and Friesland. The sea which gave them their livelihood also moulded their character, imposing a style of life, favouring certain traditions and producing strong, well-defined personalities. Despite their different occupations as fishermen, deck-hands on coasting vessels, merchant or naval seamen, or even corsairs, they all shared certain qualities, and were brusquer and more direct than land-based folk. Parival wrote of them: 'They spend most of their life at sea, out of touch with the world around them, unable to acquire refinements of manner or exercise any virtue except that of patience, though wind and storm give them frequent opportunity to practise that. They are certainly valorous, but I feel one might almost say that their valour is passive rather than active.'[4]

These temperate, sturdy, often austere men, leading a perpetually roving life, had wives and children in the coastal towns and villages; despite long absences from home and temptations in foreign lands, they remained faithful to their wives. In an age which preached the natural virtues, Grosley compared them with the Provençal sailors who kept a woman in every port of the Levant.[5] The captains were mostly men of modest origin trained in the school of hard experience and differed from their French, English or Danish colleagues in that they maintained neither servants, wine-stores nor mistresses on board. Cheese and beer sufficed for their meals, a dog provided them with company, and their sole preoccupation was the upkeep of equipment.

Their constant contact with nature's most violent aspects made mariners the most superstitious of all Dutchmen. If the sails slackened for lack of wind, the sailor would play a magical tune on his flute to entice a breeze. When a storm threatened to capsize his ship, he would thrash the cabin-boy to appease the ocean's tumultuous spirit. Even if food had run out he was careful not to kill certain birds which circled the masts, for they incarnated the souls of drowned sailors.

Despite the terribly hard life they led, sailors seldom mutinied. The first expeditions to the Far East and in the northern seas took a huge toll among the crews, until they finally became used to these climatic extremes and began to take the necessary precautions. The crews of sea-going ships were recruited in the Netherlands and neighbouring territories, sometimes from among vagabonds and impoverished workers, and were paid miserable wages; the owners were chiefly interested in keeping the running costs of their fleets as low as possible so as to meet foreign competition.

In 1630 a naval seaman was paid thirty florins a month, a sum that had remained unaltered for seventy-five years. Firm and long-term engagements were rare, and unemployment a constant threat to all on board; not just to the ordinary seamen, but equally to the junior officers, pilot, surgeon, quartermaster, lieutenant and even the captain himself, all of whom were hardly distinguishable socially from their men. It was only in 1628 that a regular corps of naval captains was established. While the shipowner made a 100 per cent profit or more on the money he had invested in a merchant ship or fishing vessel, the officers and sailors had to survive at a bare subsistence level. The population of maritime villages such as Maasluis was described as 'poverty-stricken'.[6] and the extreme sobriety of seafaring men was doubtless more a necessity than a virtue.

The captain was personally responsible for the material and social conditions on board his ship. His reputation depended on his ability to cope with the situation on the meagre sum allotted him by the shipowner or the Admiralty, and his personal profit depended on the economies he was able to make on the allowance for ship's stores, cleaning materials and medical supplies. The temptations were overwhelming for some poor devils hardened by years of such parsimony.

Although most Dutch ships were better kept and cleaner than those of other nations, some were floating jails where overloading of cargo cut down living space to a minimum and the atmosphere was one of dirtiness, squalor and starvation rations. Very occasionally a particular captain would emerge socially, after a period of years, from the mass of sea-going men, by saving a little money more or less honestly, or succeeding in cutting himself in on the owner's profits. On retirement he would buy a small house or make the supreme bourgeois gesture of having his portrait painted.

During the course of the century, the Admiralty adopted various measures of social security on behalf of the sailors in its fleets who had become victims of naval battles, including the award of compensation for the loss of a limb and pensions to widows and orphans. In Enkhuizen a well-equipped home looked after old retired mariners, but the beneficiaries of this institution were a small, privileged minority within the great mass of seafaring folk.

Although remarkable progress had been made in Dutch ship-building and navigational technique, the threat of shipwreck remained an element of the mariner's daily life. Contemporary chronicles record an endless series of sometimes overwhelming disasters: in 1657 fifty ships all sank together during a whale hunt. Some shipwrecks became famous, such as the one that befell a certain Captain Bontekoe in 1619. Bontekoe commanded a five-hundred-tonner with a crew of six hundred. During a storm, a sailor carelessly ignited a keg of brandy, and the efforts to extinguish the flames only succeeded in spreading them as far as the oil-store. This also went up in flames and the fire then reached some barrels of gunpowder which the crew had not had time to throw overboard. The ship exploded and went straight to the bottom. Bontekoe managed to cling to a piece of wreckage, and then join up with a few of his men in a long-boat. They drifted for two weeks, without food or a compass, under the tropical sun. Bontekoe improvised a crude sail with their shirts and from a small plank contrived a sort of sextant with which he steered by the stars. The men ate fish that they managed to catch with their hands, and drank their own urine. Finally, half crazed, they attempted to cut the throat of the cabin-boy and eat him, but Bontekoe succeeded in dissuading them from carrying out this crime and kept his control over the sailors until they eventually touched land at some island in the Indian ocean, from where they were later rescued by a Dutch ship.

When the *Raven* foundered under sail without sinking, eighty-three men clung for two days in raging seas to the mast of the capsized vessel. When rescuers could finally get to the floating wreck, only twenty survivors were left.

Dutch coastal waters were dangerously shallow along almost their entire stretch and afflicted by rough seas, so that when a ship went aground it ran the dual risk of being broken up by the waves or capsized by the force of the wind. Hence the importance for the inhabitants of the maritime provinces of their rights in respect of wreckages, rights which were in fact closely regulated. If all or part of the crew had been rescued, the wreck was returned to its owner on payment of an indemnity; if the crew had perished the wreck came within the scope of the fiscal authorities and was deemed to belong to the administrative district within whose limits it had been found. This faced shipowners with the problem of salvage, and in 1660 a machine was invented in Zeeland to lift submerged ships from the sea-bottom and salvage them. To commemorate this occasion, a medal was struck representing the new machine surrounded by an appropriate motto: *Soli Deo honor et gloria.*

Shipwreck rights also covered rights to the whales which were sometimes stranded on Dutch beaches. One village was able to extract five hundred florins' worth of oil from a whale washed up on the coast within its boundaries.

Peasants

The peasantry, rich or poor, presented just as much diversity as did townspeople, but this diversity was masked by a deeply felt sense of unity resulting from close contact with the soil and from a particularly stubborn traditionalism.

Both Parival and Temple[7] observed that the Dutch peasant was 'diligent rather than laborious'. The typical peasant was tall, heavily-built and brawny, with a remarkably fresh complexion resulting from his staple diet of vegetables and dairy-produce. As a group, they were simple-minded and coarse but quick to resent any brusqueness towards them. They were more easily influenced by reason than by a high-and-mighty manner, so long as they were given sufficient time for slow and deliberate reflection. Contact with large towns undermined their natural virtues, and the perfect honesty and down-to-earth wisdom which characterised them at their best remained unharmed only in fairly isolated villages. According to Parival, 'they are content with what is their due, and if you try to give them five pence for something worth only twopence halfpenny they will accept only the correct amount and give you back the remainder.'[8] They would have considered anyone mad who insisted on their keeping the larger amount. Grosley has described the ceremony attending a purchase of wool among peasants in northern Holland. When the bargaining had gone on long enough, the seller, without saying a word, would throw a ducat into a glass, hand it to the buyer and then fill it with hollands gin. They would drink a toast, looking each other straight in the face; if the buyer kept the ducat between his lips after emptying the glass, the bargain was considered settled, they shook hands on it and the buyer kept the ducat as a bonus; but if he left the ducat at the bottom of the glass, they parted without reaching agreement, but with no ill will and with mutual offers of future services.[9]

Peasants whose lands lay near a town were more aware than the others of the advantages of capitalisation. Having realised that the provisioning of the townsmen depended largely upon themselves, they exploited the situation and, as a result, there was a greater degree of prosperity among them than in the more rural provinces.

The scrupulous cleanliness of peasant houses, and even their stables, provoked the admiration of foreign visitors. They groomed their cows in this country as other lands groomed their horses, and even went so far as to tie the cows' tails back so that they should not soil themselves. Guicciardini claimed[10] that even in the sixteenth century nearly all Dutch peasants knew how to read and write. These words should be taken literally; reading and writing was the full extent of their accomplishments and the minister in charge of the village school would have been hard put to implant any less basic learning in the thick skulls of his young charges. Peasant women could neither read nor write, since girls were never sent to school. Nevertheless, the intellectual level of the Dutch peasantry was still relatively high for the period.

Relations with the towns were based on economic interests

(the disposal of agricultural produce) and on leisure activities (attending the great kermises), but the peasant mind viewed with vague, deep-rooted suspicion these urban centres, considering them vast dens of iniquity. The peasant disapproved of his daughter going out with a town boy; risks were ever present and the consequences easy to predict.

Peasants were even more assiduous than town dwellers in their devotion to the family and, beyond that, to the clan. When Descartes was living in the village of Egremond, he appeared before the local court to plead for leniency towards his neighbour, a young peasant guilty of having killed his mother's second husband. After suffering several brutal beatings she had left him, and he had subsequently threatened her on several occasions. The clan had then closed its ranks and determined on revenge; during a scuffle the enemy had been struck down, but how could any one person be held accountable for the crime? Standing around the coffin, the family had absolved the murderer.[11]

The war of liberation had cost the countryside dearly, with troops stripping the fields at harvest-time, or destroying them for tactical reasons or in a spirit of revenge. The Eindhoven region changed hands eleven times in twenty-five years. These misfortunes had given birth to a whole literature of 'Peasants' Laments' and produced a deep-seated loathing of the soldiery throughout the countryside. Nevertheless, the liquidation of the Spanish régime had benefited the more prosperous peasants in the long run; the estates of the Catholic church and of certain nobles had been confiscated or purchased by the State and then leased or sold to farmers, while all feudal rights apart from cash rentals had been abolished. The peasant's legal status had become indistinguishable from that of the bourgeois, and a fierce spirit of independence fired this recently emancipated class. The story goes that the King of Bohemia, during his stay in Holland, was chased by a pitchfork-wielding peasant through whose fields he had had the temerity to hunt. Each village had its bailiff and its aldermen, appointed by the province or the squire and exercising full judicial powers, working in conjunction with officials administering local affairs. It had its own annual feast-day, and organised regular sports contests with other villages. Some conveniently situated and carefully administered villages had achieved an enviable prosperity thanks to their association with neighbouring towns. In Jisp, well-dressed peasants were to be seen driving by in four-horse carriages, cracking their whips like any lord of the manor.

Friesland and, to some extent, Groningen were in a special category, having escaped the feudal régime in the Middle Ages. In these provinces the soil was the property of free peasants grouped in self-governing associations, and lands acquired in more recent times were governed by extremely complex rights approximating to present-day long leases. This centuries-old system had bred a wealthy peasant élite ruling, often graspingly, over farmers and piece-workers.[12]

Day-labourers and other agricultural wage-earners formed an impoverished and partially itinerant mass. In the spring, groups trailing women, children and carts trudged north to work in the forests stripping oak-bark, and this annual migration involved a high infant mortality. During whole months the labourers lived in primitive mud huts in the heart of the forests, returning to them each succeeding year to find them overgrown with vegetation and battered by storms. In a few places, associations of agricultural workers were organised during the course of the century, with members subscribing to a benefit fund, but only the better-off peasants could take part in such schemes.

PAUPERS AND CRIMINALS

A certain proportion of the population was threatened with penury at frequent intervals, as we have already seen. But more unfortunate even than these casual workers were those existing on the fringes of society in a state of permanent economic hardship. The frequency of unemployment and the nomadic tendencies of some workmen made it impossible to distinguish clearly between underprivileged workers and true vagabonds, but together they constituted a collection of humanity sprinkled with antisocial elements whose common denominator was the supreme, ever-present menace of hunger.

This segment of the nation, rejected by the very society whose economic shortcomings had provoked its existence, made its existence known through begging, a curse which afflicted town and country equally and grew worse as the century progressed. The provincial States proscribed mendicancy at regular intervals, but it was a scourge that no edicts could halt. Amsterdam swarmed with beggars and with a horde of imaginary cripples, and after the truce and the disbanding of the mercenaries the evil increased. Bands of dubious characters, leading a wandering existence or living here and there in improvised slums, exercised a variety of minor illegal trades, stole and even killed if necessary, were hunted from one province to another as a result of the banishment pronounced on them at regular intervals, and spoke an incomprehensible thieves' cant that impressed someone sufficiently for him to publish a vocabulary in 1613. It was impossible to distinguish brigands from honest wretches, and the scene was further confused by the presence of gipsies practising palmistry, drawing horoscopes and – reputedly – stealing children. However often the gipsies were imprisoned or expelled they always came back. The forces of law and order were powerless to deal with this situation.

It was dangerous to go about unarmed at night in The Hague's Wood. In 1643 a recently decapitated man's head was found there, but the police were never able to discover the assassins; and in 1661 two young women of good family were abducted in broad daylight. Towns increased their police forces, ordered the imprisonment of all beggars lacking a special permit and offered a reward to any citizen pointing out or apprehending a thief. Teams of 'beggar hunters', assisted by dogs, tracked down vagabonds in the rural areas.

The municipalities were more or less aware of the economic origins of this disorderliness and made a practice throughout the century of distributing free rations in years when famine struck or the cost of living suddenly increased. In such cases a shipload of wheat or rye was ordered and a rough bread baked and given away to needy people. In Leyden, in 1634, twenty thousand people received free bread.[1] In Amsterdam, an official allocation of alms to the poor took place once a week. The Reformed Church also dispensed charity at a local level, but only to the needy who had at least a provisional domicile; an official appointed by the deacon or the town provided these deserving poor in winter with a little butter, cheese, bread and peat. But during the summer months these supplies were discontinued and they were left to fend for themselves.[2]

The municipalities and the Church organised regular collections for aid to the poor. Bourgeois citizens were often generous contributors, and a properly launched collection in a large town could well bring in fifteen or even twenty-five thousand florins. Tradition demanded the giving of alms on special occasions such as marriages in wealthy families. In several towns the poor were presented with the pall from the catafalque after a funeral ceremony, and it was rare for a prosperous citizen to die without bequeathing a sum of money for works of charity. The reputation of the Dutch for charity was acknowledged throughout Europe, and Louis XIV himself, on the eve of his invasion of the Netherlands, reassured Charles II in these terms: 'Have no fear for the fate of Amsterdam. I live in the certain hope that Providence will save that city, if only in consideration of her charity.'

To deal with its large industrial proletariat, Leyden had instituted a body of inspectors of paupers with large assistance funds at its disposal. During the second half of the century cottages were built in several towns with private funds and rented to poor people at very low rates. Poor-houses existed everywhere, some of them taken over from the previous religious orders and now administered by the State, and the largest towns boasted several institutions serving different categories of the needy: Leyden, for example, had an alms-house for homeless paupers, another for old folk, and an orphanage as well. But the main function of these poor-houses since the beginning of the seventeenth century was the rehabilitation of vagabonds. In most districts of any importance tramps could find a reception centre, sometimes attached to the local hospital, where they received free board and lodging for three days; on the morning of the fourth day they were sent on their way again. But in some towns the influx of vagabonds was so great that the poor-houses were closed from June to October. Amenities were rudimentary in these establishments: a large communal hall, heated and provided with benches, and two dormitories, one for men, the other for women. At the end of each meal the knives were counted and locked away for safety, and at night the dormitory doors were bolted securely.

Besides a large hospital, Amsterdam possessed several orphanages, and an alms-house providing lodging for as many as four hundred aged female paupers. In 1613 a 'House of Charity' was founded to provide shelter for paupers who lived by begging, though to be eligible for admission they had to prove several years' domicile in the town. But this poor-house did provide needy travellers with a cash subsidy. A provost accompanied by officials attached to the institution scoured the town every day, rounding up beggars. At a later date the institution also housed children that the orphanage could not accommodate, and became responsible for carrying out free burials.

The administration of these various houses of refuge was vested by the town in committees of distinguished citizens, both men and women, who considered the appointment an honour. Although the day-to-day running of these charitable institutions by the junior personnel often left much to be desired, the administration at top level was usually remarkably efficient. They were often financed out of the revenues from former ecclesiastical properties, and, especially in the second half of the century, benefited from foundations and legacies. Door-to-door collections were taken once a month, and the churches held a collection every Sunday. In addition, alms-boxes were to be found at various sites in the town. The municipality put aside the income it derived from its taxes on imported cereals, auction sales, banquets and de luxe funerals for the benefit of the various institutions. And finally, charity lotteries were organised periodically and were extremely popular with the public; on one occasion, a ticket costing two stuivers won first prize of a thousand florins.[3]

Towards the end of the century the charitable institutions

became too small and their revenue insufficient. Various remedies had to be devised, including the creation of special taxes, an increase in the number of lotteries, and sending paupers back to their place of birth.

From the start of the century Amsterdam possessed two institutions for antisocial elements, combining the functions of prison and reform home, the *Rasphuis* for men and the *Spinhuis* for women.[4] A Latin inscription along the façade of the Rasphuis described its purpose: *Virtutis est domare quae cuncti pavent.*[5] The inmates were there as a result of sentences imposed by the courts and were subjected to manual labour, usually rasping logwood (whence the institution's name). Anyone who refused to work was immediately flogged, and if he repeated the offence he was thrown into a cellar that was gradually filled with water through a pipe; to escape drowning, the prisoner had to pump without stopping – an ingenious form of forced labour! Vagabonds, thieves and ne'er-do-wells of every description shared the premises of the *Rasphuis* with unruly sons imprisoned on the demand of their fathers. The *Spinhuis* ('spinning house', as its name implies) harboured prostitutes, daughters who had run away from home and wives whose husbands had had them incarcerated for misconduct or drunkenness. The more fortunate women could obtain a private room by paying for it.

A few cases taken at random from Amsterdam's criminal files of the epoch give some idea of the kind of crimes that came up for judgement, and the scale of sentences imposed. Trijntje Pieters, a servant-girl, was condemned to death for killing her illegitimate baby; Laurens Cornelisse, an inmate of the Rasphuis, was hanged for breaking open the bailiff's strong-box on the premises of the law-court which was about to try him for a previous offence; Jean Franchoys was condemned to the pillory for bigamy; the same sentence was imposed on Abraham Frederickszen, employed by a tombstone engraver attached to the Carthusian cemetery, for stripping corpses of their garments; the soldier Ernst Rip was condemned to death for murdering a comrade; Albert Alberts and his wife, notorious receivers of stolen goods, were hanged for making away with the head and right hand of an executed criminal from the pauper's grave (in their case they were doubtless suspected of sorcery as well). The list could be extended indefinitely. Murder, theft, arson and forgery were the commonest offences. One woman, Griet Andries, was sentenced on thirty-two separate occasions. The criminal law was applied with implacable severity and was especially ruthless in dealing with theft, house-breaking and the forging of signatures. Sometimes it showed incredible savagery: sixteen-year-old urchins were branded with red-hot irons; a forty-five-year-old captain, found guilty of murder, was burnt alive. The files record a repeated offender who was flogged eleven times and branded five times during the course of a single year. In the final quarter of the century two hundred and nine death sentences were carried out in Amsterdam.

Grotius justified this cruelty by the necessity for striking fear into the hearts of potential criminals. It can be understood in the context of the general callousness of feeling prevalent throughout Europe at the time, but the element of inhumanity was certainly abetted by the incoherence of the Dutch penal code. Apart from anything else, laws and customs differed from province to province and even from town to town, so that any attempt at unification ran up against the hostility of the local law-courts. In this judicial chaos crime remained wholly undefined, and the criterion, constantly repeated in judges' summings-up, was simply that 'such a thing is intolerable in a civilised state'. By this standard, blasphemy or passing counterfeit money could rank as acts no less reprehensible than murder or high treason.

Since a confession was considered to be a final and irrevocable proof of guilt, the police had an interest in securing a confession as quickly as possible and torture was used as a matter of course during interrogations, despite the fact that its use was illegal at that juncture. The same 'techniques' flourished here as in the rest of Europe: the rack, forced absorption of disgusting substances, whipping and branding. In the province of Holland judicial authorities recognised five degrees of torture; Friesland was more humane and recognised only three. These classifications were used as a basis for the scale of penalties, since torture was often included officially in the sentence after having been used illegally to force a confession.

Refined, cultivated magistrates participated without scruple or disgust in these sessions, sessions which were sometimes so prolonged that they had their meals brought in to them in the torture-chamber where the executioner was tormenting some poor devil. They had been personally responsible for the penalty, choosing it from an established, incongruous, bloodthirsty arsenal: amputation of the right hand, of the nose, or of one or both ears; burning of the tongue; gouging of eyes; slitting of one cheek; branding of the shoulder with a red-hot iron. For the smallest offence the culprit was exposed in the pillory under a wooden bell through which his head projected, with an inscription or symbol indicating his misdemeanour. Or he would be paraded through town in some ignominious garb.

The pedlar found guilty of selling forbidden books was dragged through the streets with a doctor's cap clamped on his head and a package of his merchandise slung around his neck. Petty thieves were taken by the tipstaff and exhibited to the townspeople with the stolen object tied on top of their heads. The pillory, a scaffold set up in front of the town hall, was almost as unpleasant an instrument as the rack, and the public exposure involved a dishonour that only the most miserable could accept with equanimity.

Other penalties were social or economic in character, involving deprivation of civil rights, a ban on exercising a particular profession, or fines and penalties. Banishment allowed the authorities, under some pretext or another, to get rid of individuals whom they considered dangerous; they would be expelled for a month, for life, or even for a hundred years and a day. A culprit guilty of wounding might find himself forbidden to leave his house after eight o'clock in the evening for a year; a drunkard might be prohibited from frequenting taverns for three years. During the periods when big work projects, such as building of fortifications or opening of mines in some distant colony, were under way the courts were quick to condemn culprits to these 'public works'.

The death penalty was usually carried out by hanging, but this was often preceded by tortures or else replaced by some more cruel method of execution, in which the victim was strapped down in a chair and beheaded with a sword, burnt at the stake, drowned inside a barrel, or even buried alive. Sometimes corpses were executed, as when the bodies of suicides were hanged after being dragged to the foot of the gibbet by a rope attached to a horse. For urban populations these executions provided a free spectacle regarded as a harmless popular diversion.

A gibbet stood at each of Amsterdam's gates, and the outskirts of most towns presented a similar spectacle. They consisted of two strong vertical beams about fifteen feet high, joined by a cross-beam long enough to accommodate easily half a dozen corpses at the end of their ropes. A ladder allowed the executioner to fix the ropes and adjust the nooses.

The executioner was an important official and each province had its officially designated practitioner; in Holland he entitled himself 'Master of High Works of Holland, residing at Haarlem'. His wages were calculated at piece-rates: three florins for a beheading, plus nine florins for burying the corpse. Breaking on the wheel was more profitable; at three florins a blow the total could reach about thirty florins, whereas floggings at the same rate seldom brought in more than twenty-four florins.

Prison sentences were comparatively rare, and imprisonment was considered not so much a punishment as a means of guarding the accused while he awaited trial. Wealthy prisoners could easily alleviate their conditions, but the impecunious suffered terrible privations since prisoners had to pay for their food, and the supply of provisions was a profitable enterprise for the guards. Undernourishment and lack of hygiene made these prisons centres of infection. In Amsterdam the prisons had been established in the cellars of the town hall and in the city's four oldest gate-towers, with walls six feet thick, narrow barred windows and floors strewn with a thin layer of damp straw. During the course of the century a few audacious prisoners succeeded in escaping; Johannes Palmer achieved this feat in 1652, and the court sentenced him in his absence to perpetual banishment, having failed in its efforts to recapture him.

THE ARMED FORCES

In 1601 the army under the command of the Stadtholder numbered less than twenty thousand men, most of them English, French, German and Scottish, grouped in companies or regiments of the same nationality commanded by their own officers.[1] The only Dutch units were Prince William Lewis's Frieslanders and Prince Maurice's cavalry regiment. The martial fervour of the United Provinces was no more than a memory. Of the two methods of recruitment in force – voluntary engagement and the hiring of foreign contingents – only the second was able to cover the needs of the final campaigns preceding the truce.

From 1600 until the French invasion in 1672 the wars in which the Netherlands were involved never came closer than the Republic's frontier regions, and most of them took place at sea far from its territorial waters. In the eyes of a bourgeoisie exclusively preoccupied with economic questions a land-based army ceased to fulfil a useful purpose during this rare period of immunity. Mercenaries sufficed to perform the minor tasks allocated to them, in their view, and even then their numbers were kept to a bare minimum. After the 1609 truce fifteen thousand soldiers were discharged and the remaining companies were reduced to a strength of fifty men each.[2] We have seen what were the social results of this measure. After the Treaty of Westphalia, the States of Holland considered the disbanding of half the army insufficient and demanded that the Prince should increase the proportion to three-quarters. The conflict resulting from William II's refusal might have led to civil war if the Stadtholder's death and the abolition of his post had not given the regents victory by default.

An army cost money and the States were reluctant to provide the funds necessary for its upkeep,[3] being incapable of understanding the justification of such expenditure without apparent returns of profit. The necessity of maintaining a war-fleet seemed more logical to them, since the prosperity of their international trading depended largely on its existence, but the idea of an army seemed incomprehensible. Only in the Brazilian war had Dutch troops ever been used overseas; the great exploiting Companies had their own private armies in the colonies, paid for by themselves.

When the international situation demanded it, a few extra regiments were recruited. In 1666, for instance, when war was declared on the Bishop of Munster, the States put together an army of 60,000 men; but as soon as the crisis was over they were sent packing.[4] This attitude led to so evident a disorganisation of the military machine that foreign ambassadors drew the attention of their respective governments to the fact. In 1670 the army numbered ten regiments of cavalry and nineteen regiments of infantry, totalling a little more than 26,000 men. When the French attacked in 1672, 12,000 men and 10,000 horses had to be hired very hastily from the Elector of Brandenburg.

Recruiting officers were engaged to bring in the necessary complements, contracting to furnish so many men for a particular sum. Agreements concluded with foreign sovereigns authorised these agents to scour a predetermined area, but the task was not always easy. When a war was in progress in Europe, gun-fodder became rare and expensive, and at all times recruits had a habit of deserting through sheer ill will. After extorting the enlistments, the recruiting officer consigned the men to a reliable escort which saw them to the frontier. There, they were all loaded into coaches and driven non-stop to the assembly point.

In peacetime the troops were stationed in frontier garrisons, at a safe distance from the great mercantile cities. These mercenaries constituted a foreign element in the districts they frequented, remaining somewhat apart from the local population, not so much because of their origin as because of their profession. Marriages between soldiers and local girls were frequent and Busken-Huet attributed to this fact the existence of a particular physical type characterised by small stature and dark complexion.[5]

A town harbouring a garrison was assured of considerable profit, mainly from an increased traffic in taxable goods and from payments for the billeting of troops. There were no barracks, and soldiers took lodgings in the town during the winter. But as soon as springtime provided the necessary fodder for the horses, the troops pitched camp on flat land near by. The commanding officer's tall tent formed the focal point around which were grouped those of his staff-officers, surrounded by sections occupied by the artillery park, the arsenal, the pontoneers' depot, the cavalry and then the infantry. This seasonal town, due to be abandoned in late autumn, was planned in a strict order; each company had its own street, and at the end of that street were to be found the tents of its captain, paymaster, lieutenant and sergeants. A market-place was opened up to a throng of tavern-owners, tradesmen and workmen from outside the camp. There was no shortage of women visitors, either. Bearded veterans rubbed shoulders with youths, idlers, quarrellers, gamblers and drunkards. Organised marauding, degenerating sometimes into looting, was an ineradicable evil, as was the brawling and duelling between soldiers of different nationalities.

The trooper bought his bread and beer at the commissary. Although his pay was somewhat higher than in most other European armies,[6] his position remained very precarious. It was difficult to abandon the soldiering profession, and when the unfortunate man enlisted he had usually sealed his destiny. He invariably owed money to his captain, and remained effectively tied to his company as long as he remained able-bodied. But once he was wounded or fell sick he was left to fend for himself and had to find room in some charitable institution, paying for treatment out of his own pocket. In wartime, the hastily improvised casualty wards were little better than stinking muck-heaps ravaged by epidemics, where the sick died like flies. When a veteran was finally forced to retire from active duty due to old age, he had no other recourse but to beg. A very few fortunate individuals were able to end their days as gate-keepers in some town.

In contrast, the officers were generally well-off, despite the fact that they were considered to be nothing more than servants of the civil authorities. Many of them belonged to the Protestant nobility of neighbouring countries, and being more susceptible to foreign influences than other social groups were often noticeable for their more elegant and sophisticated way of life. Even so, the army registers bore witness to the total lack of culture of some officers, incapable even of signing their own names.

The officer was entire master of the unit he commanded, whether regiment or company. The company was the basic unit in the infantry, twenty companies making up a regiment,[7] and it represented an important source of income for its commander since a captain's pay was augmented by any profit he could make on the arms and equipment he sold to his men. In addition, despite the controls operated by the government auditors, he omitted as far as possible to cross the names of dead men and deserters off his pay-lists, so that he could pocket the unclaimed money. Out of the funds advanced to him by the administration the captain bought provisions and arms, paid his men, and even gave them sickness allowances and paid ransoms. In peacetime a considerable proportion of his budget was earmarked for replacement wages, payable to the volunteers who mounted guard in place of absent soldiers. A certain proportion of the total strength did in fact disappear for quite long periods, or else the men took jobs as casual labourers with local peasants or craftsmen.

Nobody wore uniform and only the helmet and breastplate, and sometimes a scarf in the company's colours, together with a leather jacket, provided outward evidence of the soldier's calling. The sixteenth century's heroic style had vanished and the soldier or officer was now just a civilian in arms. In 1640 officers took to wearing white scarves with coloured knots; twenty years later this had become an elegant fashion adopted throughout high society.

Maurice of Nassau had founded a military academy in Breda where engineers such as Stevin taught the arts of fortification-building and general strategy. Officers from throughout Europe attended his classes. For the rank and file Prince Maurice instituted exercises in the handling of muskets and pikes, the infantry's two basic arms, and during the months spent in camp a daily period was set aside for this training. The cavalry formed a large proportion of the army, amounting sometimes to as much as a third or a quarter of the total strength. The technical corps of wheelwrights, blacksmiths and drivers made up about 10 per cent of the force together with the gunners. The Dutch artillery was reputed to be the best in the world, though it is true that in this epoch forty guns represented a formidable fire-power. In 1627 Frederick Henry was able to muster a battery of eighty pieces in front of Grol, and a hundred and sixteen pieces facing 's Hertogenbosch two years later.[8] But artillery was useless except for laying siege to strongholds, since the pieces were so cumbersome that they impeded the troops' manoeuvres on the field of battle. Sixteen horses were needed to drag the heaviest field-guns, and the appalling quality of the Dutch road surfaces made their transportation almost impossible. A sudden retreat meant the certain loss of the gun, and its slow firing-rate (one cannon-ball every ten minutes) made it ineffective in face of a fairly mobile enemy infantry.

The baggage-train made use of carriages or boats, either requisitioned or hired, according to the circumstances. Maurice used three thousand waggons on one occasion, and during the siege of Rijnbeck in 1663 he accumulated a fleet of two thousand barges on the Rhine.

The wars on land conducted by the Netherlands during the course of the century were sieges rather than orthodox campaigns, and the essentially economic aims of these expeditions made the occupation of a town or a communication network far more important than the conquest of vast territories. The eventual profit justified the initial cost: the capture in 1603 of the port of Ostend, the best defended place in Europe, cost four million florins.

When enemy armies approached a Dutch town, the peasants from the surrounding region hurried towards the town, driving their cattle before them and lugging their hand-carts. The gates were closed and teams of citizens climbed on to the ramparts, dragging sacks and bundles of faggots. The look-outs calculated the rhythm of the still distant cannonade. When the enemy forces were spread out opposite the town walls and forty-pound cannon-balls were beginning to shatter the ramparts, sappers would start digging a tunnel in the direction of the enemy battery. But the attacker might be digging a tunnel in the opposite direction, and at Maastricht the sappers from the rival armies did indeed meet in this way in the underground darkness. On that occasion the Dutch retreated in haste, threw faggots into the entrance to their hole, set fire to them and drove the smoke through the tunnel to the Spaniards' position with the aid of the bellows from the organ of the Great Church. Meanwhile, women would be boiling up oil in cauldrons on the parapets. When the town had exhausted its ammunition and eaten the last rat, the dikes were opened. This desperate measure, which had struck fear into the hearts of the Spaniards not long since, had become a regular military operation. When the Frisian deputies refused in 1673 to inundate their province to rescue it from the French, the Stadtholder had them all shot as traitors.

FOREIGNERS AND REFUGEES

Apart from the largely unintegrated military elements, a considerable foreign colony inhabited the Netherlands. In 1685 a Frenchman calculated that the number of foreigners or descendants of foreigners with established homes in the province of Holland amounted to half the total population.[1] This foreign colony was as mixed in the nationalities represented (Flemings, English, Germans, Scandinavians, French and Swiss) as in its social stratification. The cloth-bleaching industry in Haarlem employed grossly underpaid Brabantine and Westphalian labour. On the other hand, Jacob Poppen, a German from Holstein, arrived in Amsterdam without a penny in his pocket but was burgomaster of the city and a millionaire by the time he died in 1624. Frans Banningh Cocq, the central figure of Rembrandt's *Night Watch*, an important personality in Amsterdam, was the son of a Bremen labourer. The regular commercial relations established between Holland and the Levant brought a group of Armenian merchants to Amsterdam. In 1644, the Archimandrite of Cephalonia and the Metropolitan of Ephesus paid a visit to Leyden; the Patriarch of Jerusalem, prompted by the Dutch ambassador (who hoped in this way to curb the influence of the Jesuits in the Near East) had instructed them to translate into Greek the Reformed Confession of Faith and the Heidelberg Catechism.

The Flemish and Walloon Protestant refugees who had arrived at the end of the sixteenth century formed the largest group and the one that had the strongest influence on the country's development. They had originally brought not only fully formed skills with them but also considerable sheer manpower, which together constituted a decisive factor in the country's budding economic prosperity. They revived Leyden's traditional weaving craft and Haarlem's bleaching industry while introducing improved techniques. If Amsterdam replaced Antwerp as a commercial centre, it was partly because of the influx of thousands of Antwerp craftsmen and merchants from 1585 onwards. The most enterprising of these immigrants laid the foundations for the policy of commercial expansion that was to make the Netherlands a powerful nation. Willem Usselincx, a wealthy merchant, was the first to propose the founding of colonies in the New World. Moucheron and Isaac Lemaire also came from Antwerp. Flanders provided its share, too, of literary men and scholars; Heinsius and Vossius were both of Belgian origin.

During the course of the century the Netherlands gradually became the main centre of refuge in Europe, and the craftsmen, businessmen and scholars who had been drawn there by the possibility – or illusion – of a freer life and wider prospects were joined by those fleeing from persecution, political suspects and intellectuals deprived of freedom of expression in their own countries. The Republic offered considerable advantages to all these people. Most of the towns, and Amsterdam in particular, were almost impregnable; the fact that real political power was in the hands of the municipalities appeared, rightly or wrongly, as an insurance against tyranny; freedom of conscience was almost total; there were no obstacles to the importation of capital, and anyone could deposit his funds in the vaults of the bank of Amsterdam. Lastly, the States showed their determination to guarantee the right of asylum; the French ambassadors never succeeded in obtaining the extradition of a single fugitive French subject.

The large towns, particularly in the province of Holland, assumed a cosmopolitan character that was apparent at every social level. The people of Walloon and Flemish descent living in the working-class districts of Leyden were joined, towards the middle of the century, by Frenchmen, Germans, Lorrainese and Englishmen. As we have seen, the intense scientific activity displayed in the Dutch universities was already attracting students from throughout Europe before 1600. Nearly 2,700 students entered the various faculties at Groningen between 1615 and 1690. Apart from the foreign scholars, predominantly French, who had been offered chairs in the universities, there were many other scholars who came to the Netherlands in search simply of peace and freedom. Descartes lived there for thirty years (during 1618-9 and from 1620 to 1649), frequenting the schools of Leyden, Amsterdam and Franeker and establishing bonds of friendship with the Republic's most eminent figures and most inquiring spirits. Ménard was chaplain to William II and official chronicler. Even a king came to the Stadtholder to seek refuge: when Frederick of Bohemia was deposed in 1619 he chose The Hague for his place of exile and died there in 1632. His widow remained with their five sons and four charming daughters, poor and neglected, leading the modest existence of a woman of the bourgeoisie, but surrounded by the admiration and affection of the men of letters and artists who constituted her 'court'.

By the middle of the century most of the refugees were of French origin, and the proportion increased still more after the revocation of the Edict of Nantes. Frenchmen such as Isaac Angot and Gédéon Baignault (and more than twenty others during the course of the century) introduced new methods to the Netherlands' traditional clock-making craft, thus creating the basis for a future industry. On the other hand, many Huguenots whose only livelihood was their native tongue opened so-called 'French schools'. The municipalities placed these schools under common law, and after swearing an oath of loyalty the principal was given complete freedom in his choice of curriculum and teaching methods. This liberal régime and the good reputation enjoyed by the masters enabled these schools to flourish in the large towns; so much so, in fact, that after 1685 there were too many for the number of pupils available and several schools were forced to close down.

Other Frenchmen gained their living by exploiting their particular national talents; they taught fencing, or else tucked a violin under their arm and went the rounds of wealthy families giving dancing lessons. Some of them found places as master cooks in the households of princes and patricians. Later on, French hairdressers enjoyed the favour of fashionable people.

A certain number of these French refugees found a friendly reception among the Walloon community made up of the descendants of the original men of Hainault, Liège and Brabant who had come north in their flight from Spanish domination. These families continued to use their own language at least part of the time and, in matters of religion, were grouped in the 'Walloon Church' although the social unit they formed had a far broader base than this. It was the Walloons with whom Descartes was in closest touch and it was through the agency of the men of letters in their community that Cartesianism was able to exercise an influence on Dutch thought in mid-seventeenth century.

The French refugees, nearly all of whom were from small country towns, brought to their country of adoption a simple good-heartedness, graciousness and gaiety that was highly thought of by the Dutch.[2] But they found it more difficult than the Germans or English to adapt themselves to the Dutch way of life. According to Parival, it often took them two generations to become completely accustomed to the Dutch character,[3] and their social relations were not made any easier by the difficulty many Frenchmen seem to have experienced in learning Dutch (or perhaps their laziness in that respect). Pierre Le Jolle, who married a Dutchwoman, became bilingual, but he appears to have been an exception. Simple folk in the Netherlands knew no foreign languages at all; when Saumaise disembarked at Brielle in December 1636, he had to wander about the town for three hours in a blinding rainstorm before he could find an inn where they more or less understood him.

CHAPTER SEVEN

HOLLAND AT WORK

A Wealthy Country: The Organisation of Wealth, Postal and Information Services, Taxation—Commerce and the Spirit of Adventure—The Fleet: Merchant Service and Navy, Corsairs and Pirates—Trading and Colonisation: The Great Companies, Colonists and Slaves—Industry: Its Shortcomings, The Fisheries—Working the Land: Tilling and Grazing, Dikes and Polders.

A WEALTHY COUNTRY

Despite the misfortunes of war the States found sufficient funds in 1616 to buy the ports of Brielle and Flushing from the English. Antoine de Montchrestien, in his *Treatise on Political Economy* published in 1615, termed Dutch prosperity a miracle of human endeavour in a country hardly fit to live in.[1] Temple echoed this judgement.[2] The rest of Europe was first amused, then intrigued and finally alarmed by this growing prosperity. Even as late as 1700 the young Duc de Rohan was able to claim that he detected more genuine signs of wealth in these provinces than in the whole of Italy and Germany.[3] It was partly a critical study of this situation that led English theoreticians to formulate the principles of eighteenth-century economics.

The Organisation of Wealth

Dutch wealth was based not only on hard work and ability but also on the extreme prudence governing the administration of their national income. Temple analysed the situation in the following fashion: the Dutch, he claimed, organised their existence in such a way that 'their common riches lie in every man's spending less than he has coming in'. And the State followed the same course, absorbing a considerable proportion of private savings through taxation but investing it in its turn. This system safeguarded both private interests and public morals.[4] The family budget of an upper middle class citizen came under four headings: upkeep of the household, embellishment of the home, taxes, and capital gains. His other expenses were negligible. Fiscal documents of the time allow one to measure the fluctuations of fortunes in Amsterdam and The Hague between 1625 and 1675. Thanks to this system of hoarding money, large fortunes increased more rapidly than small ones. The investment of small monetary surpluses was generally limited, as we have seen, to the acquisition of articles of luxury, whereas large capital sums were usually invested in real estate and, after 1650, mainly in State bonds.

Credit was the principal stimulus of this wealth, and the law punished insolvent debtors by imprisonment. It is true that the two free towns of Vianen and Culemborg possessed rights of asylum, but to flee there was tantamount to an admission of bankruptcy. The confusion surrounding the various currencies encouraged illegal practices by cashiers and in 1600 still constituted a major obstacle to the country's development. For this reason, Amsterdam created an Exchange bank (*Wisselbank*) in 1609, designed to take the place of the money-changers and provide some control over the cashiers by instituting a system of payment by cheque. Originally conceived as a deposit and exchange centre, the bank's close relations with the East India Company soon resulted in expanded activities that included loaning money and handling government bonds, and extended its sphere of activity to far beyond the Union's frontiers.

Throughout the century, the Exchange bank and the Stock Exchange were together the two most important single institutions in Amsterdam and, consequently, in Holland. The burgermasters held the keys of the bank as they held the keys to the city itself, and its doors could be opened only in the presence of one of these magistrates. Fabulous sums of money were popularly supposed to be deposited in its vaults, and wild guesses were made as to the amount. Parival was more non-committal and remarked that the secrecy with which the bank surrounded its operations made it 'impossible to know precisely, or even to conjecture, what was the actual proportion between its cash funds and its credit'.[5] Nevertheless, he was able to confirm the 'prodigious' number of gold and silver bars, objects of precious metal and bags of money stacked in the vaults of the Town Hall behind massive doors; here lay the bank's treasure, made up of the merchants' deposits that provided it with its capital.

Once every six months the bank closed for a fortnight during which period holders of accounts submitted to the auditor a summary report of their deposits, transfers and balances. The cashier checked the details against his own invoices, and if the account-holder was found to have made an error he became liable to a proportionate fine. The bank had in fact developed into a sort of savings-bank for the town's merchants, giving them hitherto unknown security under convenient conditions. The town of Amsterdam guaranteed the bank's credit, and since the city settled its accounts in hard cash it became customary for large sums due for payment within the town to be effected by transfers on the bank, a method soon adopted by the whole Union and then by the colonial empire.[6] By 1700 the volume of business in which the bank was involved amounted to several million florins a day.[7]

In 1614 social as well as financial considerations prompted Amsterdam to create an additional bank specialising in loans (*Bank van Lening*), designed to take the place of private money-lenders. By lowering rates of interest, this institution put a brake on the gradual impoverishment of the petty bourgeoisie and so helped to create general solvency. Supported by advances from the Exchange bank, the Loan bank was mainly a commercial credit establishment until 1640. Thereafter, this particular function was largely taken over by the private banks founded for the purpose.

The creation of banks had no effect whatsoever on the monetary situation, which remained in a state of considerable confusion until the end of the century despite all attempts to rationalise the currency. Ancient concessions going back to the Middle Ages governed the right to change money, varying according to the district. Each province had its own coinage; in Holland there were several, though Hoorn, Medemblik and Enkhuizen possessed a common coinage and supervised the minting processes in turn, in seven-year cycles. National currencies of innumerable weights and values circulated side by side, including Flemish pounds, ducatoons, rix-dollars, crusados and the Carolus. Several Spanish and German currencies had an official standing. Even the florin, the principal money of account, varied in value according to whether it was minted in Holland, Deventer, Zwolle or Kampen.[8] The resulting inconvenience was particularly marked because of the high rate of circulation of coinage throughout the country; Temple remarked on the extensive use of specie at every social level, claiming that 'more silver is seen in Holland, among the common hands and purses, than brass either in Spain or in France'.[9] From time to time, the authorities succeeded in abolishing an undesirable currency, and in 1667 Amsterdam imposed a fixed rate of exchange for all units in circulation.[10] From its creation in 1544 until 1680 the Dutch florin underwent a gradual devaluation which stripped it of more than half its original value, being finally stabilised in 1681 at a defined weight of 9.45 grammes of fine silver.[11] Meanwhile, forgers flourished: experts among them prepared baths of gold-dust blended with mercury, dipped into this mixture their forged coins made of lead, tin, or even iron, then suspended the pieces over a hot flame so that the mercury separated, leaving a wafer-thin layer of gold. This crime was punished ruthlessly – the culprit was condemned to death and his goods confiscated.

The system of weights and measures was just as chaotic as the currency situation. Each town had its own regulations and customs, and definitions remained very ambiguous: the 'ton', for example, a weight much used in wholesale trade, varied from four *oxhoofd* (about forty-seven gallons) to half a *last* (about 330 gallons); the pound-weight used in retail trade was equivalent to 494 grammes, but the merchant service made use of an entirely different pound three hundred times heavier.[12]

Schemes of maritime insurance covering transportation risks had existed since the middle of the sixteenth century, the premium being included in the purchase price and varying, in 1650, from 5 per cent to 1¼ per cent of the price.[13] The ship transporting the goods was deemed lost after a predetermined period without news of it, depending on the port of origin and route; a year and six weeks in the case of a European port or the Levant, two years when originating in the Indies. An indemnity then became recoverable after three further months had elapsed.

Postal and Information Services
To serve their commercial enterprises, the Netherlands had created two entities without parallel in Europe at that time: a regular postal service and news-sheets.

Amsterdam had employed a certain number of municipal messengers since the middle of the sixteenth century, supplemented subsequently by others engaged by the merchants' corporation, and in 1621 the town was in regular touch with about twenty centres of trade in the Republic and as far beyond its frontiers as Rouen and Hamburg. Other towns followed this example and the post developed rapidly as a public service controlled by the municipal councils. The male or female messengers had to deposit a sum as guarantee during times of trouble, and specialised in a particular route. As their numbers increased, a hierarchy developed. An overworked messenger would assign a part of his load to associates, despite the official ban on such arrangements, and this tendency created an élite of chief messengers who were soon able to make a fortune. Finally, vast postal enterprises came into being, managed by a few powerful 'postmasters'. Hendrik van der Heide had originally showed his initiative by establishing postal services with several more or less inaccessible towns, and in 1655 he obtained a monopoly on mail addressed to France, Italy, Germany and England. It was an exceedingly profitable office; Amsterdam was spending about 168,000 florins a year on postal services by the end of the century and the job of postmaster consequently became the object of intrigues and corruption, with the position being awarded occasionally even to women or children.

Each postal route had its own sorting-office. Amsterdam had four, designated respectively as the depots for Antwerp, Hamburg, Cologne and domestic destinations. The Antwerp line handled correspondence for Belgium and France (a letter took four days to get from The Hague to Paris), and for Spain and Portugal by sea, while Rotterdam had a branch-line for England, and the Hamburg and Cologne depots forwarded mail to Scandinavia and the Rhineland. Amsterdam thus became an international communications centre and profited greatly thereby. A letter sent from Hamburg to Utrecht (for example) passed through its post offices, and so Amsterdam merchants had the advantage of always being the first to be informed about price fluctuations in foreign cities, ships and cargoes lying in foreign ports, natural disasters and shipwrecks. All of these were matters for financial speculation.

Originally, messengers within the Union's frontiers used public transport. Until 1663, those employed on the Amsterdam – Friesland line crossed the Zuider Zee by sail-boat, a method of transport that resulted in heavy delays when there was no breeze. Later, the messengers went by horse. Those working on the long-distance lines delivered their post-bag to the point of departure of the stage-coach or ship chosen to transport the mail to its destination. The Amsterdam – The Hague line, handling diplomatic corre-spondence and connecting with Rotterdam and England, received more mail than it could handle, so in 1659 it was decided that letters delivered to the office after the departure of the last coach should be transported overnight by horse. The messenger left Amsterdam at 9.30 in the evening, rode as far as Haarlem, crossed the Spaarne by boat and continued as far as Lisse where he met a colleague who had left The Hague at 10 p.m. The two men exchanged post-bags, had a drink together and went off in opposite directions. In 1662 this night service was extended to Rotterdam, where an agent of the Amsterdam office consulted tidal tables enabling him to calculate ships' arrival and departure times and so ensure that the mail was dispatched expeditiously. A simple system made it possible to work directly with ocean-going vessels without having to make use of harbour services. The post-office employee simply deposited the outgoing mail in a special boat, anchored at the mouth of the Maas, which then distributed it to the appropriate ships. The ships, in their turn, transferred the letters addressed to Holland that had been entrusted to them, the operation being carried out by throwing water-tight bags from one deck to another. A launch from the collecting vessel took the incoming mail to the pier, where a horseman was waiting to deliver it to the local office which sent it on its way to Amsterdam.

The importance of the postal services to the country's economic development was fully recognised, resulting in the appearance of the inevitable community of touts and swindlers. In Amsterdam the quays were infested by suspicious characters who swarmed aboard the ships the moment they tied up, begging the officer in charge to hand over letters addressed to merchants. Bribing the personnel, if necessary, to get hold of the mail, they hurried to the addressees and demanded an exorbitant sum for delivering the packages. Things went so far that individuals even managed to get hold of the letters illegally and sell them to the addressees for the highest price they could get. The only means the authorities could devise to stamp out this traffic was to forbid entry to the docks to anyone unable to prove his honest intentions. Thenceforward, pilots were ordered to deposit their mail at an office set up on the New Bridge, where the letters were registered and copies of the registration immediately posted in the Stock Exchange.

The correspondent always sealed his letter. At the start of the century he used wax, but in 1625 the practice began to develop of sealing letters with lacquer. He then handed it over to the post office or put it in one of the boxes situated in specific localities. The delivery charge was fixed by the burgermasters and either paid over at the post office (where the employee would stick a stamp bearing the town's arms on the envelope) or debited to the addressee. In the latter case, the envelope was marked: 'the messenger will pay'.[14] Postage rates were high and the service consequently something of a luxury.

Since the end of the sixteenth century the States-General had maintained a few agents abroad, in such places as Cologne, to keep themselves informed on foreign political developments. After each voyage, captains in the Dutch fleet made a report on the news they had gleaned during their travels and submitted their log-books to the Admiralty. Several municipalities, including Leyden and Dordrecht, began around 1600 to send special reporters to Italy, Germany, England and other countries. Important merchants not only got reports from their own foreign correspondents but also had agents at The Hague to provide them with information about happenings at court and acts of government. By 1611 Amsterdam had regular intelligencers stationed in Antwerp, Cologne, Hamburg, Wesel, Munster, Ghent, Lille, Tournai and Valenciennes; for four years the town had one in Lisbon as well, but the Portuguese finally imprisoned him. From 1613 onwards, the brokers' guild published a bulletin on the movement of international prices, while the East India Company established its own commercial information sheet in 1616 at so high a subscription rate that it was practically a confidential document.

Pamphlets and broadsheets commented on national events for the public at large. These had originated during the recent war as bulletins on the political and military situation and were now an established feature. Usually illustrated with engravings or drawings and couched in impassioned, sensational language, these controversial and sometimes scurrilous pamphlets were to be found filed on boards in booksellers' stalls or in the markets; their influence on public opinion was sufficient for successive governments to take them into account. They not only provided a running commentary, sometimes in verse, on political and military events but also gave news of natural disasters, crimes, epidemics and miracles.

Real gazettes began to appear for the first time in

Amsterdam between 1617 and 1619, increasing rapidly in number. By 1630 the competition reigning between them in Amsterdam obliged them to solicit official recognition, but the municipal administration remained cold to this type of publicity. On the other hand, these gazettes were fantastically popular with the general public and the passion for reading them became as widespread as the use of tobacco. By mid-century The Hague, Delft, Leyden, Rotterdam and Haarlem all possessed their own gazettes, sheets appearing once or even three times a week in the form of two columns on quarto paper. In 1650 the monthly *Dutch Mercury* was founded.

The international news provided by this Press was based on official bulletins and subject to considerable delays in transmission as a result. A Haarlem organ included in its issue of 9th January 1627 dispatches dated respectively Linz, 12th December, Venice, 18th December, Paris the 21st of that month and Berlin the 22nd, all of the previous year. In addition, most of the news they published was completely trivial, the smallest events at the Stadtholder's court being the subject of copious commentaries. From 1660 onwards certain articles filled with unconfirmable rumours and dubious gossip began to assume an aggressive attitude towards Louis XIV's political policies. The French ambassadors protested several times in vain and La Fare attributed partial responsibility for the 1672 war to the tone of the Dutch Press.

Hopes of wider circulation among immigrant circles and abroad prompted several booksellers to publish French-language periodicals, including the *Elegant Mercury*, read mostly by the aristocracy of The Hague, the *Amsterdam Gazette* and the *Leyden Extraordinary News*. The most important of these reviews had a literary rather than political or commercial character.

Local small economic interests soon made their appearance in the Press, in the shape of advertisements. The first one was printed in an Amsterdam news-sheet on 23rd May 1626 to announce the publication of the tenth volume of Wassenaer's *History*. After 1632 advertisements became a normal feature in all such journals, being placed at the foot of news items, in the margins or on the back of the sheet. Eliasar Bassan, a chocolate-maker, announced that his 'excellent chocolates would remain at the same price for several more months', a pharmacist recommended his 'universally reputed tea with Swiss herbs'. The usual aim of these messages seems to have been to persuade the reader of the honest price of the goods, though their function was eventually broadened to include advertisements such as: 'Lost, a Pomeranian wolf-dog, in the area of the docks. . . .'[15]

Taxation

Most foreign observers were astonished by the very high rate of Dutch taxation, marvelling that a nation could survive such a heavy burden,[16] or that trade could flourish despite these shackles. It is true that the system weighed most heavily on small consumers and tended to favour large companies, leading to occasional protests and campaigns among the poorer classes. In 1618 Amsterdam found it necessary to appoint inspectors to investigate tax frauds. After 1666, the various associations of journeymen weavers clashed frequently with the authorities over tax matters. The main source of discontent was the vast debt accumulated by the State during the war; now the country was having to foot the bill for its liberation. In 1660 the States-General still owed about thirteen million florins, mainly to the 'regents', who thought first of their own personal advantage in their administration of public affairs and so maintained the interest on this sum at a high rate.[17]

Direct taxation affected private income (the so-called 'two-hundredth' tax), real estate in proportion to the rent paid, household goods (the so-called 'redemption tax') according to a scale dividing taxpayers into several classes: the top or 'capitalist' category brought together all citizens with an annual income exceeding two thousand florins and those giving exterior evidence of wealth. Auction sales and building leases entailed the payment of very heavy fees. Whenever a military expedition or some major scheme of public works had to be financed a special tax was immediately levied; the property-tax was doubled or tripled, a special tax was imposed on peat or chimneys, a provisional poll-tax was established or the income-tax was raised to 1 per cent.

Indirect taxation was both commoner and far heavier. The salt-tax rose in Leyden to 100 per cent the value of the salt, beer was taxed at a rate of 60 per cent, bread at 25 per cent, meat at 14 per cent. Scales varied according to the district. In Amsterdam wine was assessed at twice the rate of beer when sold to individuals, but tavern owners had to pay half as much again. No article of consumption escaped; vinegar, sugar, cattle and fish were all taxed. A duty on oil was instituted in 1621, on tobacco in 1623, on butter in 1625. Legal stamped paper was invented in 1624. By the end of the century things had become so complicated that a plate of meat served in an Amsterdam inn had been subject to fifteen different duties before being served to the customer, and a plate of fish with a sauce was involved in thirty separate taxes. Moreover, the excise service was extremely thorough-going. In Utrecht the municipal official in charge of collecting the beer-duty inspected the brewers' cellars, candle in hand, to count the barrels. Each cask leaving the establishment had to carry the excise office's seal and have the name of the consignee inscribed in a register. If he suspected some irregularity, the inspector was empowered to hold an enquiry, during which he would interrogate under oath the tradesman, his wife, children, servants and neighbours. It was difficult to pass through the meshes of so fine a net. The innumerable tolls, vehicle duties based on weight and canal charges affecting the transportation of goods in the interior of the country, aggravated the situation and was in complete contrast to the relatively light rate of customs duty which was a source of profit only to the great ports.[18]

The collection of these various taxes was the responsibility of the provinces, who remitted a certain proportion to the Union's treasury. Official tax-collectors were established in 1672; prior to this date the provinces farmed out the collection of the various taxes to the highest bidder, the contract being for a relatively short period of three, six or twelve months. The tax-farmer paid wages to his assistants so that the full amount of the sums extracted could be paid into his cash-boxes. If Parival is to be credited, the duty collected on beer in 1650, in Amsterdam alone, amounted to one and a half million florins.[19] Contemporary rumour had it that this town's fiscal revenue exceeded fifty thousand florins a day. In 1665 the Union's total revenue came to about forty millions, of which twenty-two came from the province of Holland; Amsterdam furnished half the province's budget and the province in its turn furnished half the Union's budget.[20] The administration of general funds was carried out by various executive departments responsible to the States-General and the officials delegated by the local governments. As a result, the use of tax revenues depended entirely on the approval of the provinces, that is to say on the provincial notables.[21]

COMMERCE AND THE SPIRIT OF ADVENTURE

The Dutch soil produced almost nothing and, with the single exception of dairy products, the little that it did produce was insufficient to cover the needs of a teeming population in any particular domain. Everything had to be imported: wheat, rye, coal and basic industrial materials such as leather and metals, wool, hemp, ship-timber and dyes. As national wealth and demand for goods increased, the ties binding the Netherlands to France, Germany, England, Scandinavia, Poland and other producing countries increased and became firmer.[1] This poverty of natural resources led to the setting-up of an industry specialising in the manufacture of finished goods from imported raw material, some of whose products, including textiles and paper, were re-exported. The one profitable activity available to the country seemed to be the carrying trade. In an epoch when Europe's economic progress was fast outgrowing local market facilities, the increased demand for a variety of commodities and the relative slowness of communications together imposed the establishment of a large distribution centre. The Netherlands were ideally adapted to fulfil this role, being situated at the juncture of the maritime routes linking north-east and south-west

Europe; in addition, they had possessed a large merchant fleet since the fifteenth century.

Even so, the seven provinces benefited unequally in this respect. Apart from the Hanseatic town of Groningen, which remained an important trading centre, the northern part of the country, Friesland, Ommelanden, Drenthe and Overijssel, was principally engaged in sheep-farming and peat-cutting. The same applied partly to Gelderland. In the so-called country of the States-General south of 's Hertogenbosch, devastated by the war, wool-growing had largely superseded agriculture.[2] Economic activity was concentrated in the maritime provinces of Zeeland and, more particularly, Holland, the part of the country geographically best suited to handle a largely sea-going trade. At the height of their prosperity, Holland and Zeeland often considered the land-bound provinces to be a sheer nuisance, and their political policies sometimes betrayed these sentiments. Holland, with its huge industrial centres of Leyden, Delft, Haarlem and Zaandam, was the economic head of the country, but its vocation and essential function remained overseas trade. Amsterdam, the head of Holland, depended entirely on sea-traffic for its prosperity, and by being the first to launch out into the northern seas – particularly the Baltic – obtained an advantage over rival cities like Middelburg and Rotterdam that it retained throughout the century.

Being relatively isolated from the continent by forests and swamps, connected with the south-east only by waterways, the Netherlands were more easily accessible by sea. Even then, there were only three navigable channels along the whole stretch of sandy coast with its treacherous swells and strong tides; these were the mouths of the Scheldt and the Maas, and the Zuider Zee between the Straits of Texel and the Ij's narrows or by way of the Straits of Vlie. A certain number of ports had sprung up along these three approaches. Neither the French nor the English thought much of the natural facilities and were particularly critical of the fact that the shallow straits were in constant danger of being silted up.[3]

Although these ports demanded constant upkeep they did at least present the advantage of security, and a practically minded sixteenth-century Dutchman judged their virtues in terms of local conditions rather than ideals. Amsterdam was a case in point.[4] The Ij was over a mile wide where the town lay, constituting an excellent harbour, but access to it was through seventy-five miles of dangerous shallows extended at the south-west extremity of the Zuider Zee by the Pampus gulf where sandbanks built up and defeated all attempts to control them by breakwaters.

The progressive silting up of the Pampus during the course of the century became an increasing hazard to sea-traffic. In 1690 a hoisting system had to be introduced to allow the passage of the heaviest ships. Two barges, filled with water so that they were submerged as far as their gunwales, were brought alongside the ship on each side. Iron-reinforced wooden beams were lashed horizontally to the ship's hull so that their ends rested on the barges. These were then pumped dry, thus lifting the ship sufficiently to allow it to cross the shallows. When these had been negotiated, the procedure was reversed.

Long piers of wooden piles connected by planks ran out from the quays, forming a series of docks. The ships docked here and unloaded their cargoes into smaller vessels which made the journey to the quayside. Two buildings in the outer harbour housed the main commercial and maritime services. On the outskirts of the town, in the Pampus area, one of the East India Company's warehouses stood on a pile foundation and here ships could berth directly. All around were small islands connected by bridges, containing rope-making shops, anchor smithies and naval carpenters' workshops. By the end of the century these services were employing more than thirteen hundred workmen, working from four in the morning till six in the evening. Further down the river, the Admiralty building was also built on piles and included an arsenal, while the docks surrounding it sheltered fifty warships in a constant state of readiness. The port's activities remained almost as hectic throughout the night, and Ogier, crossing the Zuider Zee during the night of 23rd July 1636, reported that the water was bright with the lights of sailing-ships making their way to Amsterdam.[5] The fleet returned from the Indies during August, consisting of about twenty of the largest ships in use during that era, all popularly supposed to be carrying two hundred tons of gold apiece. In April the Baltic fleet of two hundred or more vessels set sail. The port of Amsterdam was in fact particularly concerned with trade to the Far East, the northern seas and the Mediterranean. The different Dutch ports all specialised in a particular activity and destination: the towns along the Zuider Zee sent their cargo-vessels and fishing-boats into the north Atlantic, while Rotterdam took charge of most of the traffic between France and England. If Parival is to be believed, he saw four hundred ships hoisting sail in the outer harbour of Brielle.[6]

The extraordinary Dutch success can be explained by the conjunction of various more or less favourable natural conditions and the existence of a national character well adapted to make the most of these conditions. The Dutch had a horror of idleness and were extremely frugal in their tastes, so that domestic consumption was low in relation to the volume of imports and re-exports. Temple insisted that 'never any country traded so much, and consumed so little: they buy infinitely, but 'tis to sell again, either upon improvement of the commodity, or at a better market. They are the great masters of the Indian spices, and of the Persian silks; but wear plain woollen, and feed upon their own fish and roots. Nay, they sell the finest of their own cloth to France, and buy coarse out of England for their own wear.'[7] The high output achieved by the workers kept prices low. The spirit of individualism encouraged the taking of risks, while prudence tempered the tendency by canalising it into boldly conceived associations – the Companies – very different from the old medieval corporations. The war against the Spaniards, originally political and religious in motivation, had gradually assumed an economic character. At the beginning of the seventeenth century the Dutch had started exploring distant seas from sheer necessity imposed by the struggle in which they were engaged, but at the same time the war had created a new love of money and a longing for peace among the people.

Although the Dutch were to be found, from then on, in every conceivable part of the world, very few of them were actually immigrants. They travelled but did not settle down. During the first half of the century the Dutch created sugar refineries at Bordeaux, La Rochelle, Angers and Rouen; Colbert persuaded a few weavers to settle in Picardy, establishing the celebrated master van Roubaix at Abbeville; we have seen that wine-brokers had established themselves in the Loire region. But although the Dutch colony in France was economically important (and never suffered any discrimination during Colbert's time despite its Calvinist persuasion) it remained small, except in Nantes. Louis de Geer, an Amsterdam citizen originally from Liège, had obtained the post of administrator of Sweden's iron ore from Gustavus Adolphus, but this vastly wealthy ironmaster and cannon merchant was only able to induce a very few of his compatriots to join him in his enterprises. In 1609 an Amsterdam merchant became burgermaster of Gothenburg, and a little later a Haarlem man became commissioner of the Swedish crown in this town. But these were isolated adventurers. There was a tiny group of expert Dutch weavers in Frankfurt and Silesia. The czars of Russia attracted a few skilled workers, mostly from Haarlem, to their country, and the saltpetre works, the budding metallurgical industry of Toula and Kalouga, the shipyards of Oka all made use of the services of Dutch pioneers. One of the first to settle in Moscow, Isaac Mossa, had drawn the attention of the Amsterdam merchants to the potential importance of the Russian market; thenceforward, there was a constant though modest flow of Dutch labour to Russia, a fact which explains the visit that Peter the Great paid to the Netherlands at the end of the century.

During this era three-quarters of a century had produced ever-widening horizons to spark Dutchmen's spirit of adventure. In this type of enterprise the profit was in proportion to the risks run and privations endured. It took between three hundred days and a year to sail from Amsterdam to the straits of the Sunda Isles. In 1601 Olivier van Noort, a debt-ridden adventurer staking his last farthing, left for a trip around the world with four ships and 248 crew; he arrived back eventually with a single ship and forty-five men. Two great voyages of discovery had already been undertaken by that time, one ending in heroic failure, the other opening up a route successfully. In 1596 Heemskerk and Barents obtained permission to explore a north Asian commercial route that would allow ships to reach the Far East without falling into the clutches of Spanish galleys. The States had promised them a reward of twenty-five thousand florins in solid cash if they reached a Chinese port. The expedition, consisting of two ships, left on 18th May. On 5th June it ran foul of floating ice for the first time – the sailors mistook the floes for giant swans! Spitsbergen was reached, and then Novaya Zemlya. Here Barents' ship was blocked by autumn ice-formations, hit by a storm and separated from Heemskerk's ship; Barents and his crew of seventeen (including two sick men) had no option but to winter on the island. Their first necessity was a house, but the only wood available consisted of huge tree-trunks brought from Siberia by tidal currents in summer, and these were hard as stone and impervious to their saws. Starving polar-bears attacked the exhausted travellers. But despite these hazards the house was finally built; working with axes they erected a fine Dutch-style frame, and when the house was ready in October they followed Dutch custom and hoisted a bough to the roof-beam. The interior remained to be completed, but at that moment the ship's carpenter died; it was impossible to bury him because of the hardness of the frozen ground. There were no planks left, so they tore bulkheads and fittings from the ship and used them instead; the roof was finished by nailing a sail over the framework. When the polar night fell, a guard was mounted on the shore in the fond hope of seeing the ice start to break up shortly (they were entirely ignorant of climatic conditions in these regions). In the windowless house with its caulked walls the fire gave out more smoke than heat. The snow blocked the chimney and by Christmas had completely covered the house. The clothing of these ill-equipped explorers became covered in rime and their shoes froze solid, but they managed to improvise footwear from fox-skins. On Twelfth Night the unfortunate band threw all discretion to the winds and decided to celebrate the occasion as they would have done at home. So they drank their last remaining wine, made pancakes from the last of their flour and elected a king. On 16th January the sun reappeared and the men made feverish preparations for departure, but by mid-March the ship was still icebound seventy-five feet from open water. In April and May they were blocked by icebergs. By the end of May, Barents became desperate, abandoned his ship and embarked his men on the ship's two longboats, hauling them over those sections where the sea remained ice-covered. Barents died during the course of this journey but his companions finally reached open seas on 19th July 1597 and made land at the Kola peninsula, where they met up with Heemskerk.

One month later another expedition, that had set out in April 1595, finally negotiated the Texel straits and re-entered the port of Amsterdam. The States of Holland had been sufficiently encouraged by reports of increasing weakness in the Portuguese fleets to authorise Cornelis de Houtman and the pilot Keyser to take four small armed ships on a voyage prospecting routes to the Indies by way of Africa. The States furnished the ships and the 249 crewmen. Only eighty-nine of them were to see their homeland again. The itinerary was crudely calculated from old reports and charts and led the small fleet first to Saint Helena and eventually to the Cape of Good Hope. They made port in the land of the Hottentots; seeing negroes for the first time, the Dutch were mistrustful and found that these natives had 'the air of hanged men'. But trading with them was easy and pleasant, since they would offer an ox in exchange for a knife. The expedition reached Madagascar on 18th August, by which time seventy sailors had already succumbed to various diseases, and recorded that they were offered a beautiful eleven-year-old girl in exchange for a fine pewter spoon. However, a sailor had his throat cut while bargaining with a local trader. The crews remained several months in this island. In January 1596 they put in to Antongil bay, where three villages were clustered. One day, the inhabitants of one of these villages stole a longboat from a Dutch vessel in order to extract the nails. The Dutch promptly answered this theft with musket-shots, and were pelted with stones by the natives. At the end of the battle, the village's hundred or more huts had been levelled to the ground. From that point they headed out into the ocean with sails set for Sumatra, passing Malayan boats with sails of plaited straw and cordage made from tropical creepers. Their destination, Bantam, appeared on the horizon on 23rd July. No sooner had they cast anchor among the junks and the Portuguese craft than a mass of Javanese, Chinese and Arabs invaded the bridge, and a fairground atmosphere soon prevailed. Houtman embarked a cargo of two hundred and fifty sacks of pepper, twenty-five crates of nutmeg and thirty bales of *fouli* spice. He wanted to make for the Moluccas but he had trouble with the Portuguese, who took hostages. His men had had enough and mutinied, demanding to go straight back to Holland.

One of the ships, the *Amsterdam*, sprang a leak, and since it was impossible to repair it, it was set on fire. They landed at Bali, remaining there until February 1597. The king of this island received this new and strange people cordially and expressed curiosity about their origins; the sailors unrolled a map and traced the supposed frontiers of their country – embracing Holland, Germany, Norway and Russia! They claimed to have a great king named Maurice who possessed an army of thirty thousand cavalry and fifty thousand foot-soldiers. The Balinese were suitably impressed but showed astonishment at the fact that this Maurice was thirty years old and still a bachelor; in Bali the kings took their first wife at the age of twelve and by the time they were twenty had two hundred. Thus were the Dutch initiated into the peculiar morals of the 'Indians'. But Houtman's main achievement was to have seen at first hand the failure of the Portuguese to consolidate their earlier enterprises in the east.

Now the way was open and the signal had been given for the great race to start.[8]

Two centuries' accumulated experience in coastal navigation[9] had built up among the Dutch an élite of skilled mariners, engineers teeming with inventive ideas and expert shipbuilders, not to mention jurists; navigation laws of ports such as Brielle, going back to the fifteenth century, or that of Amsterdam, developed from older French or English customs, provided the foundation for the international maritime laws which still operate today.

The taste for adventure so noticeable during the first half of the century by no means excluded an intelligent awareness of scientific problems among many sea-going men, and the best families were quite content to see their children depart on distant expeditions. The reports written by mariners of that era demonstrated a really conscientious attitude allied to courage and curiosity. They mentioned everything: the birds they had encountered, coast-line formations, currents, diseases, climatic extremes, essential repairs. On the island of Waygatsch in the Arctic ocean the sailors had discovered four hundred wooden statues embedded horizontally in a great stretch of ice; they surmised that this might be the kingdom of the dead. Annotated travel-journals began to appear, with particular publishers, such as Gerard Ketel of Franeker, specialising in these publications. It was usual to get some local poet to write an introduction in pompous verse which was then printed on the title page. The public was so enthralled by the descriptions and illustrations of animals and natural objects that a sort of naturalist mythology sprang up, made fabulous only by virtue of credulity and optical illusion.

THE FLEET

In 1655 Colbert estimated that the number of hulls navigating the world under the tricoloured flag of the Netherlands amounted to fifteen or sixteen thousand (that is to say, seventy-five per cent of the European fleet) but this figure was greatly exaggerated; in 1670 the Dutch fleet numbered two thousand four hundred ships at the most, though it is a fact that France possessed only a few hundred at the time.[1] The low cost of gear and crews, the latter's consistent efficiency and the competence of the staff-officers allowed the Dutch maritime transport system to eliminate all foreign competition during three-quarters of a century.

In the sixteenth century Holland and Zeeland used only small boats of eighty to a hundred tons burden, but by 1590 ships were already being built of three or four hundred tons. After 1600 tonnages of six hundred and even a thousand were occasionally to be met with; the latter figure designated the largest vessels intended for the Indies run, but most of these were of not more than five hundred or six hundred tons burden. The increase in tonnage was accompanied by technical improvements, and only the smallest ships retained the old-fashioned single-decked construction. In 1590 a new type of ship came into being, the so-called *flûte* or 'store-ship' with a circular poop, particularly suitable for navigating European waters and destined to exercise a considerable influence on the development of Dutch trade. A little later various kinds of 'stern-framed' vessels appeared, flat-pooped and designed for long journeys. The rigging became more complicated; the main mizzen-sail was supplemented by a small sail athwartships and the bowsprit was lengthened by an additional jib. Soon the only ships to be found on the high seas were mighty three-masters with several decks and a double forecastle. Each maritime route had its own particular type of vessel and sometimes several different types, depending on its needs – transportation of heavy or light cargoes, privateering or escort duties. Early in the seventeenth century the States were so impressed by the Spanish galleys that they had several ships of this type constructed in their shipyards, but these proved unmanoeuvrable in the Atlantic and were very soon abandoned.

Merchant Service and Navy

Until the end of the sixteenth century the Dutch fleet did not really constitute what we would call a 'sea service', if we take the term to indicate some minimum standardisation and central organisation. The first heterogeneous squadrons involved in the war against Spain were put together at random by local authorities, who commandeered private vessels by means of municipal edicts. Strategic necessity resulting from the rapidly developing use of artillery in sea-battles allowed the Princes of Orange and the great Amsterdam merchants to introduce an element of organisation into this chaos, in virtue of the increasing military and commercial responsibilities devolving upon seafaring men.

These factors resulted in the foundation of the great Companies and of the Admiralty, but even so, a clear distinction was never established during the seventeenth century between the privately run merchant service and the state-controlled navy. Their interests remained closely linked: the leading figures in both units were in constant contact, the equipment and material were largely the same and the roles assigned to them often almost identical; the fact that the Admiralty furnished naval convoys to the merchant fleets enhanced the international reputation of Dutch carriers. In any case, the sea services were carefully nurtured by the state, since both their mercantile and military aspects seemed to be the sole instrument of national prosperity. Nevertheless, commercial considerations were always uppermost, and whenever the world situation seemed to improve, the governments slashed the navy's budget. The Admiralty had to make do with improvisations until the next crisis, borrowing, dismissing personnel and selling ships at a loss. This explains the astonishing fluctuation in the size of the nation's fleets during the course of the century: the year after the Treaty of Westphalia, national tonnage was reduced by two-thirds and naval crews by 60 per cent.[2] Even so, the thirty or forty escort-vessels considered sufficient in peace-time cost, with their gear, provisions and crew, at least six million florins a year.

The Admiralty had been created in the final years of the sixteenth century, being presided over by the Stadtholder in his capacity of Admiral of the Fleet, and consisted of five colleges composed of deputies from the provinces, with administrative headquarters in Amsterdam, Middelburg, Rotterdam, Hoorn-Enkhuizen and Harlingen. As a central administration, the Admiralty performed a vast assortment of duties, including the management of the ships, the recruitment of crews, the choosing of staff-officers and the application of the law to maritime crimes and contraband. An independent treasury under its control was supplied from the revenue of customs duties, and if this proved insufficient in times of trouble the provincial governments sent special contributions. The Admiralty's freedom of action was thus doubly limited by the provincial regents' control. In fact, general authority over the navy soon slipped from its hands, each college indulging in its own politics without thought of collaboration.

In its early years the Admiralty – or 'the Admiralties' as it was generally called – used to hire the ships it needed from the merchant service, and at the start of the seventeenth century it was still occasionally buying merchant ships. These purchases ceased during the truce period and the strength of the Admiralty's fleet fell to almost nothing. After 1650, it needed the war with England to reawaken the regents' interest. From then on, the Admiralty built its own ships, paying for them out of its own funds. It employed a whole array of sworn officials, commissioners, controllers and collectors, charged with administering naval equipment and supervising the disposal of war-booty.

Despite changes of fortune, the Admiralty fulfilled important representative functions during the great era of Dutch expansion. Several serious incidents occurred with the English over the question of dipping the flag. The government heaped honours upon its admirals and captains, often appointing them to diplomatic missions in overseas countries. The sailors themselves were chosen in a haphazard manner from whatever sources were available, but officers were nearly always selected by sole virtue of their talents, authority and character.

These officers, although mostly of modest origin, formed a genuine élite in the Republic. Men like Tromp and de Ruyter (who as a child worked a tread-wheel in a rope-works) were the heroes of their time, adored by the masses, so that people flocked to the coast to pray during naval engagements.

Despite the high bounties they were awarded for their prize captures (from six thousand to fifty thousand florins) and the natural advantages they enjoyed, they remained simple people. When the Comte de Guiche paid a call on de Ruyter on his flagship, the day after the victory of 15th May 1666, he found the great man in the throes of sweeping out his cabin and feeding grain to his chickens. De Ruyter was pious, and every sea-battle was preceded by psalm-singing and praying on board his ship. As the responsible authority, the Admiralty encouraged all manifestations of religious sentiment and national ideology in its navy.

Private fleets engaged in commerce or fishing were completely free of any central administration, the boats being managed by the shipowner or fishing-company director as a family concern, while the great companies (whose organisation we shall study later in this chapter) ran their fleets as a big business. The companies had so many ships that they sometimes found it difficult to recruit sufficient crews. In that case they hired a recruiter, advancing him letters of credit worth a hundred and fifty florins for each man furnished. Since this agent was usually in need of ready money he would sell his letters to a jobber, sometimes for a quarter of their nominal value. So the future sailors found themselves endowed with a speculative value before they had even trod a deck.

Corsairs and Pirates

The war and the necessity of hurting Spain by striking at the roots of her wealth allowed piracy to become acceptable to the Dutch maritime code from the end of the sixteenth century. Before the truce, towns or Admiralties distributed 'letters of commission' on demand to shipowners, authorising them to privateer over a specified area. Every social level was more or less involved in this enterprise. A burgermaster of Amsterdam, Johan Corneliszen, was generally considered in 1610 to have been a former sea-rover. The 'corsairs', licensed agents of maritime pillage, ended up by abandoning all scruples and attacking indiscriminately enemy ships, neutrals and even their compatriots; they gradually assumed the status of 'pirates', brigands acting on their own. The governments made a few attempts to exercise some control: in 1605 a decree ordered the registration of letters of commission; the following year it was decided to issue new letters only on deposit of twenty thousand florins, while the authorities tried to recall to Holland the hundred and thirty corsairs roving the high seas throughout the world. But the truce put an end to these official interventions, and the State decided to remain neutral in the future, in accordance with the truce agreements. Private piracy thrived accordingly.[3] It was commonly held to be more profitable than the Indies trade.

The next half-century was a golden age for these long-haired, black-bearded sea-wolves, bare-chested under a sleeveless jacket, waistbelt bristling with pistols and daggers. These 'freebooters' (the word is derived from the Dutch *vrijbuiter*, 'seeker of free booty') were drinkers, gamblers and masters of profanity, and were almost certain to end up with their throats cut or swinging at the end of a rope. A typical specimen was Klaas Compaan of Zaandam, nicknamed 'the terror of the seas', who on first hoisting sail had hurled over the forecastle-rail his Bible, psalm-book and ship's log, so that he could work freely without any inhibitions of conscience. He was a brave man who never failed to send a sack of silver and jewels to his wife after a profitable capture (he was credited with 358 during his career), and ended his days peacefully in their small house in Oostzaan.

Any merchant ship was fair game, whatever flag it might be flying. The concerted efforts of Henri IV and of the English government finally rid the north Atlantic of these corsairs and pirates, but there were plenty of other seas left. Booty and prisoners could easily be sold in the ports along the Barbary coast, relations being established in this way between the Dutch pirates and the coastal inhabitants of the Magrab. Indeed, from 1600–10 onwards, renegade Dutch-men masquerading under Arab names settled down there and joined up with the Moorish pirates.[4] The celebrated Morate Reis was in reality a certain Jan Janszen of Haarlem; Soliman Buffoen was originally Jacob de Hoereward of

Rotterdam.[5] The infamous Veenboer, going under the name
of Soliman Reis, was slain in 1620 during an attack on a
Christian ship. As for Coert Siewerts, he had entered the
service of Venice and privateered against the Turks on
behalf of His Most Serene Highness. Covered with glory, he
ended up as Admiral of the Fleet of Denmark!

TRADING AND COLONISATION

Although trading between towns within the Union was
vigorous, it still represented only a tiny and unimportant
fraction of the total volume of business. A curious dis-
proportion seemed to govern the nation's trading, by which
its value increased with the distance covered. The country's
closest neighbour, Germany, provided transit routes of which
the Rhine was the most important; she was also a source of
staple goods such as cereals, wood and wine, but imported
very little in return. Dutch businessmen had interests in the
Angoulême paper-mills, while the textiles of Normandy,
Anjou and Brittany were dependent upon Dutch carriers.
Before 1672 the latter handled most of France's foreign
trade and even ran the coastal services between the kingdom's
ports. Hence the jealousies, and also the epithets flung at
them in the time of Henri IV and Richelieu, the sneers of
'bloodsucker' and 'starving louse'. Until 1650 there were
ten laden Dutch boats leaving the Netherlands for England
for every single one making the opposite journey. This
practically one-way traffic, based on agreements concluded
at the end of the Middle Ages, was such an irritation to the
English that the court secretly encouraged piracy against
Dutch ships in the North sea.

One of the main commodities in Anglo-Dutch trade was
cloth, bought raw in England by the Dutch as a right granted
by treaty, then cropped and dyed by them and re-exported.
The English used various customs measures to limit this privilege which filched part of their own industry's profits. Amid
the confusions of all this legislation, smuggling prospered.

Trade with Spain had never ceased despite the war, and
when Henri IV proposed in 1595 to forbid communications
with the Iberian peninsula, panic swept through Holland.

The important transit traffic of cereals, wood and fish in one direction and oil, fruit and wine in the other was vitally necessary for the Netherlands prior to the establishment of the great colonial enterprises. After 1609, the volume of business appears to have diminished, though shortly before 1648 discussions took place with a view to quoting Spanish silver on the Amsterdam market. These negotiations were successfully concluded after the Westphalia peace treaty. In 1650 the 'marine treaty' granted the Dutch fleet various privileges relative to the transportation of certain goods to Spain, Portugal and America. Smuggling remained a popular occupation in these waters, and even dealt in arms and ammunition.[1]

By mid-century the volume of imports of Norwegian wood through the ports of Enkhuizen, Hoorn and Harlingen, destined for merchants in Amsterdam and Zaandam, exceeded a hundred thousand tons. A special type of ship, with a deep hold and heavy draught, was designed for this trade. Since Norway bought nothing from the Netherlands in return except a little wheat, the balance of trade was unfavourable in this instance, and in 1635 one ship en route to Bergen is recorded as having carried a thousand or so florins in coins, while another carried three barrels filled with rix-dollars.

The Baltic trade, on the contrary, was an immense source of profit for the Netherlands. In 1600, 55 per cent of the ships touching at Swedish and Russian ports carried the Dutch flag, while fifteen years later this proportion had risen to 67 per cent.[2] The Dutch transported cereals from these northern countries to western and southern Europe. On the outward journey the ships carried cargoes of colonial produce, textiles and light-weight merchandise, posing the problem of ballast in this long, difficult sea route. Sand was used in the first place, but since it was emptied into the sea on arrival at the harbour entrance there was a risk of eventually silting up the channel. Sand was then increasingly replaced by bricks, which were sold afterwards to local merchants. This fact may explain the presence throughout the Baltic basin of Dutch construction methods and architectural style.

Access to the Baltic was at the mercy of the powers controlling the Sound and accordingly subject to political hazards,
but from the second half of the sixteenth century onwards
the Dutch had an alternative route at their disposal via the
North Cape and the White Sea, where the port of Archangel
suited their needs admirably.

The near-monoply of commercial transportation exercised
by the Dutch in northern and western Europe led to increasing international tension from the mid-century onwards,
and it was with the intention of breaking this hold that
Cromwell promulgated his famous Navigation Act in 1651.[3]
The wars of 1652 and of 1665 followed. In France Colbert's
economic policy demanded the raising of the Dutch mortgage,
whence, partly, the war of 1672.[4] In the long run these
conflicts were to lead to recession and then to the ruin of the
great Dutch trading system.

Until 1650 Dutch trading in the Mediterranean was
limited to Italy: Leghorn in particular but also Civitavecchia,
Naples, Sicily and, to a lesser extent, Venice. Even before
1600, when they had been engaged by Henri IV to provide
transportation between France and Turkey, the Dutch had
fully realised the great trading possibilities of the Levant.
But it took them half a century to ensure safe navigation
among these waters infested with Barbary pirates. At the
suggestion of a Dutch merchant in Istanbul in 1611, the
States dispatched Cornelis Haga secretly to make contact
with the Porte. Despite the opposition of the French ambassador, Haga obtained a treaty after a few months' negotiation,
specifying freedom of access to Ottoman ports, protection
against pirates, and the opening of Dutch consulates with
exclusive jurisdiction over their own nationals. Haga remained the representative of the States at the Sultan's court
until 1639 and succeeded in opening the ports of the Mussul-
man world to his compatriots. Consulates were set up
successively in Aleppo, Algiers, Tunis and Morocco, and
treaties were signed with the Moroccan and Algerian authorities. The contracting parties saw to it that these agreements
were strictly held to, and when a Dutch captain attacked and
sank an Algerian ship off Leghorn the Dutch consul in Algiers

was arrested and put in irons. In 1625 Haga persuaded his government to create a 'Directorate of Levantine trade', charged with examining and resolving all the questions relative to navigation in the Mediterranean. This organisation, consisting of seven Amsterdam merchants, functioned for about twenty years.[5]

The Great Companies

In 1594 a dozen Amsterdam merchants engaged in the spice trade grouped themselves into a 'Society of Distant Lands' designed to finance the building and equipment of a fleet of ships, and other similar associations soon sprang up. Houtman's voyage revealing the importance of the sea-route round the Cape provided an enormous stimulus to these undertakings, and in 1601 fifteen private fleets totalling sixty-eight ships set sail for the Indies. But lack of organisation led to the disastrous failure of this expedition. The intervention of Oldenbarnevelt led the States-General to create, in 1602, an 'East India Company' regrouping the existing associations under statutes similar to those of our limited companies, with sole rights to engage in Far Eastern trade. The capital reached nearly seven million florins at its inception[6] and was made up of private shares. Even the most modest contributions were accepted, offering investment possibilities to those with small as well as large savings. In fact, the East India Company avoided increasing its capital and soon ceased to attract large-scale investments. Its beginnings were difficult, but by mid-century its share certificates were returning 500 per cent. [7]

The Company was directed by a seventeen-man board selected from among the country's chief merchants, the administration being shared between five agencies enjoying a certain autonomy, based in Amsterdam, Middelburg, Enkhuizen, Delft and Rotterdam. Each branch's rights and obligations towards the Company were calculated according to the particular town's contribution to the original capitalisation; in Amsterdam's case, 60 per cent. In the Company's six capitals, the 'East Indies House' became a landmark, and those of Middelburg and Amsterdam were considered particularly magnificent.

In a relatively inorganic State, the Company served the purpose of concentrating the national resources, not only financially but in terms of equipment. It possessed its own ships (and often lent them to the Admiralty), its docks, warehouses and banks; its military influence resided in a general staff and a thirty-thousand-man army, as well as a war-fleet of forty or fifty ships; it was politically entrenched through its eventually dominant position in the Indian Archipelago, administering territories and dealing both with the local sultans and with the European powers. Its monopoly was breached, nevertheless, by the initiative of various individuals who refused to go along with the Company and founded other companies under the aegis of foreign powers.

The East India Company secured a foothold in Java and the Moluccas from its earliest years. The Dutch seafarers who had followed Houtman in making the 'Indies' voyage had run up against the Portuguese and engagements had been fought in both 1600 and 1601. The native population, resentful of the missionary zeal of the Portuguese, supported the Dutch on these occasions, viewing them as newcomers interested only in trade. The time was ripe for the creation of permanent establishments in these islands.

In 1609 the Company appointed a Governor General of overseas territories with headquarters on the island of Amboina, and when the directors, the so-called *Heeren XVII*, awarded the post in 1618 to Jan Pieterszoon Coen it became a real government. Coen was a complex and strange personality, one of the most inscrutable figures of the era: he imposed his will ruthlessly on the sultans who had been encouraged by the English to threaten his depots, yet at the same time he dreamt of breaking the Company's monopoly and conceived a colonial policy owing much to Spanish practice in America. He swept the natives out of the territories he controlled and asked the States-General to place at his disposal a group of Dutch pioneers of high moral standing, together with their families; around this solid kernel he intended to concentrate an army of slaves bought in other parts of the world, and so establish with this dual edifice a solid military force allied to cheap manpower.

Nothing came of this plan, but at least when Coen captured and razed the town of Jacatra in 1619 he was free to build Batavia on its ruins and make this new town the centre of Dutch domination. This sort of colonial Geneva, referred to by people in Amsterdam and The Hague as an 'honourable prison', was a strange conglomeration: Japanese and Chinese artisans and planters, a mixed European population of Dutch and English; a fort, a garrison, a court-house and even a church; a lawyer and a doctor; a police force, laws against drunkenness and concubinage. Fifty years later this had become a real town, designed in imitation of Amsterdam, and the heart of an empire.

Even so, Dutch influence for a long time to come was to be limited to the trading enclaves along the coasts. The governor's jurisdiction went no further than the Sino-European cluster protected by a citadel housing the Company's soldiers. Nothing at all was known about the hinterland. It does not even seem to have occurred to anyone prior to 1630 that Java might be a fertile country, and it was 1648 before the first expedition into the interior was made. The Company had no thought, originally, of territorial conquests; in 1644 it declared to the States-General that 'the towns and fortresses conquered in the East Indies should not be considered as acquisitions of the State but as the personal property of the interested merchants who have the right to sell them to whomever it may please them, even to the King of Spain'.[8] It took a century for the Company to assume control over the entire island of Java, in slow stages and without premeditation.

Meanwhile, the Company had set up a profusion of trading-posts throughout the Far East. They occupied Formosa in 1624 but Chinese pirates reconquered the island forty years later without being challenged; the small Dutch colony, including women and children, was massacred or reduced to slavery. Malacca was seized from the Portuguese in 1641 and Colombo in 1656.[9]

Relations with continental China and with Japan were of an entirely different, pre-colonial character. Chinese and Japanese officials viewed these Dutch clowns with benevolent disdain. After their expulsion of all foreigners, the Japanese government granted the Dutch sole rights to enter her ports, and once a year a Dutch embassy was permitted to proceed to Edo; on one occasion its members were invited to sing and dance in the manner of their country, to make the Shogun's concubines laugh! As for the Chinese, whose own trade routes were constantly crossing those of the Dutch, they summed up their rivals shrewdly in these terms: 'The Red-beards, that is to say the Dutch, live on the western ocean. Greedy and cunning, good judges of precious commodities, they fight with skill to obtain the greatest possible profit. For this aim they will risk even their lives and do not hesitate to penetrate into the most distant lands. Whoever meets them on the high seas will assuredly be looted by them.'[10]

The most important colonial enterprise was the foundation of the Cape of Good Hope colony. The Cape was an important staging-post on the India route, and by mid-century it became apparent that security demanded a permanent Dutch garrison there. In 1651, therefore, the *Heeren XVII* sent three ships loaded with colonists and cattle, under the command of Jan van Riebeck. Thereafter, thirty or more large vessels touched at the port annually. Blessed with a favourable climate, the colony prospered, living by stock farming and by fruit- and wine-growing. However, this peasant settlement – an unusual phenomenon in the Dutch empire – remained of very little importance for a long time. In 1672 a similar attempt was made to colonise the then uninhabited island of Mauritius, when the East India Company settled forty farming families there.

Since the end of the sixteenth century, Usselincx had tried to turn his countrymen's eyes towards America, where they might have struck Spain at the very roots of her power. Only the corsairs listened to him, and it took the truce to launch a two-pronged commercial movement in this direction. In the north, the Dutch landed on the coast of what is now New York State; this territory was called the 'New Netherlands' and gave its name to a Company founded in 1614 to supervise fur trading. In the south the trading route reached Brazil.

Towards the end of the truce period, the Dutch were handling two-thirds of the cane-sugar exports from these regions. In 1621 the States-General authorised the creation of a 'West India Company' and granted it a trading monoply along the west coast of Africa and the east coast of America. This enterprise was dogged by misfortune, and it seemed that the Netherlands were better attuned to Asia than to America. The capital was raised mostly in Amsterdam but was slow to come in, so that it was a full two years before the first ship could be fitted out. Finally, a few depots were opened in Brazil. But despite the eight hundred ships the Company sent across the Atlantic in thirteen years, it was only the capture of the 'silver fleet' in 1628 that allowed the Company to pay a first dividend to its shareholders.

Encouraged by this success, it sent John Maurice of Nassau to Pernambuco as Governor General. During his seven-year administration he was able to make some progress in developing the plantations and storage-depots of Olinda, Pernambuco and Paraibo. But back home in the Netherlands discord reigned on the subject of these colonies. John Maurice demanded troops for action against the Portuguese, but the troops never arrived. The settlement was doomed and in 1640 the Dutch began to withdraw. In 1650 the commander of the relief army finally sent by the States resigned his commission after a series of disputes with the Company's agents. He was placed under arrest. But in 1661 The Hague sold their Brazilian possessions back to the Portuguese for eight million florins.

In 1626 the Company had paid sixty florins to the local Indian chiefs for a stretch of land on the island of Manhattan, in the 'New Netherlands', upon which they constructed the colony of 'New Amsterdam'. This settlement appeared to have great future prospects,[11] but it was left to fend for itself, and when it had already accumulated a population of almost ten thousand the States ceded it to the English in exchange for Surinam on the unexplored jungle coast of Guinea. This double reverse finally checked the Company's ambitions, and in 1674 its statutes were modified and its activities reduced to much more modest dimensions. The only possessions retained by the Dutch in America, apart from Surinam, were Curaçao and a few small islands in the Caribbean.

From this moment onwards, the great Dutch carrying-trade went into a steady decline. An over-development of foreign trading activities had given rise to excessive domestic competition, while the Westphalia peace treaty had given the other European powers a fresh freedom to intervene and block several of her foreign outlets. The markets were overstocked with colonial products. Prices fell, although development costs had risen as a result of the wars undertaken to consolidate the Company's positions. Sir William Temple relates a typical anecdote: 'As I remember one of their seamen, newly landed out of their East Indies fleet, in the year 69, upon discourse in a boat between Delft and Leyden, said, he had seen, before he came away, three heaps of nutmegs burnt at a time, each of which was more than a small church could hold.'[12]

During the same period, nutmeg-trees were being chopped down in the Moluccas so as to reduce the crop and maintain prices.

Colonists and Slaves
The Dutch settlements always remained underpopulated. A handful of adventurers, orphans, sons estranged from their families were the main groups among the colonists. The governors repeatedly asked for women to be sent out and, from time to time, a boatful of girls recruited from the municipal orphanages arrived. But what the Companies really needed was soldiers. A roving population of fighting men knocked about the empire, grouped here and there in garrisons of dubious efficacy. Sommelsdijk, governor of Surinam, was assassinated by a dozen mutineers. On the other hand, the men on whom the heaviest responsibilities rested, admirals and governors, remained for a long time honest people of humble origins who had risen through sheer talent and efficiency. But an increasing social prestige attached itself to their functions, and by the end of the

century, when Coen's calvinistic austerity was a thing of the past, people saw nothing unusual in their displays of luxury, their palaces and slaves and their thirst for honours, despite the contrast that such pomp presented to the relatively simple manners and morals of the home country.

As far as the Companies were concerned, the colonies' sole function was to provide security for their trading operations. The Company vested legal control in its vassals, the sultans, being interested only in retaining real power in its own hands and ensuring that no rival power emerged. This policy led to a series of bloody wars, such as that waged by Coen against the Sultan of Mataram in 1627-9, accompanied by atrocities committed by the Japanese auxiliaries employed by the Company for such purposes. So, from war to war, the governors of Batavia were increasingly caught in the meshes of their own policies, and in a hundred years found themselves the unwilling masters of Java.

After the first wave of colonisers had established itself in the second half of the century, a few predicants came out to the Indies in their turn. Only the Formosans gave them a good reception and allowed themselves to be converted voluntarily to Calvinism; at one time there were as many as thirty-two pastors on the island. Everywhere else, these missionaries' activities were limited to the circle of their compatriots. But several of them in Malaya, Java and the Moluccas became expert linguists, historians and naturalists, though their researches remained unknown in the Netherlands for a long time and were thus unable to correct the simplistic notions held there about oriental peoples.

Having no outposts in Black Africa, the Spaniards had made use of Dutch and English traders since the sixteenth century to furnish them with slaves for their American colonies. The West India Company took up slave-trading on its own account,[13] but prosperity depended upon the fixity of the supply markets, and de Ruyter's expedition to the Gold Coast had the aim of consolidating such bases of operations. In 1637 John Maurice occupied the Portuguese settlement of São Jorge del Mina, with a view to extracting fresh manpower for his Brazilian plantations; four years later the Portuguese ceded the entire coast of Angola to the Company for exploitation. The Company could now buy annually up to fifteen thousand slaves at thirty florins a head and resell them in America at prices ranging from three hundred to five hundred. It was partly the need for a place where this merchandise could freely be offered for sale that prompted the acquisition of Surinam after the loss of Brazil.

From a financial point of view the risks involved were fully justified by the vast profits involved. And the risks were many: risk of capture, for the taking of a slave-ship meant a fortune for a corsair; risk of shipwreck for these light-weight skiffs; risk of damage to the living cargo, for these negroes jammed, men and women, in the depths of the hold died off like flies. In his own interests, the captain looked after the health of his cargo and, in cases of epidemic, would fire a musket into the air to draw God's attention to this human misery. These slave traders from Flushing, Hoorn and Amsterdam were, after all, decent folk who read their Bible every day; they lacked imagination and would have been astonished had anyone questioned the morality of their industry. The fact that laws of the United Provinces forbade slavery provided these unfortunate negroes with one single hope. If ever one of them was able, heaven knows how, to set foot on Dutch soil, he was automatically free and his master lost all rights of repurchase. In the larger Dutch towns it was not so unusual to come across such freed slaves among the domestic households of wealthy families.

INDUSTRY: *Its Shortcomings*

Dutch soil yielded only two exploitable products, sand and peat. Sand, banked up or spread out in beds, had the resilience which made it the best foundation for constructional work in marshy areas. Here was a paradox for this Bible-quoting nation: to build on sand was to build for eternity! Dikes, ramparts and foundations were all made of sand. This precious material was extracted mostly from the dunes; the Oegstgeest dunes, for instance, owned by the town of Leyden, provided the raw material used in the maintenance of the town's buildings and installations. In the north of the country, villages erected in the Middle Ages on artificial elevations of sand dug pits in their own land and lived on the proceeds of the sand they extracted. The standard fuel was peat rather than wood.[1] In some regions, its intensive and careless exploitation had broken up the soil and produced ponds which aggravated the shortage of ground from which the country suffered. At the beginning of the seventeenth century the town of Groningen made an effort to rationalise this industry within its territorial jurisdiction by digging a network of navigable canals in the vast marshlands of the Sappemeer, along which 'colonies' of peat-workers were established according to a regular plan.

The peat was extracted in slabs, cut into bricks, dried in the open air, then stored in lofts where it gradually hardened. Frisian peat, more porous and crumbly than that of Groningen, was used mainly for the bakers' and brewers' ovens.

Dutch industry concerned itself essentially with the production of finished goods from imported raw material, but its development was throttled by guild restrictions and it remained generally at handicraft level. Its economic importance in the Union in comparison with the carrying-trade was relatively small. As a result, this lack of a solidly established industrial base constituted a serious handicap, in the long run, for the trading interests, while industry, in its turn, remained dangerously dependent upon the trading situation.

However, Dutch industry had been no less quick than the traders to profit from the skills of the Flemish refugees, and it possessed, above all, one enormous technical asset: its windmills, producers of almost cost-free energy, whose uses multiplied rapidly from the start of the century. Saw-mills, paper-mills, oil-works and gunpowder factories all functioned with the aid of windmills. In the flour-mills, special millstones allowed barley to be polished without being ground, after which others ground it into flour. Windmills were also used to pump water. The windmill designer was an individual comparable in importance to the present-day engineer, and Jan Adriaenszen Leeghwater, for example, counted among the great men of his age. The oldest type of windmill was composed of a more or less square main body, one storey high, in the framework of which the sails' axle was embedded; the entire structure pivoted on a base of thick horizontal cross-beams that rested, in their turn, on a fixed lower stage. In 1600 the cylindrical windmill with a fixed frame was invented, in which a roof unit which could be swung around with the aid of levers carried the sails. Shortly beforehand, Cornelis Corneliszen had invented the giant saw-mill known as a *paltrok*,[2] designed to cut up the heaviest lengths of timber, especially in naval dockyards: the windmill itself formed a single unit with the workshop it surmounted, providing the driving power for the circular saws beneath it in the framework encasing the whole structure; the workshop was one storey high and opened up like a warehouse, allowing the cut planks to be loaded onto lighters; the entire building could be rotated, being mounted on a stonework base by cross-struts whose ends were fitted with wheels moving along the rim of the base.

The windmill was an integral part of the country land-scape, and with its moat and drawbridge formed one of the most charming and unique features of the Dutch scene.[3] It was surrounded by a complete folk-lore, the sails of the windmill serving to express popular feelings. The sails were sometimes decked with flags. Or, in the case of some great event, the millstones were stopped just when the sails formed a vertical cross, and a flag was then sometimes hoisted to the top of the uppermost sail. When there was a wedding in the village the mill was bedecked with flowers on two successive Sundays. In Holland and Zeeland, the death of someone related to the miller involved setting the sails at a particular angle, according to the relationship between him and the deceased: an angle of forty-five degrees indicated a very close loss, or sometimes even a public disaster.[4]

The first windmills appeared during the Middle Ages and they were first used for industrial purposes during the fifteenth century, Zaandam being the pioneer town in this respect. By 1600 this town and its surrounding districts had fifty or more windmills. Their number increased throughout the century to such a point that the Zaanstreek, with its 600 windmills, had become the greatest industrial complex in the Netherlands by 1700. They were used principally for sawing the building timber, imported by way of the Rhine, which Amsterdam consumed in huge quantities for the new districts it was constructing, as well as for ship-building. The opposition of Amsterdam's guild of sawyers, obstinately attached to its ancient traditions of hand-sawing, was powerless against this competition, and by 1630 Zaandam was in absolute control of that particular industry.

This triumph benefited all the branches of industry which had been concentrated in the hands of the local millers for a quarter of a century: oil-works dealing with colza, rape-seed or hemp; dye-works using Brazil wood, chalk or starch-blue; white-lead factories; tobacco- and mustard-grinding works; works for processing the raw materials used in rope- and cable-making; fulling-mills, known locally as 'stinking mills'; spice-mills; and finally paper-mills. At the end of the century a freight-boat left Zaandam every half hour for Amsterdam, six miles away. This proximity, combined with the existence of its saw-mills, had given Zaandam the opportunity to set up naval dockyards rivalling those of Amsterdam in importance, and its skilled carpenters had the reputation of being unexcelled in 'pegging, joining, carving, squaring, planing, drilling, sawing, cutting planks and knot-burning'.[5] Winches were used to wind and stretch ropes, and hulls were hauled by means of tread-wheels twelve to fifteen feet in diameter, set in motion by workmen treading the flat-boards.

By the end of the century Zaandam could claim at least fifty master builders and was producing from thirty to thirty-five ships a year, despite the inadequacy of its installations. Ships longer than 130 feet had to be transferred to a different dock after preliminary work had been completed, and this provided a typical example of the sheer illogicality of the Dutch industrial substructure; the moving operation was carried out by manual labour, the hull being dragged over a seven-foot dike, then through a curving street whose maximum width was just twenty-six feet.

Apart from Zaandam, only Leyden really deserved to be called an industrial town. Ancient craft traditions had made Leyden the main textile-manufacturing centre, especially of wool, and the influx of Flemish refugees had allowed it to modernise and develop its methods of production. In 1619 the town marketed 110,000 bolts of woollen cloth – homespun, serge and fustian – or four times more than in 1584. After 1615 Leyden also wove 'English-style' cloth. A gradual mechanisation of techniques had aided this expansion, with windmills replacing the old treading-vats. Even so, manpower and horse-power remained the principal sources of energy, since a huge additional labour force became available between 1630 and 1640, largely because of the immigration of working-class refugees. This period saw the first use by master wool-merchants and drapers of capitalist methods in the use of credit and the struggle against foreign competition. Competition was strong in international markets, and the profits of Leyden's industrialists never approached those of Amsterdam's merchants.[6] Even within the Netherlands, Tilburg was able to challenge Leyden's supremacy at one point in 1630 by obtaining supplies of cheap, contraband, Spanish wool. Subsequently, the family-operated enterprises of Brabant and Gelderland lost their independence to the manufacturers of Holland and ended up working for them. Similarly, Haarlem's cloth-bleaching industry came under the control of the big merchants.[7]

Haarlem and Delft were the first two centres of the beer-brewing industry, but competition increased rapidly in this field during the seventeenth century: Rotterdam, Groningen, Nijmegen, Amsterdam, Deventer, Arnhem and Dordrecht each established its own brewery sooner or later. This development affected Delft in particular. At the end of the sixteenth century a third of the town's craftsmen were brewers, but by 1600 twenty-nine breweries had closed, and fifty-seven more closed during the first half of the century. By 1667 there were practically none left.

Gouda made pipes and ropes. Brick-kilns were to be found throughout the country. Immigrants from Antwerp had set up a few industries in Amsterdam, making use of raw materials handled regularly by the port; they included soap-works that became world-famous, and cane-sugar refineries whose number had increased to thirty or more by 1630. After the loss of their chief supplier, Brazil, sugar-cane was introduced into Java, and in 1662 a fleet of a hundred ships sailed into the Ij, bringing the first cargo of raw sugar from the Antilles, the Indian Archipelago, Formosa and Siam.

Diamond-cutting had been introduced into Amsterdam by an Antwerp expert, Peter Goos, but the industry never employed sufficient craftsmen for them to form a guild. It therefore remained a free activity, and one of the few open to Jews. But the diamond-cutting craft did not really achieve fame and prosperity until the eighteenth century.

The Fisheries
Fishing had provided the original base for Holland's and Zeeland's economy and, as a combination of exploitation of natural resources, craftsmanship and trading, remained one of the maritime provinces' most fruitful activities. The Netherlands overflowed with fish, and the raw material provided both food products and a commodity of exchange. A special guild governed the ubiquitous fishing industry, regulating its distributing and selling activities as well as supervising the freshness of the condition of fish in transit and on delivery. The extension of the guild's activities in Amsterdam led to a split and the setting up of a separate guild for merchants dealing in smoked fish. In some places, too, regulations reserved to bakers the right to sell fried fish. At the corner of every street a strong odour heralded the presence of a fishmonger's stall with its sign representing the miraculous draught of fishes from the Bible story. Here, barrels of fresh fish of different kinds were ranged along the shop-front and took up most of the pavement space as well, while lobsters hung from the awning. In the markets, fishermen and dealers bargained, standing among the barrels of fish and the fishwives' long benches, and drank brandy together.

The point of departure for Dutch prosperity had been the

invention in 1385 by a Zeeland fisherman of the process of curing and barrelling herrings. As soon as the herring was taken from the net it was gutted, its gills and entrails (apart from the milt) discarded, and the fish barrelled in brine. This method allowed the fishermen to exploit the huge seasonal shoals of herring in the Atlantic, and traditional fishing with its purely local alimentary function gave way to a vast international trade.

The industry prospered from the beginning of the fifteenth century. The municipal administrations were fully conscious of its capital importance for the country's development and surrounded it with protective measures which survived all political upheavals to make herring-fishing the most regulated of all occupations in the seventeenth century. This type of fishing was originally confined to the ports along the Zuider Zee, especially Enkhuizen, which owed its wealth to the herring and showed its gratitude by featuring three crowned herrings on its armorial bearings. Then Rotterdam entered the herring circuit, and during the seventeenth century these two towns practically monopolised the industry. Together with the small neighbouring ports that they dominated, their total annual output was worth ten million florins, obtained with a fleet of five hundred herring-boats. The importance of herring-fishing led to the creation of an entire industry in the towns concerned. The curing and barrelling process was no longer adequate to ensure the prolonged preservation demanded by such a rapidly expanding business[8] and processing plants had to be set up in the ports to put the herrings through a second pickling operation. The profit to be derived from this secondary industry led to Amsterdam's interest and participation.

The many small ports strung along the coasts of Friesland, Holland and Zeeland, excluded from the herring monopoly, fished for cod, whiting and sole, on the high seas or inshore, depending on their equipment. Dordrecht exploited the Rhine salmon. Some coastal villages, too poor to possess boats, transported fish to nearby towns by means of dog-cart. Vlieland, the most isolated of the Frisian islands, lived partly from gathering mussels.

The fishermen of Zaandam had specialised in eel-fishing since the Middle Ages. Periodical migrations of these fish brought them into Dutch waters in huge quantities, and after being caught they were transferred to vast fish-ponds specially constructed on the outskirts of the town, where they were kept until the onset of winter and then put on the market. The Zaandam fishermen also paid Denmark for the right to net eel off the island of Amager. Each autumn, a fleet of boats equipped with tanks for transporting the live fish left Zaandam. After fishing, the fleet sometimes sailed back as far as the French coast to dispose of its haul. The drainage works carried out from 1610 onwards in the inland waters of the province of Holland gradually reduced the areas frequented by eels and some varieties disappeared altogether. After 1640, eel-fishing became less and less profitable.

Throughout the first half of the century, the fishing-fleets were under constant threat of a grave menace. The Duke of Parma had conquered the town of Dunkirk in 1583 and armed its fleet for commerce destroying against the Dutch. Dunkirk lived for sixty years from the proceeds of this piracy. These privateers operated mostly along the coast and sometimes sailed right into Dutch harbours in surprise raids, smashing installations and setting fire to fishing-boats. The truce had no effect whatsoever on this activity; in a single year Enkhuizen lost a hundred herring-boats and reprisals were useless because the port of Dunkirk had no commercial traffic at all. Some Dutch sailors, tempted by visions of easy profits, even deserted and went over to the pirates. When the herring fleet set sail in the spring it had to be escorted by warships. The States-General proclaimed that Dunkirk prisoners should be given no quarter and thereafter captured pirates were thrown into the sea.[9] This situation continued until 1646, when a Franco-Dutch army succeeded in recapturing Dunkirk and placing it under French rule once more.[10]

The search for a navigation route to the north of Scandinavia at the beginning of the seventeenth century enabled first the English and then the Dutch to discover the schools of whales that frequented these seas. In 1611 the English equipped two whaling vessels; the following year Amsterdam also built one and placed it under the command of a generously bribed English pilot. Enkhuizen, Zaandam and Delft followed suit. But English competition was so fierce that a united command became necessary and, in 1614, a group of Dutch whalers formed themselves into a 'Northern company' which was granted official status three years later and the exclusive right to hunt whale between Spitsbergen and Greenland.

The founders of the Company nourished vast ambitions. They built three huge warehouses in Amsterdam, equipped with stone-surfaced cellars forming wells for storing the oil, with a total capacity of over 200,000 gallons. To extract the oil a factory was set up in Spitsbergen, and a village for its staff, named Smeerenburg, was erected; this was inhabited during the summer and abandoned when work was finished for the year. A second seasonal colony was established in Jan Mayen island.[11] These establishments were not of much use. The company's monopoly was not respected and was, in any case, ill-defined. The whales fled to other grounds from this human invasion, and it then became necessary to hunt them on the high seas and extract the oil on board. The whaling-ships thus became more vulnerable to attack by the English and their Danish allies. Finally, in 1642, the States-General refused to renew its charter and whaling then became a free activity, with Amsterdam as its commercial centre. Temporary syndicates, set up for the duration of a single expedition, raised the funds necessary to cover the high costs of equipping a flotilla, with the merchants involved contributing shares of a quarter, one thirty-second or one sixty-fourth, as the case might be. One of the interested parties took over the management of the enterprise and was paid a salary.

A whaling-ship measured from a hundred to a hundred and thirty feet long; the largest was thirty-two feet wide and about twenty feet high including a thirteen foot draught. A shell of oak beams bolted together with iron reinforced the massive hull and helped it withstand the pressure of ice-floes.

With its seven longboats, such a ship cost twenty-five thousand florins, new, in 1700. The equipment included, besides the navigational instruments, a large amount of necessary arms and containers: 450 barrels, sixty lines of 125 fathoms each, tarred ropes made of ninety plaited strands, oak-hafted harpoons, saws, axes and various kinds of cutlass. Fitting-out was begun in the autumn. The crew comprised fifty to ninety men, according to the size of the ship, and the recruiting-officer established his office in some dockside inn and raised a flag; in Zaandam, a tavern called *The Spitsbergen* was traditionally used for this purpose. Engagements were made by contract, with clauses dealing with conduct on board as well as wage-rates. The sailors received an advance of 100 or 150 florins, which they promptly spent on drink. The rest of their earnings came mainly from their individual quota in the eventual value of the haul. The ships got under way in April, steering north-north-east. After passing the sixtieth degree of latitude, the arms were brought out and the skipper formed teams of harpooners, lancers and cutters. At about seventy-five degrees they would encounter the first ice-floes, and the whales themselves would appear between the seventy-seventh and seventy-ninth degree, somewhere south of Spitsbergen. The technique of whale-hunting was already exactly similar to that described in the nineteenth century by Melville in *Moby Dick*.

WORKING THE LAND: *Tilling and Grazing*
Wartime devastations, especially the breaching of dikes (in 1576, two-thirds of the province of Holland had been inundated) had contributed to the decline of agriculture well before the advent of the seventeenth century. In the decade following 1600 a slight temporary recovery was made as a result of the rise in prices, but agriculture never really shared in the general prosperity. Only the southern regions of Holland and some of the islands of Zeeland seem to have produced cereals or industrial plants such as colza and madder-wort.[1] The nature of the soil made the growing of cereal crops a hazardous business, rendered more uncertain still by the archaic methods used. Crop yields were too small

for reserves to be built up and, to make matters worse, the towns were indifferent to peasant economy and imported much of their corn from abroad, thus depressing still further the market value of home-grown corn. The great majority of the peasantry was content, during the first half of the century, to cultivate vegetable gardens and raise cattle. Years of famine, or at least scarcity, were by no means rare.

Stock farming, rather than land cultivation, provided the main source of agricultural revenue. Foreigners admired the abundance and hardiness of Dutch livestock,[2] and the excellent quality of the pasture-land enabled the farmers to import thin cattle in the spring, bought from Denmark and Holstein, and fatten them so that they could be resold with a profit in the autumn. But the scale of dairy produce seems to have been small in comparison with modern standards.[3] Cattle-breeding flourished in the rich terrain of Holland, Zeeland and Friesland but suffered in the country's eastern regions from the sandy nature of the soil; one prolonged drought or a single poor harvest could spell catastrophe.

In 1621 the Drenthe suffered from a severe shortage of fodder, as a result of which two thousand five hundred horses, ten thousand cattle and fifty thousand sheep perished; half the land under cultivation could not be dressed because of the lack of natural manure and the subsequent harvest suffered accordingly. It was not until major drainage operations were carried out in mid-century that agriculture was able to overcome its prolonged crisis.

It was important for the peasant to extract the greatest possible profit from his cattle. He kept the whey for his own consumption and, in the absence of any official control, was also quite likely to dilute the 'full' milk he sold in town, either retail (going from house to house, or in the markets) or to wholesalers. He was equally liable to adulterate his butter by adding excessive salt. Cheese, being the most successfully commercialised of the various kinds of agricultural produce, escaped such dangers. After being made on the farms it was disposed of in central markets, like that of Alkmaar, where it was bought in bulk by middlemen. Parival describes seeing a thousand peasant carts driving past in a single day at the Hoorn market, carrying more than 150,000 pounds of cheese to be weighed at the town's office of weights and measures.[4] Towards the middle of the century Edam was exporting five hundred tons a year of its famous red-rinded, ball-shaped cheeses.

Apart from the ordinary markets where current produce was disposed of, fairs were held at particular times of the year; some of these fairs had a traditional privilege of ordering the suspension of all actions for debt during the period they were open. The Valkenburg horse-fair in September was one of the most famous of these many fairs.

Dikes and Polders

A senior Dutch minister declared to Temple that the Netherlands '. . . employ yearly more men, than all the corn of the province of Holland could maintain.'[5] Such was, indeed, the paradoxical situation in which this country found itself and which was well expressed in the saying: 'God created the world, but the Dutchman made Holland.' The greater part of the two richest provinces, Holland and Zeeland, formed a depression slightly below sea-level, a situation that exposed these provinces to tidal onslaughts and to the actions of their inland waters. They were protected from the sea along part of their coast-line by a chain of high dunes, and to supplement these the provinces gradually erected, during the Middle Ages,[6] a series of barrages designed to protect the deltas of the great rivers and to dam them up. By the seventeenth century the coast outline and the river courses had been stabilised, and although many bodies of unharnessed water, lakes and marshes, still remained, the whole country was enclosed by an intricate network of dikes.[7] The work continued; in 1682 Amsterdam constructed a dike on the south bank of the Ij designed to protect an area of land containing some two thousand houses from inundation during unusually high tides. These works were accompanied along the rivers by the building of lock-gates, such as the technically remarkable lock with which Amsterdam cut the Amstel in 1674.

Facing the sea, a palisade of tough beams fixed together by iron clamps was driven into the mud and acted as a breakwater. Behind it arose the dike itself, a rounded earth-bank covered with grass. It was important that the material used should possess a certain elasticity so as not to break under the irregular pressure of the waves; sand, bound together by plants, fulfilled these conditions. In the seventeenth century a new method was used, by which kelp was mixed with earth. In exposed regions, several lines of dikes were constructed in depth. Those who lived along the banks of the Zuider Zee would stretch lengths of sail-cloth over the dikes to strengthen them during stormy weather and high tides.

These protective cushions of earth, sheltering the Dutch who lived behind them, were tremendously fragile and constantly eaten away by erosion. As a result, their upkeep ranked as a basic public service; numbered markers at regular distances along the dike indicated the sections for which each coastal village was responsible, the maintenance work being co-ordinated and controlled by a special administration presided over by a central council headed by a *Dijkgrave*.

The dikes constituted a line of defence. When the struggle against the encroaching waters entered an active phase, pumps operated by windmills were brought into use, following techniques devised at the start of the fifteenth century. This procedure was carried out at the end of every winter to drain the infiltrating waters which covered the countryside of Holland every year from November to February. During this winter period, the country was one immense sheet of water lashed by the winds, with houses, hills and dikes emerging like islands. In 1638, when breaking-up ice had breached the Ijssel dike, the water which invaded the surrounding flat lands was entirely drained off again by the aid of windmill-pumps.

There was no catastrophe during the seventeenth century to equal the tidal wave of All Saints' Day 1570,[8] but, even so, disasters like that of 1638 were not uncommon. The worst disaster of the century occurred on 16th November 1650, when ice-floes brought down by the Rhine breached several dikes. The Ijssel rose and overflowed. Most of the peasants were taken unawares by the sudden calamity and had no time to escape. Taking refuge on their rooftops, they were nearly dying of starvation when they were finally rescued by an expedition hastily organised by the authorities, who sent a fleet of boats.

Along the coast, the sea's periodical assaults ate away inexorably at the peripheral land of villages such as Catwijk. Throughout the 1650–1 winter torrential rains swelled the rivers and canals; shortly before the vernal equinox, a violent north-north-west wind blasted the coast of Holland; then, on 5th and 6th March, a hurricane hurled itself against the dikes, while the entire coastal population watched and waited in anguish. The dikes held. But a breach in the Saint Anthony dike near Amsterdam almost flooded the town; the local authorities succeeded in plugging the breach, but not in time to save the town's cellars from being inundated, and huge quantities of merchandise and foodstuffs in warehouse basements were submerged.[9]

The year 1550 marks the date when the first concerted efforts were made, under the compulsion of a shortage of living space, to drain dry the various bodies of stagnant water to be found throughout the country.[10] Similar efforts during the first half of the seventeenth century were attributable more to financial interests and the search for new fields of investment. The number of acres drained annually continued to rise, and by 1640 had reached a figure of 4,450 acres. Improvements in the design of windmill-driven pumps allowed considerable stretches of water to be drained dry; from 1609 onwards chains of mills were situated at different levels, allowing the water to be drawn off at successive graduated levels, a method which was both labour-saving and more efficient.

The first really far-reaching project was initiated in 1607 by Dirk van Oss, a member of the directorate of the East India Company. With the support of a few other Amsterdam capitalists and of some high-ranking officials he requested permission from the States-General to drain the Beemster lake to the north-west of Amsterdam, justifying his application on various social and agricultural grounds. In reality, this represented the first large-scale speculative enterprise in such a field undertaken by a powerful financial group. Work began in 1608 with sixteen and then thirty-two mill-pumps in operation. But since they disposed of the water pumped from the lake by simply spreading it through the surrounding land, the peasants were soon up in arms and tried to sabotage the dikes; finally, the States had to intervene. By the summer of 1609 pumping was almost completed. Then, in January 1610 a violent storm breached the Waterland dike and the sea poured into the newly drained Beemster basin. Some of the capitalists concerned in the scheme withdrew in disgust, but the enterprise succeeded in the end, and in the summer of 1612 a government delegation presided over a solemn inauguration of the new *polder*.[11]

The promoters harboured the illusion that they would be able to put the whole reclaimed surface of the lake under cultivation, but they soon discovered that the nature of the soil was ill-adapted to such purposes. By 1632 only a quarter of the Beemster was cultivated; a fifth was in use as grazing-grounds; a third was meadow-land; the rest had been turned into gardens and orchards.[12] It is interesting to note that in 1640 there were four hundred dwelling-houses on these lands, of which only half were occupied by peasants; fifty-two of them were country-houses belonging to wealthy patricians. The capital invested in these drainage operations seldom originated in peasant savings; most of the money came from surplus trading profits. There was not a great return on money invested in such enterprises and, after 1650, the largest investors avoided this type of financial outlet despite the legal advantages attached – a thirty-year tax exemption and perpetual hereditary entitlement to the land.

From 1612 to 1640 most of the lakes in the province of Holland were drained, including those of Wieringerwaard, Purmer, Wormer, Hugowaard and Schermer. The town of Amsterdam undertook to drain the Diemen lake on its south-east outskirts. During the same period twenty marshes were made fit for cultivation, amounting to over 120,000 acres. The farmers who settled in these reclaimed areas seem mostly to have been immigrants.

The engineer Leeghwater claimed that he was entirely responsible, technically, for the successful draining of the Beemster, although it must be admitted that modern historians are sceptical on the subject. But Leeghwater had a good sense of publicity. His fame spread throughout Europe, and the towns of Bordeaux and Emden, the province of Friesland, the dukes of Epernon and Holstein, the Stadtholder himself all had recourse to his services and advice. However, Leeghwater nourished a more grandiose scheme. The so-called Haarlem lake, the largest in the country, stretched between Amsterdam and Leyden; its choppy, dangerous waters (in which one of the King of Bohemia's sons drowned in 1629) constantly eroded its banks and it was popularly supposed to have doubled its surface in less than a century; it covered twenty-four thousand acres at the time. Leeghwater claimed that he had studied the composition of the lake bottom and was convinced that it was potentially fertile soil. He spent years perfecting his project and drawing up plans and maps; then finally in 1641, he presented his report to the States of Holland and to the burgomasters of the towns concerned. The air was soon full of objections and quarrels. Amsterdam was in favour, but Leyden refused on the pretext that it got all its water from the lake. Partisans made much of the fact that the drainage operations would not cost more than 140 florins an acre, a sum far less than the real value of the lands to be reclaimed; opponents could think only of the total expenditure involved and were scared stiff at the thought of spending three and a half million florins; they brought up technical difficulties, asserting that the scheme would involve the use of five hundred windmills. Leeghwater's project was buried in oblivion.[13] No doubt it was too ambitious for the technical means at the disposal of his contemporaries.

CHAPTER EIGHT

CONCLUSION

'THE DELIGHTS OF FREEDOM'

Writing to Scaliger in 1593, to inform him about the country to which he had been invited by Leyden University, the French Ambassador in The Hague, Buzenval, lauded 'the delights of freedom' reigning there.[1] These 'delights' became apparent to the foreigner the moment he crossed the Republic's frontier. Contemporary documents are almost unanimous on this point, and the more or less caustic asides provoked by the manners or character of the Dutch rarely invalidated what passed for an axiom in the eyes of European liberals.

Only those who, like Temple, were personally acquainted with this nation's political institutions were able to distinguish its complexities, paradoxes and contradictions. What did these commentators, unaccustomed as they were to sociological reflection, mean by 'freedom'? As far as the individual was concerned, the word certainly implied a broad margin of choice and initiative within the framework of the community. Yet, as we have seen, Dutch life was governed by a sometimes narrow conformism, a ponderous moral austerity and an unshakeable belief that success and virtue were identical; in addition, the triumph of bourgeois values in relationship to work, economy and welfare at every level of society smothered effectively any sharpness of character and, finally, any true audacity. The government was the very opposite of democratic, in the sense that we understand the word to-day. A monopolistic structure ruled several sectors of the economy. Nevertheless, the Netherlands remained throughout two centuries a haven of refuge to which people flocked from every corner of Europe.

It is difficult to form a balanced judgement. One must perhaps conclude that freedom in the Netherlands was more the fruit of the people's customs than of their institutions, and derived even more strongly from the very contradictions within their society; considerable incoherence in practice,

317

allied with a dearth of general principles, produced an empiricism in behaviour and even thought-processes, at all levels, which could be exploited by any individual who was aggressive, heroic or simply clever at discovering the weaknesses of the system through which he could infiltrate and make his presence known.

As we have seen, the new-found ethics had by no means disposed of the old ancestral tendencies. The Dutchman was deeply religious but remained easy-going and pleasure-loving. Attached superficially to ideals of propriety and clear-thinking, he still retained a strong element of peasant cunning and could lose all restraint at the prospect of a quick profit, however sordid. He was naturally staid, contemplative and cautious, unvengeful and rarely aroused to wrath; but once aroused he became doggedly determined.

Temple relates that he knew one Dutchman, 'that was employed four and twenty years about the making and perfecting of a globe, and another above thirty about the inlaying of a table.'[2] But this patience, thanks to which no Dutchman ever abandoned an undertaking, and this sense of realism, thanks to which he never committed himself without first weighing up all the relevant factors,[3] was rarely accompanied by any long-term sagacity, or adaptability of mind, or by that natural talent for improvisation inseparable from political genius.

The seventeenth-century Dutchman had achieved a high level of administrative and cultural progress and turned these benefits to his own advantage. He was not overawed by them. In fact, he found his Republic perfectly suited to his temperament, particularly, perhaps, because of its hesitations and inconsistencies.[4] He viewed the diversity of mankind serenely and took few things very seriously – at the most, God and money. This is why his pleasant disposition was so immediately noticeable in everyday transactions. No country counted fewer bluffers and hagglers. And despite the deep-rooted distinctions between social castes, any excuse to drink together was sufficient to unite the whole gathering.

In public life the same contradictions were apparent. Foreign ambassadors were received in The Hague with tremendous ceremony; delegates from the States came from twenty miles outside the town to meet them, with a suite of fifty carriages. But when the French ambassador had to retire in 1654 because of blindness, the government expressed its opposition to his receiving a present. This was not a hostile gesture but simply a demonstration of impartiality, since the ambassadors from the United Provinces had just been forbidden to receive presents themselves. On the other hand, these Dutch ambassadors were expected to be absolutely punctilious in matters of precedence and were maintained in a style of luxury quite unknown in the Netherlands.[5]

The autonomy of local administrations relied on practices some of which appear to have been deliberate breaches of the Act of Union.[6] But this same spirit of independence gave the impression that everything in this country was moulded in human dimensions, resulting from practical wisdom and being within the reach of all.[7] Saint-Evremond remarked that the Dutch did not so much love freedom as that they hated oppression.[8] They detested scandal and anything else which challenged respectability directly. In 1650 the Amsterdam players went so far as to represent on the stage William II's adulterous love-affairs. What greater sign of freedom can one envisage?

On the other hand, the commercialisation of people's instincts made public opinion unsusceptible to financial corruption. The fact that major scandals were rare was due mainly to a certain shopkeeper's cunning and prudence in concealing practices that had become accepted since the beginning of the century – bribing of electors, judges and tax officials, embezzlement of state funds and all the other misdemeanours involving widespread nepotism and favouritism in what was essentially a society of tradesmen and merchants. In 1615 the burgomasters of Amsterdam are known to have taken advantage of their supervisory rights over the cadastral registry to conceal the extent of their vast real estate from the tax authorities. It seems that Oldenbarnevelt himself accepted twenty thousand florins from Henri IV in suspicious circumstances. Following the suicide, in 1650, of Cornelis Brusch, registrar of the States-General, an enquiry unearthed a scheme of embezzlements totalling two million florins in which no fewer than sixteen deputies were involved. The seventeenth century had seen worse in France and England. Corruption in the Netherlands remained within the permissible limits of personal freedom and was, in any case, faced with a vigorous criticism that became an accepted part of the social system. The opinions expressed in pamphlets and from the pulpit may not have had much effect, but they acted as a safety-valve for public opinion, were inoffensive to trading interests – in fact such outbursts were considered effective in promoting commercial efficiency – and were consequently permissible; ultimately, no one cared much.

Passions were more easily aroused in the field of religion. At the time of the quarrel between Arminians and Gomarists, the tone of the polemics descended to an exchange of insults liable to provoke breaches of the peace; so, in 1632, the Amsterdam municipality put an end peremptorily to this quarrel by judging it prejudicial to the efficient exercise of business. The religious equilibrium which gradually established itself in the country seemed to be a victory for tolerance, but it was just as much the fruit of a desire for enrichment which, in its turn, demanded a peaceful atmosphere.

So a style of life was fashioned that was unique in Europe at that time. 'Men live together, like citizens of the world, associated by the common ties of humanity, and by the bonds of peace, under the impartial protection of indifferent laws.'[9] This phrase of Temple's expresses the consequences rather than the causes of an original, complex array of factors impossible to reduce to simple elements. It indicates an average rather than an exact measure. But it is in the nature of causes to be less immediately apparent than their effects; and it is the average, rather than the extremes, that the ordinary individual perceives. It was not pure illusion which prompted Parival to say, before leaving the country, that he 'never tired of admiring the happiness of the subjects of the States of Holland and could not help envying their condition.'[10]

BIBLIOGRAPHY

It would be impracticable to give here a complete bibliography of the period under review; a large volume would be necessary. A few references, relating to the contents of the notes that follow, will be more practically useful. Most of the works I mention include material for critical study and numerous references. Particularly important are the bibliographical lists included in the beautifully produced anthology entitled *De tachtigjarige oorlog*, Amsterdam, 1941. The daily life of the Dutch during the seventeenth century was made the subject, about a hundred years ago, of two large works by the historian G. D. J. SCHOTEL, which remain indispensable today: *Het oudhollandse huisgezin* (Haarlem, 1868) and *Het maatschappelijk leven onzer voorouders* (Rotterdam, 1869). Later studies derive from these works and add very little. The following may be worth mentioning: A. L. J. de VRANKRIJKER, *Het maatschappelijk leven in Nederland in de gouden eeuw* (Amsterdam, 1937); A. W. FRANKEN, *Het leven onzer voorouders* (The Hague, 1942); finally, A. MULDER, *Zeven eeuwen Nederlandse levenskunst* (four volumes; Amsterdam, 1940–52), a largely superficial and pseudo-literary work. A. STARING, *De Hollanders thuis, gezelschapstukken uit drie eeuwen* (The Hague, 1957) resumes the same theme, basing itself mainly on the evidence of the visual arts.

These last-mentioned books should all be used judiciously, since the work of their artists and engravers is permeated with anachronistic elements. I have been able to clarify and amend some information given in these works by consulting the collections of the Mauritshuis in The Hague and the Prentencabinet in Amsterdam.

The *Accounts* published by foreigners who had visited the Netherlands constitute an important source of information. J. N. JACOBSEN-JENSEN has made an inventory of these accounts in his *Reizigers te Amsterdam* (Amsterdam, 1919). R. MURRIS, *La Hollande et les Hollandais au XVIIe et au XVIIIe siècle, vus par les Français* (Paris, 1925), analyses the impressions recorded by some thirty Frenchmen, several of whom had spent many years in the country, prior to 1700, in various capacities. The book written in 1669 by JEAN-NICOLAS PARIVAL, ex-professor of French at Leyden, and published in Amsterdam in 1678, anonymously, under the title *Les Délices de la Hollande*, has been particularly valuable to me; I have used the 1738 re-edition. An interesting *Voyage en Hollande fait en 1719 par Pierre Sartre* has been published by V. ADVIELLE (Paris, 1896). The most complete source of this type is the report drawn up in 1673 by the English Ambassador, SIR WILLIAM TEMPLE, *Observations upon the United Provinces of the Netherlands*, whose original text has been re-edited by G. N. CLARK (Cambridge, 1932). Page numbers of references to this work are those of the Cambridge edition.

There are several excellent works of synthesis on the numerous aspects of the history of the Netherlands' 'golden age'. I have consulted, in particular, the following works: *Algemene geschiedenis der Nederlanden* (twelve volumes; Utrecht, 1949–58), volume V (for the period 1567–1609), VI (1609–48) and VII (1648–1748); especially important are the chapters devoted to social and economic questions, in volumes V and VI by T. S. JANSMA, and in volume VII by J. G. VAN DILLEN; I refer to this collective work under the initials AGN; *De tachtigjarige oorlog*, mentioned above, which I refer to under the name of *Oorlog*; J. and A. ROMEIN, *De lage landen bij de zee* (Utrecht, third edition, 1949); P. J. MULLER, *Onze gouden eeuw* (three volumes; Leyden, 1896–8). One should add, on the theme of colonial expansion: K. GLAMANN, *Dutch-asiatic trade 1624–1740* (The Hague, 1958); and G. M. DE BOER, *Van oude voyagien* (Amsterdam, 1912) which gives illustrated accounts of a number of voyages of discovery from the end of the sixteenth to the beginning of the eighteenth century. Those who read French may find useful the small book by M. BRAURE, *Histoire des Pays-Bas* (collection *Que sais-je?*, no. 490; Paris, 1951).

Although partially out of date, the basic work on the century's intellectual and artistic culture remains that of C. BUSKEN-HUET, *Het land van Rembrand*, to which I refer in the Haarlem re-edition, 1941, and one must also mention J. HUIZINGA, *Holländische Kultur des 17. Jahrhunderts* (Jena, 1933), as well as the attractive *Atlas van de Nederlandse beschaving* (Amsterdam, 1958); this last book's range and choice of illustrations make it particularly suitable as an introduction for the foreign student to Dutch civilisation. J. and A. ROMEIN, in their *Erflaters van onze beschaving*, present a series of monographs on various individuals whose influence made itself deeply felt in their particular epoch; the second volume is devoted to the seventeenth century (Amsterdam, 1938).

There is a good recent history of Dutch literature: *Geschiedenis van de letterkunde der Nederland*, a collective work published in 's Hertogenbosch; the seventeenth century is covered in volumes IV (1948) and V (1952), for which G. A. VAN ES, G. S. OVERDIEN and E. ROMBAUTS are responsible. G. DERUDDER devoted a book in French to one of the most typical representatives of this literary era: *Un poète néerlandais: Cats, sa vie et ses œuvres* (Calais, 1898).

As far as painting is concerned, the classic work by FROMENTIN, *Les Maîtres d'autrefois*, has retained all its charm and much of its usefulness. The two splendid volumes of W. MARTIN's *De hollandse schilderkunst in de 17e eeuw* (Amsterdam, n.d.), centre around the figures of Franz Hals and Rembrandt respectively.

A certain number of particular studies are mentioned in the following notes. But titles mentioned above, unless otherwise indicated, are referred to only in an abbreviated form: the name of the author and, where required, one of the title's words.

NOTES

CHAPTER ONE

THE BACKGROUND OF DAILY LIFE

THE TOWN

1 Temple, p. 103.

2 Some of these signs were later revived and used as trade-marks by tobacco merchants.

3 Murris, p. 37 and Advielle, p. 31.

4 A wooden keyboard, with pedals, operated levered keys furnished with wires attached to the bells. A new system, of hammers moved by a drum, was introduced in the seventeenth century: removable pegs, placed in particular holes in the drum's perforated surface, determined the melody, which could thus be varied. Originally, bells were cast in moulds of a very few standard sizes, so that the notes they gave out were limited in variety. But, in about 1645, someone had the idea of filing the outer shell of newly cast bells in order to vary their tone: the thinner the metal, the higher the note.

5 *Amsterdam, die groote stad,*
die is gebouwd op palen.
Als die stad eens ommeviel,
wie zou dat betalen?

6 It is extremely difficult to give any equivalent of the seventeenth-century florin in terms of contemporary currency. The archives of the Bank of Amsterdam provide information as to its absolute value; but its relative value and purchasing power remain obscure. At the most, one can calculate entirely approximately and theoretically, on the basis of data presented by N. W. Posthumus (*Nederlandse prijsgeschiedenis*, Leyden, 1943), that the florin of 1650 was worth one-ninth of a napoleon which, at the average rate of the napoleon on the free market in 1958 would make it equivalent to four new French francs (approximately 6/– or 85c). But it must be borne in mind that the elements of a Dutch seventeenth-century budget are hardly comparable to those of an average present day budget; and that, between 1600 and 1660, the florin underwent a series of devaluations which resulted in its losing nearly half its value in relation to gold. The florin was divided into twenty *stuivers*, the stuiver into sixteen *penningen*.

7 Temple, p. 150.

8 Murris, p. 193.

9 Franken, p. 211.

10 The Calvinist Church was hostile to statuary art, tolerating it only in its application to tombs: for example, the statues of William the Silent and Tromp, both in Delft. The erection of the statue of Erasmus in Rotterdam provoked a violent quarrel. The habit adopted by some patricians during the course of the century of decorating the parks of their country houses with statues did not, unfortunately, contribute to the development of an original art form – on the contrary. It is interesting to note that, on the whole, flat countries seldom appear to provide inspiration for budding sculptors.

11 AGN, p. 95.

12 Advielle, pp. 51 and 55. A 1632 report records the number of lodgings available in the principal towns of Holland: Amsterdam, 15,000; Leyden, 8,300; Haarlem, 6,000; Rotterdam, 4,900; Delft, 4,800; Enkhuizen, 3,600; Dordrecht, 3,200. Compared with the statistics provided by the 1622 census, these figures would indicate an average density per lodging of about : four persons in Rotterdam; five in Delft; six in Leyden, Enkhuizen and Dordrecht; seven in Haarlem; and nearly ten in Amsterdam, which thus appears to have been an over-populated town, to say the least.

13 The sedan chair, introduced at the end of the century, had no success at all.

14 Parival, p. 83.

15 The municipal accounts of 1679 contain four items under this heading: upkeep of lamps; rape-seed oil and linseed oil; twenty pounds of cotton for the wicks; wages of the lamp-lighters, making a total expenditure of 358 florins.

16 Murris, p. 138; Parival, p. 199; Temple, p. 96.

THE COUNTRYSIDE

1 The impression of French travellers; Murris, p. 2.

2 G. Cohen, *Ecrivains français en Hollande dans la première moitié du XVIIe siècle* (Paris, 1920, pp. 317 and 320). Foreigners making a rapid voyage through the Netherlands were more favourable in their judgements. But most of them visited the country during the summer, and their impressions often consist of impermissible generalisations. Some authors of

Accounts go so far as to compare the charm of the Dutch countryside with that of Italy (Murris, p. 22).

3 The construction of one of these farms, at the end of the seventeenth century, required the following materials: 114 cubic feet of oak-wood, ninety-eight cubic feet of clay, forty cubic feet of earth-and-dung mixture, and twelve tons of straw.

4 A splendid open-air museum in Arnhem has preserved specimens of these various peasant styles, to which it has devoted an annotated catalogue.

HIGHWAYS AND CANALS

1 Temple, p. 103.

2 Today's trains, following more or less the same route, take two hours and forty minutes.

3 From Groningen to Amersfoort, six florins five stuivers in 'first class', five florins five stuivers in 'second class' and four florins fifteen stuivers in 'third class'.

4 Temple, p. 93.

5 As, for example, *De Amsterdamse Trekschuyt geladen met vrolijke geesten* ('The Amsterdam passenger-boat, filled with jolly fellows').

6 The *Doelen*: this word is still used today for many hostelries in the Netherlands.

CHAPTER TWO

THE DUTCH INTERIOR

THE HOUSE

1 Some particularly elaborate cupboards cost as much as a thousand florins.

2 Murris, p. 139.

3 Advielle, p. 30.

4 Murris, pp. 73–4.

THE TOILET

1 De Vrankrijker, p. 15.

2 Murris, p. 141.

3 The extremely high price of the wig made it an object of luxury and prevented its general adoption.

4 F. Van Thienen, *Das Kostüm der Blütezeit Hollands* (Berlin, 1930), p. 50.

5 And jewellery as well. This was similar to what is worn today: ear-rings, necklaces, rings, bracelets, and jewelled hair-pins. Jewellers used mostly gold and pearls.

6 Schotel, *Huisgezin*, p. 156.

FOOD

1 Particularly for drinking wine, since it was usual to drink beer from pewter mugs.

2 A European porcelain-making industry only came into being at the beginning of the eighteenth century, when Delft asserted and retained its supremacy in that field.

3 The cauldrons made in Aix-la-Chapelle were quoted on the Amsterdam Exchange throughout the century (Posthumus, table 187).

4 Advielle, p. 30.

5 In 1650 nutmeg cost, wholesale, two-and-a-half florins a pound; pepper, a half-florin (Posthumus, tables 69 and 74); one should add to these figures the very high fiscal taxes and the apothecary's retail profit.

6 In Dutch. V. Franken, pp. 93–4.

7 Schotel, *Huisgezin*, pp. 349–51.

8 Because, being an agricultural product delivered directly by the producer to the consumer, milk-production was not answerable to any guild.

9 Murris, p. 94.

10 *Een ey is d'armen troost met oly wel gebraen.*

11 J. Van Loenen, *De Haarlemse brouwindustrie voor 1600* (Amsterdam, 1950), p. 53.

12 Franken, pp. 94–5.

THE EVENING AT HOME

1 *Kaart, keurs en kan bederven menig man. De gelegenheid maakt de dief.*

2 Schotel, *Huisgezin*, pp. 179–83, quotes several hundred similar titles.

3 Parival, p. 216.

4 Quoted in Schotel, *Maatsch*, p. 111.

CHAPTER THREE

THE COURSE OF LIFE

RELIGION

1 Temple, p. 127.

2 The iconoclasm of the years 1560–70 was as much revolutionary as religious in character: see Busken-Huet, p. 355.

3 Quoted by Romein, *Lage L.*, p. 416.

4 Schotel, *Huisgezin*, p. 170.

5 Busken-Huet, p. 320.

6 An annual income of 500 florins represented a fortune for a predicant.

7 Advielle, p. 43.

8 Temple, p. 125.

9 Romein, *Lage L.*, p. 367.

10 In 1596 the only people to be barred from public office were former pupils of the Jesuits or the Belgian universities.

11 The capture of 's Hertogenbosch from the Spanish in 1629 was accompanied by a brief crisis of fanaticism (ransacking of the cathedral, sequestrations) which had no effect upon the general situation.

12 L. Leuven, *De boekhandel te Amsterdam door katholieken gedreven tijdens de Republiek* (Epe, 1951), pp. 11 and 27–30.

CHILDREN

1 Parival, pp. 31–2.

2 Parival, p. 32.

EDUCATION

1 According to Schotel, *Huisgezin*, p. 84.

2 Quoted by de Vrankrijker, p. 131.

328

3 Such as 'The post office of Cupid and Mercury' (Schotel, *Huisgezin*, p. 254).

4 Despite the efforts made during the course of the century to improve manuals of reading and reckoning.

5 The seventeenth century possessed one good poet writing in the Frisian tongue, Gijsbert Japiks (1603–66), an impoverished schoolmaster of Bolsward, who remained unknown by his contemporaries.

6 On the question of the Latin schools, see E. J. Kuiper, *De hollandse schoolorde van 1625* (Groningen, 1958).

7 School fees varied from three to eight florins a year; text-books (published by the State at cost price) cost only four florins for six years of studies, in 1626, according to Kuiper, p. 87.

8 If one judges by the amount of his salary, a rector's social importance varied considerably according to his location: the rector of Edam's Latin school received 150 florins a year in 1625, while his colleague in Utrecht received 1,300 florins in 1637 (Kuiper, p. 87).

9 A 1626 document concerning the publication and distribution of school text-books gives, incidentally, some indication of the relative importance of the Latin schools in the different towns of Holland: Amsterdam took 16 per cent of the edition; Dordrecht, Haarlem, Leyden, Delft and Rotterdam each took 8 per cent; Gouda, Alkmaar, Hoorn, Enkhuizen and The Hague each took 6 per cent; nine small towns shared the remaining 14 per cent. From 600 to 1,200 copies were printed of each of these text-books, which gives one some idea of the minimal influence of the Latin schools. (Kuiper, pp. 86–7).

10 The age of admission to the Faculties was not governed by any regulations. In practice, students were seldom less than sixteen years old, and diplomas were seldom awarded to anyone under twenty-three.

11 Parival, pp. 69–70.

12 Cf. the table in Cohen, pp. 351–2. This figure of fifty can be divided as follows: twenty-two in letters (philosophy), two in law, three in medicine, seventeen in theology and three in mathematics; thirty-eight came from France's western maritime provinces. In 1630 Leyden's professor of mathematics had six French pupils, including Descartes.

13 A regular annual budget covered normal purchases.

14 In 1642 the Utrecht municipal council intervened in this way in the quarrel between Descartes and Vossius.

15 Parival, p. 77.

LOVE LIFE

1 Temple, p. 105.

2 Murris, p. 83; cf. also p. 57, and Temple, pp. 105–6.

3 Murris, p. 84; Parival, p. 39, emphasises, too, the contrast between the chastity of the married women and the easy morals of the girls.

4 In prosperous households, where marriage contracts were drawn up, these were signed on the day the parties were engaged.

5 All this was extremely expensive. In 1640, the costs of an elegant wedding could well exceed 4,000 florins.

6 Letter quoted by Cohen, p. 308.

7 Murris, p. 72.

8 Reported by Regnard; Murris, p. 100.

DOMESTIC EXISTENCE

1 A poem of 1680, quoted by Murris, p. 59.

2 Murris, p. 61. An identical remark made by the Swiss de Haller is quoted by Busken-Huet, p. 531.

3 Murris, pp. 85–6 and 97.

4 Poem quoted by Franken, p. 96.

5 Temple, pp. 105–6.

6 Cohen, p. 537, and Busken-Huet, p. 338.

7 These regulations applied also to manservants.

8 Parival, p. 30.

9 Murris, pp. 119–20.

10 For instance, 'The untidy household', painted in 1663–5, now in the Wellington Museum, London.

11 On the other hand, they did use spittoons.

12 Parival, p. 40.

13 Reported by Busken-Huet, p. 436.

14 Schotel, *Huisgezin*, pp. 323–5, and Franken, pp. 83–4, list a great number of these cries, some of them in verse.

THE GUILDS

1 Originally, the governing body was elected by the members of the guild.

2 Murris, p. 113.

3 The different trading interests were not all represented at the central Exchange. For example, the important cereal trade had its own special Exchange in Amsterdam.

SICKNESS AND DEATH

1 Temple, p. 113.

2 A recent thesis, presented at the University of Paris by Dr T. M. Torillon, examined, from a clinical point of view the maladies exhibited by some of the characters in Brueghel's pictures. Despite the dangers presented by such analyses, and the fact that Brueghel did not, of course, live during the period under discussion, it may be interesting, nevertheless, to list a few of Dr Torillon's 'discoveries': gangrene through obstructive thrombo-angina, syphilitic tabes, spastic paraplegia, various thyroid troubles, and no less than five types of blindness. . . .

3 Temple, p. 113, and Murris, p. 33.

4 Temple, p. 113.

5 Water-divining was practised fairly widely, though frowned upon by authority. Nevertheless, competent judges recognised its scientific value.

6 Digby's treatise on this medicament had been translated into Dutch. The formula called for green vitriol oxidised in the sun, pulverised and blended with gum arabic.

7 On the other hand, it was considered perfectly permissible to go and take treatment in the waters of Spa.

8 The examination fee was very high : 250 florins, that is to say, four or five times as much as the doctorate fee imposed by the faculties.

9 Translation of an example quoted in Schotel, *Maatsch*, p. 285.

10 The name given them by Parival, p. 228.

11 Murris, p. 34.

CHAPTER FOUR

RECREATIONS

1 In the coastal regions, this animal was decimated by the sea-eagle.

2 Parival, p. 218.

3 Mentioned in Cohen, p. 604.

4 Parival, pp. 218–19.

5 At least during the first half of the century. The taste for open-air games diminished subsequently.

6 Quoted by Franken, p.176.

7 Quoted by Schotel, *Huisgezin*, p. 74.

8 Franken, pp. 170–1.

BANQUETS AND DRINKING-BOUTS

1 Murris, pp. 124–5.

2 Temple, p. 107.

3 Temple, p. 113.

4 Temple, pp. 142–3.

5 Quoted by Cohen, p. 260.

6 On this question, see AGN, pp. 103–5.

7 In 1670–5, Schiedam hollands was worth, wholesale, about thirty-six florins a cask of thirty gallons, while the same quantity of brandy from Bordeaux was worth about seventy. As regards wine from Bordeaux, the Amsterdam Exchange quoted 160-gallon barrels at prices ranging from eighty to 156 florins between 1620 and 1670. See Posthumus, tables 96, 99 and 100.

8 This medical prescription was fashionable throughout Europe at the time.

9 Advielle, p. 21.

10 Advielle, p. 22.

11 The best tobacco was imported from America. Virginia tobacco was particularly esteemed, and, for making into snuff, different varieties grown by the Spaniards. But from the beginning of the century tobacco was planted at enormous cost

in Zeeland, and then in Gelderland, Overijssel and the Utrecht region.

12 Murris, p. 121.

FEAST-DAYS AND HOLIDAYS

1 Parival, p. 172.

2 Temple, pp. 135–6.

3 The cult of this saint had once been very popular in the Utrecht diocese; the territories it had covered (the greater part of what were to become the seven provinces) numbered more than a hundred churches or chapels dedicated to Saint Martin.

4 Quoted by Schotel, *Huisgezin*, p. 218. – The feast of Saint Nicholas was illustrated by a vast folk-lore of children's songs, some of which have come down to us.

5 Marionettes, on the other hand, did not appear until 1686.

CHAPTER FIVE

ARTS AND LETTERS

FINE ARTS

1 See Romein, *Lage L.*, pp. 403–31, particularly p. 421. And yet, several Dutch architects created important work in Hanseatic towns. And the sculptor Adriaan de Vries, who left no work whatsoever behind him in his native Holland, was hugely successful in Italy and Bavaria, and later in Austria where he worked for the Emperor.

2 Parival, p. 29.

3 I mention here the towns where the painters in question received their training, even if they were not born there.

4 It is impossible to quote any average tariffs.

5 Quoted in Schotel, *Huisgezin*, p. 198.

BELLES-LETTRES

1 The literary techniques practised in the chambers of rhetoric, in both 'lyrical' and dramatic fields, go back to the fifteenth

333

century and the French 'great rhetoricians' of the Burgundian school.

2 Despite, or because of, the extremely popular nature of their language, the rhetoricians played a considerable part in the formation of everyday Dutch parlance and modern literary language.

3 J. Prinsen, *Rekeningen van de kosten van het rederijkerfeest te Leiden in 1596* (*Historisch Genootschap*, XXV, pp. 444–89), studies the accounts of the rhetoricians' convention in Leyden in 1596; the expenses amounted to nearly two thousand florins, a considerable sum for the period.

4 Parival, p. 100.

5 Mulder, IV, p. 126.

6 An established actor was paid two florins; a walker-on, provided by the old folks' home, rated a third of a florin.

7 Murris, p. 179.

8 On this question, see J. Fransen, *Les Comédiens français en Hollande au XVIIIe et au XVIIIe siècle* (Paris, 1925). From 1605 to 1655 French troupes are recorded as having passed through on twenty occasions, including twelve visits to The Hague.

9 The first literary reviews appeared during this era: in 1684 and 1686, two French-language magazines appeared in Amsterdam, *La République des Lettres* and *La Bibliothèque universelle et historique*, giving critical extracts of recent books; then, in 1692, *La Bibliothèque de l'Europe*, in Dutch, modelled on the first two.

10 This strange second Christian name of Maria's was given her by her father in memory of a shipwreck that had occurred off the isle of Texel; it means 'Texel calamity'.

11 Quoted by P. Brachin, *Le Cercle de Muiden* (*Archives des Lettres modernes*, no. 4; Paris, 1957).

12 On this question, see Brachin.

13 In 1642 a philosophical-medical factum, of strictly academic interest, printed in a three hundred copy edition by a Utrecht publisher, sold out in a few days.

14 Reproduced in Cohen, p. 503.

CHAPTER SIX

DUTCH SOCIETY

THE POWER OF THE HIERARCHIES

1 In the development of which it played a part that was at once anticipatory and causative; the French resurgence in the eighteenth century, and the emergence in England of schools of political economy were partly due to the reactions provoked in these countries by Holland's commercial competition.

2 Quoted by Franken, p. 19.

3 As far as the cost of foodstuffs is concerned, we know only the wholesale rates as recorded by the Exchange.

4 AGN, p. 139.

5 Temple, p. 100.

6 A high-ranking municipal official might occasionally receive an annual salary of 5,000 florins. A municipal physician in Amsterdam received less than 1,500 or 2,000 florins. The public authorities treated the matter of salaries in a completely off-hand manner; Paludanus, the municipal physician of Enkhuizen, saw his own salary progressively increased, then suddenly reduced by half. A university professor engaged by personal contract received from 500 to 800 florins at the start of the century; thirty years later, he received 1,000 or 1,200 florins. But there were great individual discrepancies. Nearly all high officials possessed private fortunes.

7 Leuven, p. 43; AGN, p. 122; Busken-Huet, p. 429.

8 Figures given by de Vrankrijker, p. 116. Working hours and hourly wages varied according to the season; as far as possible, the guilds prohibited working by artificial light. In 1664 wage rates varied by about a third in a naval dockyard.

9 From the contracts offered after 1668 by Peter the Great to the Dutch workers he wished to attract to Russia, we may conclude that 250 florins a year, plus board and lodging, represented an enviable position for a workman at that date.

10 Wages reached their highest level, nominally, in 1663. But the growing practice of employing women and children, who provided a new, cheap labour force, succeeded in depressing wages once more, although the cost of living continued to rise. On these questions, see AGN, pp. 142–3.

11 AGN, p. 141.

12 Romein, *Lage L.*, p. 289.

13 Romein, *Lage L.*, p. 356.

14 In the collection of the Amsterdam Rijksmuseum. The date is contested. In some opinions it was painted as late as 1672

15 Parival, p. 239.

16 Temple, p. 79.

THE PEOPLE

1 AGN, p. 144.

2 *Oorlog*, p. 200.

3 Incidents of working-class agitation recorded during the course of the century all resulted from purely economic discontent; only the public disturbances of 1618, and those of 1672 leading to the savage assassination of the de Witt brothers (the corpses dragged through the streets by the crowds, then displayed on gibbets), had any political significance. Economic grievances also lay behind such incidents as the frustrated attempt, in 1622, by the stonemason Balthasar Paul to burn down the Amsterdam Stock Exchange; this artisan was a native of Namur and worked for the Spanish.

4 Parival, p. 24.

5 Murris, p. 106.

6 AGN, p. 145.

7 Parival, p. 23; Temple, pp. 97–8.

8 Parival, p. 23.

9 Murris, p. 143

10 Murris, p. 113.

11 Cohen, pp. 589–90.

12 In 1745 a revolt broke out in Friesland. – For further details concerning the disturbances provoked by the Frisian peasantry from the end of the seventeenth century onwards, see C. Pauw, *Strubbelingen in stad en lande* (Groningen, 1956).

PAUPERS AND CRIMINALS

1 An enormous number for a town whose population was probably about fifty thousand at the time.

2 In 1611 more than two thousand families in Amsterdam were assisted in this way, in 1615, 2,500. In 1600 the deaconry distributed 200,000 florins in cash and six tons of goods.

3 These various schemes provided the Amsterdam poor-house with an income of 80,000 florins in 1665.

4 The Hague also possessed a Spinhuis.

5 'It is the property of Virtue to master that which the whole world fears.'

THE ARMED FORCES

1 Nearly 7,000 English, 2,500 French. Out of a total of 18,942 men, only about 17,000 were fighting men, including a few cavalry units.

2 Instead of 120 to 150.

3 The military budget of 1619, one of the lowest of the century, was a little over 500,000 florins; in 1670 it reached 6,000,000; the States' net revenue at the time was about 40,000,000 (Temple, pp. 153–4 and 160).

4 In 1683 Amsterdam and several other towns of Holland refused William III's demand for troops for his campaign against France.

5 Busken-Huet, p. 611.

6 Before the truce, about thirteen florins each thirty-six day period; see the tables quoted by Cohen, p. 35.

7 A regiment of cavalry was divided into five 'troops' or squadrons.

8 The ordnance in the Dordrecht arsenal provoked the admiration of contemporary experts. From the start of the century the Dutch used breech-loading guns.

FOREIGNERS AND REFUGEES

1 Parival, p. 22. – A very vague assessment which the author fails to support with any precise figures. It can be stated, however, that from 1575 to 1619 63 per cent of the residents of Leyden came from Belgium or France.

2 Their influence on the country's economy became apparent especially after 1685 (though without lasting effect); the wave of Huguenot refugees swept into Holland by the revocation of the edict of Nantes included a certain number of manufacturers.

3 Parival, p. 33.

CHAPTER SEVEN

HOLLAND AT WORK

A WEALTHY COUNTRY

1 Murris, p. 36.

2 Temple, pp. 128-9.

3 *Oorlog*, p. 192.

4 Temple, p. 102. The author gives what are probably very approximate figures; he claims that private savings amount to 60 per cent of the revenue, and that taxation takes a half of that figure. He adds that in France or England a tax of 2 per cent would provoke violent protests.

5 Parival, pp. 119-20.

6 Any promissory note of more than 600 florins was supposed to be paid over the counter, otherwise the transaction was liable to be cancelled.

7 Advielle, p. 22. Middelburg in 1616, Delft in 1621 and Rotterdam in 1635 all created their own exchange-banks, but none of them ever rivalled Amsterdam's bank in importance.

8 All these currencies were silver. The few gold coins in circulation were mostly of foreign origin. They were exchanged according to the current market-rate. Thus, the sovereign was quoted at fourteen florins in 1613, fifteen in 1622, fifteen and a half in 1644, and fell to fourteen again the following year. A few towns, including Groningen, Zwolle, Nijmegen and Deventer, struck gold florins. Regarding the value of gold during the century, see the tables in Posthumus, pp. 120 and 543 onwards. Amsterdam had become a world market of precious metals.

9 Temple, p. 143.

10 Several foreign currencies were quoted regularly on the Amsterdam Exchange: those of Frankfurt, Paris, London and Venice, from 1609; those of Nuremberg and Lille, from 1634; that of Stockholm, from 1664; and of Leipzig and Madrid, from 1676.

11 It was only established as the single official currency of the Union in 1694.

12 Posthumus, pp. LIV–LV.

13 5 per cent for goods coming from Turkey and the Mediterranean, the risks of piracy being particularly great on this

route; 4 per cent for cargoes from Brazil; 2½ per cent from Bordeaux. Unnecessary changes of route voided the agreement, but justified delays (due to storms or other similar circumstances) gave the insured person the right to claim against the captain. See *La Richesse de la Hollande*, London, 1778 (an historical report on the East India Company), pp. 81–106.

14 From Utrecht the carriage of a letter for Nijmegen or Haarlem cost two stuivers; from Deventer, three stuivers; for Aix-la-Chapelle, four; for Brussels, seven; for London, twelve.

15 Examples given by Mulder, III, pp. 38–9.

16 The uneven distribution of taxes (small import duties, high domestic taxation combined with numerous special taxes) made it difficult for contemporary observers to assess the real volume, and their judgements are, therefore, contradictory at times.

17 The individual debt of the province of Holland reached 65,000,000 florins, covered, after 1655, by bonds paying from 4½ to 5 per cent interest.

18 The charges varied according to the place. Customs duties in the port of Amsterdam were modified in 1603, 1609 and 1651. Special rates applied in 's Hertogenbosch and Tilburg made these towns economic enclaves on Dutch soil.

19 Parival, p. 121.

20 The official proportion of provincial contributions to the general budget, in units of 100,000 florins, was: Holland, 58,000; Friesland, 11,500; Zeeland, 9,000; Utrecht and Groningen, 5,800 each; Gelderland, 5,600; Overijssel, 3,500 (approximate figures).

21 With whom more or less legalised methods of defrauding the tax authorities were widespread.

COMMERCE AND THE SPIRIT OF ADVENTURE

1 See the lists given by Posthumus, pp. XLIX–LII. The only national products exported by the Netherlands during the seventeenth century were those deriving from the fishing industry and stock-breeding. In 1672 the importation of French hats reached a value of a million florins.

2 Textile crafts had been developed around Tilburg, Eindhoven and Helmond.

3 See the remarks by Temple, pp. 128–9.

4 Not only was Amsterdam a relatively new town; even the site on which it was built – the mouth of the Ij – quite possibly did not even exist in the early Middle Ages, in an age when Rhineland cities, Utrecht, Nijmegen and Deventer already had a long history behind them.

5 Murris, p. 40.

6 Parival, p. 152. This specialisation in the various ports was by no means exclusive; it simply indicated the predominance of a particular local interest or commodity. As a means of comparison, these are the trading figures for some ports of Holland and Zeeland, according to AGN, p. 96, in 1624 and 1648 (in multiples of 10,000 florins) – in 1624: Amsterdam, 1,069; Rotterdam, 189; Enkhuizen, 120; Flushing, 105; – in 1648: Amsterdam, 1,728; Rotterdam, 180; Enkhuizen, 79; Flushing, 141.

7 Temple, p. 142. Superficial observers tended to perceive only sordid avarice; cf. Murris, pp. 92–3.

8 These two voyages were described by participants: that of Novaya Zemlya by Gerrit de Veer; that of Java by Frank van den Does. See De Boer, pp. 18–95.

9 From the end of the Middle Ages, sea fishing was one of the principal sources of income for the northern Netherlands. By the sixteenth century, the carrying-trade in the North Sea and the Baltic had assumed a vital importance for Holland.

THE FLEET

1 This was one of the reasons which prompted Louis XIV's minister to give his approval to the 1672 war.

2 Examples of these variations, which follow exactly those of international politics at the time: in 1607, seventy-five ships and 10,000 tons; in 1615, fifty and 20,000 in 1628, 125 and 30,000; in 1652, seventy-five and 20,000; in 1658, fifty and 10,000; in 1665, 125 and 60,000.

3 The capture of the Spanish 'silver fleet' by Piet Hein, in 1628, may be considered as a privateering exploit. Few war events in the seventeenth century struck the popular imagination so forcibly. Piet Hein got away with sixty-six pounds of gold, 177,000 pounds of silver and large quantities of valuable merchandise. The total value of the loot amounted to 12,000,000 florins. This sum served to pay off the Company's debt, with enough left over to be divided as follows: 50 per cent to the shareholders, 10 per cent to the Stadtholder, 1

per cent to each member of the government . . . and $\frac{1}{10}$ of 1 per cent to Piet Hein! The crews and the Company's officials received large gratuities, and there was still some money left to finance the expedition against 's Hertogenbosch. During the era of letters of commission, booty was divided between the government (20 per cent), the admiralty (10 per cent), and the shipbuilder, captain and crew (70 per cent altogether).

4 The measures taken in Holland during 1606 and 1609 against corsairs were doubtless the main cause of these 'desertions'. In addition, some corsairs captured by the Berbers embraced Islam to save themselves from becoming galley-slaves.

5 One of these Dutchmen, Simon the Dancer, is credited with having introduced to the Algerians a type of light sailing-boat whose lack of a galley increased the mobility and efficiency of the Moorish pirates.

TRADING AND COLONISATION

1 Arms smuggling from Amsterdam was a regular activity from 1609 onwards, and even seems to have been encouraged occasionally by the local Admiralty against the wishes of the States. During the 1672 war Louis XIV's armies were partially equipped with munitions bought from the Dutch.

2 Total figures for traffic in the Sound given in AGN, p. 97.

3 The document stipulated that foreign ships could only bring into England the products of their country of origin.

4 Mention should also be made of the Dutch-Danish naval battle of 1644, caused by the raising of transit dues in the Sound. The English wars took place at sea. Louis XIV invaded the actual territory of the Republic and so struck at her very heart.

5 In 1623 the East India Company made contact with the opposite extremity of the Islamic world, when it opened up a trading-post in Ormuz, Persia. During 1626-7 a Persian embassy visited Holland.

6 That is to say, more than seven times the capital of the English East India Company, founded in London in 1600.

7 Parival, p. 56, notes that, taking market fluctuations into consideration, they returned an average of 300 per cent.

8 Quoted by Busken-Huet, p. 430.

9 In 1606 Abel Janszoon Tasman of Hoorn reached Australia.

The southernmost tip of America, Cape Horn, is named after his home town.

10 Quoted in *Oorlog*, p. 178.

11 A contrast with one founded, in 1620, in Cape Cod, by the Pilgrim Fathers! The *Mayflower*, in fact, left from Holland. But no one in that country was interested in the venture.

12 Temple, p. 149.

13 During the first twenty-five years of its existence, the West India Company did seven million dollars' worth of business in slave-trading.

INDUSTRY

1 Coal was also imported from Scotland and from the Liège district.

2 This word designated a kind of peasant overcoat, reapplied in this case because of the building's shape.

3 That far more ancient device, the water-mill, was used mainly in Gelderland, providing motive power in particular for the paper-mills.

4 At the turn of the century, mills in the Zaandam area were sometimes used in this way to transmit special messages.

5 According to the terms of the certificate granted to Peter the Great, after he had completed his apprenticeship in Zaandam at the end of the century. Quoted by Mulder, IV, p. 10.

6 In Leyden itself a section of the textile industry remained in the hands of small artisans.

7 Nevertheless, this was an important industry capable of treating some 100,000 pieces annually by mid-century.

8 In 1630 80 per cent of the 13,000,000 gallons of pickled herring produced by the herring-fishing industry was re-exported.

9 During the same period, in the Far East, prisoners were abandoned on desert islands: see, on this subject, Busket-Huet, p. 560.

10 The new régime did not succeed in suppressing piracy completely.

11 The workmen sent there lived in terrible conditions, of which some idea can be gained by studying the themes in prayer-books used at that time in the merchant service: 'prayer to be said during the Northern summer', 'prayer to be said when

hemmed in by ice', and so on (see *Oorlog*, p. 186). The existence led by the teams who remained on the spot during the winter to look after the installations was even worse.

WORKING THE LAND

1 According to Parival, p. 101, the price of land in peacetime was very high: from 1,200 to 1,400 florins an arpent (roughly equivalent to an acre) for meadowland, 1,800 to 2,000 for farmland, 2,500 to 3,000 for gardens.

2 Parival, p. 11.

3 Guicciardini (quoted by Schotel, *Huisgezin*, p. 327), in his *Description* of the Netherlands, written in 1565, noted with admiration the fact that the village of Assendelf produced 4,400 gallons of milk daily. But the herd comprised four thousand cows. The average output was therefore nine pints of milk per animal, a ridiculously small amount compared with present-day yields. It is very doubtful whether stock-breeding conditions and productivity improved between 1550 and 1650.

4 Parival, p. 208.

5 Temple, p. 95.

6 During the Middle Ages the territory of the Netherlands, north of the 'great rivers', consisted of: a band of solid land forming an extension of the German plain and reaching as far as Utrecht; a line of dunes bordering the North Sea; and, between these, a region of shallow lakes and marshes formed during the fifth century by breaches made in the dunes. The work of draining this central region could be undertaken only as a result of the combination of three factors during the fourteenth century: a financial factor (resulting from the creation of the herring fisheries), a political factor (the creation of a central authority) and a technical factor (the introduction of the windmill from East Asia).

7 The system of dikes was universally admired by foreigners, and represented an astonishing technical achievement for the era.

8 One of the worst natural disasters ever to strike Holland: 30,000 people perished during this flood.

9 For an account of these happenings, see Parival, pp. 387–8.

10 During the twenty-five years preceding the war, nearly 100,000 acres of marshland were reclaimed in this way for agriculture.

During the war, drainage operations continued on a more modest scale: 750 to 1,000 acres annually.

11 This word designates any reclaimed land converted to agriculture or grazing uses.

12 The total annual value of these exploitations was 250,000 florins.

13 The Haarlem lake was not drained until the nineteenth century.

CHAPTER EIGHT

CONCLUSION

'THE DELIGHTS OF FREEDOM'

1 Text quoted as the epigraph of this book; Cohen, p. 201.

2 Temple, p. 106.

3 According to Temple, p. 103: 'No man offers at any undertaking, which he is not prepared for, and master of his design, before he begins; so as I have observed nor heard of any building public or private, that has not been finished in the time designed for it.' As we have seen in the first chapter, the Amsterdam municipal council refrained from taking such a measure when arranging for the construction of the new town hall.

4 In the opinion of Sorbière, in 1650, reported by Murris, p. 229.

5 The composition of embassies was apportioned among the most powerful provinces: Holland named the ambassador to Paris, Zeeland the ambassador to London. The general interest came second in these private politics. Zeeland, for instance, sent a mission to Paris with the specific task of circumventing the Holland ambassador.

6 *Oorlog*, p. 223.

7 According to Temple, pp. 133–5. This was one of the causes of the influx of refugees.

8 Murris, p. 78.

9 Temple, p. 126.

10 Parival, p. 219.

INDEX

Dutchman, the, in his home, 47, 53–5, 63, 67–73, 74–7, 95, 97, 132–3, 170, 195, 267; his clothing, 56–8, 59, 62–3; as a gambler, 76–7; his attachment to science, 114–15, 118–19; his temperament, 119, 318; and the theatre, 209; a great reader, 219; an inveterate brawler, 238; as a trader, 280; not an emigrant, 281; his public life, 318–20
Dutchwoman, the, in her home, 41–2, 54, 55, 68, 74–7, 130, 133–9, 137–9; her clothing, 56, 57, 58–61, 62; and childbirth, 94–8; and her children, 100, 101; education of, 111, 134, 246; her temperament, 120, 133; and marriage, 122, 126, 130, 132; her appearance, 133; and servants, 136–7; and drinking, 173, 175; and smoking, 180; in industry, 238
Dutch Mercury, 274

East India Company, xvi, 66, 267, 273, 279; formation of, 294–5; its trading activities, 295–9; its colonists, 299–300
Edam, 195, 312
Elzevirs, the, 221, 222
Engagements, 125
England, influence of, 38, 39, 56, 76, 212; Dutch trade with, 277, 291
Engraving, 198–9, 221
Enkhuizen, 9, 15, 27, 269; individual features of, 29, 51, 155, 171, 244, 269, 307
Epidemics, 148–50
Erasmus, Desiderius, 133, 219

Farmhouses, 27–8, 46–7, 326 n3

Farming, 310–12
Feast-days, 180–1, 183–7
Fire-fighting, 20–22
Fish, control of, 22–3, 306
Fishing industry, 163, 306–10
Fleet, the, 285–6, 340–1
Florin, the, value of, 269, 324 n6
Flowers, the Dutch and, 49–50, 122–3
Food, 67–8, 70–3, 170; cooking of, 68–9
Foreigners in the Netherlands, 261–5
France, influence of, on the Dutch house, 14, 38, 39, 43, 47, 54; on travel, 15–16; on gardens, 28, 50; on fashion, 55, 56, 59, 60, 156, 231, 264; on drinking and eating habits, 173–4, 231; on manners, 77, 109, 170, 225, 226, 230, 321; on culture, 112, 193, 209, 210, 222–3; refugees from, 263–5, 274; Dutch colony in, 281; trade with, 291
Franeker, 112, 114, 115, 118
Frederick Henry, Prince, 109, 209, 230–1, 233, 260
Free-thinkers, 94
Frein, Henri de, 77
Friesland, xvii, xix, 88, 231, 253; characteristics of, 25, 28, 62, 105, 125, 163, 187, 248, 278, 311
Frisian islands, 25, 124, 162, 261
Funerals, 159–60, 250
Furniture, 38–40, 43, 46–7, 54, 94

Games, parlour, 76–7; ball, 167; children's, 169–70
Gardens, 28–9, 48–9, 75; pleasure, 164
Gazettes, 273–4

Library of Congress Cataloging-in-Publication Data

Zumthor, Paul, 1915–
    [Vie quotidienne en Hollande au temps de
    Rembrandt. English]
    Daily life in Rembrandt's Holland / Paul
Zumthor ; translated from the French by Simon
Watson Taylor.
        p.   cm.
    Originally published: London : Weidenfeld and
Nicolson, 1962.
    Includes bibliographical references and index.
    ISBN 0-8047-2200-5 (cl.) —
    ISBN 0-8047-2201-3 (pa.)
        1. Netherlands—Civilization—17th century.
    2. Netherlands—Social life and customs.
    I. Title.
    DJ172.Z8613   1994
    949.2′04—dc20   93-27947
                                            CIP

⊗ This book is printed on acid-free paper.